山下有風

Wind

Against

the

Mountain

Harvard-
Yenching
Institute
Monograph
Series
42

Wind Against the Mountain

The Crisis of Politics and Culture in Thirteenth-Century China

Richard L. Davis

Published by the Council on East Asian Studies, Harvard University,
and distributed by Harvard University Press,
Cambridge (Massachusetts) and London   1996

The Harvard-Yenching Institute, founded in 1928 and headquartered at Harvard University, is a foundation dedicated to the advancement of higher education in the humanities and social sciences in East and Southeast Asia. The Institute supports advanced research at Harvard by faculty members of certain Asian universities, and doctoral studies at Harvard and other universities by junio faculty at the same universities. It also supports East Asian studies at Harvard through contributions to the Harvard-Yenching Library and publication of the Harvard Journal of Asiatic Studies and books on premodern East Asian history and literature.

Library of Congress Cataloging-in-Publication Data

Davis, Richard L., 1951–
Wind against the mountain : the crisis of politics and culture in
thirteenth-century China / Richard L. Davis.
p.   cm. — (Harvard-Yenching Institute monograph series ; 42)
Includes bibliographical references and index.
ISBN 0-674-95357-6
1. China—History—Sung dynasty, 960–1279.   2. China—Politics and
government—Sung dynasty, 960–1279.   3. Martyrs—China.
4. Martyrdom.   I. Title.   II. Series.
DS751.D38   1996
951'.024—dc20   96-25667
                                                                CIP

Index by Richard L. Davis

To my family,
for their generous forbearance

Contents

Figures

Maps

Tables

Preface

This rendering of the last years of Song, with a focus on loyalist resistance to Mongol domination, is an outgrowth of earlier work. It was during research, in particular, for the last of my three narrative chapters of *The Cambridge History of China*, volume 5, that the magnitude of the loyalist phenomenon and the complex motives of its participants started to sink in. I soon realized that this political episode had ramifications beyond mere politics and Song martyrs were dying for more than just dynasty—the traditional slant on Song loyalism. Rather, marytrdom came to be linked to many other powerfully compelling symbols, including masculine virtues and gentry dominance. This second layer of meaning was often understood by Song men and sometimes even alluded to in their writings, especially the literary pieces, but never elaborated upon in any detail. A similar dearth of interpretive discussion exists in later historical writings, where the heroic feats of men enshrined in dynastic legend would become too sacred to be dispassionately dissected and analyzed. I did not begin with the intent of imposing Western constructs of gender and class on this body of traditional Chinese literature. Indeed, I would have been happier simply to narrate a stirring story of dynastic collapse. But as unanticipated messages began to leap from the pages, those other issues became impossible to ignore. I have attempted here, in consequence, to add a cultural history dimension to this political story, relating political loyalty to cultural values in the broadest sense, fully recognizing the risks of attempting to satisfy multiple constituencies of readers.

The research in primary documents for this study was largely done in

the mid-1980s. In the intervening years, a sizable number of new monographs have been added to our expanding stock of scholarship on the Song, largely in intellectual and social history. These monographs have helped me to identify sources and clarify problems in areas where my own expertise is limited. Of special value among the few works in political history is Jennifer Jay's recent book, *A Change of Dynasties* (1991), published just as I was completing the first draft of this book, and her contribution here is documented in the many references that follow. Yet my work is radically different from hers. Most obviously, her study begins where mine ends, focusing principally on the Yuan dynasty. She deals with loyalism as an avocation, whereas my concern is with loyalism in general, especially martyrdom, as a conduit for expressing other concerns: frustrations with political and institutional traditions; ambivalence toward material and cultural life; anxiety over relations between ruler and ruled, men and women, *wen* and *wu*. My efforts have also been made easier by an impressive body of recent research on Song political and military history out of Taiwan and mainland China, most notably Li Tianming's seminal *Song Yuan zhanshi* (Taipei, 1988), a comprehensive survey of military history for the thirteenth century.

My continuing work in Southern Song politics has also been spurred on by an exceptional cohort of colleagues and friends stretching from China to New England. Huang K'uan-chung of the Academia Sinica, in Taipei, most immediately comes to mind—a scholar whose near encyclopedic command of the sources and stunning sensitivity to historical nuance continues to humble and inspire me. I owe other debts of gratitude to fellow historians Maggie Bickford, Valerie Hansen, Horst Huber, Thomas H. C. Lee, Denis Twitchett, and Don Wyatt. They all read the manuscript at different stages and it is much enhanced by their help. The manuscript was similarly enhanced, later in the process, through input from two anonymous readers for Harvard's Council on East Asian Studies, whose conscientious rigor was balanced by constructive objectivity. I should also thank those who helped turn my rough draft into a finished book: Lee Ann Best and Katherine Keenum provided the kind of editorial stewardship rare for most presses today while cartographer Dennis O'Brien produced maps of the first order. Still, only one person, the late James T.C. Liu, saw this project evolve from conception to near completion—always prodding and probing as he selflessly steered many a valuable document my way. As scholar, Professor Liu had a wonderful knack for identifying the many layers of distortion and levels of meaning in Song sources, displaying in the process

an enviable sense of history and humanity that seemed as much intuitive as learned. He will be sorely missed, not only by me personally, but by two generations of Song historians who looked up to him as mentor and friend.

Finally, I must acknowledge my family—an exceptionally large but genial group of brothers and sisters, aunts and uncles and cousins—common folk from Buffalo, N.Y. who have indulged my personal and professional priorities with unrelenting compassion and support. I owe the same to Chiang Jung-yuan, who has taken the long absences in stride. To my parents, Darcy and Jessie Williams, the debt is greater still. In devoting their lives to caring for children and neighbors in need, they were my earliest models of moral fortitude—living proof that we can always be better than the circumstances of our existence.

Wind Against the Mountain

In the middle of the earth is water:
*The image of **the army.***
Thus the superior man increases his masses
By generosity toward the people.

The Changes, VII.[1]

1·Shi:
The Army at Sea

The Song stands out among Chinese dynasties as perhaps the least obsessed with imperial spectacle: no majestic capitals of perfect symmetry symbolically linking the orders of man and cosmos, no great walls nor grand canals in pompous display of wealth and power, no far flung expeditions by land and sea in assertion of the supremacy of the Middle Kingdom. Its emperors and politicians proved far too timid, inclined more toward conservation than expansion and content to sacrifice intangibles like dynastic image for concrete gains in material life and border stability. Yet this principle of minimalism, which had so characterized and constrained the dynasty for three full centuries, gave way at the very end to a drama of unthinkable intensity as Chinese royalists made their last stand against Mongol conquerors.

That final contest of imperial wills, Song versus Yuan, occurred at Yaishan, or "Cliff Hill" as the island holdout was called. Located among a dense cluster of islands in a bay some eighty to a hundred kilometers due south of Canton (modern Guangzhou), Yaishan represented the southernmost fringes of civilization as the Chinese knew it, beyond which lay only an endless expanse of water.[2] A largely mountainous island scarcely fifty kilometers around, Yaishan was heretofore of scant import, agricultural or commercial. This is not to deny, however, its very considerable strategic assets. The northern approach was protected by waters so shallow as to impede free passage for all but the smallest of enemy ships, while the southern approach was surrounded by steeply precipaced islets from which sentries could conveniently monitor waters of the South China Sea. The island must have been largely desolate when

1

the Song entourage arrived in the summer of 1278, the child emperor Zhao Bing (Modi, b. 1272) accompanied by his retinue of courtiers and soldiers. By most accounts, that entourage consisted of up to 200,000 men and women, but mostly men.[3] This represents an incredible number for a force in persistent retreat since the outset of 1276 and confined to an area of relatively small size and unaccommodating terrain. Then again, sources allude to the bulk of the Song military being housed at sea, on the larger warships, while on the island upwards of a thousand temporary barracks and other quarters had been rushed to completion in a few short months, suggesting a rather stupendous demand for housing. Even at half or a third of their reputed numbers, Song holdouts were far too numerous for the Mongols to ignore and they clearly had no such intent.

In fact, both sides seemed to be racing feverishly yet methodically toward a final solution to their old feud. Through the autumn and early winter, Song defenders struggled to fortify their tropical citadel while Mongol forces, growing stronger and more militarily astute with each victory, progressed south by land and by sea on a steady course clearly targeted at Yaishan. The six year-old Zhao Bing, last male heir to the deceased Duzong (r. 1264–1274) and sole source of legitimacy for Song loyalists, was throughout sequestered at the Yaishan sanctuary. Attending to the young emperor was the Dowager-Consort Yang Juliang, the thirty-four year old concubine of the former Duzong. Only recently had she lost her own son, the short-lived monarch Zhao Shi (Duanzong), and she now reigned as senior regent to the new ruler, her stepson.[4] It appears that Zhao Bing's biological mother, a lesser concubine of Duzong surnamed Yu, attended him as well, along with a grandfather and other close relatives. These rather shadowy characters were assisted and prompted, in turn, by Chief Councilor Lu Xiufu (b. 1238). A dedicated overseer of civil affairs, he remained in steadfast service to the heirs of Duzong throughout their three-year ordeal of retreat and exile. As for military affairs, these were directed by Zhang Shijie, a common man of imposing dedication and discipline who represents certainly the most critical, if not necessarily the most celebrated commander of the late Song.[5]

The Mongol regime was represented by mercenary sailors of varied ethnicities. Of their chief commanders, Li Heng (1236–1285) was Tangut and Zhang Hongfan (1238–1280) was northern Chinese. They would direct several tens of thousands of other non-Mongols, in turn.[6] Having recently snatched from Song control the vital port city of

Guangzhou, Li Heng approached Yaishan from the north and west, Zhang Hongfan from the high seas to the south. It was the middle of the first lunar month, late February 1279 by Western reckoning, and Zhang Shijie had prepared Song armies for a decisive confrontation. He even arranged for the emperor to be present, no doubt to rally his war-weary troops. In the company of Dowager Yang and Councilor Lu Xiufu, the child monarch occupied one of the larger ships, which was protected by over a thousand other ships, large and small, strung out in a single line like a veritable wall in the South China Sea.[7] As a symbol of immovable resolve, the entirety of Song military assets would be invested in the contest, which by most indications stood at two to three times enemy strength.[8] Victory must have seemed a certainty and a decisive win was critical to stemming the tide of enemy victories which had occurred throughout this, the last corner of Song resistance, the last hope of dynastic survival.

The Song could scarcely have been better prepared. It went so far as to cover the sides of its wooden ships with matted linings, enhancing their resistance to the enemy's incendiary arrows and catapults.[9] But Song strategy hinged on one critical, indeed fatal assumption—belief that the enemy would act swiftly, in which case its own superior numbers would win handily. Unfortunately, Yuan aggressors proved unexpectedly patient. Refusing to be lured into hasty action, they first cut off all escape routes by securing their flanks to the north and south. The next two weeks involved an unrelenting harassment of Song ships, isolated as they were at sea. This situation left the Song progressively short on fresh supplies of water and weapons for its sailors, while the morale of all suffered irreparably. Its only alternative was to break the enemy blockade and flee to the safety of the high seas. But nothing seemed to favor the south, nature included.

On the morning of March 19, the southern navy awoke to depressingly dense clouds and persistent rains, a sight not uncommon to springtime in the Chinese tropics.[10] But there seemed, this time, some measure of preordination in such dreary weather: as one eyewitness saw it, Heaven had already begun to mourn the certain losers.[11] Their vision impaired, southern ships were hit from the north by the forces of Li Heng, who exploited the outgoing morning tide to sweep across the ordinarily shallow waters and launch a surprise strike. Following this onslaught, only hours later when the afternoon tide flowed in the opposite direction, came an attack by Zhang Hongfan. It was as if the enemy was propelled by some divine wind as they struck the southern flank of Song

defenders with the precision and impact that pincer actions were designed to deliver. Casualties mounted on both sides, for the high stakes had incited intense exchanges, indeed some of the most ferocious fighting the dynasty had seen in the past half-century of war. When hostilities broke sometime before dawn, an ignominous defeat thickened the sea and air: for as far as the eye could see, lifeless bodies floated on the warm waters, largely casualties of the Song in a carnage of stupefying dimensions. Wen Tianxiang (1236–1283), the sole eyewitness for whom written record survives, alludes to the magnitude of the disaster with stirring eloquence:

> Arriving at the southern seas
> Upon which human corpses are scattered like fibers of hemp,
> Foul smelling waves pound my heart to bits,
> Billowing winds beat at my frosty temples.[12]

Another writer alludes to "a vast sea of red," in confirmation of a massive bloodletting.[13] By most accounts, including sources for the Mongol side, the Song had lost an incredible 100,000 to violent death—the entirety of its military and civilian contingents.[14] Yet an amazing number of these, perhaps even most, did not vanish in the heat of battle: they perished of their own volition. The deaths of Jia Chunxiao and his family, including his wife and daughters, are said to have been suicidal; an executive at the Ministry of Personnel, the specter of defeat seemed too much to bear.[15] Many others shared their sentiment, it would seem. One anonymous chronicler, apparently a subject of the Yuan, estimates one-third to one-half of the deaths to be suicidal. He writes: "Numbering in the *tens of thousands* were the esteemed officials, literati, and women who leaped into the water with gold weights attached to their waists."[16] We should rightfully question whether weights of any composition, let alone gold, would have been so readily available to our shipbound victims; and if so, whether the drowned bodies could possibly have surfaced in time to document the deed of willful death. But extant records are consistent and emphatic in attributing such an end to Zhao Bing, the seven year-old emperor. Clutched in the arms of Councilor Lu Xiufu and clad in a gown of royal yellow, the imperial seals of gold strapped to his waist, he joined the others in a ritual of death whose symbolism far exceeded the powers of his tender mind to comprehend. No record was made of the whereabouts of his mother, Lady Yu, who may well have died sometime earlier, but historians did record the fate

of the senior consort-dowager, Yang Juliang. Somehow, almost miraculously, she had succeeded in eluding Yuan armies, commander Zhang Shijie having arranged a hasty departure. Fate had not doomed her to follow the others in death. Free to take flight, she could have started anew in a different place or under an assumed name. Yet once informed of the fate of the others, Dowager Yang threw herself into the sea, ostensibly out of loyal devotion to a dynasty which had so uniquely honored her with power and status.[17] Her body would later be retrieved from the water by Zhang Shijie and given a proper burial, before the commander himself drowned, apparently by accident.[18]

Not everyone on the Song side perished at Yaishan: among the civilian and military officers then present, a hundred or so are reported as having surrendered to Yuan forces—individuals hereafter relegated to the sidelines of history.[19] But for the vast majority whose lives met an abrupt end, the eulogies would follow for countless years hence, including eulogies by men who had no vested interest in the dynasty and bore no personal witness to the heroic last stand of its loyal subjects. Particularly stirring is a poem by Fang Feng (1240–1321), a nostalgic sort just shy of forty when the Song fell.[20] In his "Mourning Lu Xiufu," he personalizes this political tragedy by focusing on the innocent child, who least deserved so violent an end, and his dutiful minister:

> At the hour of crisis he clutches the child,
> Conditions extreme, on the verge of toppling over;
> The sea turtle's back conveys the Middle Kingdom,
> The dragon's whiskers, Heaven at the bottom of the sea.[21]

It seems only appropriate that the Son of Heaven, pillar of the terrestrial world, should be juxtaposed to the giant sea turtle, symbolic pillar of the abyss to which the young emperor was now permanently consigned. By tradition, the turtle's back is so broad as to be capable of supporting the entire earth. But both are now powerless and the Middle Kingdom is left adrift, at least from the perspective of Fang Feng and countless others who bemoaned the loss of their political and spiritual master.

MAKING SENSE OF INSANITY

One distinguished survivor who refused to confine his loyalist fervor to the lament of mere verse was Wen Tianxiang. A one-time councilor for the dynasty in its waning years and principal commander of its land

forces, he mourns in more personal terms the loss of close colleagues and death of a cause which in recent years had consumed his every energy. Yet he also saw beyond the morbid vista of Yaishan to the example of moral rectitude inspired by the dead. Steadfast loyalty even in the face of certain death—the martyr's subordination of self to a higher moral cause—would live on long after the individual actors in this drama had been forgotten, lending immortality to mere mortals. He writes:

> A mountain refuge exchanged for a grave at sea,
> Without empire is to be without family.
> For men with wills of a thousand years,
> Our lives have no limit.[22]

These lines were composed, by all indications, in early 1279 at the outset of a four-year incarceration that would take Wen Tianxiang from Yaishan to Beijing, from the southern fringes to the northern stretches of an empire now wholly occupied by alien conquerors. These years were filled, in part, with assorted literary undertakings: an autobiographical sequence intended as a personal account of the controversial last years of the dynasty, as well as poetic elegies for the important people and events of those trying times. Yet the more Wen Tianxiang reflected on the values and deeds of himself and his cohort the more convinced he became that virtue must shape itself, can only shape itself, through deed.[23] Conscience dictated that he offer up himself as a sacrifice.

Contemporaries report that he twice attempted suicide, once by poisoning and then by starvation, both early on in his captivity.[24] And despite repeated high-level attempts by the Mongol court to convert him, including the personal intervention of Khubilai Khan (r. 1260–1294) and the khan's chief adviser, Wen Tianxiang would accept nothing short of death.[25] He writes of the Yaishan martyrs, "the minor subject who dies ten thousand deaths has nothing to regret."[26] Death is necessary, he argues, because "the loyal subject cannot serve two masters."[27] This may seem like formulaic verse gleaned from some teenager's text of Confucian precepts and, indeed, Wen Tianxiang admits to being strongly influenced by the plethora of didactic literature on loyalism current in his youth.[28] Whether as allegorical history or historicized fiction and poetry, that literature had reiterated the duties attendant to public service as it celebrated death for a noble cause. But for the ethically obsessed Wen Tianxiang, life did not imitate art so much as life imitated history.

En route to the north, for example, Wen Tianxiang reports coming upon a tombstone crowned with the words, "Grave of the Man without Ruler."[29] Cut in 1188, the inscription employed the reign title of the fourth monarch of Jin, descendant of Jurchen conquerors who in the mid-1120s had swept the Chinese heartland from their Manchurian base and imposed minority rule on virtually all of North China. By then, those conquerors had ruled for six full decades, certainly the bulk of the dead man's life. Yet by refusing to acknowledge Jurchen rulers as his own—by claiming to have no ruler at all—the deceased was implicitly challenging the legitimacy of current overlords. He was further affirming an enduring loyalty to the Song, the dynasty which had formerly governed all of China and still aspired to effect a grand unification from its southern base. For the dead man and the survivors burying him to offer such a bold statement of protest—one tantamount to sedition against the new dynasty—must have involved a rather staggering store of courage and conviction. In 1279, as the forty-three year old Wen Tianxiang hurriedly scanned this tombstone under the careful eye of his captors, he found anecdotal immediacy to Confucian abstractions about political loyalty, abstractions otherwise sterile in their impersonal remoteness. The incident also left him convinced, more than ever, of the senselessness of passing so many decades as a man without master, an empty existence. Better to die young and morally proven, a symbol of something greater than himself.

Adjustment to life without a master would be a decision not his to make; in January 1283, after four long years of incarceration, Wen Tianxiang would be carted off to Beijing's sprawling firewood market where, before a vast crowd of spectators, he was executed. His last words, "I have completed my service," would confirm his dogged devotion to the memory of Song.[30] But the totality of his commitment to public service demanded near-superhuman levels of personal sacrifice, sacrifice that may have appeared to most contemporary admirers and later observers alike as assuredly unreasonable and perhaps even immoral.[31]

There were, first, the mishaps visited upon his young and growing family due to the ethical extremism of their patriarch. In the eighth lunar month of 1277, Mongol armies closed in on his hideout in the vicinity of Square Rock Ridge (Fangshiling), in the heart of Jiangnan West circuit and not far from the Wen ancestral home at Luling county. Two of Wen Tianxiang's six daughters would die in the chaos accompanying the conflict, while the Lady Ouyang (d. 1305), his legal wife, along with two concubines, two other daughters, and the younger of two sons were

taken prisoner. It appears that this vulnerable family of women and children, which had otherwise kept close to their patriarch, had been permanently separated in the course of the conflict, compelling Wen Tianxiang to move on without them.[32] They would later be escorted to Beijing and placed under house arrest—except for the younger son, who never survived the early days of captivity.[33] The only members of his immediate family to elude pursuers and follow him in flight were his aging mother, Zeng Deci; two younger daughters, Jianniang and Fengniang; and the only son born to Wen Tianxiang and Lady Ouyang, Wen Daosheng. But it was precisely those free members of his family who were lost, in rapid succession, by the end of the next summer: the sixty-four year old matriarch died of an unspecified illness, as did the twelve year old Wen Daosheng, and his two younger sisters.[34] Constant movement in an unfamiliar and often hostile environment had simply taxed their frail bodies beyond all reasonable limits. As for the children incarcerated in Beijing, the son died a year later while the daughters—the sole surviving offspring of the fugitive statesman—would spend the remainder of their lives up north, permanently severed from their southern roots. A disconsolate Wen Tianxiang likens the children to "young swallows without nests, shivering in the autumn chill."[35]

No ordeal, however, was as long or bitter as that of Lady Ouyang. She stood alone in confronting the untimely deaths of her children and the four-year incarceration of her husband, with all of its false hope and lingering despair. She also withstood, undaunted, a detention up north that spanned nearly three decades: not until 1298 did Mongol authorities consent to her release.[36] It was only then, upon returning to the family's native Luling, that the widow was reunited with Wen Sheng, a former nephew who had been adopted in 1278 as heir to her husband's temporarily broken line. The son, now middle-aged, must have seemed a veritable stranger.

The youth entrusted with maintaining the ancestral line of Wen Tianxiang, not to mention the assorted ethical legacies that he as martyr came to represent, was born in 1268 to Wen Bi (1237–1298), the sole surviving brother of Wen Tianxiang. Yet for all the fraternal intimacy implicit in this sharing of sons, the relationship between the two brothers was severely strained by political turns and moral priorities. The two men, separated in age by only a year, had passed consecutive doctoral examinations. They also served the Song court-in-exile at the highest levels, Wen Tianxiang as honorary councilor and Wen Bi as prefect of Huizhou (Guangnan East) and fiscal intendant for the strategi-

cally vital Guangnan region.[37] Yet on the heels of the Yaishan debaucle, Wen Bi not only surrendered Huizhou to the enemy, he readily accepted high office under precisely the rulers who still held his brother in captivity.[38] Wen Bi's motives were never made public, and we should not necessarily assume a selfish disregard for his brother's plight. Nonetheless, the elder Wen understandably agonized over the matter. He is rumored to have rejected monetary gifts from a well-intentioned Wen Bi, deriding these as the tainted "spoils of treachery."[39] On the occasion of his brother's arrival in Beijing, as Wen Tianxiang entered his second year of captivity, he writes of the growing distance between them:

> Last year, leaving my camp and then the mountains,
> This year, coming all the way to Yan [modern Beijing]:
> Brothers, one confined to prison while the other mounts his horse,
> Same father, same mother, but not the same Heaven.
> How pitiful is the scattering of flesh and blood
> Among men who are not even fifty.
> For the Three Benevolents, life and death has its own individual meaning,
> Distantly, the white sun intrudes into the azure mist.[40]

Wen Tianxiang never demanded that his younger brother conform to his own high standard of ethical propriety, as demonstrated by his refusal to sever ties with Wen Bi in anger or disgust. This may be because, as some writers speculate, Wen Bi had clandestinely assisted in the dangerous task of smuggling out of prison his older brother's prose and poetry.[41] Sheer possession of such politically sensitive material, if detected, might well have cost his very life. The senior Wen would certainly have known of his brother's assistance and secret empathy for him, in that case; still, the political wall dividing them could not be easily forgotten. In declaring that the two no longer share the same Heaven—by accepting different masters, their loyalties stand in diametric opposition—Wen Tianxiang is suggesting the presence of a nagging tension for which the passage of time offers no reasonable remedy. Tensions would persist, as well, due to the elder brother's adamant insistence on dying a martyr's death.

The senior Wen seems to have accepted the ethical improprieties of his younger brother, despite glaring inconsistencies with his own values and priorities, in part because he saw no single "ethically correct" response to a given set of political circumstances. The "three benevolents" whom he invokes in the above poem, for example, were officers of the declining Shang dynasty, in the twelfth century B.C., who opposed the

policies of their monarch. In consequence, one would be murdered, another imprisoned, while the third elected to withdraw from office and serve his family. As narrated in the *Analects* of Confucius, each of the three had responded to events in a manner which was "individually meaningful," the response of one being no less legitimate than the other. One aspect of such individual circumstance is, of course, one's station within the dual communities of state and family. Of the two Wen brothers, Tianxiang was senior in age as well as political stature, so his sacrifice should presumably be greatest.

Another factor in Wen Tianxiang's eventual acceptance of his brother's ethical choices was, doubtlessly, his own growing sense of guilt with reference to family responsibilities. While in captivity, he mentions the care required by an aging mother; her death would soon follow, demanding the elaborate rituals appropriate to a woman of her social station.[42] That responsibility was rightfully his, as eldest son, yet political preoccupations had prompted Wen Tianxiang to delegate most of these ritual duties to younger siblings. What greater breach of filial piety, Confucianism's most cardinal virtue, than this! And sadly, absolution of conscience would have to await the afterlife:

> My mother formerly instructed me in loyalty
> And I have not forsaken my mother's ideals.
> When reunited at the Eternal Springs,
> Our ghosts and spirits will rejoice together.[43]

Such moral malaise masked in religious resignation reemerges with reference to another important family responsibility which Wen Tianxiang failed to undertake—"collection of the bones and flesh" in advance of proper burial for the daughters who died at Square Rock Ridge.[44] The consequent "shame" seemed to haunt him interminably. Elsewhere, he laments the disrupted lives of two younger sisters who paid dearly for the political activities of their brother: one was surrendered to authorities by her own in-laws while the other endured years of aimless flight.[45] "Since antiquity," he writes, "the completely loyal were not completely filial." "The two are not mutually perfectable," he writes elsewhere.[46] In a funerary inscription for his brother, author Liu Yueshen (b. 1260) waxes eloquently on the marvel of "a single household producing both loyal subjects *and* filial sons"—the Song dynasty's equivalent to the Three Benevolents of old.[47] This would offer little consolation to Wen Tianxiang, however, who in effect admitted that his own resolute pur-

suit of loyalty came consciously and consistently at the expense of filial and fraternal duties to family.

But Wen Tianxiang, in placing loyalty before filiality—public duty before private obligations—was taking a radical and perhaps even unorthodox stand, one not explicitly sanctioned by the Confucian canon. The classical philosopher Mencius, however strong his sense of civic duty, was unequivocal in recognizing the superior claim of family commitment. "There are many duties that one must discharge," he declares in the fourth century B.C., "but fulfillment of one's duty to parents is the most basic."[48] A century earlier, Confucius had similarly suggested that such private obligations as filial piety take precedence over civic duty, at one point chastizing a son who had reported to authorities the illicit deeds of his father.[49] This principle is affirmed elsewhere, when Confucius states, "filial piety and fraternal devotion constitute the root of benevolence."[50] As a benevolent heart is rooted in filial commitment, filiality must by implication precede, if not necessarily take precedence over loyalty, private virtue preceding public virtue. Still more explicit are the sentiments expressed in the *Classic of Filial Piety*, a text that Neo-Confucian moralists of Song times found particularly inspiring: "Filial piety begins with serving one's parents, it later evolves into serving one's ruler, and ends with establishing one's own self."[51]

Nonetheless, for all of the explicit affirmation of family's priority in shaping a larger moral order and the implicit assumption of family over state, there existed in early Confucian thought a stubborn disinclination to articulate such *a priori* status. Loyal duty (*zhong*) and filial devotion (*xiao*), according to most early writings, represent altogether complementary goals. In the words of the *Book of Rites*, a conservative Confucian text of the early empire, "In the loyal subject's service to his ruler and the filial son's service to his parents there is a single root. To obey the ghosts and spirits on high, while obeying rulers and elders outside the home and offering filial devotion inside the home—this serves the completion of man."[52] Clearly, the suppression of the self as exemplified by filial submission at home is expected to facilitate, not complicate or contradict, submission to authority outside the home. This principle would be affirmed a millennium later by Ouyang Xiu (1007–1072). Perhaps the most compelling of the many Song historians to articulate convictions about civic duty, his *Historical Records of the Five Dynasties* was widely read among the literati of Wen Tianxiang's day. And part of the work's appeal lies in its author's daring engagement of assorted ethical conundrums in Confucian society. He writes: "Without a father

how can one be born, without a ruler how can one live? Yet it has long been said, 'loyalty and filiality are not mutually perfectable.' How is this so? . . . If one acts on self-interest then both will be harmed, yet *if one acts on righteous propriety* then both will be attained."[53] To the extent that the propriety of one's actions, according to Ouyang Xiu, hinges so critically upon the intent of the actor—a selfless sense of righteous duty—the measure of soul-searching undertaken by Wen Tianxiang during those several years of imprisonment can well be imagined. Might he have done more to spare his family the suffering that was, rightfully, his alone to bear? Could he confidently affirm that it was devotion to a noble political cause, not an obsession with historical standing and other forms of male vanity, which fueled his fierce will to die?

Fortunately, in the case of Wen Tianxiang, the strength of his commitment to dynasty and the process through which he resolved attendant moral dilemmas are abundantly documented in his collected writings, much of it autobiographical prose and poetry with specific focus on the last years of his life. A leading actor on the late Song political stage, he also served as chief chronicler, and we will turn to him frequently in the pages to follow, as he doubtlessly would have wanted. Yet there are many thousands for whom little or no written record exists, even though the measure of their sacrifice and the dilemmas they confronted were equally wrenching. In so many cases, entire families and communities were obliterated, their singular crime being loyalist resolve. Moreover, martyrdom occurred in a manner, quantitatively and qualitatively, unique in China's long history prior to Song. The case of Li Zifa offers but one example of such devastating loss.

A low-level administrator for his native Nan'an commandary, in the empire's heartland, Li Zifa had assisted in the region's defense in 1276.[54] That defense proved so dogged that Mongol belligerents had been forced to retreat in frustration. But they returned with reinforcements in late 1278, intent on eliminating this Song holdout, one of the last in the circuit of Jiangnan West. With defeat imminent, Li Zifa returned home where his extended family of forty-seven was assembled. They apparently assisted him in sealing up the place before setting it afire. Their morbid wish to perish together came too quickly to permit second thoughts—thoughts about the death of innocent children and the disruption of family lines in a society that values nothing more than these.

More staggering still was the loss of Chen Yuzhi (doct. 1265), a native of the coastal city of Yongjia, less than four hundred kilometers from the Song capital at Lin'an (hereafter simplified as "Linan").[55] In

residence when northern armies began their assault, he organized "sons, nephews, and other villagers" into militias that offered a resistance so stiff as to keep the enemy at bay for two long years. But when the region fell, his men exhausted and wealth spent, he slit his own throat. And most, if not all of the Chen clan joined loyal villagers—an estimated eight hundred persons in all—as they "followed him in death." Similar to circumstances at Yaishan, the precise number to die by willful act of suicide, and not through hostile exchange with the enemy or coercion from fellow clansmen, will never be known. Use of the term "follow" in the various accounts of the incident, however, clearly suggests death as a volitional act. Another point to be made about the actions of this community of martyrs at Yongjia: certainly not everyone or even a majority of the eight hundred lost souls were members of the literati class, individuals with a vested interest in and commitment to the Song order. A considerable number must have been common people, individuals perhaps swept up in the fear and frenzy, but imitating as well the conduct of their social superiors.

There is less precision in reports of another suicide, Jiang Youzhi. It is only known that he was a professor at the Huizhou prefectural school, some two hundred kilometers west of Linan. In early 1276, when the Mongols took the capital, he led a sizable body of students in starving themselves to death.[56] This was no act of impetuousness or insanity, no last recourse for men and women trapped hopelessly by a dreaded enemy. Rather, it was a premeditated act of suicide by individuals who consciously chose to place "righteous principle," according to contemporary observers, before parochial concerns of simple survival.

Righteous principle had also motivated the deaths of literatus Yuan Yong and his family, it would appear. Their native Mingzhou, just south of modern Shanghai, was a prefecture with exceptionally close ties to the dynastic enterprise, a great generator of commercial wealth and literati talent, and among the region's leading families were the Yuan. Yuan Yong never held office under the Song, his doctoral degree earned only in 1271, as the dynasty entered its tumultuous last years.[57] He vigorously opposed, all the same, the decision of the local political establishment to surrender Mingzhou to the enemy in early 1276, their resistance having never been firm.[58] His first act, one of espionage, involved misinforming the enemy of reserve military strength. And when the hope of inducing an early withdrawal eluded him, he fought off the intruders as much as meagre resources would permit before being taken captive. By most accounts, he recognized his mission as suicidal from the very

outset. "Having lived as an official of Song," he declared, "I will die as a ghost of Song." Even under an excruciating and ultimately fatal "fire torture," Yuan Yong refused to submit to Mongol captors. His death had coincided with *Qingming*, the grave sweeping rites of early spring, and his family was busy tending to their ritual duties at gravesites beyond the city. Only after returning home did news of his demise reach them and their response was one of utter hysteria. Wives, children, grandchildren, and others—seventeen in all—committed suicide en masse by drowning. None in that group of seventeen seemed seriously distressed over the absence of a male heir to Yuan Yong, a son to conduct ritual sacrifices in his memory. It was, in the end, a mere servant who rescued Yuan Yong's five year-old son from the water and thereby prevented extinction of the entire line. There is no indication here of female survivors being coerced into taking their own lives, as is occasionally documented in other family suicides, for they were separated from Yuan Yong during those last critical days. Neither can the extreme response of Yuan women and youths be attributed to the extraordinary duress or destitution attendant to enemy siege. The self-assured dispatch with which they executed their deed, in all its awesome finality, can be explained only by a sharing, at some level, of the loyalist convictions of their fallen patriarch. Through death, they could celebrate the unity of the Yuan family as the ethical conscience for their community.

In the chronicles of earlier dynasties we read of elite men who commit suicide in the wake of a devastating turn of political events, instances where their honor or integrity is threatened so thoroughly that death seems the only respectable way out. There are records as well of men coercing their wives to die with them, perhaps in anticipation of the violent rape and murder that vengeful conquerors have historically perpetrated on the defenseless.[59] Prior to the Song, however, it was exceedingly rare for family leaders, with such willful premeditation, to take part in the annihilation of their entire progeny. Equally inconceivable is the notion that communities of hundreds and thousands, even tens of thousands, might band together in mass suicide. But in the last years of Song, such stories emerge over and again on a scale and frequency that simply staggers the rational mind. These stories suggest not only a convergence of historical conditions altogether unique in the long history of China, but also a radical change in the values, public and private, of the men and women of Song. The contrast with earlier times is perhaps nowhere more striking.

In the late sixth century, on the eve of the reunification of China

under Sui and Tang, historian Wei Shou compiled a *History of the Wei*. Writing under court auspices, he was the first to cluster together the biographies of loyalist exemplars under the title "Virtuous and Righteous." But the tone of his preface is one of rage, not revelry, as he laments the ethical void of recent times: "those who revere loyalism are rare and those who practice it are few."[60] Authors of the dynastic history for Tang, writing in the mid-tenth century, make no similar protestations. On the contrary, they consciously crammed their loyalist chapters with the biographies of men who seem scarcely to fit the loyalist mold—individuals whose private sacrifice for public cause seemed at best marginal, certainly not of the degree expected of martyrs.[61] In their anxiousness to make moral heroes out of mere exemplary statesmen, writers of the original Tang History were implicitly acknowledging a certain angst about the ethical standards of the age. Precisely such lack of discrimination would prompt revisionist historians under the direction of Ouyang Xiu, a century later, to purge roughly one quarter of the old biographies from the loyalist cluster of their *New History of the Tang*, replacing them with more credible entries. In the process of reordering moral categories, revisionist historians set a higher standard for the evaluation of prospective loyalists in future chronicles; they also set a higher standard of ethical conduct for statesmen who would aspire to such distinction.[62]

Compilers of the dynastic history of Song, writing in the mid-fourteenth century, would largely embrace the more stringent standards of the eleventh century. To earn inclusion among the ranks of loyalists, individuals were now expected to exhibit an uncommonly intense and selfless dedication to dynasty, on the one hand, and willfully jeopardize their very lives and careers as a consequence, on the other.[63] Even with such inflation in ethical expectations, they had no shortage of candidates: the biographical cluster for the "Loyal and Righteous" in the *History of the Song* (*Song shi*) ends up at least twice the length of comparable chapters in the Tang official histories, relative to total volume. This would suggest a veritable revolution in the ethical constitution of Song China. They may have been writing under Mongol auspices, yet official chroniclers made scant effort to camouflage their enthusiasm for the Song and its unparalleled attainments in moral culture:

> The spirit of loyalism among literati had, by the Five Dynasties (907–959), degenerated to the point of near extinction. And at the inauguration of Song there were the deplorable likes of Fan Zhi and Wang Pu [officials with no

remorse at changing dynastic loyalties]. Need we add more! But the accomplished founder's initial praise of Han Tong and subsequent honoring of Wei Yong [men staunchly loyal to preceding dynasties] was enough to express his aspirations. Later, officials along the northwest border often proved utterly fearless in the face of deadly contests, [having found inspiration in their example]. . . . By the time the Song perished, the loyal and virtuous were so prominent that they could be chronicled one group after another. The accomplishment reflected in this reforming of the old and nurturing of the new was scarcely achieved in a single day [it had grown incrementally over the centuries].[64]

The reader should not be deceived by our commentator's allusion to loyalist exemplars of dynasties past. For all of the earlier models and precedents, the loyalist phenomenon of Song times is unique in the depth of literati devotion to empire. That rare devotion is owed, in part, to the new relationship forged between ruler and ruled over the course of the dynasty's three hundred years. Historians have documented the evolution of this relationship in considerable detail and the implications of such changes are reflected in the lives of the men and women to follow. Other factors informed this new ethic as well.

The Song had presided over an explosive economic and technological revolution, an explosion which enhanced the quality of life for every sector of society, but perhaps for none more than the leisured classes.[65] This induced, in turn, a cultural rejuvenation the intense dynamism and enduring influence of which has few peers in the history of China. Although operating within the confines of an imperial edifice now over a millennium old, the dynasty stretched that system to its limits as it overhauled virtually every aspect of political and social organization. Yet by the late thirteenth century, these were all glories of the past whose legacy had come increasingly under attack.[66] Not merely were the old innovative impulses persistently suppressed as an inhibiting conservatism set in, but the entire monarchical order of Song grew progressively lethargic and dysfunctional. Most indicative of this dysfunction was the failure of the royal family to provide suitable heirs, the extent to which in 1274—and for the first time in the recent two centuries of Song rule—the throne would pass to a series of very young children. To the politically astute, the message this conveyed was perfectly clear: the Mandate of Heaven was on the verge of expiring, this regime going the way of countless others before it. Confronted with so unpropitious an augury and denied the inspiration of mature male monarchs that such times so desperately demanded, one would scarcely expect the kind of

radical expressions of loyalty to the royal house that are so abundantly documented for the late 1270s. The conduct of Wen Tianxiang and cohorts appears, to wit, as irrational from a political perspective as it was from the perspective of family obligations, noted earlier.

Some might attribute such seemingly irrational behavior to the unique character of the Mongol conquest of China, with its inordinate levels of hysteria and fear. Since the early years of their marathon forty-five year conflagration with the Song, the Mongols had annihilated entire populations partly as retribution for prolonged resistance, but also to set an example for other would-be resisters. Such mass brutalization of civilian populations occurred out west at Hanzhou, back east at Changzhou and Zhenchao, along the coast at Chaozhou and Xinghua, and in the heartland at Yingzhou and Jingjiang, to name the more notable locations.[67] At inaugurating his final campaign against the Song in 1274, Khubilai Khan seemed to be breaking with this ignominious tradition by instructing his chief commanders to refrain from unnecessary pillage and murder.[68] But most such travesties occurred after his injunction and their repeated occurrence suggests that Khubilai's commanders operated on an altogether different code of conduct. Citizens of the Song must have intuited as much, which would, perhaps, explain their desperate reaction to the enemy advance. If annihilation of one's entire family is a reasonable expectation in light of the brutal record of northern armies, then preemptive intervention is wholly rational as the most humanely dignified way out.

Were this the case, it would seem that these men and women responded preeminently to concerns of personal dignity—an instinctive preference for an honorable death for oneself and loved ones—not some ethical abstraction about dynastic loyalty. The problem here, however, is that other regimes of those turbulent decades confronted similar brutalization at the hands of the same enemy without triggering a comparable response from their subjects. The Jin dynasty of northern China, for example, ruled by Jurchen conquerors from Manchuria, had come under Mongol assault beginning in 1211. This was the heyday of Chinggis Khan, a time when Mongol notoriety as despoilers of the civilized world seems to have approached its terrorizing peak. With reports of millions being lost in a single region, the conquest of Jin scarcely departed from this tradition.[69] Still, Jin loyalists who willfully partook in the annihilation of entire families and communities in the manner and magnitude of Southern Song were exceedingly rare, exceptions to the rule confined almost exclusively to the military elite.[70] The

institution of minority rule with its blatant juxtaposition of privilege for some and abuse for many, however perverse the political species, cannot wholly explain the rather impassive response of Jin subjects at-large to such a terrifying assault on their homeland.

Apart from the totality of loyalist commitment, the Song experience differs from Jin, and indeed all Chinese dynasties before it, in the relative diversity of its loyalists, politically as well as socially. Prior to the Song, martyrs to dynasty were principally men of military stock. More likely to be confronted with life-threatening situations, soldiers were also most thoroughly indoctrinated in codes of glory and honor—or "righteous principle" (*yili*), in the idiom of Confucian China. Civilians were cut of a wholly different cloth. As agents of the throne, they might occasionally lose their lives in the execution of sensitive court policies or in the chaos of local insurrection. But as a rule, in times of dynastic transition when the state needed their leadership the most, society's most privileged tended to recede into the background, no doubt retreating to the safety of their walled compounds or rural retreats. This historical inclination of the literati elite to place survival of family before the interests of state is glibly acknowledged, as early as the eleventh century, by Ouyang Xiu. In his *Historical Records of the Five Dynasties*, for example, he bemoans the absence of civilian representatives among loyalist martyrs and attributes this to the shamelessness of littérateurs who so readily surrendered moral leadership to their social inferiors, mere military men. With compelling indignation, he writes:

> Rites and righteousness are the premiere methods for regulating the self. Integrity and shame are the premiere maxims for anchoring the self. Without integrity everything is acceptable. Without shame anything is done. . . . For the entire Five Dynasties era, I have found [only] three literati of complete virtue and fifteen officials killed-in-action. Curiously, many others with the trappings of Confucians would pride themselves as students of antiquity, enjoy the emoluments of men, and serve the empire of men. But when it came to loyalist virtue, our candidates came solely from the ranks of military leaders and foot soldiers. How could men of virtue be altogether absent among Confucian civilians?[71]

This tendency toward social irresponsibility among the literati ostensibly peaked, according to Ouyang Xiu, during the Five Dynasties era. This was ostensibly a time of pervasive corruption and degeneracy in the lives of royals and their courtiers, a time when civilian leaders were eclipsed by their martial inferiors, *wen* eclipsed by *wu*. Thus, Ouyang

Xiu called for the restoration of a reinvigorated *wen* to a position of natural dominance. But his characterization of the Five Dynasties as an historical aberration—the values of its literati antithetical to the past—should not be accepted uncritically. Rather, the acute ethical crises of that era had merely highlighted a problem of literati ambivalence toward the state that existed long before the Five Dynasties and may be as old, indeed, as the empire itself. It was at precisely this convention of ambivalence that men of the Song—especially historians like Ouyang Xiu, but also an assortment of other intellectuals and ultimately the state itself—directed their efforts to cast the old ethical laxity into a new order of moral rigor. The measure of their success lies in the preponderance of civilian leaders among the ranks of martyrs, most notably those who willingly laid down their lives for righteous principle.

EXORCISING DEMONS OLD AND NEW

In narrating the response of Song men and women to the demise of dynasty, our objective is to understand the changes in culture—political, social, and moral—behind those responses. Our temporal focus is the 1270s, when the military tide finally began to turn decidedly against the Song, the extent to which the extension of Mongol domination over all of China became depressingly inevitable and irreversible. Unlike a century and a half earlier when Song royalists still had the option of flight further south, this time there would be no safe sanctuary from which to launch a dynastic revival, no remote refuge for royal pretenders. For the first time in three centuries, southern men and women were confronted with the prospect of life without the Song as they came to terms with, simultaneously, the high moral expectations of a newly invigorated Confucian order. So many of the ethical abstractions of the eleventh and twelfth centuries had evolved in a vacuum: the empire had enjoyed such enduring prosperity and stability that the prospect of conflict between state and family seemed remote. Only as the empire stood on the verge of collapse would its leadership finally discover whether the new morality had acquired any practical relevance, whether it could inspire coherent public and private agendas, whether it could survive the dynasty that had nurtured it. But political ethics represents only one dimension of the loyalist problematic in Song times. The other was cultural—a function of conflict between southern contexts and northern values, material life and moral culture, feminine power and masculine privilege.

The last years of Song were a time when court women, who for most of the dynasty had kept a low political profile, emerged as powerful managers of child monarchs and arbiters of state affairs. Away from court, women filled many a vacuum left by absent or deceased husbands, no less confident in ethical conviction than their men. No contemporary observer could miss the obvious implication of *yin* in ascent over *yang*, the weak leading the strong—an unhealthy and potentially lethal imbalance, by the standards of traditional Chinese politics. Sensitivity to the image of invirility would prove particularly acute for a regime of China's southeast. No region was more removed, contemporaries believed, from the gravitational energy or *yang* dominance of the north. In the words of Chen Liang (1143–1193), an eminent political philosopher of the late twelfth century, the "proper" or "vigorous energy" (*zhengqi*) of the Middle Kingdom resides in and resonates from the northwest.[72] It is precisely this gravitational force which traditionally made for the creative and martial superiority, or vigor, of the northwest as cradle of Chinese civilization. Contrastingly, the south contains varying degrees of mere "peripheral energy" (*pianqi*). The most peripheral or "enfeebled" is ostensibly the Wu/Yue region, south of the Yangzi River and gravitating on the eastern coastline, a region far removed from the northwest and populated by Han peoples much later. This was, historically, the "small land of the southern barbarians," according to Chen Liang, an allusion to the fragmentation, political as well as cultural, common to this geographically insular area.[73] Even regions farther west—the old Chu domain of the central Yangzi and the Shu domain of the far west—by tradition considered less peripheral than the southeast, are nonetheless consigned to political and cultural marginality relative to the Central Plains. Such presumed disparities in regional stamina and will were echoed elsewhere, in the writings of the twelfth-century poet Xin Qiji and the seventeenth-century historian Wang Fuzhi, as will be shown.[74]

One aspect of this purported "peripheralness" is the proclivity of the southeast, its government as well as residents, to be distracted by the material amenities uniquely abundant in this region. Linan presented the Song elite with a range of amenities and diversions that rivaled the biggest and best of premodern cities.[75] A coastal site provided easy access to commodities from Japan and southeast Asia, fueling a diverse influx of exotic imports. An abundance of lakes and rivers yielded an amazing array of fresh fish for the city's hundreds of restaurants while augmenting the possibilities for local leisure and distant travel. And the

terrain surrounding Linan, in contrast with the arid and monochrome vistas of the northwestern loess, is exquisitely varied. Rolling hills of verdant green lie to the south and to the west a massive lake whose natural endowments are rivaled only by the magnificence of its human enhancements. Over ten kilometers in circumference, West Lake provided the rich and powerful with a seemingly limitless supply of public restaurants and private villas, dancing girls and singing boys. It is a "kingdom of amusements" (*leguo*), in the words of Chen Liang, where the will to war is weak.[76] Such consumption-driven debauchery has long been associated with the Wu region, but the magnitude of it all in Southern Song times had no apparent precedent.[77] Moreover, the formality of planned capitals like Chang'an and Luoyang, including the strict allocation of space by principles of ritual symbolism, did not exist in Linan. A dense population consigned to this new and less formal configuration made for a spontaneous interaction across traditional lines of class and gender, bringing together men and women, rich and poor in culturally dynamic yet subversive ways. Even students at the various university campuses, commonly considered the moral conscience of Linan, were widely addicted to the city's consumption habits.[78] In this way, the south's material assets evolved increasingly into a political and social liability, an unhealthy distraction from the agrarian simplicity exemplified by the northwest. A moralist-inspired backlash, coinciding with the declining fortunes of dynasty, would be a source of constant anxiety throughout the last years of Song and powerfully inform the actions of its defenders, as we will see.

The guilt induced by material comfort, the angst attendant to geomagnetic inferiority, and defensiveness about a court dominated by women and children all proved conducive to overcompensation. The male courtiers of the Song seemed intent on dramatizing the virility of the fledgling dynastic cause that they represented through acts of exaggerated heroism. The very notion of "loyalty" (*zhong*), in the context of China's middle period, had become increasingly associated with masculine heroics and manly virtues. It would even represent the premiere moral component of an ideology of manhood. This occurs, in part, because loyalty was traditionally expressed through public deeds and men dominated the arena of politics. It also occurs because loyalty was identified with an impassive selflessness and rigid discipline for which women presumably lacked capacity. In the words of martyr Wen Tianxiang: "Those seeking to perform the deeds of men can scarcely afford the sentiment of mere wives."[79] Like most men of his day, he assumed

women to lack the emotional detachment and civic commitment of men. And it is this "natural" inadequacy of women that naturalizes male domination and, in the process, justifies their subordination to men. Moreover, to the extent that war is principally a male vocation, military contests can serve to distinguish the sexes—achieving precisely the "differentiation between husband and wife" that Neo-Confucian moralists had come to advance so aggressively in recent generations.[80] This affirms, in turn, the principle of dominance by the physically stronger sex. Certainly in the West, it has been the aggressive and competitive qualities of the male, originating in his role as hunter and warrior, that later came to define his character and behavior as a social being.[81] Remarkably, the Chinese subscribed to a similar logic. "Men are prized for their physical strength, women venerated for their weakness," goes an old Confucian adage.[82]

Just as the battlefield provides the context for demonstrating the physical superiority of men, the battle itself provides the occasion to exhibit male virtues such as loyalty to state—a masculine code of absolute ethics as an alternative to the moral ambivalence of material society.[83] It is no coincidence, therefore, that the loyalist literature of the late Song contains frequent reference to Chinese manhood: *zhennan, nanzi, zhangfu*. Far more than sheer political affinity or personal honor was at stake. In the process of affirming masculine virtue, Song men implicitly affirmed the social agenda associated with it, an agenda of hierarchical submission where women defer to men and the effete defer to the virile. Also implicit in that agenda is a certain fundamentalistic revival of traditional distinctions of gender and class—a cultural conservatism, if you will. In reacting to the urbane decadence of the day, the Southern Song male sought to recast himself into a more respectably virile mold. Material comfort, in this context, emerges as incompatible with the higher standard of masculine discipline now expected of men.[84]

There is evidence, in fact, that Song men were quite conscious of the links between political ethics and social hierarchy, male virtue and female submission. Again, Ouyang Xiu's *Historical Records of the Five Dynasties* emerges as critical to this insight. As noted earlier, he seemed to speak most passionately when denouncing the ethical depravity of the day, particularly with reference to men at the top of the social pyramid—the *shi* literati who, since the time of Confucius, were presumed best suited to lead society along the proper moral path. In the literati leadership of the Five Dynasties, however, Ouyang Xiu found a moral vacuum that threatened more than merely the political order of the day:

it jeopardized the larger social order in dangerously pernicious ways.

Ouyang Xiu hints at his anxieties about the literati leadership of recent generations in a lengthy preface to a cluster of biographies for morally deficient men. Here, he introduces the Woman Li, the wife of Wang Ning, a minor official who had died on assignment near the western capital. Having gathered his remains and the belongings of her and son, Woman Li was headed for Shandong, roughly a thousand kilometers to the east, when she was denied accommodations by an innkeeper. The improper spectacle of a woman with a young child on the highway without an appropriate male companion had left him suspicious. There ensued an appalling confrontation where the widow refused to leave the premises and an intemperate innkeeper grabbed her by the arm, as a first step to forceably evicting her. She responded with near violent rage at an indignity that seemed tantamount to sexual violation: "With head facing the heavens, the woman let out a prolonged wail as she proclaimed: 'How is it that I, someone's wife, have failed to protect my chastity by permitting this hand to touch me. And surely a single hand cannot be permitted to defile my entire body!' So drawing an axe, she lopped off her own arm."[85] The reader never learns if the widow eventually secured lodging at that particular establishment, but news of her plight inspired the imperial court to bestow gifts on the woman while punishing the innkeeper with public flogging. Ouyang Xiu then concludes: "Literati with no similar regard for physical self who countenanced untold indignities merely to save their own lives, must feel some measure of shame at learning of the character of the Woman Li." This line leads directly into the biography of Feng Dao, chief councilor under four of the Five Dynasties whom Ouyang Xiu would emblazon in infamy as a symbol of the prevailing indifference to ethical duty.[86] In his own words:

> Although personal witness to the death of rulers and dissolution of empires, Dao never evinced much concern for these. At the time, the world was gripped by universal chaos and alien invasion, nearly turning on its head the mission to propagate the race, while Dao would style himself Old Man of Eternal Joy and write a book of several hundred words where he narrates with pride his service under four separate houses, plus the [barbarous] Khitan, and the ranks and honors earned.[87]

By juxtaposing this virtueless man against a woman of great gravity and inner strength, Ouyang Xiu exposes the longstanding presumption of males as morally superior to be in serious jeopardy. He also suggests grave social repercussions as an outgrowth of this shift in political ethics.

He is never explicit in defining the problem solely in terms of gender, he never directly links the superior virtue of women to the subversion of male power and privilege. Yet through the context and the terminology employed, gender-related identities and interests are clearly implied. Our objective here is to treat Song men as men, individuals with anxieties and agendas that are informed as much by gender as other things like profession and class.[88] It is a perspective lamentably lacking in secondary scholarship on traditional China, despite the abundance and diversity of primary sources for the recent millennium of history.

Apart from class and gender, another lens through which men of the late Song saw their own times was dynastic history and precedent—a vulnerability which the enemy quickly learned to exploit. In early 1276, as Mongol troops entered the final weeks of their assault on Linan, chief commander Bayan would make an exquisitely astute observation as he spurned overtures of peace: "Your Song once acquired the realm at the hand of a child and will lose it at the hand of a child as well. This is simply the Way of Heaven. Need we say any more?"[89] This was no off-the-cuff comment, for in his supreme confidence in the impending victory of his cause, Bayan draws inspiration from political and historical traditions native to China and compelling to its people. After all, some three centuries earlier another six year-old had sat on the throne of the Later Zhou, only to reign in insularity and impotence. He similarly met with border war and domestic instability, conditions conducive to the coup that came in 959, after less than a decade in power. It was a largely bloodless act that permitted the chief of the Palace Guard, Zhao Kuang-yin (927–976), to catapault himself to the throne as Supreme Ancestor (Taizu) of Song. Neither the child nor his regents, male and female, had done anything to warrant their fate. Theirs was perhaps the finest of the Five Dynasties, after all, their leadership far more responsible than most. Power would pass uneventfully, all the same: few deeds of loyalist heroism occurred in the form of royals committing suicide or commanders resisting defiantly. Heaven had simply withdrawn its Mandate, so it seemed to many, inducing literati resignation in the inevitable. For a people inclined to view history as a progression of repetitive episodes and accustomed to intuiting the will of Heaven through the repetition of human events, this recollection could be utterly disabling. But the collapse of a towering Song would follow none of the familiar or foreseeable patterns—predictably perhaps for a dynasty that broke with so many other conventions of the past. Balancing the expectations of region, class, and gender, incalculable numbers of southern men and

women willfully laid down their lives. Cognizant of the eyes of history upon them—their minor deeds much magnified by the uniqueness of the times—they acted on a confused agenda where political culture and cultural identity converged in guiding their rendezvous with fate.

The wind blows low on the moutain
*The image of **decay.***
Thus the superior man stirs up the people
And strengthens their spirit.

The Changes, XVIII.

2 · Gu:
Decayed and Volatile

There would be no need to consult the soothsayers, the auguries of the year 1274 being anything but subtle. It was late that summer, in the eighth lunar month to be precise, that the Mountain of Heavenly Visage yielded to pressures from the depths of the earth, tremors within inducing landslides without. In turn, these triggered floods of ominous proportions. Utterly "beyond calculation" is the number of men and women who perished, according to official sources, in the floods and ensuing chaos.[1] After all, Tianmu Shan was at its nearest point a mere fifty *li*, roughly twenty kilometers, from the capital of the Song empire, Linan—a city which had grown far beyond the size anticipated for, or even appropriate to, a purportedly "temporary" capital. A circumference of merely ten miles around made Linan significantly smaller than the capitals of most dynasties, its urban squeeze and rural sprawl stretching the upper limits of premodern technology. City borders were extended to accommodate in excess of one million residents, while the southern and western suburbs swelled with the vast overflow.[2] Their rapid growth with scant planning had left these communities acutely vulnerable to nature's caprice. It was out of this desperate sense of vulnerability, perhaps, that locals so readily embraced longstanding traditions which attributed magical powers to Tianmu Shan.

The mountain range seems to have towered over the surrounding hills, although peaks of two to three thousand *zhang*—nearly 30,000 feet according to the 1271 gazetteer for Linan—is most assuredly an exaggeration. A circumference of 500 to 2,000 *li*—up to a thousand kilometers with thirty-six separate caverns—may represent overstate-

ment as well, although admittedly the range did span four separate prefectures.[3] Yet a mountain's auspicious powers rest less with sheer monumental qualities and more with subtleties of location, qualities in this case eminently abundant. As if by some divine design, Tianmu Shan culminated in imposing twin peaks beneath which vast streams of water cascaded and careened, initially forming two massive ponds before flowing down in every direction. Such majestic elegance inspired countless myths and legends. Some suspected immortals to inhabit its caverns, others believed its shrubs to contain magic elixirs of immortality. The famed poet Li Bo, of the eighth century, spoke of "the celestial golden pheasant" hovering above.[4] Back in the third century, the distinguished geographer and adviser to royalty, Guo Pu, hailed the geomantic propitiousness of Tianmu Shan. This land where "the dragon flies and the phoenix dances" he annointed as the birthplace of future kings.[5] In the twelfth and thirteenth centuries, emperors of the Song ensconced in nearby Linan built temples to honor the spirits of the mountain. They had hoped, no doubt, to benefit politically from its perceived powers to nurture and legitimize pretenders to the Mandate of Heaven.[6]

A second event of momentous import to residents of metropolitan Linan was the sudden death only weeks earlier of Duzong, fifteenth emperor of the Song line. Stricken at the youthful age of thirty-four and scarcely a decade into his reign, his unexpected demise came at the worst conceivable time. The Chinese word for a momentous death, *beng*, reserved solely for emperors and empresses, has the original meaning quite literally of "landslide." Such dual usage implies that both events can be equally cataclysmic from the perspective of mere men. Embodied in the idiom is compelling symbolism as well. To the extent that a shifting earth was long perceived as heaven's most emphatic vehicle for intervening in earthly affairs in general and political affairs in particular, so a monarchical death shares a similar aura of divine designation. But Tianmu Shan was no ordinary mountain. Associated with the dragon and phoenix, the natural world's complement to the human world's emperor and empress, any irregularity at such portentous heights was certain to induce scrutiny and fear on the surrounding plains. Indeed, contemporary records depict residents of Linan as utterly "convulsed" by the landslides, as if to suggest that the event's political import weighed heavier in the minds of common citizens than even the coincidental loss of life.[7]

This is not to say that the deceased emperor had somehow, through personal example or political style, instilled the measure of respect among his officials or endearment among ordinary subjects the extent

to which they should have genuinely mourned his premature death. He
was adopted into the royal family as Zhao Qi—to employ the emperor's
personal name, a practice which by tradition was strictly taboo thus the
widespread use of the posthumous designation Duzong, the "Measured."[8] Unfortunately, the self-restraint so prominently exhibited prior
to his accession and the inspiration behind such complimentary characterization had failed to transform itself, afterwards, into the temperance demanded of the Son of Heaven. Rumors of excessive indulgence
in wine and song persisted throughout his reign. The illicit deflection of
public funds as subsidy for private entertainment are rumored as well,
the emperor seeking every excuse to feast and make merry. It was a lifestyle which would have sapped the stamina of any mortal, yet the strain
on Zhao Qi seemed greater than most. He had been born with congen-
ital defects of some gravity which stemmed, according to credible informants, from his mother's unsuccessful attempt at aborting her pregnancy.[9] In youth, this left Zhao Qi visibly maladroit in the simple use
of arms and legs, while later it required frequent medication. Critics also
seethed at the emperor's inexplicable dependence on the lameducks of
the preceding reign: he seemed merely "to fold his hands" in ambivalence and resignation as power passed from one unworthy surrogate to
the next.[10] Even in ordinary times such deficiences in political savvy and
fiscal restraint would have outraged observers at court, who readily saw
in the new reign too many semblances of its predecessor, the tumultuous
times of Lizong (see Figure 1). But the dynasty's vigor had further deteriorated in recent years, a border menace once simply annoying having
now assumed crisis dimensions. And this ruler, an average man in his
prime forced to bear personal witness to the sad spectacle of his empire
crumbling before him, possessed neither the vision nor vigor to challenge an inscrutable Heaven. The material and sensual were his only an-
tidotes to a paralyzing depression.

The sense of crisis was reinforced by the third catacylsmic event of
the summer of 1274—the official declaration of war by the Mongols
against the Song. The enemy edict, issued only twenty-three days before
the death of Duzong, was masterfully timed and crafted. Placing blame
for the war on the south, it asserted Mongol objectives as fundamentally
humane but finished with a declaration of ruthless commitment to unconditional victory. Composed as instructions from Khubilai Khan to
his troops, a dissemination beyond the barracks and borders of the
north was nonetheless clearly intended:

Since the time of Emperor Taizu [Chinggis Khan], we have communicated diplomatically with the Song. And in the age of Xianzong [Möngke], I received orders from my frontier post to join the punitive drive against the south. [Chief councilor] Jia Sidao, at that juncture, repeatedly dispatched envoy Song Jing to visit me and request a cessation of hostilities and respite for the people. Since my accession [in 1260], I have reflected on this prospect and thus commissioned Hao Jing and others to forward a correspondence of inquiry. This could have provided a plan for all humanity. Yet he arrested Hao Jing and continued to dispatch troops year after year. The dead and injured now pile up while prisoners and hostages grow. This all suggests that the Song has brought peril to its own people. . . . Today, I charge you to advance by land and water and inform both near and far [of our intent] so that all may know: among the enemy, the innocent without advance preparation will be spared callous murder or plunder by our soldiers; those who eradicate treason and promote submission or otherwise achieve special distinction will be duly advanced; but for those who stand firm in opposition or defiantly resist, there will be no question of capture and perhaps death.[11]

This proclamation of war came at a curious time, preceding both the death of Duzong and the disaster at Tianmu Shan. Moreover, the Mongol war against the Song—following immediately on the heels of their 1234 conquest of north China—was already forty years old, the conduct of which had never before required formal declaration on either side. And the fifty-nine year old Khubilai was already fourteen years into his reign, newcomer to neither the politics nor the prosecution of this conflict. New conditions, however, suggested that the old stalemate might be about to end.

By the spring of 1273, the Mongols had finally succeeded in their five-year assault on Xiangyang. The collapse of that strategic plum in central China, as we will soon see, had jeopardized Song command of the Yangzi River to a degree unprecedented in its history, jolting the south like a bolt of lightning. It also confirmed the Mongol ability to adapt to new technologies and modes of warfare: the natural barrier of water, which historically insulated southern China from nomadic occupation, had been breached with daring decisiveness. Astutely, Khubilai was exploiting this new sense of vulnerability. His declaration of war further represents an indictment of the Song political establishment and its mismanagement of border affairs. It is as though he and his advisors had intuited a groundswell of negative sentiment against the besieged government in Linan, especially among the politically astute literati, and were adding political propaganda to their already lethal arsenal of weapons now targeted on the south. In this context of growing military

Figure 1. Emperor Lizong (r. 1224–1264).
Courtesy of National Palace Museum, Taipei, Taiwan ROC.

strength and political deftness on the part of its dreaded foe, only a bold initiative from Linan—an imaginative deployment of the empire's still considerable resources—could spare southern China from the dreaded fate of virtually every other empire heretofore to lock horns with the Mongols: a painfully decided defeat.

Writers of the dynastic history, evincing little empathy for the beleaguered monarch, characterize Duzong as "lucky" to have died of natural causes in palatial comfort as his empire's fortunes hung slimly in the balance.[12] He would never experience the violent death or humiliating surrender that awaits most final monarchs. Not so lucky were his surviving sons: Zhao Shi, Zhao Xian, and Zhao Bing. Ranging in age from three to five years old, none were even remotely ready for the responsibilities thrusted upon them. It is perhaps for this reason that few senior statesmen spoke out against the court's decision to bypass eldest son Zhao Shi, born to a lesser consort, in favor of a younger son born to Empress Quan, Duzong's legal wife (see Appendix A). Just two months shy of his fourth birthday, Zhao Xian (Gongdi) became the sixteenth emperor of Song on the ninth day of the seventh lunar month, 12 August 1274 by western reckoning. He was the youngest ever to sit on the Song throne, yet being constantly prompted and pampered by swarms of senior officials and palace ladies, the boy must have sensed however innocently the tension and trepidation which informed the actions of all.

THE LADIES IN WAITING

Many would direct the child monarch toward his rendezvous with fate but none was so pivotal as his step-grandmother, the Grand Dowager, who presided over the first female regency since the eleventh century.[13] Born as Xie Qiao (Daoqing, 1210–1283), she hailed from a family of distinguished service but modest means.[14] Her grandfather, Xie Shenfu, had enjoyed the favor of a succession of monarchs and the respect of most colleagues in the bureaucracy. This was no easy feat for the late twelfth century, when factional strife and collegial rivalry had increasingly paralyzed the court. Yet Xie Shenfu was cast in a rare mold where the several traits most critical to political success converged in a single personality. He could be critical yet fair, serious yet approachable, principled yet flexible, and scrupulous at rising above factional demagoguery—traits so extraordinary that the discriminating Emperor Xiaozong (r. 1162–1189) once characterized him as possessing "the deportment of the ancients."[15] No compliment could be greater for a Confucian bureaucrat under the empire.

The granddaughter of Xie Shenfu seems never to have known him personally, his long career having ended shortly before her birth. But the political legacy of this senior statesman would command the respect of courtiers for generations to come, benefiting his granddaughter in more ways than one. Xie Qiao entered the harem of Lizong soon after his 1224 accession and rose in a few short years to legal wife and empress. Her grandfather may have been dead for at least a decade or two, yet few would deny him some role in her steady climb up the harem hierarchy. It was surely not physical assets which carried her there, for on this score she was sadly deficient.

According to official chronicles, Xie Qiao was born with an inordinately dark complexion; she also had cataract-like obstructions in one eye, unsightly afflictions whose traces remained visibly with her even at the time of entry into the imperial harem. Under ordinary circumstances, this would have critically handicapped her candidacy as consort, for physical beauty and grace while not exclusive qualifications were assuredly of some relevance. Her extraordinary selection, by most accounts, came only after some aggressive lobbying by the Dowager Yang, stepmother of Lizong and widow of Ningzong.[16] A politically savvy and enterprising woman, an accomplished calligrapher as well, Yang Yan must have seen so much of herself in this younger woman: both were highly literate and intellectually gifted, both had known financial hardship due to the loss of fathers at an early age, and the two seemed seriously handicapped relative to other women of the harem in their physical beauty and appeal to the emperor. It was Xie Shenfu who had promoted Yang Yan's installation as empress in 1202, seeking to counter Emperor Ningzong's seduction by a certain mesmerizing beauty. This represented for Empress Yang a political favor now over two decades old and she would scarcely, for reason of sheer cosmetics, forgo this opportunity to repay that outstanding debt. Emperor Lizong first procrastinated, designating no one as empress for the initial five years of his reign, but he would ultimately defer to his stepmother in 1230, just two years before her death. He did so partly due to his own insecurities as adopted son to Ningzong with rather weak blood ties to the royal family. He also knew better than to challenge the palace's senior women, who expected a strong voice over such domestic arrangements. Still, never happy with the choice, he responded by lavishing his amorous energies on a series of lesser consorts.

Other empresses burdened with similar neglect have often responded by growing bitter and vengeful, perpetrating acts of violence on the favored woman or women. Palace violence of the sort had erupted only a

few decades earlier, in the age of an impulsively jealous Empress Li, wife of Emperor Guangzong (r. 1189–1194). Her chilling assassination of rival consorts and terrorizing of the emperor himself would drive him to near insanity and force an early abdication, in the end—a lesson angry courtiers would not soon forget.[17] Empress Xie was cut of an entirely different cloth. Dynastic historians evince a highly favorable bias in depicting her as "proper and serious," a thoughtfully measured woman. Despite marriage to a man whose reputation for obsessive romance and even lechery persisted well into his fourth decade in power, as he approached his mid-sixties, the empress maintained not only proper but ostensibly "generous" relations with her husband and fellow consorts.[18]

Another curious trait of Empress Xie, which is at the source of her estimable standing in the traditional historiography for the Song, is a strong disinclination to extend her influence from the palace to the court. Her grandfather's political legacy and her own considerable acumen, contrasted so starkly against her husband's bumbling ineptitude in managing bureaucrats and border affairs, should have drawn Empress Xie into court affairs regardless of her own predisposition to restraint. Those occasions were by all indicators exceedingly rare, but there is record of one notable exception that, with hindsight, emerges as highly suggestive of the political courage and confidence of Xie Qiao, as she approached fifty years old and the third decade of her reign.

The incident occurred in the summer of 1259, at the height of an intense Mongol offensive out west against Sichuan. Nothing in the two earlier decades of hostilities between north and south was as massive and focused as this, for the first time confirming to the Song its greatest fear: the Mongols, who for long seemed content merely to harrass and pillage a belligerent south, had grown intent on outright annihilation. They had even acquired the requisite skills to succeed. For too long, decisionmakers in Linan had "toyed with the enemy," contemptuous of them and smug in their own conviction of superiority. But in the recent month or so the Mongols had seized Sichuan's ten leading cities while intensifying activity in central China. This suggested the imminent opening of a second front farther east, probably the central Yangzi region. Emerging from this emotionally pitched context was a proposal to relocate the capital to a more defensible location, a coastal site perhaps. After all, residents of Linan had long learned to live with the strategic liabilities of their ostensibly "temporary" capital. Precisely the city's most valued asset in peace—accessibility—turned out to be its greatest liability in war and no amount of human engineering could wholly offset the designs of na-

ture. To the east, an enemy could too easily access the river which linked Linan to the Hangzhou Bay, cutting off supply as well as escape routes; and they could approach the western suburbs with still greater ease from one of the several points along a meandering Yangzi River, which at its nearest point was only a few hundred kilometers away (see Maps 1a and 1b). So the relocation proposal stood on firm strategic ground. Politically, it triggered a flood of acrimony.

The dynastic history attributes this memorable gaffe to Dong Songchen, a manipulative eunuch whose favor by the emperor seemed to correlate in direct proportion to the bureaucracy's disdain.[19] Yet debate at court was far too intense and wide ranging, drawing in even regional officials, for the relocation proposal to represent the view of a single castrate in isolation from the outer court. Broader political support for relocation is also implicit in the emperor's initially sympathetic reception. Yet the idea evoked a stiff rebuke from Empress Xie. Any move would "alarm the masses," she argued, inducing a dangerous hysteria which could only benefit the enemy.[20] She might have added an equally unsavory consequence of a quick imperial exit: it would present an image of the royal family as irresponsibly desperate, willfully jeopardizing the lives of millions in metropolitan Linan merely to protect the person of the emperor. Others favoring a firm military stand soon followed her lead, perhaps intuiting that the court's overreaction to the Mongols might wreak a domestic havoc exceeding even the effects of the incursion itself. It was this rejection of desperate hysteria and reliance on iron will that ultimately prevailed. The Mongols had already withdrawn by late August, acting chiefly on domestic considerations back north, which included the death of their khan on a Sichuan battlefield. But motives mattered less than end results and these seemed to confirm the wisdom of an assertive approach—the empress's approach—to the border crisis.

The role of Xie Qiao in this controversial debate is noteworthy not only because it reflects her considerable confidence in political conviction, nor simply because it documents her decisionmaking input at the highest level. More importantly, her public challenge of a policy associated with the favored Dong Songchen, a fellow member of the palace, suggests a rare sensitivity to the interests and concerns of the outer court, and the male literati who manage it. For a woman whose confinement to the palace had now exceeded three decades, this was no mean accomplishment—certainly, such independence of eunuch aides was not normative for earlier dowager-regents.[21] And fifteen years later, this record of promoting the interests of the empire at large, not merely

or even principally the inner court, must have made the prospect of a Dowager Xie regency in the 1270s far more palatable to an outer court of men instinctively wary of women in power. Equally reassuring and increasingly relevant, in light of the changing political arena of the 1270s and the war councils that now commanded centerstage, was the dowager's demonstrated strength at border management. Even in the face of deteriorating and sometimes desperate conditions, she retained until the end perhaps the calmest head in the capital.

Dowager Xie could be equally circumspect yet courageous when it came to domestic concerns. During the first year of her regency, for example, she faced growing pressure to elevate the posthumous standing of Zhao Hong, her husband's long-deceased stepbrother and rival.[22] This political hot potato had been tossed about for fully a half-century, ever since 1225 when imperial prince Zhao Hong, having been purged from the palace, was executed on charges of conspiracy against the state. Posthumously stripped of titular honors, the young man was buried as a commoner; and the throne which came so close to being his would pass to the future Lizong, the second adopted son of Ningzong. His fate seemed tragic to many, his penalty unduly harsh. Dowager Xie was, of course, the wife of Lizong and any proposed reversal of actions associated with her deceased husband and his disgraced brother was certain to be received with instinctive reluctance. At the same time, as dynastic fortunes declined in the 1270s, court officers would acquire a heightened sensitivity to issues of ritual propriety. Out of this sensitivity grew a festering angst over the absence of an heir to the dead prince—a male descendant whose ritual sacrifices could appease his angry ghost. Few could have found fault with the dowager had she chosen simply to ignore the pleas, as had her husband for so many decades. She did not, but instead instructed her History Bureau to review the relevant precedent and prepare a recommendation. After months of consideration, she acted positively on that recommendation, restoring princely status to Zhao Hong and designating an heir to his line. Neither of her predecessors, not her husband nor her stepson, had responded so constructively to this shameful blight on so hallowed an institution as the imperial succession and the courage displayed by her action was nothing less than extraordinary.

Dowager Xie, as adoptive mother of the previous emperor and widow of the one before him, was the senior representative of the palace in the regency of the child emperor Gongdi, in 1274. Documentation may be scant, but there is every reason to believe that she shared some measure of power with, or at least regularly consulted, other imperial wives and

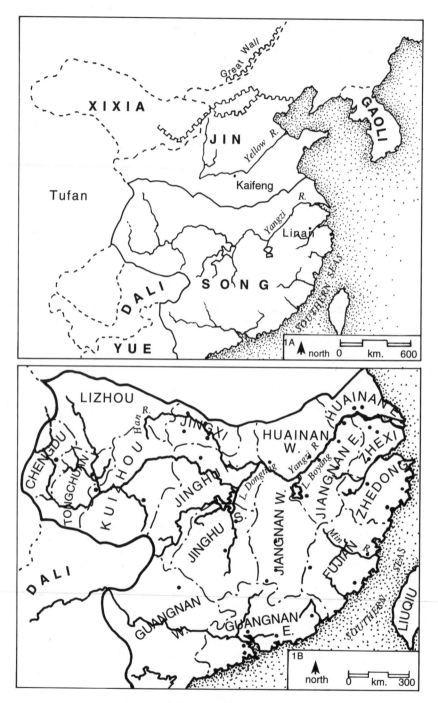

Maps 1a and 1b. Song China by Circuit

mothers, particularly the women who gave birth to her three grand-sons—all potential heirs to Duzong. Of these, the thirty-three year old Quan Jiu (1241–1309), wife of Duzong, probably commanded an especially attentive ear.[23]

Quan Jiu possessed like the senior dowager an exceptionally sharp and savvy political mind, and an equally impressive pedigree. On the one hand, she was the grandniece of Lizong's mother, the Lady Quan, making her and the former emperor close cousins. The Quan matriarch had married a distant cousin of the royal Zhao clan and her son grew up in the Quan household at Shaoxing, to be plucked by the palace as heir to Ningzong when already a young adult. This left the future Lizong uncommonly close to his maternal relatives, for whom in later years posthumous honors were so generous as to provoke the repeated reproach of officialdom. On the other hand, Quan Jiu could boast a distinguished father, Quan Zhaosun, an administrative level official who died on assignment in the provinces. Biographical sources portray his daughter as far more worldly than most young recruits for the harem. Having traveled extensively with her father and observed him in office, she emerged as remarkably conversant in current events and confident in her own views. Those qualities largely inspired Lizong's selection of her, at twenty years old, as consort for his own son-by-adoption. Thus, he willfully ignored her rather advanced age—advanced, that is, for a position where virgin innocence is imperative and early puberty the preferred time of recruitment.[24]

The dynastic history offers a rare record of the first meeting, in December 1261, between the aging emperor and his son's new bride. Lizong was initially struck by her arrestingly auspicious physical traits: broad forehead, prominent eyes, and thick eyebrows that extended to her temples.[25] Yet even these could scarcely have prepared him for the grit and gravity of her intellect, which caused their first meeting to be so unconventionally spirited that it was twice recorded in the same dynastic history. The fullest account, found in her official biography, begins:

> Officials spoke [favorably] of the manner in which Lady Quan accompanied her father, Zhaosun, as they traveled about the Yangzi and Jinghu regions and experienced both hardship and danger [due to Mongol hostilities there]. In her treatment of the statused and wealthy, she was certain to exhaust the Way of vigilance and restraint. Emperor Lizong, in memory of his mother Lady Cixian, ordered the future empress to enter the palace, where he addressed her: "Your father Zhaosun died in the service of his majesty in the Baoyou reign [1253–1259], the very thought of which makes me grieve."

The future empress responded: "My father can be remembered, but even more should the plight of the masses of the Huai and Hu regions be remembered!" The emperor came to regard her as truly exceptional and said to his high officials: "The words of this daughter of the Quan family are particularly *grandiloquent*. A betrothal should be arranged with the heir-apparent to permit continuation of the ritual line."[26]

One can well imagine the level of consternation among those in attendance on that December day. The response of Quan Jiu contained, after all, a strong satirical sting as she alluded to the emperor's most fatal flaw—perennially placing domestic trivia before the escalating crisis at the border. Lizong quickly intuited this, as evidenced by his characterization of the woman as "grandiloquent" (*shenling*). The phrase here represents an allusion to the *Analects*, where Confucius suggests that those clever in words and appearance are rarely benevolent.[27] Lizong was not necessarily suggesting that his cousin lacked moral virtue, merely that she spoke with an imposing measure of craft and forcefulness. Nonetheless, a sense of civic responsibility exceeding even his own seemed not to threaten the monarch, who apparently viewed the humanistic thrust of Quan Jiu's comments as due compensation for her cutting words.

For our two empresses, independence of their husbands on issues of public policy and personal decorum were luxuries afforded them as empresses, the legal wives of the emperor and maternal symbol of the empire. Pedigree made it easier as well. A proper family background provides educational and social exposure, but also the kin group supports that could nourish these women while insulating them from the potential wrath of the world's most powerful man, the emperor. More vulnerable were the lesser consorts of Duzong, née Yang and Yu. Yang Juliang (1244–1279) was the senior of the two, her son being older and her title as the "Pure Consort" (*Shufei*) more advanced as palace protocol goes.[28] Some scholars believe her to be descended from the influential family of Empress Yang, wife of Ningzong, and closely related by blood to Lizong.[29] In fact, the assumption lacks foundation in existing scholarship and stands as pure conjecture. We can establish, however, that Yang Juliang hailed from a highly literate family, father Yang Zan among the most celebrated poets and literary tutors of mid-century Linan.[30] Poetic celebrity notwithstanding, the fact that his daughter would enter the palace as mere "Beauty," the lower rung of the consort ladder, suggests negligible political clout for the Yang clan. Rather than family influence or imperial favor, the critical factor in her subsequent advancement was apparently fertility—her nomination to Pure Consort

coinciding as it did with her first pregnancy. Even then, despite having given the emperor his first son, she would never receive the highest of harem honors, that of Precious Consort (*Guifei*). And by some accounts, she continued to identify herself as "slave," a self-effacing term used by lesser women of the palace, even after her elevation to dowager—a sign of unusual humility perhaps, but more likely a reflexive response to humble origins.[31]

Much the same holds for Consort Yu. A woman of obscure origins, she never rose above the middling rank of Cultivated Countenance (*Xiurong*), despite having provided the emperor his third and last son.[32] This is clear confirmation of humble beginnings and helps to explain why these women, in the initial years of the child regency, remained mere shadow figures whose activities were rarely recorded. They would emerge as political forces, in their own right, only with the demise of their handlers male and female, especially the empresses dowager and grand dowager.

The scrupulous circumspection of dowager-regents toward the end of the Song—their insistence on deferring to the authority of the outer court—is partly in reaction to events earlier in the dynasty. The eleventh century, after all, had produced an astonishing succession of female regents, women whose free-wheeling and even unorthodox conduct alienated many a court officer. The decade-long regency of Dowager Liu (969–1033), the stepmother of twelve year old Renzong (r. 1022–1063), was the first in Song history and a controversial one at that (see Figure 2). Courtiers resented her assertiveness at governing and vindictiveness toward critics, but also her attempts at stretching ritual protocol—personally conducting sacrifices at the Temple for Imperial Ancestors and erecting shrines to her own ancestors.[33] No less controversial was Dowager Gao (1032–1093), wife of Yingzong who surfaced as regent over grandson Zhezong (r. 1085–1100), who was eight years old at the time of his accession. A frugal and disciplined woman, Dowager Gao wins high marks among conservative historians, having rescinded the unpopular reforms of Wang Anshi and purged the court of reformist elements. Yet the ultimate effect was to further polarize courtiers over the reforms and set the stage for generations of crippling factionalism.[34] A more recent empress to assert a public role for herself in political affairs was Yang Yan, wife of the mediocre and muddled Ningzong. Without ever becoming regent, she struck a rare alliance with the outer court to assassinate an unpopular councilor in 1207 and purge an unpromising heir in 1224.[35] None of these were particularly villainous

Figure 2. Empress of Renzong.
Courtesy of National Palace Museum, Taipei, Taiwan ROC.

women, none acted recklessly or at whim. But they demonstrated the potential for palace women, at a time of monarchical incapacity, to accumulate dangerous levels of power in a manner threatening to male handlers in the civil service—an image that our women, at a time of such acute vulnerability for the dynasty, could scarcely afford to convey.

AS FOR THE CRAFTLESS CARETAKER

Contrasted against this palace cohort of responsibly circumspect women was an outer court of men neither circumspect nor responsible. And none seemed more representative of that male leadership of the mid-1270s, with its glaring deficiencies of character and conviction, than Jia Sidao (1213–1275). He represents, without a doubt, one of the most colorful political figures of the thirteenth century. He was also exceedingly well connected, making him an ideal candidate to serve as principal liaison between a male bureaucracy and a female regency.

He was the younger brother of Emperor Lizong's greatest love, the beauty he most desired to make his empress but dared not once the omnipotent Dowager Yang had intervened.[36] That woman, Precious Consort Jia (d. 1247), would bear the emperor a daughter prior to her own death at middle age. This would be Lizong's sole daughter and only offspring, male or female, to survive infancy. The death of Consort Jia when the child was merely six would further cement the emperor's attachment to his daughter, later ennobled Princess of Zhou and Han (1241–1262). The strength of those ties was reflected in his insistence, upon her marriage at twenty, to erect a home for her just outside his own palace. This enabled Lizong to slip away unnoticed for the informal visits that he made with some frequency. When she died only a year into the marriage, very likely in childbirth, the sense of loss seemed paralyzing. The monarch had been robbed earlier of his favorite consort and now the sole legacy of their love, all as the clock on his own mortality raced toward sixty—for China, the end of a sexagenary cycle and the transition from middle to old age. With Jia Sidao, brother of his consort and uncle to his daughter, he could share this sense of personal loss while at the same time celebrating a common kinship. The two men also bonded, they simultaneously discovered, through a shared passion for reckless abandon—the emperor acting on pent-up fantasy, his brother-in-law on years of indulgent living.

Lizong's combination of personal and professional ties to Jia Sidao

began early on and would last for the duration of his long reign. The two had first met in 1238, on the occasion of the Lady Jia's advancement to Precious Consort.[37] These events for the monarch's in-laws were part of standard court protocol, which along with the imperial conferral of title and office served to cement ties between the two families. This is the earliest known contact between the thirty-three year old emperor and his twenty-five year old brother-in-law, but Jia Sidao had already acquired a reputation in the capital far greater than one would expect for a man so young.

Reports of Jia Sidao's tireless carousing in Linan once circulated in such profusion that many have survived to this day.[38] They made their way to the emperor as well, who proved anything but embarrassed. Instead, he acquired a wholesome envy of his brother-in-law and the uninhibited freedom of sensual expression afforded ordinary men of means in this extraordinary city. Frolicking around West Lake—and the luxurious restaurants, tea houses, and brothels for which it is famed—was a common pastime for the capital's teeming population of literati. But Jia Sidao seems to have elevated occasional leisure to an art of perpetual sensuality. Whether on yachts on the lake or villas on surrounding hills, he demanded entertainment of decadent sumptuousness.

The number of metropolitan lots owned personally by him or made freely available to him is difficult to calculate, but they could be counted in the dozens, it appears. In the hills overlooking West Lake he built a reception hall dubbed "Partial Repose" and a pleasure garden known as "Nurtured Cheer." By all indications, the two were fabulously grand, for birthday celebrations each year reputedly drew in several thousand men and women with no indication of overcrowding. More famous, indeed infamous, within the leisured elite of Linan was Jia Sidao's "Garden of Clustered Fragrances." Built in 1262, construction costs for this residence with attached ancestral temple mounted into the millions in bolts of silk and strings of cash, costs assumed largely by the state, it is alleged. The building of an official residence for a councilor-level appointee and subsequent transfer to him as private property has ample precedent in the court protocol of Song, but even in the most prosperous of times, state subsidy rarely occurred on a scale of this sort. The spot was nestled between two mountains and the natural vegetation so thick as to obstruct most sunlight even at the height of day. The various halls, pavilions, and vistas each had an elegant name to describe its aesthetic properties: "Resplendent Lodge of the Dawn's Light," to name but one.

Such names were often conferred by the emperor, in which case large tablets of rare wood or stone would be commissioned to provide an appropriately ornate acknowledgement.

Surroundings of such exquisite sumptuousness required, of course, décor of commensurate elegance and Jia Sidao cronies brazenly broke many a social convention, if not necessarily imperial law, to do so. There is record of a one-time imperial tomb with origins in the tenth century being pilfered to this end. Jia Sidao had a particular penchant for calligraphy and among the works eventually netted by his art procurers, many were undoubtedly pilfered as well. In fact, a collection of more than a thousand scrolls, in combination with a vast array of other objects, so swelled his several homes that Jia Sidao was compelled to erect a separate tower to store it all. Still more unsettling than such ostentation were rumors of illicit raids on the palace collection, with its vast trove of eleventh-and twelfth-century works. Emperors Lizong and Duzong appear never to have begrudged their favorite unrestricted access to this official repository, nor even beyond. In an act tantamount to *lèse-majesté*, so rumor has it, Jia Sidao once laid personal claim to a former consort of Lizong—in effect, raiding the imperial harem![39] Recognizing no bounds of discretion or decorum, his lifestyle seemed an unsettling statement on the men of his time and their priorities.

For those familiar with China's long history and the abuses of power so eminently documented therein, these may seem minor improprieties. In contrast to the decadent last reigns of other major dynasties, there are no stories for the late Song of endless streams of gold and silver witlessly diverted from state coffers merely to lay idle in some private repository, no wholesale parceling out of the empire's greatest wealth and highest offices to members of some favored clan, no surreptitious deployment of secret police to terrorize political enemies. No, the Song took great pride in the consensual constraints that governed the use of state power and resources, constraints not necessarily dictated by law but no less binding. Jia Sidao's problem was preeminently one of image: all too frequently, and publicly, he would test the limits of those constraints. Never in traditional China were sensual or material indulgence considered crimes: however compelling the Confucian case for moderation, refined tastes and conspicuous consumption scarcely disqualified one for political leadership. It was also quite commonplace for emperors of the Song to reward distinguished service to the state with generous gifts—valuable commodities and *objets d'art*, luxury villas and gardens as well.[40] But for an emperor to offer such gifts, and a chief-of-state

guilefully to accept them, at a time no less of diminishing resources and ravaging war, does irreparable injury to the image of any leader, still more so for men of such visible eminence. These were scarcely the salad days of old and to continue spending at former levels of lavishness betrayed an offensive insensitivity—insensitivity to commoners worn weary by ever escalating wars and taxes, insensitivity as well to a literati elite increasingly doubtful of the martial will of a leadership unduly distracted by the material. Few observers would miss the resonances with an earlier Song emperor and his minister—the artistically gifted Huizong (r. 1110–1126) and the materially distracted Cai Jing (1046–1126)—men most blamed for the loss of the north to foreign invaders.

Quite apart from his arrant indifference to the times, Jia Sidao seemed grossly insensitive to the new standards of social propriety associated with the School of the Way, *Daoxue*—also known as the School of Principle, *Lixue*, due to its rationalization of the human and natural orders through universal laws or "principle." Enshrined as state orthodoxy since 1241 with its proponents ever eminent in stature, the school emerged as intensely hostile to the leisured frivolity of the day. It challenged southerners to reject the obsessive materialism around them and literati males, in particular, to shun the effete adornment common to the era. Focusing specifically on the etiquette of marriage ceremonies, for example, Neo-Confucian conservatives such as Sima Guang (1019–1086) and Zhu Xi (1130–1200) had decried the wildly escalating cost of wedding dowries.[41] The prevalence of dowry contracts executed with businesslike precision, in lieu of the old informal exchange of wedding gifts, irritated them as well. It suggested that profit had eclipsed propriety even in the conduct of family affairs. In a related issue about wedding proprieties, Zhu Xi railed against the current practice of bridegrooms donning the popular crown of flowers, in its "unmanly" ornateness, instead of the single flower of times past.[42] Here again, material abundance seemed to be eroding traditional austerity, urban decadence having a feminizing effect on the Song male. Having become "slaves to things"— that is, to "desires of the ears, eyes, mouth, and nose"—elite men, in the process, had lost their moral focus or "sincerity" (*cheng*), as Confucian purists dubbed it.[43] And the court had finally begun to listen, it appears. A proscription, issued in 1206, against military officers assuming the ornate attire and material lifestyle of civilian counterparts clearly reflected an urge to impose limits on material corruption, particularly with reference to the men entrusted with the empire's defense.[44]

The Neo-Confucian urge to material and sensual denial, dubbed by

one writer as "moral rigorism," would receive new and enlarged emphasis in the thirteenth-century writings of men like Zhen Dexiu (1178–1235).[45] A one-time emissary to the north and tutor to royal princes, he scrutinized the conduct chiefly of emperors and their close advisors, cautioning against the prevalence of the four "wayward desires"—desires for excess drink, sex, amusements, and possessions.[46] Restraint of such urges had made sound political sense for a very long time in China, but the whole process of cultivation through regulation would assume, in Song times, almost spiritual dimensions for a society where secular values had historically dominated. It is thus in a context where material possessions had acquired such potent symbolism that the lifestyle of Jia Sidao came to symbolize everything wrong with the southeast and its male leadership. To appease these critics, the councilor had only to follow the example of self-restraint set by Empress Xie, who faced with rising military expenditures chose to reduce significantly her own personal allowance.[47] The symbolism behind such displays seems to have eluded him and, in this regard, Jia Sidao alone bears responsibility for the political consequences of his own lifestyle decisions.

An unconscionably lavish lifestyle cannot entirely explain the Song literati's utter contempt for Jia Sidao. Part of his political baggage, as it were, relates to background. He may have hailed from a family of distinguished officials and favored consorts, but his own credentials were shamelessly slim. Although royal in-laws were commonly selected for prominent posts in the military services, the higher echelons of the civil service remained the almost exclusive preserve of doctoral degreeholders.[48] Lacking such credentials, Jia Sidao's high-level regional appointments in the 1240s and nomination as chief councilor in 1259, at a youthful forty-six no less, ran against longstanding political convention.[49] And none would be more incited than the thousands of credentialed and experienced bureaucrats who were categorically passed over in his speedy advance. For this reason, his performance in and out of office was certain to be scrutinized with a diligence much greater than most. Yet this favorite son frequently acted with such unbridled abandon that a veritable immunity to the censure of colleagues seems his working assumption. This may be seen in the caprice and hypocrisy with which Jia Sidao formulated government policy. Beginning in 1263, for example, his administration embarked upon a desperate and ultimately disastrous course of economic restructuring, the Public Fields Program (*gongtian fa*).[50] It was a program intended to augment revenues for the state through the reallocation of private wealth—the only at-

tempt at major reform in the thirteenth century, indeed the only sweeping overhaul of the landowning system in the entire dynasty.[51] But set against the reform was the political record and image of its promoter. Meanwhile, the tactics employed in executing the program exposed Jia Sidao as more adept at identifying the problem than constructing a viable solution, better at conceiving policies than orchestrating politics. The consequence, alas, was doom for the policies themselves.

The problem was not particularly complex. The Song empire, due to its overall laissez-faire approach to economic management, had nurtured a vast and influential community of entrepreneurs, persons amassing prodigious levels of private wealth. Repeated reference is made, already in sources of the eleventh century, to "monopolists" who turned hefty profits through moneylending at usurious rates. In this way, they eliminated petty traders in the cities and soaked up peasant properties in the countryside.[52] Yet through assorted acts of manipulation, they commonly paid only a fraction of their tax obligation. The shielding of fixed assets from assessment could sometimes be done by falsifying land deeds. A simpler solution involved mere reassignment of property to a duly designated "official household." Here, blanket tax exemption was the rule and the aggregate of such households, for a bureaucracy with over *thirty thousand* active members, stood in the hundreds of thousands. In theory, Confucian society aspired to a scrupulous separation of literatus and merchant, status and money. In practice, however, fluidity and overlap was commonplace: the marriage of daughters and adoption of sons often brought together benefits otherwise reserved to each class. Yet such behavior could only be perceived by the state, especially a state with the centralizing impulses of Song, as a conspiracy against itself. Through their deprivation of potential revenues, the elite threatened the empire's very ability to function. And at a time of military crisis when revenue needs are greatest, this fiscal problem assumed a pressing strategic import.

The Public Fields program was intended to curtail such tax evasion through the most radical of all conceivable methods: expropriation. In effect, one third of all landholdings in excess of two hundred *mou*—a scant sixty acres later to be reduced to thirty—had to be surrendered to the state. If aggressively implemented, the effect on most elite families would be devastating. The legitimate cost of supporting their large households, inflated as a consequence of concubinage and the attendant profusion of male heirs, could scarcely be met with those assets alone. Further inciting the divested were the rates of state reimbursement, set

so arbitrarily low as to border on outright confiscation. This seemed scarcely different from the long succession of other attempts at state ownership, which history had proven a uniform disaster, symbolic more of destitution than courage. Undeterred by such resentment, Jia Sidao and cohort went on to extend this daring divestment of official wealth to non-official households. Indeed, the entire scheme was executed with such sweeping effectiveness that the government ended up possessing, in some circuits, up to twenty percent of all lands. In token ceremony, Jia Sidao may have offered up a sizable chunk of his own land, but this hardly entailed any notable dimunition in a lifestyle of conspicuous consumption that stood in stark contrast to the heightened austerity expected of others. Such hypocrisy would not be lost on an angry elite.

Beyond resenting the duplicitous demands of court reformers, the landed elite was perhaps most incensed by another fact: economic measures so extreme seemed wholly unjustified by existing conditions. Even up to its very last days, the Song had far from depleted its cash reserves. Admittedly, the thirteenth century had been struck by a succession of wars that seriously drained the Song exchequer. This, in turn, encouraged the printing of unbacked paper currency—an issue which over the course of the thirteenth century had grown at least twenty-five times![53] Nonetheless, since the outset of the Southern Song, hefty sums had been squirreled away in various treasuries as part of a Privy Purse under the direct control of the throne.[54] Of more recent origin was a so-called "Reserve Treasury for Peace along the Border," a special defense fund.[55] The size of this surplus is not specified, but in the annals of the 1260s and 1270s, there is frequent reference to the withdrawal of countless millions in strings of cash to defray military expenses with no indication of exhaustion. There is also record of the last monarch Zhao Bing, as late as 1278, still possessing cash reserves sufficient to build *thousands* of housing units at the Yaishan holdout.[56] Thus, the appearance was one of a monarch clinging obsessively to secret stockpiles while relentlessly escalating his exactions from a populace left ill-tempered by successive imposts.

We may never know what motivated Jia Sidao, only four years after his unorthodox appointment as chief councilor, to embrace a reform agenda so certain to alienate him and the monarchy he represented from precisely the class whose support they both so desperately needed. With some measure of certainty, however, we know that he acted more on a desperate cynicism than the idealistic impulses of the eleventh-century. Unlike the moderate reformer Fan Zhongyan (989–1052), his economic

platform was propelled by the conviction that the interests of the court and the regional elite were fundamentally antagonistic. And unlike the radical reformer Wang Anshi (1021–1086), he made no distinction between modest wealth and great wealth, unneeded bureaucratic perquisites and legitimate commercial profit. At a time of hostilities abroad and declining fortunes at home, this image of cynical indifference was one that the Song state could ill afford. Then again, Jia Sidao and his two imperial patrons, Emperors Li and Du, were perhaps nowhere more deficient than in their insensitivity to public image. The only palace figure to possess such sensitivity was Empress Xie, as demonstrated by her enduring temperance, personal as well as political. But with reference to the Public Fields, there is no record of an opinion favorable or unfavorable being expressed by her.

ALAS, THE WIND SHIFTS

After a decade and a half as chief councilor, court observers must have come to regard Jia Sidao as wholly immune to political challenge. Not the ill-conceived domestic policies which alienated the landed elite, nor the death of his first sponsor Lizong in 1264, nor even the demise a decade later of successor Duzong seemed capable of shaking him. The only force capable of toppling Jia Sidao was Jia Sidao himself.

Brief mention was made earlier of the loss, in early 1273, of Xiangyang commandary, Jingxi circuit (modern Hubei). In the heart of the Song empire, this strategically vital city sat sandwiched between the political seat of Linan to the east and a resource-rich Sichuan to the west. But it also lay a scant sixty kilometers south of the Mongol border and was accessible, from the north, by a multiplicity of waterways which flowed into the nearby Han River (see Map 2). The Han itself flowed west to east, along the city's northern and then eastern banks before proceeding in a southeasterly direction into Jinghu North circuit. Some three hundred kilometers downstream lay not only a prosperously sprawling Hanyang but also the Yangzi River—the commercial and strategic lifeblood of the entire south. Precisely because of this direct link between Xiangyang and the Yangzi, or "Long River" (Changjiang), strategists on both sides invested militarily in this city far more than its modest size ever seemed to justify.

With walls a mere five kilometers around and a population of some 200,000, Xiangyang was scarcely a large city, by the standards of a highly urbanized Song.[57] All the same, the central government's invest-

ment proved as vast as it was varied. The Mongol siege on Xiangyang and its sister city directly north, Fancheng, had begun in 1268. After 1271, the monitoring of nearby waterways and land routes was so intense, according to one source, that not even fish or shrimp stood a chance of slipping through. In response, the Song entrusted supreme command of the region to Zhang Shijie and Li Tingzhi, two men of exceptional fortitude and experience.[58] It also transferred from the eastern to the central front troops numbering in the hundreds of thousands.[59] The court's investment extended to material support as well. Over a five year period, it released from metropolitan coffers some fourteen million strings of cash, supplemental appropriations for the region specifically targeted at the fortification of defenses and compensation of troops.[60] Song defenders also proved remarkably innovative, both in technique and technology. Records for the opposing side document the erection of wooden "palisades" (*zha*) along the bed of the Han River: formerly used as simple barricades but now fixed in place by iron locks, these posts provided support for a network of suspension bridges whose span across the river served to connect the two cities.[61] Also deployed in the theater, apparently for the first time, were small ships propelled by "rotating wheels" and thus capable of maximum velocity by exploiting natural currents.[62] Technological innovation is further evidenced by the "floorless ship." Sandwiched between and apparently propped up by two legitimately manned vessels, these decoys had the usual masts and rigging, but a bottomless hull. The decoys thereby not only served to deflect arrows and catapults, they would also drown the hapless aggressor who succeeded in scaling its sides while not noticing, due largely to deceptive camouflaging, the abyss only a leap away.[63]

Unfortunately, the massive military mobilization of Linan rested upon political alliances and assumptions so untenable as to jeopardize the entire effort and leave the southern leadership critically vulnerable to the aggressor. In a region some one thousand kilometers removed from the capital back east, there had emerged two festering maladies with reference to military deployment, maladies intimately intertwined and at the same time set on a course of certain collision with one another but also with the court. On the one hand, the entire military infrastructure for Jinghu had grown highly personalized, in glaring contravention of Song ideals of a bureaucratically detached mode of management. In the mobilization of men and materiél, therefore, the individual commander often proved more important than the command itself. Worse yet, military organizations often gravitated on the kin

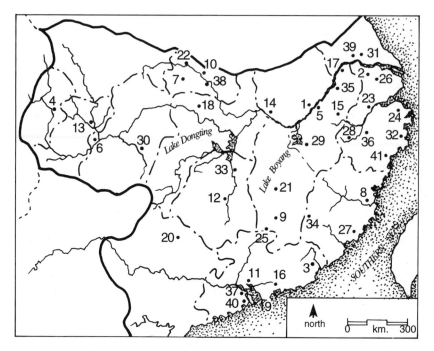

Map 2. Cities of Song China

group, a self-perpetuating and defiant brood. While Linan had a long history of tacitly accepting some measure of hereditary power, especially in its military bureaucracy, it was never altogether comfortable with such power. Destruction of the preceding Tang dynasty, after all, had occurred at the hands of military hegemons in the provinces and the Song would not passively permit the resurgence of similar threats to the center.[64] On the other hand, the regional military was itself divided, the activities of formal armies and informal militias having rarely been coordinated for maximum effectiveness. This may belie administrative negligence on the part of overseers, but more likely it grows out of a panoply of conflicting interests between the capital and the circuits politically, the professional and the amateur militarily. Yet these militias of locally conscripted men, "people's armies" in the vernacular of the day, often fought with the dogged determination lacking in the seasoned professional. In the absence of effective deployment of such dedicated militiamen, southern defenders held exceedingly dim prospects for prevailing over the north, whose recent expansion owes much to its flexible approach to marshaling scarce military resources.

More specifically, Jia Sidao served for fifteen years as chief councilor and, after 1267, as special military councilor (see Appendix B).[65] For the duration of that tenure, the preeminent military figure in the central theater—that is, the two interior circuits of Jinghu north and south, plus the critical border circuit of Jingxi—was Pacification Commissioner Lü Wende (d. 1270). Although native to the east, the lower Huai, his professional network prospered at Jinghu like nowhere else. And an enviably thriving network it was indeed![66] At least two of his several brothers held influential commands in this and other regions. Younger brother Lü Wenhuan even managed the local defenses as prefect of Xiangyang while Wende coordinated affairs intraregionally. He had a first cousin overseeing operations along the eastern border, a son managing defenses on the southwestern fringes, and a son-in-law ranked high in the metropolitan Palace Guard. That son-in-law, Fan Wenhu, subsequently won reassignment to the Xiangyang front as head of a special imperial force. Many others of high military stature launched their careers under the protective wing of Lü Wende and, although unrelated by blood or marriage, were nonetheless identified closely with his Jinghu establishment. The general destined for loyalist fame at Yaishan, Zhang Shijie, is among the more prominent of these. In fact, some of the most thriving cities up and down the Yangzi River were commanded, so it is said, by associates of the omnipotent Lü Wende.[67] Local

autonomy of the sort had long been commonplace farther west, in the heart of a mountainous Sichuan, but it was less common for the Song heartland—and the drift of military power downward was a dangerous one from Linan's perspective.[68]

In the personal case of Lü Wende, the court had less reason to worry. After all, he had formerly joined Jia Sidao in the heroic defense of Yingzhou, the same Jinghu hinterland, and by all indications emerged in the councilor's good graces. The loyalty of subordinates was not so certain. So, the commissioner's sudden death in the early days of 1270 prompted Linan to intervene, selecting a replacement from outside the Lü circle. The office went to Li Tingzhi (d. 1276), a native of nearby Suizhou with a doctoral degree and impressive resumé. Having served principally in the east, Li Tingzhi possessed no local constituencies and this caused the Xiangyang establishment to greet his appointment with hostile resentment.[69] Locals also saw in the capital's selection of an outsider some measure of suspicion toward regional loyalties. It was as though these provincials had ready access to a sensitive memorial from Councilor Jia to Emperor Duzong, which had demanded, as much out of political fear as policy principle, that "military power cannot go without reclamation even for a day, just as border affairs cannot be neglected even in the slightest."[70] The utterances of Jia Sidao were made in a context of broader rifts between center and periphery. As modern scholars have shown, the Song court under Jia Sidao had adopted new regulations for military expenses, beginning in 1261, which effectively stripped local leaders of discretionary clout over their own military budgets.[71] Councilor Jia doubtlessly saw this as a way of maximizing return on military expenditures. Local commanders would obviously see things differently and the conflict growing out of such differences undermined, in the end, the interests of all.

Fan Wenhu, the former commissioner's son-in-law, appears among the first to make explicit his intent to take orders only from the court, not the new commissioner.[72] In his case, as head of a Palace Guard unit on regional assignment, this fell somewhat short of insubordination. But after a year or so in the region, he scrupulously evaded engagement of the enemy while flaunting his apparent immunity to censure.[73] The entire defense effort would suffer in the process. During a critical 1272 maneuver to break the Mongol blockade, for example, he arrogantly withheld his men—a force estimated at one hundred thousand strong. His pretext of awaiting orders from Linan proved uncompelling to most and the fall of Xiangyang a half year later seemed largely his doing. Yet

Fan Wenhu was never punished. Even in the face of vociferous protest, the court transferred him to Anqing, a city farther east along the Yangzi River. Scarcely a year into his term and after scant resistance, he negotiated the surrender of that city to the north. This enabled him to hold onto his post as prefect, even arrange for a nephew to succeed him when Mongol patrons offered new opportunites for his own advancement. He quickly became one of their most effusive clients, volunteering for their campaign against the Song with an enthusiasm that baffled even them. The exact reasons for his alienation from Linan and eventual defection may never be known, but surely a contributing factor of some significance was the threat to Lü power as represented by the appointment of Li Tingzhi.

Sharing a similar ambivalence toward the Song state and its agenda in the region was Lü Wenhuan, the late Commissioner Lü Wende's younger brother. He left no record of resentment against his new overseer, Li Tingzhi, but understandably so. After all, as prefect of Xiangyang and assistant commissioner of surrounding Jingxi circuit, Lü Wenhuan's very survival rested upon the generous and unequivocal support of the region's supreme commissioner. Even the appearance of discord had to be avoided at all costs. All the same, his degree of commitment to dynastic interests should rightfully be questioned in light of subsequent conduct. It was Lü Wenhuan who negotiated the surrender of Xiangyang to the Mongols, he who went on to accept the supreme commissionership under them which had eluded him under the Song, and he who figured prominently in the Yuan campaign against Song remnants farther south. He would even commit, two years later, the ultimate act of infidelity to Song royals—joining personally in the occupation of its capital by northern armies. During that ethically awkward moment as he addressed Dowager Xie face to face, he assumed a patronizing humility, as reported by sources favorable to him: "My coming to engage southern troops, in accord with instructions from the north, should be seen as nothing more than the deed of a vile servant who exacts the revenge of his master. It scarcely compares to a son's attack against his parents, for I had no choice in the matter."[74] By suggesting a lack of volition and employing such self-deprecating terms as "vile servant" (literally, a mere "dog or horse"), Lü Wenhuan succeeded in casting himself, in the eyes of history, not as an unrequited renegade consumed by ambition and indifferent to his disgraced masters: rather, he seems a mere pawn without independent input in a contest of greater wills. The humility implicit in this often quoted phrase would strongly

influence the relevant historiography. His surrender of Xiangyang came to be portrayed as an inevitable consequence of dwindling men and supplies.[75] It even emerged as a humane means of sparing innocent lives, the alien conquerors having sworn mass murder for all cities engaged in prolonged resistance.[76] Never was Lü Wenhuan censured for selfish duplicity, even though overseer Li Tingzhi had grown increasingly suspicious that he might be conducting a dialogue of sedition with the enemy—suspicions which he repeatedly communicated to the court during those final weeks, all to no avail.[77]

Yet when the behavior of this individual is duplicated so widely throughout his larger kin group, a group whose material interest was served so consistently well by defection, it is difficult to deny self-interest as chief motivation. One after another, Lü clansmen would follow Wenhuan's lead in capitulating to the enemy. And it was the timeliness of their apostasy, for most, which enabled them to prosper under the new regime. Among these turncoats were assorted nephews and cousins, but more notably Lü Wenhuan himself. When he retired in the mid-1280s and his son succeeded him as pacification commissioner for the entire Huai and Yangzi valleys, there was no question of prearrangement.[78] The Mongol political order, being based as much on personal ties as bureaucratic rules, could more readily accommodate regional networks and hereditary privilege. For exclusively martial figures such as Lü Wenhuan who cared little for bureaucratic accountability or dynastic precedent, the Song regime must have seemed obsessive in checking their power and thwarting their aspirations. Frustrated by the old regimen of centralized and impersonal management, a new order of local autonomy had irresistible appeal.

The Song had only one other way of undercutting a locally entrenched military establishment, while harnessing the spiraling cost of defense—by maximizing use of regional militias. In the Xiangyang theater, for example, some of the most heroic fighters were non-professional conscripts. Direction of these irregulars had been entrusted to Zhang Shun and Zhang Gui. Men of humble origin, they possessed neither the wealth nor power to corrupt their civic commitment to region. Their effectiveness as mobilizers was further enhanced by an exceptional familiarity with local conditions and intimate ties to commoners.[79] As a rule, the Song preferred assigning largely supportive missions to the militias, but important missions all the same. The two men had been instrumental in maintaining Xiangyang's vital link to the outside by breaking the Mongol blockade. Due to the intensification of that blockade

starting in 1271, these were death-defying assignments. Yet in the summer of 1272, with only a few thousand men and a hundred small warships, they slipped past enemy barricades by rediscovering an alternative water route to the upper reaches of the Han; then, beating off Mongol sentries on the return leg of the trip, they delivered a vast store of supplies from Junzhou, nearly one hundred kilometers up the Han River. Unfortunately, Zhang Shun would perish at the end of this mission, ambushed by the enemy just outside the walls of Xiangyang. A similar fate awaited Zhang Gui scarcely three months later. In storming another blockade to the south of Xiangyang, he met with stiff resistance. His men largely dead and his own body punctured by dozens of wounds, he fell into hostile hands and accepted death over surrender.

Some scholars argue that Zhang Gui, and the non-professionals that he represented, were senselessly sacrificed by the powerful establishment—the likes of Fan Wenhu who refused to jeopardize their own regulars in support of the militias.[80] This would suggest that however useful the militias might have been, the local military establishment ultimately considered them expendable all the same. Surely the court would not concur with its senior men in the field, but it was hardly in a position to challenge their ethical priorities without jeopardizing an alliance already perilously fragile. In the absence of such prodding, however, Linan would lose the staunchest of its local warriors.

The valor of lesser military figures was not isolated to Zhang Shun and Zhang Gui. In the same theater, there is the widely heralded case of Niu Fu and Wang Fu, mid-level officers who in the last days of Fancheng consciously chose death over capitulation to the enemy.[81] Both responded to the city's impending collapse by leaping into burning buildings. The region's only executive-level officer known to share their totality of commitment was Fan Tianshun.[82] As commissioner for the circuit, he was Lü Wenhuan's superior. He was also Fan Wenhu's nephew, the only member of that network known to have committed suicide just prior to the demise of Fancheng. He strangled himself. Why Fan Tianshun's personal reaction to events would depart so radically from the rest of that group may never be known. Perhaps he had been condemned to death by circumstances beyond his control and merely seized the initiative, acting in defense of personal integrity, not civic duty. Or maybe he was, in fact, cut of a radically different cloth, ethically, from the bulk of his Fan and Lü kinsmen.

In the early weeks of 1273, it was not the frustration of reining in provincial commissioners nor even the senseless waste of militia re-

sources that most commanded the attention of the Song court. Fan-cheng had fallen to the enemy in the first lunar month, Xiangyang in the second, and the circumstances surrounding their demise contained some terribly unsavory implications for the south. The leadership of Fancheng had included such staunch loyalists as Fan Tianshun and Niu Fu, men adamant in their refusal to surrender. Once the victors led by Arigh Khaya and Aju stormed the city by force, they quickly instructed their underlings to conduct a general massacre as retribution. No distinction would be made between young and old, male and female, civilian or military. Corpses perhaps in excess of ten thousand were then piled up to form a mound so high as to stand visibly in view of holdouts on the lower bank of the Han River, at Xiangyang.[83] Not the dramatic display of enemy firepower nor the rapid depletion of their own men and materiél—nothing could demoralize Xiangyang defenders like this grotesque sight and the terrifying message it so forcefully conveyed.[84] After all, mirrored before them was their own potential fate. The city, in the end, would be spared through the timely defection of Lü Wenhuan. But back at Linan, the unfolding of events along the Han River could only have confirmed the court's greatest fear: in the arsenals of war, no weapon is more lethal than the threat of mass annihilation. As alien conquerors, the Mongols faced few ethical obstacles to embracing such strategies. Yet Song warriors could scarcely reciprocate in kind when their potential targets to the north shared a common bond of blood and history. This inability to exploit that critical weapon of terror may well have been the most debilitating of Song China's strategic handicaps, the miscalculations of muddled policymakers notwithstanding.

Traditional historians have been merciless in blaming Jia Sidao for virtually every negative development of the 1260s and 1270s, the fall of Xiangyang included. An indictment so sweeping involves inevitable exaggeration, but with reference to border policy these critics speak with some degree of insight. As special military councilor, the decision to appoint Li Tingzhi as commissioner was certainly his to make and he stood the most to gain, politically, from a successful tenure where central authority is reaffirmed. Jia Sidao cannot be spared responsibility, therefore, for the actual outcome of that tenure, which included devastating rifts that started with the local military establishment and reverberated beyond. Neither can anyone but he be blamed for the failure to respond to Li Tingzhi's repeated warnings of impending treason at Xiangyang. All too frequently, he tabled petitions and deferred actions, as if to suggest a lack of full confidence in his own appointee. But per-

haps most irresponsible was Jia Sidao's inequitable dispensation toward commanders defeated at Xiangyang. Understandably, Commissioner Li was recalled to the capital and then stripped of power. But this important act of military discipline acquired the unfortunate image of political scapegoating: the commissioner had done nothing more than his court had instructed and the court seemed intent solely on camouflaging its own miscalculations. The inscrutably self-serving Fan Wenhu, perhaps the most negative factor in the Jinghu military equation, got away with a mere reprimand and immediately proceeded to his new post in the same hinterland. As metropolitan censor Chen Wenlong would observe with livid cogency, "this is tantamount to rewarding someone who rightfully deserves punishment."[85] The court's appearance of impotence—that is, its inability to act consistently on established rules of military discipline—seemed certain to further compromise the center's vigor and credibility as shepherd of regional surrogates. The consequences of such inconsistency were borne out in the first lunar month of 1275, when the once reprieved Fan Wenhu abruptly defected to the Mongols. A month later, Jia Sidao was purged from power and soon thereafter assassinated.

The summer of 1274 lay halfway between the collapse of Xiangyang and the purge of Jia Sidao, a time of near paralyzing military and political uncertainty. Yet coinciding with the dynasty's bleakest hour was a revelry of sorts, a period of partial redemption for the dynasty's fading image. Dowager Xie may have been well into her sixties when the regency began, yet she came to rely increasingly upon a younger generation of promising bureaucrats. These men of imposing intellect also emerged as exceptionally committed to the cause of dynasty. They leapt into the political fray fully cognizant of dangerous changes on the horizon and the extraordinary sacrifice that such change would likely demand. Anticipation of epochal change is confirmed in a passage from the official history, where one of these devotees to dynasty, Wen Tianxiang, reportedly had a chance encounter with a one-time teacher now retired as chief councilor, Jiang Wanli. This occurred in 1273 shortly after the younger man's nomination to an important civil post in lower Jinghu. The seventy-five year old Jiang, congratulating him on the appointment and expressing his personal confidence, nonetheless did so in a voice uncharacteristically somber for such occasions: "In my witness of imminent change in Heavenly episodes and human events, I have observed a good number of people in my many years. But my dear sir, it is with you that responsibility now rests for finding a proper path for

this troubled age. To this end, I trust that you, Sir, will exert yourself fully."[86] Jiang Wanli's allusion to "imminent change" and "Heavenly episodes" clearly suggests his anticipation of the radical turns commonly associated with the transfer of dynastic power. The mere thought of such weighty responsibility would have absolutely terrified most men, but for a select few like Wen Tianxiang, trying times presented a rare challenge as well. They may have lacked the power, individually or collectively, to change the course of history, an inscrutable Mandate of Heaven often seeming to possess a will and reason of its own. But while the dynasty's ultimate fate may have been fairly certain, the course it would follow in meeting that fate most certainly was not. Our committed few, as revelers for a doomed cause, might actually turn their last service to Song into something greater—an opportunity to immortalize the dynasty with their deeds.

Under Heaven, wind:
*The image of **gathering**.*
Thus does the prince act when disseminating his commands
And proclaiming them to the four quarters of heaven.

The Changes, XLIV.

3·Gou:
Gathering Unpropitiously

Success in defending the Song, in the final analysis, would rest not just on the deeds of heroic men, but also the rhetoric of a pivotal woman—the Grand Dowager, Xie Qiao. In the aftermath of new setbacks at the border, she grew all the more determined to mobilize the resources and stir the hearts of her subjects. Such determination was behind the most daring step of her short but stormy regency—summoning loyal subjects from the four quarters to shield their capital from advancing armies. For the hundreds of military and civilian leaders to receive her edict during that final month of 1274, the plea to "succor your king," *qin wang*, struck an emotionally inspiring yet painfully familiar chord. Gleaned from the classical canon, the *Narrative of Zuo* in particular, the phrase conjured up images of feudal heroism where loyal vassals hastened to defend their lords against the infidel.[1] In the intervening two millennia, kings of old may have been recast as the Son of Heaven, domestic rebels replaced by the alien intruder, yet under the insular and vulnerable conditions of the day, the Song monarchy more closely resembled a partitioned feudatory than a unified empire. Vulnerability is not always a liability, however, and could be transformed to a strategic asset if exploited astutely. Precisely for this reason, the empress begins her rescript with an allusion to her own advanced years and the emperor's youth. She then strengthens her rhetorical appeal by swallowing political pride and accepting full responsibility for the sad state of affairs. This strategy of turning external weakness into internal strength is executed with deft eloquence when the Grand Dowager declares:

The empire's progression toward impending peril is entirely, I regret, due to the insubstantiality of Our moral virtue. The heart of a benevolent and caring Heaven was expressed through the stars, yet We failed to stir. Mutations in the earth's orbit were portended through flooding, yet We failed to reflect. The sound of woeful lament reverberated throughout the countryside, yet We failed to investigate. The pall of hunger and cold enveloped the armed forces, yet We failed to console.

The regency of Dowager Xie had scarcely entered its fifth month, so her personal culpability in recent mishaps is clearly overstated. Perhaps she is acknowledging the excesses of earlier monarchs, her husband now dead for a decade and her stepson whose cold corpse still lay in-state awaiting its final interment. Or she may have sought, shrewdly, to juxtapose the diligence of her own governance to the deliquency of years past and benefit from the favorable comparison. Yet the message in her dramatic call to arms is more positively purposeful than defensive—it speaks to the rare unity of state and society achieved under Song rule, the interdependency of ruler and subject that links their two fates and demands reciprocity. In her own haunting words:

Over three hundred years of moral and charitable rule have left deep imprints on the hearts of humanity. The souls of countless millions beseech Heaven to render assistance. . . . I can only trust that you, the literate warp and martial woof of the empire, having lived on the emoluments of your monarch will not forsake him during distress and that those infused with loyal and righteous vigor will offer their services in engaging the enemy of their prince.[2]

The summons reputedly brought tears to the eyes of Wen Tianxiang when it reached him a month later, the early weeks of 1275. His native Jiangnan West, where he was on official assignment, lay some nine hundred kilometers southwest of Linan—distance and duty thereby preventing him from responding with the expected urgency.[3] He agonized over the sad spectacle of greatness reduced to desperation, the same court which not long ago had singled him out for top honors in the doctoral exam now reduced to such deplorably dire straits. Still more agonizing was the powerful sense of *déjà vu* that certainly gripped him and any other reasonably learned subject to receive the *qin wang* rescript. History seemed set on a path of cataclysmic change all too eerie in its familiar contours.

A century and a half earlier, indeed during the same lunar month, a similar plea to "succor the king" had gone out to the circuits. Again, a

monarch of Song, the forty-four year old Huizong, was held virtual hostage to a capital under alien assault. The 1126 rescript also began with apologies for the misguided policies of the past followed by a rousing call to protect the dynastic enterprise, an enterprise begun in the mid-tenth century which by the early twelfth was revered no less than it was entrenched.[4] The edict of 1126 did not achieve its objective. The Jurched tribes of Manchuria continued their encroachment, occupying the capital at Kaifeng in 1127.[5] Only one son of the royal family, the future Gaozong (r. 1127–1162), would elude the captive fate of his many siblings and flee south where the rule of Song continued under his auspices. North China was permanently lost and the dynasty nearly expired. To the extent that the call to *qin wang* was identified with the futile efforts of rulers soon to be dethroned, its reinvocation by Empress Xie in 1274 ran the risk of frightening off potential supporters through negative association. Modeling her own actions on a difficult past also ran the risk of highlighting the single greatest contrast: leadership now resting with palace women, an exclusively male literati might prove less responsive to their summons. Political concerns of the sort were compounded by the ponderous military implications of an indiscriminate call to arms. The prospective militias would surely prove difficult to direct: characterized by poor education and military inexperience, militia units were also unmanageably small in size and diverse in regional background. As many as 100,000 men—a respectable but not inspiring show—would eventually surface at the capital, only several of these in groups exceeding ten thousand.[6] Moreover, many of these "volunteers," as Wen Tianxiang personally admits, were ethnic minorities from the mountainous southwest with dubious loyalties to the cause.[7] The clumsy convergence on the capital of hundreds of motley militia, many of them present only through the coercion of local leaders, threatened to induce a chaos far greater than any army of alien conquerors.

ACTIVIST REVELRY IN THE ACADEMY

Grand Dowager Xie must have appreciated the ramifications of her decision and, quite frankly, it is difficult to imagine a person so perennially cautious undertaking an action so daring and decisive. Perhaps she was swayed by the junior dowager, Quan Jiu, a woman with estimable powers of persuasion, plus an enduring faith in the goodwill of common subjects. Pressure doubtlessly came from the court's rising star as well, the complex and fiery Chen Yizhong. No personality figured more

prominently in the politics of a waning Song, his talents for shaping literati opinion and then stirring colleagues to action almost legendary. Chen Yizhong represented, after all, a large community of idealists who dominated the cultural circles of the capital but seemed peripheral to its power politics. His personal sense of alienation from power may relate, in part, to the social obscurity of his family and the poverty of his youth. Yet it appears most powerfully informed by his years as a student at the Imperial University or *Taixue*.[8]

With roughly sixteen hundred students at its height in the Southern Song, this was the empire's premiere institution of advanced learning— a modern "academy" of sorts where students, often mature in age, took an independent approach to their studies. The university had historically served, since its inception in the second century B.C., as a hotbed of political dissidence. But under the Song dynasty, and especially during the thirteenth century, its clout in the capital was truly exceptional. A generally tolerant political climate—the "charitable rule" to which the Grand Dowager refers—had made student activism possible, while mounting crises made it increasingly necessary. The university's expanding influence is confirmed by Song contemporaries, who warned of a dangerous shift of power from the court to the academy. The anecdotist Zhou Mi (1232–1298) writes in his memoirs: "Beginning in the early Kaixi era [1205–1207] and again following the 'era of change' [post-1234], public discourse empire-wide did not revert to men on high but often to the gentlemen of the two schools [i.e., the Imperial University and the Military Academy]. . . . The Son of Heaven emptied out his own thoughts to listen to them, chief councilors bowed their heads and trusted them, and the entire empire bent its heart to applaud them."[9] A critical symbol of this shift in political clout was Chen Yizhong.

Two decades earlier, he was among six students to stage a fiery campaign against favorites of the emperor and their illicit sway at court.[10] Their chief target had been the ubiquitous censor Ding Daquan (doct. 1238). A lackluster bureaucrat with suspiciously close ties to eunuchs and consorts of the palace—the *yin* faction, as students saw it—he jeopardized the integrity of the civil service while deflecting power away from the throne. It was through such contacts, critics believed, that Ding Daquan could harangue, ridicule, and ultimately orchestrate the purge of Chief Councilor Dong Huai (doct. 1213), a figure popular on the university campus. Student sympathy for the chief councilor is reflected in the measure of their antipathy for his erstwhile enemy. Pejorative nicknames like "Ding the Blue Face"—an allusion to the blue

veins running close to the surface of his face—were but one expression of that contempt. Students resented as well the political arrogance of Ding Daquan, which had long exceeded the bounds of mere indecorousness to border on treacherous insubordination. Perception of him as a "loose cannon" was reinforced in the summer of 1256, upon the dismissal of Dong Huai. Having clearly orchestrated the purge of his rival, Ding Daquan would add insult to injury by personally leading palace guardsmen to the chief councilor's official residence, where Dong Huai was hounded out of home and town. This had occurred under the cover of night and before the imperial rescript of dismissal had been formally issued. Students protested the action by flooding the court with memorials and staging demonstrations in the capital. In the recent past, similar acts of civil disobedience had worked favorably for students. This time, the court responded with a rare measure of severity. It expelled Chen Yizhong and fellow provocateurs from the university and banished them from the capital. And to curb the activist impulses of those to remain, it condemned the university's conduct and proscribed future demonstrations. This represents, by the standards of most dynasties, a rather mild rebuke. But by the standards of a dynasty known to celebrate civil restraint, it seemed unthinkably severe.

Rarely, however, did the late Song fully enforce such proscriptions and still more rarely did it remain vindictive toward one-time dissidents. Chen Yizhong thereby returned triumphantly to Linan within a few short years, competed for doctoral credentials in 1262, and won second place on an examination list of over six hundred. Ding Daquan had been purged by then, politically discredited as well. Contrastingly, as one of the "six gentlemen" persecuted for political conviction, Chen Yizhong could now command a rare credibility within an expanding group of alienated intellectuals in and out of the capital. At the same time, he had acquired a virtual immunity to further intimidation by the newest autocrat at court, Chief Councilor Jia Sidao.

The later advancement of Chen Yizhong to high metropolitan office is portrayed as less a victory for Confucian moralists and more a political trick hatched by Jia Sidao.[11] This may seem curious for a councilor whose conflict with the intellectual establishment is legendary. But according to the dynastic historians who formulated this argument, Jia Sidao expected to benefit personally from association with this former student and the voices of "righteous" idealism that he represented. The revival of Chen Yizhong would foster an image of political tolerance as contrasted against the artless whimsicality of Ding Daquan, whose

tenure had only recently ended. And with both men native to the Zhe-jiang coast, Jia Sidao may have had personal ties to Chen Yizhong, al-though a generation separated the two in age. Yet the measure of his con-trol over the bureaucratic process, the extent to which Jia Sidao alone bears responsibility for the sensitive nomination, is perhaps overstated in official accounts. Since his own advancement from chief councilor to special military councilor, in 1267, he shared power with a succession of bureaucratic chiefs, including such seasoned and savvy politicians as Jiang Wanli (1198–1275) and Wang Yue (doct. 1220).[12] These men can scarcely be dismissed as mere puppets of a colleague clearly their intel-lectual and professional inferior. Moreover, beginning in 1270 precisely as the Chen Yizhong revival got underway, the court audiences of Jia Sidao were voluntarily reduced to only three per month. These are all signs of diminished input into decisionmaking, despite Jia Sidao's re-tention of some strategically-placed allies at court.[13]

It may well be that the principal sponsor of Chen Yizhong was nei-ther the special military councilor nor those directly beneath him, but rather the Grand Dowager herself. It is hardly coincidence that his leap from executive at the Bureau of Military Affairs to assistant councilor (10th/1274) and then chief councilor (3rd/1275) occurred in the early months of her regency. Later, it was Chen Yizhong's advice that she most often solicited and most scrupulously followed, sometimes to her own considerable detriment. Despite the many years which separated them—and Dowager Xie must have been Chen Yizhong's senior by at least twenty years—they shared remarkably similar attitudes toward current affairs. Her firm opposition to the 1259 proposal to relocate the capital farther south, the eunuch gaffe alluded to in the preceding chapter, sug-gested two critical aspects of her political thought. On the one hand, she opposed the presently passive response to the border menace, preferring instead a more intense and adamant belligerency. On the other hand, she preferred that the throne, in formulating policy, rely less on a few palace favorites and more on an outer court of civically conscious advi-sors. Not by coincidence, these represent exactly the two issues around which the university most frequently and fervently rallied, the extent to which they had evolved into something akin to a university platform.

It should be noted that the political posture of the Imperial Univer-sity, on court policy in general but border management in particular, made it the most radically militant community in the capital. This refl-ects the influence of an intellectual establishment far more militant than

the civil service mainstream. Ethical purists such as Zhu Xi saw the purge of foreign occupiers from north China as a moral imperative. Having humiliated the dynasty by seizing its lands and imprisoning its royalty—violating the sanctity of both state and family, in the process—retribution became the premiere obligation of filial sons in the south. "One cannot live under the same sky with the murderers of one's father," Zhu Xi writes indignantly.[14] Utilitarians such as Chen Liang and Ye Shi (1150–1223)—another influential group at the university—might be more pragmatic in their domestic agenda, but in foreign affaris they shared the militancy of Confucian moralists.[15] In fact, they went still further in seeking to accelerate the timetable for reunification of north and south, arguing that prolonged division would sap the empire of its will and vitality to fight. Through the lens of either moral duty or strategic expedience, a wide range of late-Song intellectuals thus rallied around a cause that utterly terrified the generally cautious officers at court. Idealistic students were more easily drawn to the visionaries, but at the cost of serious frictions with a political establishment so close to its campus yet remote from its heart.

The university's determined battle against Ding Daquan, the wily censor who went on to a brief stint as chief councilor, was fueled by more than mere outrage at the breaches of court policy and protocol noted earlier. It further branded him with "bringing harm to the loyal and good." He had nurtured, as students saw it, a dangerous complacency in military affairs and discipline, jeopardizing the lives of dedicated soldiers and innocent civilians alike.[16] A similarly militant rhetoric characterized the university's campaign against an earlier chief councilor, Shi Songzhi (1189–1257). Here again, memorials were weighted heavily with accusations of arrant pacifism, charging the councilor with appeasing the northern aggressor and demoralizing his own troops.[17] The charge seems, on surface, highly implausible in the case of Shi Songzhi: it was his personal command of border armies that had stemmed a massive Mongol blitzkrieg in the late 1230s. But students were unimpressed by such isolated feats. Shi Songzhi hailed from a family of prominent pacifists and seemed, to them, guilty by association. His family was also among the richest in the realm—a background similar to Ding Daquan and Jia Sidao. This left Shi Songzhi a highly incredulous advocate of martial discipline and resolve to university students, who held fast to the Neo-Confucian ideal of fixing one's emotional focus and restraining material impulses.[18] In the university's relentless campaign against him, it

was the university that triumphed. And the court, unable to function with Shi Songzhi at the helm, had no alternative to terminating his six-year term in 1244.

Joining the hundred and forty odd university students in signing petitions against Shi Songzhi were a still larger number of students from other campuses in the capital. Involvement of the national Military Academy, *Wuxue*, is especially significant in this regard. As training ground for future leaders of the armed forces, the inclination there toward militancy was particularly strong. And the revanchist zeal of the military academy, in turn, served to reinforce similar predispositions at the civilian-oriented university. Angry frustration over an insensitive political machine prevailed at both institutions, but the university preferred to protest through rhetoric and demonstration. The academy sometimes went a step farther, taking recourse to arms. Surely no one could forget the abortive attempt on the life of Chief Councilor Shi Miyuan (1164–1233), in 1209. The perpetrator was an academy graduate then serving in the Palace Guard, Hua Yue, who allegedly resented the humiliating terms of a recent accord with the Jurchen, an accord endorsed by the councilor.[19] After uncovering the plot, a throne intent on dissuading future zealots could not but exact the death penalty of Hua Yue, despite widespread sympathy away from court for his idealism. The outcome had been quite different two years earlier, when the university and the academy joined forces in support of Shi Miyuan.[20] Their extraordinary secret alliance then, in 1207, had led to the assassination of Han Tuozhou, the special councilor behind a military adventure against the Jurchen. For militants at the academy to assist in defeating a fellow militant at court may appear confused and contradictory, especially when their action ultimately strengthens the hand of a common enemy, the pacifists. But Han Tuozhou lacked authenticity to them—a politician who exploited war for personal gain, as they saw it. A counterfeit militant courting their empathy, he was perhaps more threatening to the cause of dynastic restoration than the genuine pacifist, and more deserving of his fate.

It seems terribly anomalous that the Song, a dynasty inclined toward civility over intrigue in the resolution of court conflict, should be struck with a succession of such violent episodes in the thirteenth century. Repeated contravention of political norms of the sort is due partly to the acute ineptitude or ambivalence of reigning monarchs. Only when the institutionalized checks on surrogate power break down—only when the separation of executive power fails and remonstrance is silenced at

the Chancellery and the Censorate—do ordinary men feel compelled to take extraordinary steps to restore the traditional balance. Also contributing to political violence are the passions of relatively young men in their twenties and thirties, which unleashed into an already combustive political atmosphere, have the potential for paralyzing disruptions in metropolitan order.

No sane statesman would welcome such disruptions. Yet in rallying Song citizens behind the dynastic banner, the passion associated with student activism proved too compelling for the Dowager Xie to resist, even though this may well represent the greatest single miscalculation of her entire regency. Nearly two decades had lapsed since the student days of Chen Yizhong and he had long ago proceeded to the civil service. There, a high examination ranking and an established political record permitted easy access to choice appointments. Now a member of precisely the establishment once targeted for attack, he nonetheless continued to cast himself in that familiar role of the outside critic, the displaced student who acts on noble aim, not political exigency. He apparently aspired to govern the realm by employing the same strategy which had served university interests so well in recent decades—the politics of polarization. Rather than compromise with critics, he preferred to employ rhetoric of escalating intensity to isolate and then discredit them. Chen Yizhong most assuredly knew that the court, by tradition, operated not on such confrontationist principles. Yet the art of strategic alliance and subtle compromise was nearly impossible for him to assimilate and anguished attempts to do so would visibly torment colleagues in the capital, dowager-regents at court, and most importantly, commanders in the field.

MILITANTS ALIENATING THE MILITARY

Chen Yizhong's enigmatically pugnacious political style would trigger a succession of crises, the first to occur in the second and third lunar months of 1275. As coadministrator of the Bureau of Military Affairs, Chen Yizhong astonished all when he entreated the throne to execute Jia Sidao.[21] There had been no indication, heretofore, of tension between the two men. On the contrary, the younger man is believed to have quite consciously cultivated close ties to the special military councilor. The souring of relations seemingly occurred almost overnight and was due to a single action—an action which would expose the old administration as spineless and self-defeating.

In the recent two months, northern armies had begun advancing rapidly eastward along the Yangzi River from Huangzhou, in central China, to Anqing and Chizhou, several hundred kilometers downstream. Such uneasy proximity to its capital required a quick and dramatic response from the south, prompting Jia Sidao to assume personal direction of what mushroomed into a massive storm up the troubled Yangzi. He had hoped to arrest the enemy advance, perhaps even restore a Song presence there. At other times, it was the emperor who would likely lead such legions to rally his men, but in recent generations they preferred to direct armies from the safety of palaces at Linan. Nor were absent emperors replaced at the border by councilor-level surrogates. Shi Songzhi seems the premiere exception for the thirteenth century and his historic supervision of frontier armies had occurred some three decades ago. Precisely due to the political and strategic symbolism of his enterprise, Jia Sidao would spare nothing. With 100,000 troops under his command, their formation reportedly stretched across one hundred *li*, some forty kilometers, as it exited the capital! Accompanying ships sat deep in the water, so heavily laden as they were with armor, weapons, and supplies. Yet combatants had scarcely made their trek of some 250 kilometers from Linan to the Yangzi city of Wuhu before news reached their camp, at Dingjiazhou, of new defections in the central theater. A reassessment of the entire mission was now in order and a desperate Jia Sidao, to win time, offered the treasure aboard his ships for a temporary truce, an offer rejected by the Mongols. He then fled east to the security of the walled city of Yangzhou. From there, he would convey to Dowager Xie a message certain to incite his enemies at court: he urged an immediate evacuation of Linan for Pingjiang, modern Suzhou. Some two hundred kilometers up the Grand Canal, the site seemed less vulnerable to naval assault from the coast and had the added advantage of proximity to troop concentrations near the Yangzi. The dowager responded calmly by soliciting the views of leading court officers in a debate that raged on for six full days. The radical call for Jia Sidao's death emerged in this context of intense fear but also amid sentiments of angry betrayal.

Perhaps he was acting on idealist reflexes rather than political reason when Chen Yizhong made his extreme demand. After all, for decades he and his fellows at the university had stood unequivocal on the relocation issue: they had demanded nothing short of a staunch defense. This principle would be reiterated by students in the current debate as well. A memorial from the Imperial Clan Academy, one of the more modest

sized institutions of Linan where the cream of the crop of Zhao imperial clansmen studied, proved pragmatically succinct: "Your Majesty de-
bates whether or not to relocate to Qingyuan [Mingzhou] or Pingjiang
[Suzhou], or in the event of extreme conditions take the ocean route to
Min [Fujian]. It makes no sense to contemplate where to proceed, for
where we go they can go as well. Meanwhile, debate only alarms and
incites the people with no advantage to the court."[22] The original proposal had merely anticipated a local repositioning of political and military assets, not distant flight. Over the course of debate, however, other
options had clearly emerged and these included sanctuary farther south.
The Dowager Xie's position on holding ground had not changed since
the 1250s, however unfavorable the recent turn of military events. Her
own well-known beliefs could only have reinforced the defiant instincts
of Chen Yizhong himself, although traditional historians see his stand
as politically calculated.

The timely demand to execute Jia Sidao is often portrayed as a calculated play for more power, Chen Yizhong seeking to distance himself
from a one-time associate while appealing to the well-known political
instincts of the Grand Dowager herself. Yet there exists too great a con-
sistency in the rhetoric of this former activist, from the 1250s through
the 1270s, to justify the cynicism of historians whose hostility represents a retrospective based on his later deeds. Dowager Xie no doubt
intuited the proposal as genuine as well, for she required only six days
to dismiss Jia Sidao. She further conceded to his opponents by confis-
cating family property and ordering a distant exile. Under no circumstances, however, would she sign her former councilor's death warrant.
It would have been bad form: he was, after all, the brother of her husband's favorite concubine. The appearance of jealous retribution, on her
part, had to be avoided at all cost. Moreover, the dowager's restraint reflected a genuine commitment to political civility and reprehension of
violence. "Sidao has diligently served for three reigns," she declared.
"How can We countenance compromise of the etiquette appropriate to
a high official due merely to the transgression of a single day?"[23] He fell
to an assassin all the same, a half year later, but with neither the authorization nor foreknowledge of the Grand Dowager. For the second time
in the century, court enemies had exacted violent retribution against a
councilor-level official. And this time Chen Yizhong appears seriously
implicated in the plot.[24]

The dismissal of Jia Sidao should have put to rest the relocation issue,
but only a few days later it triggered an event of still greater import for

the fledgling Song cause. Throughout those six days of court debate, the chief officer of the Palace Guard, Han Zhen, had gone beyond mere public endorsement of the evacuation proposal to begin actual preparations for flight. He had acted on secret instructions from Jia Sidao, instructions received with the duly designated imprimatur or "wax seal" of the special military councilor.[25] Han Zhen's actions, more than formally authorized by the appropriate civil overseer, reflected as well the consensus of his colleagues in the Guard and their genuine concern for the security of the royal family. Yet an overreactive Chen Yizhong, assuming some secret agenda of insubordination or treachery, seemed utterly irrational in his response. Han Zhen appeared to challenge his authority as the court's new chief executive and overseer of the Palace Guard. The guardsman's close links to the Jia Sidao administration had, quite simply, compromised his credibility with the new leadership. Yet the radical response of Chen Yizhong to the pressure of Han Zhen was also informed by historical experience. It had been the chief of the Palace Guard, some three centuries earlier and in an episode now enshrined in dynastic legend, who purged a child monarch and inaugurated the rule of Song. In so similar a context of vacuum on top, suspicion and paranoia were certain to drive the instincts of civilian overseers of the military. Han Zhen should have intuited as much.

Sadly, it was paranoia that prevailed. At the outset of the third lunar month, Chen Yizhong summoned Han Zhen to his official quarters on the pretext of policy discussions. Once there, he drew from his sleeve an iron cudgel and struck a paralyzing blow to the palace guardsman's head. Han Zhen was further brutalized before death: the bones in his feet and legs were painfully broken, his severed head later to hang from the Facing the Heavens gate, the principal portal through which officials passed each day enroute to their offices in the imperial city (see Map 3). The intent of intimidating other potentially insubordinate sorts was unmistakable. It all backfired. The death of Han Zhen triggered a rare mutiny among loyal officers in the Guard. Marching on the palace gates in a shocking act of protest, the angry assailants sprayed palace grounds with incendiary arrows before fleeing under the cover of night. Soon joining them in flight would be countless others, particularly military men estranged from their civilian overseers. The incident quickly incited a broader desertion as well, reflecting a shattered confidence in decisionmakers at court. Most such deserters found santuary in nearby cities; the family of Han Zhen fled all the way north, seeking asylum with the enemy.

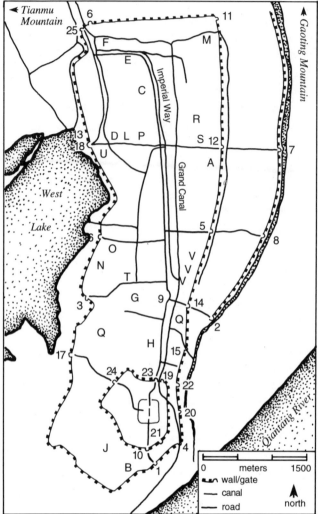

Map 3. Linan

Official sources, in their rather cursory treatment of the incident, tend to portray Chen Yizhong as acting on personal whim. Yet a highly credible contemporary then residing in Linan, Zhou Mi, insisted that he was merely following the orders of Dowager Xie.[26] Court authorization is certainly implied by public exposure of the guardsman's corpse so soon after his death. It is also implicit in the advancement of assassin Chen Yizhong to chief councilor only four days later, clear expression of the dowager's enduring confidence. Yet so much in this violent act contravenes the all too consistent political style of Dowager Xie. Her very recent insistence on maintaining "the etiquette appropriate to a high official," the extent to which she withstood a near avalanche of pressure to execute Jia Sidao, represents a statement of principle which should have applied equally to Han Zhen. After all, her objective went beyond upholding the humanistic traditions long associated with the dynasty and critical to the loyalty of its literati subjects. A more immediate concern was the maintenance of metropolitan order. In originally opposing relocation of the capital, in 1259, the dowager had invoked the cause of "not inciting the minds of the masses."[27] Surely, little would be more disruptive to the metropolitan order than an unjust assassination of the capital's chief military officer.

If Dowager Xie did have a hand, however reluctantly, in the death of her chief guardsman, then she may well have lived to regret it, for the action went well beyond merely alienating a few high-placed military men. Equally outraged were civil service mainstays such as Zhang Jian. He was among the more senior men at court, having earned his doctoral degree in 1223, some five decades earlier.[28] He was also perhaps the most amiable and generous character there, colleagues dubbing him "Mr. Cheerful"—a sobriquet often used satirically. In the aftermath of the Han Zhen assassination, however, a somber Zhang Jian abruptly abandoned his office, fled the capital, and ignored repeated summonses to return. His motives were made unmistakably clear in official correspondence, where he writes: "Although Han Zhen requested relocation of the capital, he clearly had no other motive. To send him to his death for simply this, inducing the attendant commotion and anxiety, seems surely excessive."[29] For a man whose entire career was marked by the meticulous avoidance of controversy, this is an uncharacteristically strong statement. Unfortunately for the court, the sentiments of Zhang Jian reverberated elsewhere. The dowager would herself acknowledge the disaffection pandemic within literati ranks and her own frustration at addressing it. In an edict posted weeks later just outside the audience cham-

ber, on April 16 by Western calendar, she assumed a rare virulence in denouncing such weak spirited men:

> For over three hundred years, our dynasty has employed *propriety* in its treatment of the literati class. Yet when the successor and I met with assorted personal hardships, officers high and low offered not a single proposal for saving the empire. Within the capital, officials now abandon commissions and forsake audience; away from the capital, custodians relinquish seals and desert cities. Censorial officers are already incapable of investigating and indicting for us while the two or three remaining executives cannot lead and direct the efforts of the group. Superficially they cooperate with us, but in succession they flee by night. . . . .The Mandate of Heaven has not yet changed, the laws of the empire are still in place. Be advised that military and civilian officials who remain at court will be advanced two salary levels, but those who forsake their empire and abandon us will be investigated by the Censorate and reported to me.[30]

Hers was a difficult tightrope: combining carrot and stick in shepherding men so conflicted and fickle. It is noteworthy that Dowager Xie would portray official alienation as reflecting sheer cowardice in reaction to recent setbacks at the border. This seems a clever shifting of guilt. Yet the Han Zhen affair had occurred only eighteen days earlier and this domestic fiasco surely offered equally compelling reason for the capital's rank-and-file, in fear but also anger, to abandon ship.

FORTITUDE AT THE FRONT

The dismissal of Jia Sidao and death of Han Zhen may well have represented a conscious move, on the part of desperate decisionmakers, to set a higher standard of discipline and dedication for their surrogates in the military and civilian services. Perhaps the Song problem, heretofore, had been an excess of compassion and empathy. After all, the empress and her advisors continued to be haunted by the controversial pardon of Fan Wenhu by ex-councilor Jia Sidao; he defected to the enemy only a year later, it will be remembered. If the court could only demand punishments for failure as consistently as it dispenses rewards for success, if it could only instill a measure of fear into its men commensurate with the terror struck by the enemy, if it could cast in masculine forcefulness the orders emanating from a court of women and children—then perhaps the recent rash of defections and desertions could be stemmed. Thus, coinciding with Chen Yizhong's growing stature at court, there occurred an aggressive retaliation against Song defectors, their family

property confiscated and court honors rescinded.[31] The most visible targets were men of the heartland, Fan Wenhu and Lü Wenhuan, although leaders farther east were affected as well.

"In times of trouble, severe penalties are altogether fitting," goes one widely-subscribed principle of Song legal policy.[32] Yet merely resorting to heightened discipline might well convey the exact opposite message—a message of desperate vulnerability whereby otherwise loyal subjects turn elsewhere for political sanctuary. Only this can explain the strategic losses that soon stretched from one end of the Yangzi to the other. The central Yangzi cities of Hanyang and Huangzhou, Jiangzhou and Anqing were surrendered after only modest resistance, usually by the prefect or other civilian in charge. The surrenders came in rapid succession, largely in the early months of 1275, and would likely have occurred irrespective of the mettle of Song men. Quite simply, the dynasty had made too many strategic blunders over the decades and now had to face the consequences. On the one hand, it had focused too narrowly on Xiangyang and other cities along the Han River, at the expense in some measure of cities along the second line of defense, the Yangzi. With such concentrated investment in a single theater, the loss of one was certain to trigger the fall of others with domino-like precision. On the other hand, the Song had reserved for the eastern theater a vast contingent of its standing army, estimated at 700,000 regulars in all.[33] Such concentrations may have enhanced the security of the capital, but at the expense of the rest of the empire. Moreover, too many strategic edifices rested upon the goodwill of a single family, the Lü network mentioned in the preceding chapter, with its preponderant influence over the Song heartland. Not only did members of that network defect to the Yuan in large numbers, but they then helped negotiate the surrender of other cities in the region, bringing to the process their imposing clout.[34] In a context where defeat seemed preordained by decisions past, the defection of Song regional leaders to the Yuan did not always reflect their alienation from the cause of dynasty. They often acted out of necessity and against the wishes of a divided local leadership.

The veritable tug of war over dynastic loyalties that often paralyzed local defenders and culminated in a violent resolution is vividly illustrated in the case of Chizhou. Some six hundred kilometers up the Yangzi River, this prefecture of over a half million was left with only five hundred troops as enemy forces began to close in, their manpower either deflected to neighboring theaters or lost to desertion. The chief civilian officer had already absconded many months earlier, leaving As-

sociate prefect Zhao Maofa to fill the void.[35] Native to the far west with no known personal ties to Chizhou, the associate prefect remained fully committed to vigorously defending the region all the same. Only after his military overseer struck a secret agreement to surrender would he accept the futility of his cause. Having precluded a similar apostasy for himself, death offered the only honorable way out. It must have been mere hours before the final assault that Zhao Maofa moved to put his house in order. He held a banquet for family and friends, distributed family possessions to a few close relatives, and discharged assorted servants—all with ritualized precision and forethought. He also wrote parting poems to his brothers in a distant Sichuan, affirming their eternal fraternity but also his mortal debt to the Song cause:

> City walls not high, moats not deep,
> Lacking in men as well as materiél;
> Only through death can I repay the empire,
> In some future life, we may again be brothers.[36]

He and his wife, née Yong, then committed suicide, their bodies garbed in formal attire and hung from the Pavilion of Complacency, a location intentionally selected to symbolize the impassiveness with which the two met their heroic deaths. Mongol occupiers would be impressed by the civic duty of Zhao and the marital devotion of Yong: Bayan not only honored them with a proper burial, but recommended posthumous titles from the Yuan court.

Only a month earlier and a scant one hundred kilometers away, there occurred a parallel case of loyalist revelry at Anqing. The Mongols had been sweeping other cities in the central Yangzi, yet the prefectural seat here would be difficult to take, enveloped as it was in a mountainous region some sixty kilometers north of the river.[37] Yet before northerners had even begun to turn their attention to the city, the wily Fan Wenhu in his capacity as civil officer negotiated a surrender. Those negotiations were conducted elsewhere via special emissary, altogether circumventing Associate prefect Xia Yi and for good reason. He was a doctoral degree-holder and former student at the Imperial University whose loyalty to the Song was absolutely inalterable.[38] At being presented with a *fait accompli*, Xia Yi opted to take his own life. He had tucked away in his collar, prior to ingesting poison, a suicide note where he swore allegiance to ruler and family and made light of his own death at fifty-five, which he explained as "destined."[39]

During the Mongol sweep of the Song heartland, many who re-

sponded by taking their own lives stood decidedly outside the defense establishment, individuals who would have neither jeopardized life nor compromised honor by continuing to live under the new regime. Making an exceptionally strong statement in this regard was Jiang Wanli.[40] Born to a humble family and raised along a northern stretch of the Boyang Lake, some sixty kilometers south of the Yangzi River and north of the thriving city of Raozhou, he nonetheless spent most of his mature years in the empire's capital. He began as a student at the Imperial University and enjoyed the distinction of serving as its chancellor. He also served in a variety of other esteemed offices, metropolitan and regional, culminating in a brief stint as chief councilor, in 1269. Contemporaries seem to have respected Jiang Wanli most for his intellectual and political integrity. Yet radicals on the ascent resented his cordial ties to Jia Sidao, seeing in this a lingering threat to dynastic rejuvenation. When the seventy-three year old retired from government in 1273, the prospect for vindication must have seemed remote.

His return to Raozhou coincided with an intensification of Mongol pressure against this prefecture of nearly one million, which despite population density was acutely short on trained soldiers. Its indomitable prefect proved remarkably resourceful in piecing together a viable defense, all the same. Although native to another region, Prefect Tang Zhen did not hesitate to empty treasuries of their wealth and draft commoners into military service. His imagination and industry may have been commendable, yet his peasant conscripts made poor fighters while the professional mainstay often refused to fight. By the second lunar month of 1275, the associate prefect struck a secret agreement with the enemy; an obstinate Tang Zhen, refusing to be converted, was killed. The prefect's ethical endurance inspired many in the local elite including Jiang Wanli. "Although not currently in office," he concluded, "I must still live or die with the empire."[41] He thus threw himself into a pond as the enemy breached the walls of Raozhou. Following in his footsteps were his sole surviving son, plus other kin and associates, the corpses so numerous as to appear "like a pile of stones." Jiang Wanli died without male heir, perhaps even without surviving siblings, his younger brother having very recently met with violent death as well. One can only wonder whether he would have acted with similar finality had he known then that his beloved Raozhou, in a matter of mere days, would be reclaimed by the Song in an inspired if ephemeral rally.

In their nine-month offensive ending in early summer 1275, the Mongols would sweep across thirty cities and towns in central China,

which by their reckoning involved absorption of some two million persons.[42] Most of these new acquisitions lie north of the Yangzi River in Huainan West circuit or south of the river in Jiangnan East. More sporadic were their holdings farther east. Huainan East and Zhexi remained largely in Song hands despite some inroads. Moreover, as a summer respite set in and key Mongol commanders returned north for consultation with a court laying the final plans for victory, Song forces launched a major rally. Reverted to southern control were Raozhou and Ezhou in the heartland, plus a dozen or more cities to the east. Earlier respites of the sort sometimes persisted for years and the prospect, however ill-founded in this case, could only have momentarily lifted southern spirits. In the interim, the Song would move aggressively to recover lost territory by offering the post of prefect for anyone capable of gaining a lost city, subprefect for regaining a town.[43] Such *quid pro quo* office for land strategies stood in glaring contravention of dynastic traditions, but the Yuan had implemented similar policies with such remarkable success that the Song could not but respond in kind. Song defenders were also significantly heartened, that spring and early summer, by the steady stream of armies which proceeded toward Linan in response to the dowager's *qin wang* summons.[44] They came from as far as the remote southwest, Guangnan circuit, well over a thousand kilometers away, only to arrive at Linan for rapid reassignment to theaters usually near, sometimes not so near the capital. The turnout was certainly not on the scale expected: at an initial peak of thirty to forty thousand (more would arrive later), it met merely a fraction of dynastic needs.[45] Yet if the Song held any hope of retaining the eastern Yangzi, that hope rested upon these tens of thousands of common men, who joined by a still larger number of regulars, would ostensibly overwhelm the enemy with their numerical strength and rustic resolve.[46]

No less important to the south's summer revelry was the sweeping redeployment of top commanders. The court shifted Zhang Shijie, for example, from the Jinghu heartland to the newly imperiled east while entrusting to Li Tingzhi, only recently revived after the Xiangyang debacle, an expanded role in the same eastern theater.[47] The mission of Li Tingzhi was to fortify defenses at Yangzhou and thereby reinforce Song dominance of Huainan East, that strategically vital strip of land south of the Huai and north of the Yangzi Rivers. Yangzhou may well represent the plum of the region. The Yangzi flows to its south, the Grand Canal extends northward through its center. Mongol armies had repeatedly besieged the city, at times coming alarmingly close to toppling

it, but defenders held firm against staggering losses. Meanwhile, Zhang Shijie would direct the effort to reclaim Song sovereignty south of the Yangzi, retaking in the summer cities temporarily lost to the enemy in the spring. Most notably among these reclamations were Changzhou and Pingjiang, cities straddling that critical southern stretch of the Grand Canal which connects the capital to the north. This might seem a virtually impossible mission in light of enemy control over Zhenjiang and Jiankang (modern Nanjing). On the southern side of the Yangzi River near Yangzhou, the two prefectures were equally critical links in the canal life-line between north and south. Surrendered to the Mongols in the third month, these cities never reverted to Song control. The capital was indefensible without them, but reclamation by Linan never progressed beyond preparatory stages.

Through its frustrated struggle that summer to restore some measure of territorial integrity to its dissolving empire, perhaps the greatest single defect of a waning Song becomes glaringly clear. Dynastic fortunes were declining not because combatants were too few or their courage deficient, nor due to any inadequacy of sophisticated weapons or hard cash. On the contrary, these all surfaced in remarkable abundance when conditions dictated. But coordinating and deploying these resources evolved into an enterprise of escalating difficulty for a dynasty sapped of confidence in itself and faith in its men. The magnitude of the problem can be seen, in microcosm, through the battle of Jiaoshan, early in the seventh lunar month of 1275.

Sitting on the northern bank of the Yangzi River, a scant ten kilometers east of enemy occupied Zhenjiang, the hills of Jiaoshan were to provide an anchor for Song defenders to use in blocking the further advance eastward of Mongol ships. Joining Zhang Shijie, now generalissimo for the eastern theater, were Liu Shiyong and Sun Huchen, representing the local military and civilian leadership.[48] Together they committed a reputed 10,000 warships, many of them the imposing "Yellow Goose" and "White Sparrow" models designed for patroling the high seas. The magnitude of manpower invested in the enterprise is not known, but a force of fifty to sixty thousand would have been minimally necessary to man and defend so vast a naval fleet. These ships, anchored on both banks of the Yangzi and facing westward (upstream), were organized in block formations consisting of ten ships attached to one another by iron chains. This created an unbreachable wall with multiple tiers of defense and no means for southern ships to exit or even regroup. Having vastly outnumbered and overpowered the north, this

seemed an opportune moment for the Song to make public display of the best of its naval assets, the advanced technology that only the south could afford in such abundance.

Visibly absent from the Jiaoshan front was Bayan, generalissimo for the north, but his stand-ins were no less seasoned: the Mongol Aju was in command, assisted by two Chinese natives of the north, Dong Wen-bing and Zhang Hongfan, men with decades of experience as merce-naries under the Mongol banner. They reportedly deployed no more than one thousand ships, one-tenth the Song numbers and noticeably inferior in quality. Such disparity should have precluded a frontal as-sault, but northern strategists seemed masters of the unexpected. With a thousand skilled archers manning both sides of their stoutest ship, they exploited the downstream current to storm forward, pelleting Song vessels with incendiary arrows in a barrage that continued relentlessly for hours. Simultaneous with this naval action was the deployment of cavalry, which succeeded in infiltrating coastal pockets without notice. From these coastal positions they launched surprise strikes against the stationary ships of the south. A naval contingent soon emerged at the rear of the Song flank, exerting additional pressure. Pandemonium en-sued. Fixed in place by anchors and chains, the Song navy was unable to respond flexibly to this multi-directional assault and sat in the water as easy targets. Fire leaped quickly from one ship to the next, consuming initially sails and masts, soon the entire hull. Frantic sailors had no option but to lunge into the water. It ended as a mammoth fiasco: upwards of ten thousand reportedly perished while an equal number were captured alive. Also seized by the enemy were some seven hundred of the coveted White Sparrows. Zhang Shijie and fellow commanders, with whatever men and ships they could salvage, would escape via the high seas; and their defeat raised serious questions, if not about their commitment to lead, then surely their competence to do so.

The south's shameful showing at Jiaoshan grew out of strategies ob-sessive in their rigid myopia. Song commanders were handicapped by a tunnel vision which left them attentive to only a single flank. They proved enamored of positional strategies that valued endurance over responsiveness; and devoid of confidence in their own men, the leader-ship overconstrained and overregulated the rank-and-file. Their hearts seemingly weightier than their heads, they deployed the wrong boats for the Jiaoshan maneuver: mammoth hulks capable of high velocity on the ocean with its strong winds and waves, but near to immobile on the relatively calm waters of the Yangzi. Perhaps no alternative ships were

available at that time and place. More likely, the alternatives were never considered and the consequent waste of resources utterly appalling. An error of similar magnitude occurred in the deployment of human resources: the infantry of Zhang Shijie were impressed into naval service while the sailors of Liu Shiyong were impressed into infantry.[49] In the face of such stunning miscalculations, there is still a remarkable tendency even among tough-minded policymakers to exonerate Zhang Shijie. He is portrayed as the sad victim of simple bad luck but also a victim of irresponsible colleagues who failed to provide the necessary backup. An otherwise harshly critical Wen Tianxiang, for example, seems more moved by the tragic spectacle of defeat than the mismanagement behind it. Clearly, no recrimination toward the hapless commanders is contained in his elegy, "The Battle of Zhenjiang,"

> From the high seas, a thousand ships;
> Carnivores who live on the flesh of hundreds of thousands.
> The river still, it cannot flow;
> Remorse lingers to this very day.[50]

The Yuan side apparently sustained heavy casualties as well, which explains why bodies and débris were reputedly so thick that the Yangzi virtually ceased to flow. Wen Tianxiang alludes to this high casualty count in one line and "carnivores" in the next, the implication of which rings clear: it is the barbarism of northern aggressors, not the ineptitude of the southern command, which caused so many lives to be needlessly lost.

It may seem curious that the dynasty to invent the finest of military technology in the world of its day—gunpowder and cannon, power crossbows and fire lances, stone throwers and poisonous gases—would prove so consistently maladroit in their deployment.[51] Some historians attribute Song losses to the outward flow of important military technologies, where they could be improved upon by the enemies of China and eventually used against it.[52] In effect, the Song had lost its technological edge. Yet, as the Jiaoshan debaucle demonstrates so vividly, the state of military technology was not so critical as the management of that technology and late Song overseers were the worst of managers. Then again, the Song never saw itself as a martial culture; and civilian overseers of the military, convinced of the superiority of their own civil crafts, could only have been ambivalent toward any changes—particularly the creation of new technologies—that threatened their preeminent standing in government and society. They could accept the logistical utility of large armies and sophisticated weapons; yet when these

failed in battle, that failure did not so much diminish as enhance the power of civilian leaders, whose value to society ostensibly transcended the mechanical contrivances at their disposal. Those leaders must have intuited this, if only at some subconscious level, thereby compromising their confidence and commitment in deploying those devices.

LITERATI IN WAITING

The battle at Jiaoshan exposed southern strategists as bumbling and shortsighted, incompetent even to defend the imperial capital in its own backyard, that all-too-critical circuit of Zhexi which borders the Yangzi River and extends south all the way to Linan. This served further to dispirit metropolitan officials residing in the capital. The confidence of these men in their professional and personal security had already taken a severe battering in the spring, when defections at the border and mutiny in the Palace Guard drove Linan to the brink of anarchy. Many of those who had fled the capital in the spring were only beginning their return when more bad news came from the front. Added to these tensions, and perhaps feeding on them, were the personal conflicts that plagued the Song political leadership, a leadership prone to create crises over which to fight their own internecine battles. Not all such dissension can be blamed on the university ideologue Chen Yizhong, with his notoriously mercurial moods. Others of prominent station could be no less divisive in word and deed, most notably among them Wang Yinglin (1223–1296).

Few courtiers of the day could be as egotistically self-assured as he, and perhaps deservedly so. He passed admission examinations for the Imperial University at sixteen, earned his doctoral degree at eighteen, and honors as "Erudite Litterateur" at thirty-three.[53] For the entire thirteenth century, he was only the fifth man to be recognized as Erudite, where the literary and humanistic standards of examiners were set so high as to frustrate all but the most prodigiously precocious. It was also Wang Yinglin who directed the doctoral examination of 1256 and waxed so effusively on the intellect and integrity of Wen Tianxiang, the ardent royalist who headed that list of awardees. Wang Yinglin went on to serve at the Imperial University in an administrative capacity, then the Military Academy as professor. These appointments would inevitably reinforce his own predilection toward revanchist idealism. They would also augment his credibility among academic activists critical of the court and instinctively hostile to its leaders.

Wang Yinglin's militant proclivities were further inspired by his affinity for the *Spring and Autumn Annals*. This classic, a key text in the university curriculum, had particular relevance for the Southern Song. After all, the *Annals* chronicles another era of political division, albeit two millennia earlier, where the Middle Kingdom, surrounded by hostile peoples, had come to regard its civilization as under siege. The work also covers a time of redefinition for Chinese culture, a time when earlier intellectual traditions were being codified while assimilating the new. The *Annals,* at once, celebrated this cultural revival and promoted its propagation through assertively interventionist policies toward the "other"—the non-sinicized world.[54] It is a conservatively militant work, at least in the eyes of the Song reader. Wang Yinglin fully appreciated this philosophical legacy, although his specialty was historical research, ancient and modern. Like his father, he had served at the History Bureau in the capital, compiling official documents and composing contemporary narratives for the court. In later years, his own writings focused substantially on historical geography and institutional development, with a secondary interest in China's early astrology and literature.[55] Through these historical pursuits he came better to appreciate traditional rituals and their unique role in ordering society—linking past and present, high and low through a continuity of cultural forms. It was ostensibly in recognition of these interests that an aging Lizong installed Wang Yinglin as erudite of ceremonials, the palace's premiere consultant on ritual etiquette.

A century later, writers of the Song dynastic history forced to assign the biography of Wang Yinglin to some specific intellectual category, chose the "Grove of Confucians." Heretofore, this biographical cluster contained men for whom the study or practice of traditional rites consumed their principal energies. Writers of *Song Shi* apparently acted on more ambiguous and less restrictive criteria; still, they tended to expect a record of scholarly distinction in traditional Confucian crafts, either ritual or statecraft. Conspicuously absent from this group were Neo-Confucian metaphysicists, the philosophical luminaries of the dynasty. No intellectual community had similarly succeeded in integrating their rationalized vision of the natural order with a reinvigorated regimen of political and social mores. Reflecting the unique character of this new-wave Confucian, a special category in the dynastic history dubbed "Teachings of the Way," *Daoxue*, was created for them. Yet the intellectual landscape of the thirteenth century did not neatly divide into such

self-contained blocks. To the contrary, a progressive erosion of barriers between the new rationalists, the old ritualists, and assorted other rivals seemed discernibly underway.[56] Wang Yinglin hailed from the coastal city of Mingzhou, for example, where the rival School of the Mind (*Xinxue*) dominated the landscape. But that was the early thirteenth century and by mid-century these idealists had begun conceding ground to the rationalists. A pivotal figure in Mingzhou's growing acceptance of this rival teaching was Wang Yinglin himself.[57] In his scholarship are traces of an extroverted rationalism and an introverted idealism, but at the same time a fascination with the mundane crafts traditionally associated with Confucianism. What appealed to him about *Daoxue* was not its obscure metaphysic, but its moral critique of governance.

Wang Yinglin found himself perennially at odds with establishment politics, even more than Chen Yizhong. He censured the unpopular Ding Daquan, in the late 1250s, for an inept handling of border affairs—his fraudulent misrepresentation of real conditions and defeatist resignation. He later proceeded to offend Jia Sidao as well. An ally in better times, Wang Yinglin attacked him on two fronts: economic policies that wreaked rural havoc and border policies that fostered defeatism and retreat. He fulminated with perhaps greatest intensity against the political vanity of recent statesmen, men for whom the silencing of opponents came at the cost of critical input for the court. Yet his critique of government is distinguished from most others in its consistent concern with that nexus between state policy and divine designation, secular rule and supernatural intervention. This is evidenced in the scattered remnants of his memorials, where he frequently demanded a constructive response from court managers to "changes" or "warnings" from Heaven.

Wang Yinglin had long been enamored of theories on celestial "paths" and "orbits"—a sort of historical astronomy.[58] Reinforcing such scientific pursuits, however, was his belief in an interactive resonance between Heaven and Earth, man and cosmos. Such theories had proliferated in early China; they even provided the foundation for notions like Mandate of Heaven and Five Phases. So much of this nonetheless seemed antithetical to the rationalist impulses of Song. Thus, their presence in court rhetoric and historical writings had declined rather dramatically after the mid-eleventh century.[59] Only with the closing decades of the dynasty would such speculative dogma regain some of its old lustre. There was no Confucian rationalization, after all, for the impending ascent of the Mongols over the Song, the culturally inferior

prevailing over its decided superior. The only explanation—and ultimately the south's only salvation—is divine intervention, the unilateral mediation of an omnipotent Heaven.

Unfortunately, this special sensitivity to rituals and omens served more to distractively divide the court than to strengthen its resolve. Irregularities in the heavens would trigger a succession of proposals of dubious relevance to the crisis at hand. In the tenth month of 1275, for example, court astronomers reported Saturn and Venus to have crossed paths. A solar eclipse had occurred only months earlier, lending greater significance to this recent event. Wang Yinglin, as imperial secretary, responded by recommending the posthumous adoption of an heir to Zhao Hong.[60] As mentioned in the preceding chapter, this deposed royal prince had died nearly fifty-two years earlier in a bloody dispute over the throne. It was in retribution for conspiring against him that the future Lizong ordered Zhao Hong, his step-brother, to be buried on a straw mat while repeatedly refusing to designate a posthumous heir. Dowager Xie could scarcely undo so consistently emphatic a policy of her dead husband without appearing guilty of a still greater offense—infidelity to his sacred memory.

Wang Yinglin and fellow proponents of amnesty surely understood this dilemma with all of its personal and political ramifications. They must have intuited the potential here for setting one segment of the imperial clan against another: the two step-brothers represented different branches of the clan and this matter a lingering thorn in their relations.[61] Only recently, through the deaths of its principal actors, had old wounds begun to heal. Equally ponderous was the prospect of dividing the palace itself. It was common knowledge that the widow of Emperor Duzong, Dowager Quan, came from the same extended family as her father-in-law, Lizong. Certainly she would greet any attempt at elevating, even posthumously, the representative of a rival branch with consternation. The senior dowager thus ran the risk of offending the junior dowager, mother of the child emperor, were she to act positively on the Wang Yinglin proposal. She eventually elected to do so, after some astute diplomacy the details of which have eluded historians, but she should rightfully have been spared such pressures. At a time when domestic reforms and foreign conflict had already strained the loyalties of the empire's elite, a time when child monarchs and female regencies had already detracted from the regime's legitimacy, it seemed scandalously insensitive for Wang Yinglin to toss into the political arena yet another bone of hot contention.

His penchant for stirring other sorts of court controversy were legendary as well. He locked horns with Chief Councilor Zhang Jian, in the spring of 1275, over the Palace Guard affair. Absolutely and inalterably convinced that Han Zhen had plotted seditiously against the throne, he supported Chen Yizhong's provocative assassination; Councilor Zhang stood equally convinced of the guardsman's innocence.[62] This seems the basis of a feud between the two so bitter that Wang Yinglin, from his powerful post in the Censorate, would soon indict the chief councilor and secure his dismissal. Dowager Xie must have recognized the conflict as partly personal in motivation, for it was she who ruled that Zhang Jian retain full salary in demonstration of enduring favor.

In the fall of the same year, Wang Yinglin targeted another chief councilor, Liu Mengyan, and applied extraordinary pressure to have him purged.[63] His charge this time centered on favoritism. The senior councilor had allegedly arranged choice appointments for friends and associates, including men whose official records seemed blemished beyond redemption. In the rhetorical idiom of Wang Yinglin, "he finagles with legal norms merely due to crisis conditions, he opposes majority opinion merely due to personal bias." Accuracy aside, the allegations were in the least premature, coming a mere five months into the Liu Mengyan administration. And when the dowager refused to act, Wang Yinglin took recourse to a pressure tactic common at the university—the political strike. He abruptly abandoned Linan and returned to his native Mingzhou, from which he continued to forward memorials in the hope of a favorable response. It never came.[64] The dowager, no doubt wearied by her constant need to mediate between such contentious men, found governance easier without him.

Wang Yinglin dared to attack these two councilors, individuals far more advanced than he in age and experience, because he viewed himself as occupying the moral high ground. Ostensibly, he supported bureaucratic professionalism while the councilors acted on arbitrary whim, he promoted discipline while they fostered laxity, he reflected literati consensus while they represented private agendas. He seemed to demand, effectively, an end to politics as usual. For too long, personal contacts weighed heavier than professional experience, while a single executive or two on top governed in isolation from their civil service cohort and the voiceless masses. Rhetoric of such prudish pretense emerges as virtually identical to the idealism of the university, from which it clearly derived inspiration. Yet Wang Yinglin failed to exemplify personally those standards which he imposed so fastidiously on others. He argued

against personal whim and for bureaucratic procedures, but then defended the arbitrary assassination of Guardsman Han Zhen, the most outrageous act of court subterfuge in recent decades. He criticized Liu Mengyan for reassigning rather than disciplining those local officials who lost cities at the front. Yet there is no indication of similar criticism of Chen Yizhong, who as chief councilor similarly failed to discipline many a defeated officer. The two men on close personal terms, Wang Yinglin simply chose to exempt his friends from the scrutiny extended to others. Moreover, he had an annoying proclivity for pontificating on ideals without adequate grounding in reality. It was unnecessary to look beyond the court itself, with its literati ranks shrinking daily—the pool of potential replacements had long dried up. The stiffening of disciplinary standards that he demanded, however compelling as rhetoric, would make calamitous policy.

For most of 1275, Wang Yinglin commanded an exceptional measure of power without holding a councilor-level post. This relates partly to his direct access to Dowager Xie through service in several secretarial capacities. Her public pronouncements were personally crafted by him, her political will invigorated by the power of his pen. The exceptional sway of Wang Yinglin also relates to vacuum at the top. The councilors to succeed Jia Sidao being old and listless, leadership naturally devolved by default on the second tier of court men. Much the same can be said of Chen Yizhong, whose personal power seems perennially to have exceeded the authority of his office. He plotted the purge of Han Zhen without the consultation or consent of councilor-level overseers. He personally arrested and then liquidated the assassin of Jia Sidao at coastal Fuzhou, again without court authorization. He briefly commanded troops near the border without the usual experience or commission. No one ignored rules and flaunted favor as much as Chen Yizhong. A partial Wang Yinglin apparently perceived the ends to justify the means, a sentiment initially shared it seems by the grand dowager. Yet even for her, the seductive intensity of loyalist rhetoric quickly wore thin, a conclusion that others in the militant cohort of Chen Yizhong and Wang Yinglin would reach as well.

As the rhetoric of Chen Yizhong began to lose its lustre, so did his political image, which plummeted almost immediately after the reins of power passed formally to his hands. Persistent bickering and grandstanding at court seemed a mere decoy for indecision, even cowardice. This offers the only explanation for the seemingly interminable war of words that Chen Yizhong relentlessly waged with colleagues. His dis-

pute with senior councilor Zhang Jian over the Palace Guard affair, as noted earlier, culminated in the councilor's dismissal late in the third month of 1275. A court shakeup ensued where Chen Yizhong emerged as junior councilor. His senior counterpart, as left-chief councilor, would be Wang Yue (doct. 1220), a statesman probably in his late seventies with five full decades of distinguished service.[65]

Widely experienced, Wang Yue's strength nonetheless rested with fiscal administration: both in and away from the capital he held numerous posts including a stint with the fiscal intendancy for the Huai border region. With the eastern Huai now critical to the dynasty's survival, this experience had suddenly acquired a vital currency to the court. Yet he and Chen Yizhong mixed like fire and water from the virtual outset and tensions seemed never to abate. Actually, the two were remarkably similar in political style, independent and self-righteous. As critics of Jia Sidao pacifism, both had independently demanded his head. Similar impulses but separate agendas may partly explain the rare intensity of their mutual antipathy. They sometimes fought over reasonably substantive issues, like the best approach to managing the war front or punishing disgraced officials. Just as often they battled over inconsequential matters, such as appropriate use of the chief councilor's official residence or the limits of bureaucratic formality.[66] Before long, Chen Yizhong began withholding vital information from his superior while Wang Yue took to mobilizing the university against him. Months later, when Dowager Xie reluctantly accepted the resignation of Wang Yue, she made specific reference to the incompatability of her two councilors and its "disquieting" consequences—perhaps the understatement of the decade!

The distractions attendant to such conflict may help to explain the curious ambivalence of Chen Yizhong toward his new duties as chief councilor, the extent to which he would absent himself from court and capital, unexcused, for periods of unthinkable duration. Admittedly, the grand dowager had personally entrusted him and Wang Yue with general direction of all metropolitan armies, regulars and militia. These forces, with a combined strength reported at 175,000, were not merely intended to defend Linan, but to be deployed to other potential hotspots.[67] Yet precisely when border conditions were most unstable and reinforcements most desperately needed, in late spring and early summer 1275, Chen Yizhong stayed close to the capital. By all indications, it was an aging Wang Yue who repeatedly rallied for a councilor-led campaign at the front and Chen Yizhong who persistently procrastinated. Only in the seventh month would he leave the safety of a well for-

tified Linan, but not for the front and a symbolic rally of camraderie with men in the field. Rather, he proceeded south to the coast where he blended in with the landscape, leaving many questions of motive to be answered.

The departure and destination of Chen Yizhong may well relate to some secret mission for the grand dowager. After all, the royal family's only escape, should conditions deteriorate, lay to the south and coastal cities represented the sole springboard for any resistance movement. Among the most easily accessible to ocean ships yet defensible by land was Wenzhou, roughly four hundred kilometers southeast of Linan. As a native to the region, Chen Yizhong undoubtedly possessed the local contacts needed to facilitate the hosting or passage of an imperial entourage. And in light of the controversy triggered by former relocation proposals, it stands to reason that the dowager would have preferred an unexcused leave for her councilor, assuming she fully understood this to be his mission. She never named a replacement for Chen Yizhong, despite an absence of four long and difficult months.[68] On the contrary, only a day after his departure she dismissed Wang Yue as senior councilor and kept that position vacant as well. It all suggests an abiding confidence in the eventual return of her junior councilor.

Yet dynastic historians, perhaps unduly swayed by retrospective hindsight, tend to be more cynical in imputing motives for Chen Yizhong's prolonged absence. He left at a time not merely of personal conflict with Wang Yue, they argue, but ill repute throughout the capital including the all-important academic circuit. The chancellor of the university, Yang Wenzhong (doct. 1253), had only recently delivered a trenchant indictment of both councilors, who in his view, seemed to indulge vanity at the expense of duty: "Matters are truly perilous and urgent. Surely, the somber trust of the dynasty's ancestors and the innocent lives of a hundred million are vested with the two councilors. Yet today we do not engage defensively and tomorrow we will not engage offensively—all for lack of cooperation. The opportunity will never come again and regrets will never do."[69] Soon to follow in the chancellor's lead in petitioning the palace, their aim squarely targeted at the junior councilor, were students at the Metropolitan Academy. This rather provincial college of the capital traditionally tended to defer to the better regarded university when it came to political activism. This time, however, its students stepped forward to submit a memorial of intense acrimony in response to Chen Yizhong's departure from Linan.

Dynastic historians chose merely to paraphrase the memorial from

the Metropolitan Academy, probably due to the exceptional length of the original, but even in this abbreviated form the impact is powerful. Enumerating dozens of alleged "failures," students led by Liu Jiugao would denounce both the policies and character of Chen Yizhong:

> At a time when Yuan armies assault the doors of our empire, he permits *qin-wang* militias to languish in the capital without proper deployment. At a time when chief councilors should rightfully leave the capital to oversee men in the field, he frets and fears—summoning meetings for wide-ranging debate but then failing to act. He delegated Lü Shikui as envoy and peace emissary, a man with the savage mind of a wolf. He deployed [at Jiaoshan] the infantry of Zhang Shijie for action on water and deployed the sailors of Liu Shiyong for use on land—their subsequent failure a result of inappropriate direction. We fear that Jia Sidao may not be our only incompetent commander.[70]

The image here is of a politician who can never translate his high-sounding rhetoric into concrete actions, someone too tentative and terrified. Perhaps even more unsettling, from the personal perspective of Chen Yizhong, is the student characterization of him as cynically duplicitous, a loathesome pacifist masquerading as militant hero. "While overtly demanding the punishment of Jia Sidao," students state earlier in the same memorial, "he covertly supported him." No insult could be worse for a man whose words had been for decades so consistently militant. And in light of his historically intimate ties to the academic establishment, student attacks came as a personal affront tantamount to a child turning on his father. Students had little proof of some secret liaison with Jia Sidao, yet more important than proof is perception and this memorial suggests a glaring lack of credibility on the part of Chen Yizhong. His rhetoric seemed more than merely hollow, it was deviously misrepresentative. Devoid of conviction or courage, he emerges in student complaints as cut of the same cloth as a spineless Jia Sidao.

According to court rumor, this particular student attack was orchestrated by a vindictive Wang Yue: intuiting his own influence to be fading, he sought to discredit his chief competitor.[71] Dowager Xie may have concluded as much herself, for she promptly ordered the arrest of student provocateur Liu Jiugao and the dismissal of Wang Yue—a rather radical response intended to bolster the sliding stature of her junior councilor. Chen Yizhong's own decision to take leave of the capital may have been prompted by political embarrassment, it may have been intended to defuse tensions within the bureaucracy, or maybe it aspired to

appease critics whose complaints of inaction persisted. Yet the act appeared to most contemporaries as a cowardly retreat. This is partly because he spurned a succession of envoys sent by the dowager with pleas for his return. When he finally conceded, early in the tenth month, it was only after the dowager in a personal letter to his mother importuned her to intervene on the court's behalf.[72] In the interim, Chen Yizhong would communicate his desire for reassignment to the coastal theater.[73] Yet this being the one place altogether free of enemy penetration, the request only served to reinforce the appearance of abject cowardice on his part. Then, there was the changing border situation, which entered a downward spiral precisely at the time of his departure and deteriorated further in his absence.

Those still committed to the cause of dynasty could only be disheartened by the grand dowager's inclination to place her greatest trust in this man of dubious dedication, a man whose personal deficiences seemed all too characteristic of the region where he was born and raised—the "peripheral" and effete Wu region. No less unsettling was her curious ambivalence toward Wen Tianxiang, a man of grit from the interior who represented the only promising alternative. He had emerged in Linan late in the summer of 1275, after a furlough of several months in his native Jizhou, to submit some daring proposals for military restructuring. Clearly, he knew this to be the dynasty's last opportunity to alter the course of history, to reorganize its military resources with an eye for maximizing effectiveness and minimizing controls. Yet he also recognized the compelling power of tradition which stood in the way and demanded a measure of courage far greater than the palace could probably muster. Undeterred, he would write:

> Our Song, compensating for the chaos of the Five Dynasties, long ago eliminated regional governors and established local administrators. This may have provided adequate defense, at the time, against the "tail wagging the dog" malady, but it also left the empire progressively weak. Thus, the enemy could assault one prefecture after another, one county after another, until the entire Central Plains had collapsed—an inconceivably lamentable event! It is imperative today, therefore, to divide the entire realm into four commandaries, installing in each a supreme commissioner to direct them. . . . In this way, the area will be sufficiently vast and the resources sufficiently concentrated to stand firm against the enemy.[74]

This notion of a radical restructuring of military power based on the once-discredited models of Tang was hardly new. Since the initial fracturing of the Song realm into north and south, over a century ago, it had

assumed various incarnations and Wen Tianxiang's personal conversion to this notion of a decentralized military went back at least fifteen years.[75] The recent string of losses along the central Yangzi had only confirmed the vulnerable isolation of individual cities from the larger region to which they belonged. Yet his proposal, however pragmatic and sound militarily, faced insurmountable challenges, politically.

For most dynasties successful at unifying China, early monarchs tended to advance chiefly the martial enterprise while later monarchs would focus on the literary—the consolidation of power demanding methods and talents quite distinct from the inaugural spew of alliance, intrigue, and war. The Song pattern, however, deviates demonstrably from this standard. The dynasty may have begun with a coup d'etat by the Palace Guard, but for precisely that reason there emerged a suspicion toward the military which can only be described as paranoid. At the very outset, in an event later dubbed "dissolution of military power at a single banquet," the Song founder would purge his Palace Guard of its chief commanders.[76] Emperor Taizu then initiated a broader demilitarization the scope of which has no parallel in the entire history of China. Extending methodically from the capital to the provinces and in a process requiring decades to complete, military power was subordinated to civilian authority. This elaborate system of checks-and-balances had established, in effect, an antagonistic relationship between the two camps where coordination of activity would often present insurmountable challenges. Moreover, the best of martial resources came to be concentrated near the capital, as further enhancement of palace control. In that the Song had emerged from the ashes of the Five Dynasties, with its incessant conflict between feuding military factions, so tight a rein seemed perfectly reasonable. Yet in defending regional interests, the civilian comisioners of Song were never as effective as the military governors of Tang. This is due, on the one hand, to policies of rotation that valued detachment over entrenchment, and on the other, civilian checks on the military that emasculated and crippled the martial enterprise.

If implemented, the proposal of Wen Tianxiang would do more than merely revert local affairs to martial men. It would herald as well the doom of centralized checks and balances while regional overseers receive a virtual *carte blanche*. It would mean an end to the court's perceived micromanagement of the war, with the regional command enjoying full discretion in responding to border conditions. Most importantly, it would exploit provincial instincts of survival and gain to the benefit, at least short-term, of the state. This represents, however, precisely the

kind of regional autonomy against which the Song had fought so assiduously three centuries earlier, only to confront a recent challenge from Lü Wenhuan in the Jinghu interior. The immediacy of that experience would surely preclude the court's ready embrace of his proposal, however astute and necessary.

Wen Tianxiang's notion of relinquishing most civilian controls on the military never received serious consideration. It had been spawned, quite obviously, by a naive nostalgia for the martial ardor and perceived invincibility of Tang times, the desperate delusion that a lifestyle long dead could be revived through an assortment of anachronistic institutions. The proposal of Wen Tianxiang was also doomed by the political insecurity of the new councilor, Chen Yizhong. After all, he had received the official sponsorship of Wang Yue, arch-rival of Chen Yizhong.[77] There commonly comes with such ties the presumption of patron-client bonds, a presumption certain to leave the new councilor suspicious of Wen Tianxiang's every word. Added to this were assorted personal rivalries between the two men. Wen Tianxiang had placed first on the 1256 examination, Chen Yizhong had placed second in 1262; he hailed from the rugged interior, Chen Yizhong from the ill-omened coast. He was the more literarily and materially accomplished, the more articulate and refined, acclaimed and respected. Under the circumstances, making Councilor Chen fully confident in Commissioner Wen or, for that matter, the commissioner wholly responsive to the chief councilor, required a measure of time and temperance that fate would afford neither man, nor for that matter the dynasty they sought to defend.

There is no water in the lake:
*The image of **desperation.***
Thus the superior man stakes his life
On following his will.

The Changes, XLVII.

4 · Kun:
The Desperate Deeds

The summer 1275 revelry of the south and the idealistic vigor of its youthful advisors would scarcely scare off the Mongols. Their leadership, with Khubilai Khan in Shangdu and Bayan on the front, still saw the Song as ready for the taking, its power near to exhausted. After all, the northern advance of a thousand kilometers along the Yangzi River, earlier in the year, had exposed southern cities as critically lacking in the requisite regional supports—a problem not to be solved by a simple shifting of military assets, however compelling the rhetoric of Wen Tianxiang. Yet even in this context of understandably optimistic anticipation, a perceptible anxiety still gripped the Yuan court and especially its Chinese advisors. A distinguished academician, the seventy-two year old Yao Shu (1203–1280) indeed warned of the potential for court objectives being thwarted less by southern belligerents than by Yuan surrogates in the field. His personal communication to Khubilai in the autumn of 1275, on the eve of a fresh campaign directed at the Song political heartland, began with a somber observation:

> Last year, Your Majesty promulgated the order to refrain from indiscriminate murder and then Bayan crossed the Yangzi with his troops advancing ahead of schedule. Some thirty cities and over a million households would surrender. Since antiquity, never has the south been pacified with such divine triumphancy. But in the recent summer to autumn not a single city has surrendered. This is because our military officers do not intuit the larger plan of empire nor have they internalized the profound benevolence of Your Majesty; rather, they seize property, assault, and kill wherever they go. At Yangzhou, Jiaoshan, and Huai'an sizable numbers of the enemy were killed in battle and, although we prevailed, we also sustained untold injuries.[1]

This represents a rare admission of personal failure for Khubilai and his policies. Heretofore, none of his recent predecessors had persevered with similar dedication to suppress the most offensive of conquest atrocities and impose restraints on notoriously self-aggrandizing armies. His instructions to Bayan in the preceding summer, instructions reiterated in the recent spring, provide clear evidence of such dedication.[2] So Khubilai must have placed serious stock in the suggestion of a notable deterioration in this emerging discipline and, moreover, rising casualties on both sides as a consequence.

Of still greater interest to the Mongol ruler was his Chinese advisor's caution against cathartic relief. Yao Shu predicts that the final assault on the south, as it shifts focus from the hinterland to the east, should encounter a heightened resistance and not necessarily for the obvious reason—Song military resources being concentrated there. Rather, from the perspective of Confucian humanism, he asserts:

> The Song may be less than diligent in governing its empire, yet Linan will surely not surrender lightly. To cherish life and abhor death are among the constants of human sentiment. When men of the south dare not act on these instincts, it is solely out of suspicion of our own vacillation with reference to earlier promises to disavow unwarranted murder. We should therefore reissue the edict against senseless murder, the extent to which rewards and punishments are firmly established, favor and trust vigorously promoted. In this way, Sagely deliberations need not be unduly expended nor military might needlessly squandered.

The argument here is surely informed by the needs, political and rhetorical, of the day. To assume the Song resistance to be fueled by mere survival instincts and not any genuine affinity to dynasty, for example, is unjustifiably cynical for this native of Luoyang, the auxiliary capital of early times where imperial politics had long infused local values. It seems woefully naive, at the same time, to assume that after four decades of bloody feuding, Khubilai's mere reiteration of ideals demonstrably inconsistent with established practice would be sufficient to allay fear and suspicion among southern holdouts. The least compromised by political dogma is Yao Shu's prediction of a bitter struggle over the Song capital. It is insight he owes largely to history. By now, China could draw upon fifteen centuries of experience with dynastic change; and, almost invariably, imperial capitals stood at the center of this contest between old and new. Their landscape sustained more in physical destruction, their populace suffered more in retributive annihilation. Yet in the cur-

rent contest of Song versus Yuan, there is the added factor of terror. The Mongol threat of general massacre for cities that stand firm might compel Song defenders, especially in their highly fortified capital, to fight to the last man. From the perspective of Yao Shu, magnanimity to the vanquished seemed a better means of winning converts.

We have no evidence of Khubilai responding favorably by issuing, yet again, his former proscription against indiscriminate murder. Perhaps he perceived the actual abuses of policy to be less than appearances might suggest. Perhaps he feared conveying to his commanders the lack of confidence implicit in such a message. Maybe he saw no direct link between declining discipline among his men and heightened resistance in the south. But most likely, he refused to preclude the selective use of mass murder as a tool of intimidation, which probably saved more lives in the long run than it cost in the short. Khubilai could be a masterful manipulator of Confucian ideals and icons, but Confucian humanism seemed distinguished more as an ideology of governance than of conquest and conquest was the order of the day. His advisors would have to prove otherwise.

In the annals of Song history can be found a compelling caveat with which Khubilai Khan and his Chinese informants were thoroughly familiar. At the dynasty's outset some three centuries earlier, the Song had entrusted its campaign against the south to the legendary Cao Bin (931–999). That campaign entailed an initial focus on the Jinghu heartland, followed by the Sichuan basin out west, and finally the lower Yangzi to the east. With some earlier campaigns marred by excess violence, Emperor Taizu felt compelled on the eve of the Yangzi drive to admonish his chief commander against needless pillage and murder; and Cao Bin proved loyal to the spirit, if not always the letter, of those instructions.[3] He spared the lives of most defeated pretenders while treating their vanquished courtiers as "honored guests," to employ the idiom of the day. The Song conquest of the southeast, completed in an extraordinary year and a half, came to be heralded by moralistic historians and statesmen alike as testimony to Confucian humanism's ultimate efficacy as state policy. This scarcely means that Song objectives were achieved through persuasion rather than war, the enemy irresistibly drawn to the magnetic appeal of monarchical beneficence. What did occur was a rare measure of martial restraint that became enshrined in the dynasty's mythology. And those myths, embellished over the years, provided a man like Yao Shu with the rhetorical ammunition to cast Chinese political values in a light more militant and thereby meaningful to his Mongol patrons.[4]

Many aspects of the conquest strategy adopted by Khubilai seem reminiscent of the campaigns of early Song, but none so conspicuous as the decision early in his reign to focus initial military pressures on the Jinghu heartland and advance east from there. In the process, Khubilai rejected the Sichuan-first strategy of his predecessor, Möngke (r. 1251–1259). Yet for all of his sensitivity to historical analogies, he must surely have intuited as overblown the widely echoed parallels between the past and present, the late tenth and thirteenth centuries. The Ten Kingdoms possessed a small fraction of the resources of the Southern Song—economic and human, technological and military. These kingdoms also lacked, perhaps more importantly, that vital political resource of direct lineal descent from an established unifier—the *sine qua non* of dynastic legitimacy for the Chinese. It is precisely such legitimacy, reinforced by centuries of sustained sovereignty, which nurtures literati identification with dynasty. Regardless of the court bickerings or military indiscretions of Linan, regardless of the vulnerable state of defenses, obliteration of the Song as a political and cultural entity seemed likely to present the Yuan with its greatest challenge ever.

AUTUMN'S GRIM HARVEST

Growing out of this perception of Linan as still a powerful foe, the Mongols moved cautiously: to isolate and eventually starve the capital into submission, they first targeted surrounding cities. Already under their control was territory as far east along the Yangzi River as Zhenjiang and Jiankang, centering on modern Nanjing. When the two prefectures capitulated after only modest resistance, back in the spring of 1275, it brought the Mongols within three hundred kilometers of the ocean coast. And with both prefectures situated on the southern side of the river, they easily doubled as launching pads for forays against other locations in the populous and prosperous Yangzi valley. The task of autumn 1275 was, at once, consolidation and expansion. Upon chief commander Bayan's return to the eastern front, early in the tenth lunar month, Mongol attention thus turned almost immediately to neighboring Changzhou; there, they began a massive siege whose cost would prove absolutely staggering for both sides, in human terms even moreso than strategic.

This prefecture of over seven hundred thousand men and women, held briefly by the Mongols in the spring, had months ago reverted to the Song. In southern hands, Changzhou provided vital support for a

broader rally in the region. It also reaffirmed Song supremacy over the Grand Canal, whose final three hundred kilometer stretch still remained firmly in southern hands. The canal provided far and away the easiest inland approach to Linan without which Mongol ambitions, if not altogether thwarted, might in the least be seriously stymied. The stakes on both sides so uncommonly high, the investments militarily would spiral. The Mongols had devoted, according to reports, an unthinkable two hundred thousand men to the contest, an army which Bayan chose to direct personally; assisting him was Wang Liangchen, a southern defector familiar with local conditions. Song numbers must have been significantly smaller, although at court orders countless thousands from various other cities in the region had been diverted to Changzhou. The south also committed some of its finest commanders to the defense effort. Dedicated regional commissioners in the persons of Liu Shiyong and his assistant Wang Anjie, supported in turn by civilian liaisons like prefect Yao Yin and his coadministrator Chen Shao, seemed certain to stand their ground.[5]

For a month and a half, the two sides locked horns. The Song clung predictably to the defensive tactics that had characterized earlier contests, chiefly reinforcing old walls and constructing new barricades while delivering ever escalating rewards to combatants in the form of honors and office. It never had the luxury of time to rebuild city walls, which with a height of merely fifteen to twenty feet were acutely vulnerable. The Mongols, on the other hand, evinced an enviably resourceful cunning. They would succeed in thwarting all Song attempts to storm their blockade, while exploiting every vulnerability of Changzhou itself. After razing most rural communities in the vicinity, they conscripted these homeless men and women into work brigades, units used to fill the moats surrounding Changzhou with stone and earth, erecting embankments in the end. Northern regulars could then cross this initial line of defense, set fire to the wooden palisades representing the second line, and proceed to scale the city walls. From every direction they descended simultaneously on the city, flooding its streets as southern defenders continued to do battle.

Although the Mongols ultimately prevailed, no side truly won in the battle at Changzhou. There is record of extraordinary heroism among Song defenders, heroism that claimed an unthinkably large number of lives on the opposing side, including dozens of lesser commanders. The southern commissioner Liu Shiyong, for example, may have escaped the city with scarcely his own life, but he slayed a sizable number of enemy

stalkers while on the retreat.[6] Destiny did not similarly favor his second-in-command Wang Anjie, who was taken captive and killed for refusing to renounce the cause of dynasty. He had the courage of a "real man," according to contemporaries, who took inspiration in his "perfection of righteousness and benevolence."[7] In this case, moral principle would prevail over human survival, cultural forms over natural instinct. There were others. The prefect of Changzhou and his coadministrator also died as Song martyrs, along with assorted other colleagues. Southern soldiers on the retreat were rounded up and massacred. No one of any political or military stature survived to surrender the city, no one to mediate an occupation which otherwise turned savagely brutal. At taking the city on December 6, Bayan ordered his men to conduct a general massacre, the lives of only four hundred women and children reported as spared. The liquidation of Changzhou may have erupted as a frenzied fit of rage or maybe as an act of vengeful retribution for unacceptably high casualties on the Mongol side. But more likely, it was shrewdly calculated to serve some strategic purpose.

Only a day before that final assault, Bayan had conveyed an ominous message to Song holdouts in the city. Issued as a public notice and delivered on the stems of arrows, it accused Changzhou residents of complicity in no less than treason: an interim regime of northern puppets had been subverted, and at great loss of face from Bayan's perspective. The severity of their infraction notwithstanding, he still promised an unconditional amnesty in exchange for immediate surrender. Yet he finished with another less beneficent pledge: "If you persist in this senseless and staunch resistance, then not even children will survive the piled corpses and bloodletting. You should reconsider your position promptly, so as not to regret things later."[8] Having issued, and publicly so, a vow of ruthless force, Bayan could scarcely afford to retreat from his own words without losing credibility. But he surely intuited the added advantage, militarily, of setting a harsh example of Changzhou. For the first time in the eastern Yangzi River valley, Mongol conquerors had perpetrated mass annihilation on an entire city of Song loyalists, lending immediacy and credibility to a threat heretofore perhaps perceived by locals as remote. This could only have terrified, even paralyzed, holdouts in neighboring cities, and especially cities having only recently reverted to Song control.

Further confirmation of terror as a conscious motive in the depopulation of Changzhou can be found in the high visibility with which northerners conducted their merciless charge. Whereas conquerors of

modern times prefer generally to conceal such deeds, the Mongols seemed to relish in making public spectacle of them. Refusing to bury the bodies underground, in Chinese fashion, they piled the corpses high and then covered them with earth. This gruesome vista is far too reminiscent of Fancheng nearly three years earlier to be sheer coincidence. And like then, the speedy surrender of neighboring cities was the probable objective. Yet the scale now was many times greater. A vivid relic of the Changzhou atrocity stood, until recent decades, near the city's eastern gate: a mound as tall as the wall itself, some twenty Chinese feet, with an area of roughly a half acre.[9] Assuming ordinary erosion, the original tumulus may well have been twice as large and many times more emotionally evocative. The poet Yin Tinggao, writing decades after the incident, would allude to the powerful sense of death which still hung thick over the city like noxious vapors:

> A million men approach from the west, no strength to resist;
> Alone in peril and daring to die, the rancid dust of the battlefield.
> In search of past events, no elders survive to recount;
> A setting sun atop the city wall, the green iridescence of the dead.[10]

Even into our own century, human skeletons could be dug from the mound, confirmation of the corpses having never been removed for proper burial. Perhaps this contributed, more than anything else, to the aforementioned sense of a ghostly presence that persisted long after the bodies had turned to dust.

Death on such massive scale is never easy to accept, but this particular slaughter probably outraged the educated elite more than most. Changzhou was no mere military outpost like Fancheng, but rather a cultural center of the first order where men of letters and their literary relics abounded. A local gazetteer for the region, written a mere seven years before the massacre, was effusive in boasting "the assemblage of rare talent that has persisted here for generations."[11] This is readily quantified in the production of doctoral degreeholders for Changzhou, so prodigious as to exceed nearly all other prefectures in this region of exceptional prosperity and refinement.[12] In a matter of days, the bulk of these human resources were obliterated. Countless public schools and private libraries were destroyed as well, although details on the scope of such material loss are lacking.

It was precisely the magnitude of this vast cultural loss that made Song strategists think twice about offering a similarly staunch defense of the next enemy target—Pingjiang (modern Suzhou). Less than a hundred

kilometers south of the Changzhou prefectural seat and straddling the Grand Canal, this historic city of canals and gardens, learning and leisure while slightly smaller in size was no less distinguished in cultural terms. It was in confirmation of the importance of Pingjiang to the security of the capital, but also the cause of dynasty, that the Song, in recent months, had made a sizable military investment. It dispatched auxiliaries to augment local militia while entrusting supervision of the defense effort to the unflinchingly loyal Wen Tianxiang. Another loss so close to the capital had to be avoided at all cost. Only three days after the massacre at Changzhou, however, the court abruptly recalled Wen Tianxiang. The pretext was "consultation," perhaps with the intent of deployment to another nearby hotspot. Wen Tianxiang took with him a reported thirty to fifty thousand men, the cream of the city's resistance. Thus, it took only three more days before the presiding civil and military leaders surrendered Pingjiang to the enemy.[13] The negotiations occurred free of the usual pressures of battle and siege. They also occurred without explicit authorization from the court, which seems to have planned a replacement for Wen Tianxiang. Yet official endorsement is implicit in the capital's untimely decision to raid the prefecture of its finest military resources, denying Pingjiang the wherewithal to defend itself. In the end, a mass of cultural relics were preserved, along with countless human lives, but at a cost perhaps too high in strategic terms.

In the concluding weeks of 1275, a slew of other cities and counties in the region of Lake Tai were relinquished, yet less through defection by local leaders than as a result of the inadequacy of reinforcements from the capital. Decisionmakers in Linan seemed, in effect, to be making a succession of short-term decisions in a long-term vacuum. Most historians attribute such vacillating myopia to Chen Yizhong. Continuing to hope for a negotiated withdrawal of enemy forces, he adamantly rejected alternative strategies. His recall of dedicated royalists like Wen Tianxiang and concentration of residual armies closer to Linan would strengthen the court's hand in those negotiations. Chen Yizhong did not share Wen Tianxiang's optimism that one or two decisive victories might stem the Mongol tide. For the Yangzi valley at least, enemy strength had simply grown to insurmountably high concentrations. Dowager Xie appears to have deferred to the judgment of her chief councilor, a man who shared so many of her own political convictions. She also kept an abiding faith in Heaven and its powers to intervene on behalf of an otherwise hopeless cause. The depth of that faith is documented at the very end of her struggle, when only the Qiantang River stood between her defenseless

capital on the high ground and enemy hordes on the low. Even then, the Grand Dowager fully expected divine deliverance. In a final act of desperate protest, the still pugnacious dowager is reported to have affirmed: "If there are spirits in the oceans, they will surely summon forth vast waves to expel the entire lot in a single sweep."[14] Her hope was no mere flight of fancy. During high tide, after all, salt water from the Hangzhou Bay had so frequently swelled the Qiantang River and flooded the lower bank that wooden locks had long been installed, at several points, to control the flow between river and sea.[15] The locks were surely open as the enemy pitched camp on that vulnerable side, but for days the otherwise perilous tides stayed uncharacteristically tame. Heaven had spoken, but not as she expected.

A DISCOMFITTING DIPLOMATIC CORNER

The seventeenth-century historian Chen Bangzhan was describing the paralysis of decisionmaking in 1126, when another nomadic power positioned itself to invade an earlier Song capital, yet his words ring even more true for 1276. He writes: "Those advancing war did not decidedly wage war, while those advancing peace did not single-mindedly pursue peace. Even with city walls breached and peril imminent, there was still no consensus of court opinion. Their minds lacking resolve, so many things changed so radically in the passing of a single year."[16] It seemed as though the intervening century and a half had wrought little change on the consciousness of Song statesmen. It was the stunning string of Mongol victories that partly explains their chronic indecision and ambivalence. Yet late Song leaders were also straightjacketed by their own rhetoric. For decades, idealists in and out of the universities had denounced pacifists in power and the foreign policy compromises associated with them. This partly explains the notable failure of the south to strike any diplomatic settlement with the north, as the Song had formerly undertaken with the Jurchen in the twelfth century and the Khitan in the eleventh. Such settlements would, by tradition, demand annual tribute from the materially prosperous south in exchange for peace with cash-strapped nomads. By the mid-thirteenth century, however, the old diplomatic compromises had grown too politically contentious to be seriously considered as an alternative to war.

Song hostilities with the Mongols had erupted as early as 1227, initially more by accident than design and largely derivative of conflicts elsewhere. Striking an alliance in 1233 which went sour a year later, the

two powers subsequently entered a new stage of prolonged belligerency.[17] Yet neither could marshall the measure of resources and commitment needed to subdue the other. This occurred not for lack of trying, however.

The Song often behaved in a manner inexplicably callous and cavalier. It launched a disastrous campaign in 1234 against the northern capitals of Kaifeng and Luoyang, the sole accomplishment of which was to incite Mongol occupiers.[18] It further angered them by detaining and even assassinating a succession of diplomatic envoys. The earliest such incident occurred in 1231, the most recent in 1275. One northern envoy remained incarcerated, in fact, for a full fifteen years before Linan finally approved his release.[19] The Mongols evinced modestly more restraint in their treatment of southern emissaries, but they compensated with a greater persistence in harassing the border, harassment which included sometimes ambitious strikes against the Song heartland. In certain campaigns, particularly of the late 1230s and 1250s, they seemed intent on nothing short of outright conquest. Yet as early as 1238, the Mongols also approached the Song about an annual gratuity in exchange for peace; they did so again in 1260.[20] Such overtures are significant for two reasons. They represent an implicit admission of the north's inability to prevail by arms alone, as well as a tentative acceptance of an indefinite coexistence with the south. On various occasions, the Song agreed to explore other options, including unrestricted trade along the border, but categorically ruled out subsidies. Some courtiers questioned the genuine willingness of the Mongols to coexist, others warned of modest demands growing excessive with time, and virtually everyone reacted viscerally to the diplomatic humiliation implicit in such tributary ties.[21] Their reasoning seemed so compelling, for the moment at least, but proved in the end a blunder of enormous proportions. Entente was still possible at a time when the Song retained its military edge and the Mongols remained ambivalent about their goals in the region. Conditions had grown far less favorable by the 1270s.

The Song had snubbed the Mongols not because their demands were excessive nor because anyone seriously doubted, with reference to securing the border, the economy of cash subsidies over armed conflict. The opportunity was lost, instead, due to a dangerous shift in the political center at Linan. Most chief councilors of the thirteenth century may have privately preferred compromise over confrontation in the conduct of foreign affairs. Still, few dared to act publicly on their own impulses. The university had emerged as too powerful a political force even to

ignore, let alone offend. At the same time, a strident militancy also gripped the intelligentsia-at-large. Such stridency is perhaps most pronounced in the rhetoric of Chen Yizhong, Wen Tianxiang, and Wang Yinglin—all men in their middle years whose entire lives were punctuated by this seemingly interminable conflict and whose antipathy for aliens tended, in consequence, to be more intense. Their own life experiences were reinforced in turn by the Confucian idealism rampant among intellectual activists. It was many generations earlier and under administrations more pragmatically utilitarian that such border deals were struck—peace-for-payment arrangements that detracted visibly from the esteem and authority of the Middle Kingdom. An order now obsessed with ritual propriety and moral probity would not so readily countenance the compromise demanded by *realpolitik*.

Jia Sidao, for example, may have been vilified as an inveterate pacifist; yet for virtually all of his fifteen years as chief councilor, he did little to advance peaceful coexistence with the north. Blame for incarcerating northern envoy Hao Jing is commonly placed with him, an incident that seriously aggravated tensions between the two powers.[22] In fact, the initial arrest in 1260 may well have been the handiwork of border officials, yet it was Jia Sidao who permitted the envoy to languish more than a decade in jail. That he would knowingly jeopardize relations with the north in the process suggests some extraordinary pressures. For a while, a newly-enthroned Khubilai Khan would continue to pursue peace payments from the south. Those initiatives were repeatedly spurned. Only during Jia Sidao's last days in power, following his disastrous defeat along the eastern Yangzi, would he offer to meet the dual Mongol demands—hefty subsidies and a new protocol as supplicant.[23] These terms lay clearly within the guidelines of earlier agreements between the Song and former occupiers of the north. But having approached Bayan from his emergency quarters at Yangzhou, Jia Sidao had acted under conditions of duress and without advance approval of the court. Bayan summarily dismissed his concessions as untimely, a rejection which induced a sigh of relief, curiously, among ranking courtiers in Linan: Dowager Xie and her new advisors had apparently found the assumption of "vassal" status unacceptably offensive. Thus, new proposals offered two months later would concede to subsidies and subsidies only.[24] The south's diplomatic retreat was enough to incite an ill-humored Bayan. In the interim, two of his envoys and much of their sizable entourage were killed by Song border patrols. They had come within seventy kilometers of Linan and court complicity was difficult to

deny. Dowager Xie denounced the act all the same, her personal correspondence with Bayan promising prosecution for the men responsible. Such humble words would fall, by now, upon deaf ears.

A decade and a half of southern intransigence to the Mongols was chiefly due to its perception of northerners as disingenuous. All too frequently, they waged war first and embraced diplomacy second, or made demands fully apprised as excessive from the outset, or prompted indecent behavior in envoys to create cause for war. Still, a greater measure of responsibility for the diplomatic deadlock rests with the Song. Its leadership did not speak with a single voice, after all. A councilor at the front might be undercut by royal patrons in the palace or rivals at court, as occurred with Jia Sidao. However entrenched, no bureaucrat governed in a vacuum and political winds were prone to abrupt shifts. The Song suffered, in many ways, from the worst of a monarchical system given to whimsical change and a tradition of political pluralism given to divisive rhetoric. Meanwhile, the court itself might be undercut by well-intentioned surrogates at the border. It is curious, for example, that diplomatic outreaches by the north and south alike were so frequently thwarted by presumably insubordinate officers at the Song border. This is not a dynasty known to indulge military whim. Quite the contrary, the court commonly kept so tight a rein that many likened it to a veritable noose. Yet border incidents of the sort had erupted over too vast a region and too long a time span to have been orchestrated by any single personality or series of personalities in Linan. In all likelihood, court intent was blurred and provincial initiative encouraged due to tensions be-tween pragmatists and idealists, tensions originating in the capital that grew magnified in the circuits. The problem emerges as especially pronounced in the year 1275, with its exceptional array of contrary signals emanating from a volatile and fractured court.

In this year of cataclysmic change, none seem more radically affected than Chief Councilor Chen Yizhong. He began with a vitriolic denunciation of Jia Sidao pacifism, yet within months would concede to the offering of peace payments. He initially opposed any form of diplomatic submission to the north, yet by year's end could accept "uncle-to-nephew" protocol, so long as the Song assumed a role of modest seniority.[25] He even directed an expanded dialogue with the north where he committed to the process such distinguished court officers as Lu Xiufu, a staunch royalist then serving as executive at the Court of the Imperial Clan. Nonetheless, Chen Yizhong's diplomatic moves seemed perennially out-of-step with strategic realities. At this late stage, few conces-

sions short of outright surrender would likely satisfy the enemy. The times demanded an imaginative and aggressive engagement of the crisis, indeed nothing less than diplomatic coup. Yet the proposals coming out of Linan late in the year 1275 continued to fall short even of Jia Sidao's offerings at the outset. Through such rigidity, based in ideological as well as political vanity, the brash and imprudent Chen Yizhong backed the court into a dangerous corner without means of retreat. His diplomatic posturing had backfired. Dowager Xie was reputedly reduced to tears as she pleaded with him to make further concessions.[26] She even approached Bayan with a personal plea for compassion. "According to the etiquette of antiquity," she noted in correspondence to him, "rulers in mourning have never been targeted for military campaign."[27] Invoking the humanitarian protocol of an ancient China would scarcely stir Bayan, a man culturally if not ethnically Mongol. The male handlers of the dowager must surely have intuited as much; but she was never so cynical in her estimation of others nor so wedded to political convention.

DYNASTY DIVIDED

At this juncture of diplomatic impasse when the enemy was politely but persistently returning a succession of envoys, Chen Yizhong and Dowager Xie would have to reassess a host of unsavory options, ultimately to chose a course of action that offended their most deeply held convictions and sensibilities. By the early weeks of 1276, northern armies were closing in with startling speed. In a three-pronged assault involving extraordinary numbers, they approached from the east through the Hangzhou Bay, from the west through the Tianmu Mountains, and from the north along the Grand Canal. This brought them within thirty kilometers of Linan. Meanwhile, the Song capital had lost the bulk of its armed forces to desertion, regulars having fallen to a reputed thirty thousand while assorted militia peaked at several times that number.[28] Still greater and more politically revealing were the civilian losses. Following the usual respite for the lunar New Year, a mere six officials appeared at court for the scheduled audience. From chief councilors to ministry executives, from the civilian to the military bureaucracies, desertions occurred at every level.[29] It was in this context of defenseless isolation and impending peril that Chen Yizhong urged his royal patrons to do the unthinkable—surreptitiously evacuate their capital.[30] Coming from a man who had built a veritable career around assailing presumed pacifists—pro-

posals to relocate the capital striking a particularly sensitive chord—this came as a stunning reversal.

His own proposal of February 3 was one over which Chen Yizhong must have agonized for some time. Nearly ten days earlier and under conditions less extreme, he had rejected similar pleas from Zhang Shijie and Wen Tianxiang.[31] As dedicated loyalists and the empire's premiere commanders in the capital, their intent was not to save a few royal necks at the expense of dynasty, but to preserve the cause of dynasty by protecting the lives of those deemed indispensable to its survival. After all, the enemy had made virtually no inroads into the coastal circuits, a vast stretch of land shielded by the high seas to the east and various mountain ranges to the west. Capitalizing on the naval capacity still at the court's command, the plan involved fleeing east to the Hangzhou Bay and then south. The intended destination is not specified, but with Chen Yizhong the only leading official native to the coast, his home of Wenzhou seems most probable.

At a time when the Mongols were moving swiftly to secure the Hangzhou Bay and cut off escape routes, Chen Yizhong wavered inexplicably. His pretext, the need for fresh reports from his peace envoys, is not terribly compelling. A more likely motivation is sheer cowardice. When envoys returned to Linan, they had conveyed Bayan's firm rejection of recent proposals along with a new demand: face-to-face talks with the chief councilor.[32] This utterly terrified Chen Yizhong. By Song tradition, councilor-level officials did not personally conduct diplomatic exchange and, in light of the inordinately high mortality rate among recent envoys, such commissions could be more perilous than battle itself. He thus became a quick convert to relocation and proceeded, almost immediately, to convince the highly reluctant Dowager Xie. By day's end, she was packed and fully dressed when she learned of the latest desertion—like those he criticized so vehemently in the past, Chen Yizhong had himself absconded only hours before. Tossing to the floor her hatpin and earrings, the grand dowager angrily denounced the betrayal. She then withdrew to her palace boudoir, the fates of her and the child monarch but also the dozens of other court ladies now resting on the mercy of an enemy not known to be merciful.

A declaration of unconditional surrender had apparently been drafted in advance, for it was forwarded to the Mongols on the very same day along with the imperial seals—the Chinese equivalent to royal crown as symbol of court authority. Composed as if from the hand of the child-

monarch of Song to the emperor of Yuan, the rescript began with the usual humility and platitudes:

> I respectfully, as ruler of the Great Song empire, Zhao Xian, bow a hundred times in submitting this rescript to Your Majesty, the Benevolent, Brilliant, Spiritual, and Martial Emperor of the Great Yuan: . . . Your Servant and the Grand Dowager have lived, day and night, in anxiety and fear. Inevitably, we considered our own mutual preservation by relocating the monarchy, as if to entrust the fate of millions of living beings to a single person, me. Yet the Mandate of Heaven, having shifted, Your Servant chooses to change with it.

There follows a plea for clemency for the royal family, but also the larger imperial clan:

> My grandmother, the Grand Dowager, is now very advanced in age and has lain with illness for several years. Your Servant may be alone and infirm, yet my heart is full with emotions and these cannot countenance the prospect of abrupt annihilation of the three hundred year old Imperial Altars of my ancestors. Whether they be misguidedly cast off or specially preserved in tact rests solely with the revitalized moral virtue of the Emperor of the Great Yuan—a dependence that succeeding generations of Zhao men will never dare to forget.[33]

At the same time that the Song court presented itself, at least to the Mongols, as prepared for unconditional surrender, it took additional steps which clearly imply a radically different agenda—steps probably taken by Chen Yizhong following consultation with one or both of the empress dowagers.

On the one hand, in response to pressures from the imperial clan, the court arranged for the secret flight of Emperor Gongdi's two brothers, Zhao Shi and Zhao Bing. The emperor himself would remain with his mother, Dowager Quan, no doubt at her insistence. His two half-brothers, invested with nominal appointments along the remote coast, left with only their biological mothers and closest relatives. Unceremoniously, they departed Linan on February 4 consciously avoiding the bay route to the east, the route once planned for the empress but now too perilous. They headed south instead, following a network of narrow inland waterways. Dividing up the royal family in this way would frustrate northern pursuers bent on a speedy roundup of Song royalty, while affording the dynasty some alternative to outright surrender. On the other hand, the court appointed a senior councilor who only weeks ear-

lier had abruptly left the capital, Liu Mengyan, as supreme pacification commissioner for much of the empire's residual heartland, southern Jiangnan West and Jinghu circuits. Historians fail to link the two actions, but linkage seems undeniable.

The native place of Liu Mengyan to which he returned early in 1276 is Quzhou, some 250 kilometers southwest of the capital.[34] This prefecture sits adjacent to Wuzhou, the planned transfer station for the entourage of imperial sons and consorts headed for the coast. The role he did play or should have is not documented, but understandably so for a mission shrouded of necessity in secrecy. Still, his proximity to the area and new responsibilities as commissioner suggests that the court at least hoped for, if it could not fully guarantee, his assistance in securing safe passage for the royal party. More importantly, the court also hoped that Liu Mengyan could contribute to the pro-Song resistance in the hinterland. The Mongol success at securing most cities along the Yangzi River had yet to be duplicated deeper into the interior, the penetration of which still posed formidable obstacles. But this only partly explains the persistence of optimism in the south, even into the early weeks of 1276 when developments in and around the capital seemed so uniformly negative.

It was during these same challenging weeks, more importantly, that the enduring strength of Song loyalism was vividly illustrated by events at Tanzhou, modern Hunan's Changsha. In the heart of Jinghu South circuit near Lake Dongting, this thriving prefecture was home to over two million.[35] Tanzhou was the administrative center of the circuit as well as its economic hub, a leading exporter of the region's coveted teas and textiles. It was also a prefecture of "great families," an established elite accustomed to privilege and reluctant to relinquish it.[36] Such a strong consciousness of class and community is reflected in Prefect Li Fu, who hailed from an educated family of more modest means but strong political convictions.[37] A sturdy and stubborn people, Tanzhou residents had fought valiantly against Jurchen intruders in 1130, holding ground despite staggering losses; over a century later, in the spring of 1274, they had fought off the first wave of Yuan invaders with equal valor.[38] In terms of the local landscape, conditions at Tanzhou seemed strikingly similar to Changzhou, over a thousand kilometers away, and the consequences would be similarly tragic.

The Mongols had begun their second assault on the walled city in the tenth month, 1275, their commander Arigh Khaya threatening defenders with mass murder should they persist. Defenders turned a deaf ear

all the same, even in the face of glaring vulnerability. Their local militia had been reduced to only several thousand: too many thousands of fit warriors, earlier in the year, had been sent off to Linan to rescue their monarch, others fled the city for the safety of surrounding towns. Now, the young and inexperienced had to take up the task of protecting the homes and families of all. It is remarkable that Tanzhou still held out for three long months. But this was an "iron city" to employ the vernacular of the day, its walls sturdy and its people stout.[39] Their resolve owes much to the exceptional charisma and compassion of Li Fu, who mobilized much of the population including aborigines from outlying regions. They were probably not prepared, however, for the enemy storm that hit on the eve of the lunar new year—January 18, 1276 by Western reckoning—and took mere hours to run its course.

As that final assault got underway, the citizens of Tanzhou seemed to anticipate the worst. Li Fu had prearranged for a subordinate to assist in the mass suicide of his family. It would be for him a means of "exhausting loyalty," according to authoritative sources, for them insurance against the "degradation of captivity." To celebrate the past while numbing the senses, the entire brood would drink to intoxication before being put to the sword. Arrangements included the incineration of all bodies in the family home—occupiers intent on vengeance would thereby have no relics to abuse or desecrate. The subordinate, Shen Zhong, then returned home to kill his own wife. Her lifeless body lay at his side when he, now back at the Li Fu residence, slit his own throat. Prefect Li Fu was preceded in suicidal death by an assortment of other colleagues and friends. A military advisor, Yang Zhen, threw himself into a pond when the city fell.[40] His wife and concubine drowned with him, in a last minute rescue effort, whether by accident or design is uncertain. Another associate who helped orchestrate the Tanzhou defense, the local literatus Yin Gu, took his own life as well.[41] He reportedly sat squarely and impassively as flames engulfed his home—the courage of a "real man," as characterized by Li Fu. Perishing with him were "kinsmen old and young, servants male and female"—over forty in all! Included among these were a younger brother and his immediate family, plus two sons who had just completed the capping ceremony of a newly confirmed manhood.

Still more astonishing is the impact of recent events upon other locals, nameless men and women of no great political or social station. The scene is described in the Song dynastic history, a source compiled under Yuan auspices and thus generally conservative in its reconstruction of

these sensitive times, as follows: "Many of the people of Tanzhou, at learning of these deaths, annihilated their entire family. No wells in the city were empty of human corpses, while strangled bodies hung in dense clusters from the trees."[42] This astonishing case of mass suicide can be verified independently of official sources as well. The bodies of several thousand were found in a single pond, according to a well-informed contemporary.[43] Other sources allude to the expansive Xiang River, running north-to-south through the city, as thick with dead bodies.[44] Represented prominently among the dead were ordinary commoners, or "petty types," for only this can explain reports that the streets of post-war Tanzhou were nearly devoid of a pedestrian presence.[45] It is noteworthy that Arigh Khaya resisted pressure from his men to punish the city with liquidation, despite serious personal injury in this siege of three long months.[46] Thus, the high level of casualties at Tanzhou resulted either from hostilities in the final hours of battle, which were admittedly intense, or self-inflicted injury by men and women who saw no reason to survive and greater meaning in death.

The loss of valuable territory and countless lives in the Hunan heartland, coinciding as it did with staggering setbacks in the Yangzi valley, affected the Song leadership in remarkably different ways. Clearly for Wen Tianxiang, but perhaps Chen Yizhong as well, mass death at Tanzhou seemed to confirm an enduring enthusiasm for the cause of dynasty and a measure of military resolve rare for any region. This among other factors had doubtlessly inspired the nomination of Liu Mengyan as pacification commissioner, a man who only recently had completed a term as prefect of Tanzhou. Such visibility in the larger region would presumably make him highly effective as mobilizer of royal supporters. We have no evidence that he indeed acted on these expectations, for the fall of neighboring prefectures in Hunan followed very soon thereafter. Nonetheless, the mere expectation implies a new determination among some at court to carry the royalist cause from Linan to the deep south. Other civilian leaders who inexplicably disappeared from the capital, during its final weeks, also seemed to experience a sudden political conversion—resurfacing at residual Song enclaves along the southern coast or in the interior. Zhang Shijie, Chen Wenlong, and Chen Yizhong would soon rendezvous with the imperial entourage at Fuzhou before dispersing to organize local resistance elsewhere. During the final days of Linan, University chancellor Yang Wenzhong had also accepted an executive appointment along the southern coast, although for reasons of health he never made it. The various components of this complex puz-

zle fell too neatly into place to represent mere coincidence, as the dynastic history seems to suggest. High-level orchestration is a virtual certainty and the orchestrators most likely were Chen Yizhong and Zhang Shijie, the civilian councilor and his military complement.[47]

By all indications, Dowager Xie grew increasingly alienated from the agenda of Chen Yizhong and cohort. As underscored in her communiqué to Bayan, her preeminent concern at this late date was preservation of the Imperial Altars—the continuity of kinship and ritual so central to the social and spiritual identity of the Chinese. Implicitly, the ritual order takes precedence over the political order, for in the final analysis she refused to jeopardize the survival of the royal family for the larger cause of dynasty when prospects seemed so bleak. Moreover, political survival by this time would necessitate prolonged exile in the far south, perhaps years of itinerancy as well. Being of poor health by her own admission, this woman of sixty-six years would not likely have survived. Neither would her five year old grandson, Emperor Gongdi, if vague references to assorted "infirmities" can be believed. Recognition of such frailties provides one explanation for the dowager's apparently unilateral move, promptly on the heels of her chief councilor's departure, to surrender unconditionally. The only other explanation for her speedy surrender is errant duplicity. To wit, having delayed until February 3 the flight south of her two other grandsons, Dowager Xie perhaps resorted to diplomatic dickering in order to dissuade the enemy from immediate military action. And with Mongol attention diverted from conquest to negotiation, the entourage of royal sons and high officials would thereby win the critical time needed for safe passage to the coast. Sacrificed for their safety, however, were the two empress dowagers along with the reigning monarch, Gongdi.

The conscious use of peace talks as cover for a royalist rally is also suggested in the subsequent actions of Dowager Xie. In commissioning a team of negotiators to finalize the terms of surrender, on February 6, she named as chief envoy the man perhaps least suited for this humiliating task—the staunchly militant Wen Tianxiang, now credentialed as chief councilor. From the very outset of his arrival at Gaoting Mountain, the camp of Bayan located a mere twenty kilometers to the north, he took to evasive and dilatory tactics. He demanded as precondition to talks that advancing armies immediately retreat up to three hundred kilometers from the besieged capital. Nothing could be more preposterous in light of the overwhelmingly superior strength of northern forces.[48] Wen Tianxiang also mentioned annual subsidies and vassal status as if to sug-

gest a retreat from the full surrender already mandated by the court. Reference to Gongdi as "ruler of the Song empire," in official communiqués, further implied lingering imperial pretenses on the part of Linan. Then, there was his searing rhetoric, where Wen Tianxiang seems to shift from diplomatic posturing to masculine histrionics the symbolism of which may well have eluded Bayan and anyone else who failed to see the images behind the words.

In his personal record of that confrontation—a record doubtlessly embellished for rhetorical impact—he professes to chastising Bayan and cohort for the avarice and malice of mere barbarians. He then relishes in narrating a display of manly courage so daring that it reputedly humbled even a fearless Bayan: "As northern rhetoric grew inflexible, I said to them, 'I am the premiere degreeholder and chief councilor of the southern court and only a single death short of repaying my empire for its beneficence. I fear neither the swords and saws for mutilation nor the kindled vats for scaldings.'"[49] The Mongol leaders in attendance all "changed colors," according to Wen Tianxiang, "and called me a *real man*." And indeed it was this grand display of Chinese manhood—and southern Chinese manhood, in particular—that had motivated him from the outset. Switching from prose to poetry, he celebrates the occasion:

> In serving the three palaces and nine temples, which stand imperiled
> The wolf's inner thoughts can never be known.
> In commissioning envoys, if none can humble the mad barbarians
> *Then who in the southeast is a true man?*[50]

Wen Tianxiang may emerge as nauseously egotistical for those intent on reading his words literally.[51] But his goal was not so much to glorify himself as to edify the southeast, a region for too long trivialized by northern conquerors and their demeaning political theories. By contrasting alien muscle with native gall, Wen Tianxiang confirmed the continued virility of southern men and the government, however fragile, that they supported.[52] An exquisitely unassuming and jocular Bayan seemed genuinely baffled, uncertain whether to break with a smile or a scream. Politely, he dismissed the other envoys along with their improper documents, but retained this one as virtual hostage. A bellicose Wen Tianxiang personally portrays detention as proof of his own considerable powers to intimidate; modern scholarship suggests that the Mongols simply distrusted his earnestness as envoy. Based on the aforementioned

dialogue between the two men, incarceration was more likely intended simply to help cool an unpredictably hot temper.

CLEAVAGES OF GENDER AND CLASS

Not until March 28, well over a month after the Grand Dowager's official surrender, did Bayan cross the Qiantang River and parade victoriously through the gates of Linan. Diplomatic posturing, on the Song side, only partly explains the extraordinary delay. For very different reasons, the Mongols were equally anxious about occupying a city heralded near and far as the most materially and aesthetically endowed metropolis in the entirety of East Asia. Soon to become the crowning jewel of an expanded Mongol empire, the city's richly appointed palaces, literati villas, and religious establishments had to be preserved at all cost. Bayan's initial orders, therefore, prohibited the further advance of his own men under the threat of punishment by the harshest rules of martial law. Only ten days after the surrender and following the methodical mediation of civilian emissaries did he permit select contingents of armed men to enter Linan and prepare for a peaceful transition of political power.[53] In consultation with Dowager Xie, with whom they interacted largely through loyal eunuchs, this group of Chinese and Mongol occupiers proceeded to seal up government treasuries, schools, archives, and administrative bureaus. They dismissed civilian and military officers of the court, a chiefly ceremonious gesture in light of long depleted ranks. They then thoroughly secured valuables within the palace, imperial paraphenalia and *objets d'art*. The assistance of eunuchs familiar with the imperial household proved invaluable on this score.

Despite the rare restraint exercised by Mongol occupiers, the mood among residents of Linan was understandably tense. A sympathetic observer, Wang Yuanliang, portrays their acute sense of vulnerability as their southern capital prepared for the ignominy of occupation by northerners with the repugnant look and smell of aliens:

> Crowds of courtiers in lofty royal chambers,
>   pensive and speechless
> As Chief councilor Bayan presses
>   for the proclamation of surrender.
> The three palaces of Emperor and Empress,
>   behind pearl-studded blinds
> As a myriad of cavalry with curly beards lurch
>   before the chambers.[54]

Locals were first frightened by the awesome spectacle of steppe men with their coarse features and burly physique, juxtaposed against the fragility of China's most refined of regions, Wu/Yue. Still more frightening was a brief but exceedingly violent episode that struck on February 5, immediately following the Grand Dowager's proclamation of surrender. For an entire day, from dusk to dawn, roving Song guardsmen murdered innocent civilians indiscriminately on the streets, while the city's riffraff went on a wild rampage of assault and looting.[55] It was as though history prepared once again to repeat itself. Palace security had gone on a similarly insane rampage in 1127, as the Jurchen undertook their occupation of the Northern Song capital at Kaifeng.[56] They saw their honor at stake, undoubtedly the same motive of palace guardsmen this time around. The consequences a century later would prove less perilous. Through the right combination of arm-twisting and reassurance, the Mongols swiftly restored order. But residents of the capital, no less than Wen Tianxiang, never felt altogether confident with "the utterances of wolves"—northern promises that they would be spared the humiliation of death or imprisonment.

Especially vulnerable were the hundreds of female courtesans and servants, many of them young and attractive, trapped inside the imperial palaces. On the one hand, they faced the likely prospect of being morally compromised, if not in an act of anonymous rape then perhaps as the unwilling wife to some decorated warrior. They knew all too well the tragedy of Cai Yan, so somberly elegized through poetry and painting. This literarily refined daughter of a distinguished minister of Han, in the year A.D. 192, fell into the hands of invading Huns and ended up betrothed to a chieftain in Central Asia, a world away from home.[57] Consorts of the vanquished might even end up in the harem of the conquering monarchs, where they lent exotic color to a multi-racial mix but passed bitterly insular lives in a setting of foreign sounds and smells. On the other hand, even in the absence of sexual violation, these women faced another moral crisis for which historical anecdote offered no meaningful guide. Their husbands dead and the dynasty overturned, did the moral dictates of a recently reinvigorated Confucianism demand their own lives as well? Clearly, many answered in the affirmative.

On the eve of Bayan's victory march into Linan, an estimated one hundred imperial consorts and female servants committed suicide by drowning.[58] These palace women were apparently in the process of being tied up, along with eunuchs and musicians, in preparation for the

long trek north to Beijing and ultimately Shangdu, the new dynasty's northernmost capital in modern Manchuria. They may have taken their own lives out of fear of being violated en route, for eunuch companions in shackles themselves could scarcely provide the usual security. Or perhaps they were reacting to news of their Manchurian destination, only recently disclosed, which lay beyond the pale of civilization as most Chinese knew it and conjured up images of the Cai Yan ordeal a millennium earlier.[59] Yet two senior consorts who made the trek successfully without incident, née Chen and Zhu, would still commit suicide by strangulation, joined by two lesser consorts.[60]

The four women were all widows of Duzong and probably in their thirties. Arriving at Shangdu only ten days earlier, on June 15, they were even honored by Khubilai with a formal audience. No sexual abuse enroute to the capital had occurred. It must have been at roughly this time, however, that they learned of Khubilai's future plans for them—to be married off to mere carpenters.[61] More problematic than surviving their husbands was entering a new marriage in their absence. On this score, moralist philosophers of the time were emphatic. "To starve to death is a very small matter, but to lose one's integrity is extremely grave," was the famous Neo-Confucian response to a question about the appropriateness of remarriage by a destitute widow.[62] Similar moral convictions are reflected in the suicide note of Chen and Zhu, where they allude to the imperative of placing a higher cause before mere human survival:

> We did not disgrace the empire
> And fortunately have been spared personal disgrace.
> For generations we lived on the subsidies of Song
> And now endure shame as subjects of the north.
> We humble women die
> To preserve a solitary chastity.
> Like loyal officials and filial sons
> We anticipate rejuvenation in a new life.[63]

Composed in parallel prose, this note confirms the dual concern of the women with personal as well as political honor, family as well as dynasty. Chastity alone did not demand their deaths, particularly in light of the moral deficiencies of their husband, Duzong.[64] Still, in conformity with social expectations, the two women chose to stress the personal import of their deed. Reference to their "humble" station is also noteworthy. Lacking the pedigree of most harem recruits, the Widows Chen and

Zhu seemingly sensed a greater moral debt to dynasty as recompense for its extraordinary elevation of them. Being young and humble, they doubtlessly felt more dispensable as well.

Whether Chen and Zhu were joined by other indistinguished women is not known, but clearly within the ranks of captive women were many nameless individuals without ties to the palace. This is confirmed by Nie Bichuang, the manager of a Daoist monastery in the Song capital whose wife was taken north. Some years after the separation, he writes the following poem in her memory:

> In the inner apartments when you knotted your hair
> in betrothal
> We could scarcely have anticipated lives spent
> in separation.
> I still do not know if you were mistaken due to your beauty
> Or if surrounded by horses you can still buy cosmetics.[65]

This was no woman of the palace and her husband seemed genuinely baffled as to the reasons for her captivity. Was it a case of mistaken identity? Or had the Mongols been heartlessly random in their forage for southern beauties?

Curiously, the palace women to feel least compelled to commit suicide were the same women who held the greatest measure of privilege—the dowager-regents of the deposed child. As older women with greater stature, Grand Dowager Xie and Dowager Quan were least likely to be physically violated or forceably remarried. In the absence of such challenges to their chastity, death was not imperative. The influential historian Ouyang Xiu, in scrutinizing the behavior of palace consorts of the Five Dynasties era, had never criticized their mere survival of dynasty, only their subsequent marital infidelity.[66] When moralist philosopher Zhu Xi juxtaposes the male literatus who is "a loyal minister in death" against his spouse who is "a woman of integrity in life," he implicitly accepts a double standard for moral perfection in men and women, permitting female spouses to survive even as their men die.[67] Other factors also figured into the survival of our two dowagers, motives both personal and political. Dowager Quan, for example, as blood mother of child-emperor Gongdi, surely played some role in the court affairs of these two trying years and, of all decisions, she surely had a voice in that to retain her son in the capital, even as his two step-brothers fled to safety. The decision to surrender unconditionally may have been hers as well, reflecting her growing disillusionment with the literati men around her.

The strength of that disillusionment can be seen in an incident that occurred sometime in May 1276, when the junior dowager delivered a stiff rebuke of an unruly underling.

She and the deposed Gongdi were under military escort for relocation up north when their entourage of several hundred, just after crossing the Yangzi River, was intercepted by Song loyalists.[68] The interloper was Li Tingzhi, the relentless commander of Yangzhou, who continued to defend his charge despite dynastic collapse at Linan. Now, he had laid a nighttime ambush with the intent of liberating these Song royals from their Yuan captors. A six-hour exchange with northern guards ensued, Li Tingzhi unable to prevail despite a force estimated at forty thousand. His failure was inevitable: the principal captives, quite simply, did not care to be liberated. Dowager Quan would disavow the plot and denounce its protagonists in the strongest of terms. Communicating by letter with this isolated holdout, she wrote: "Through official rescript, you were ordered to accept the generous terms of surrender, yet failed to respond even after many days. How can you fail to understand Our intent, still seeking to secure the frontier? By now, We and the Successor have already submitted as subjects of the Yuan. On whose behalf do you persist in defending the city of Yangzhou?"[69] The dowager emerges here as utterly livid at the insubordination of regional leaders who dared to flaunt court orders, men seemingly intent on reducing royal patrons to mere puppets in the service of some partisan agenda. She was angered as well by the jeopardy to royal life and the larger peace accord presented by this belated rally. After all, the court had already fallen to foreign conquerors through the fickle cowardice of male managers—men who only recently had abandoned her and her son and now, in a seemingly compensatory display of masculine theatrics, would risk personal harm to the royal family.

Yet embedded in the dowager's seemingly casual comments lies a probing query on political ethics for which Li Tingzhi had no ready response: to whom or what do civil servants owe their fealty? By continuing their fight against Mongol occupiers already two months after the monarchy had been formally relinquished, Song loyalists were affirming devotion to a cause that surpasses any individual representative of that cause, devotion to the institution of monarchy that exceeds any individual monarch, devotion to traditions once nurtured by dynasty that now have a life of their own. Historically in China, political responsibility had been expressed in personal terms—namely, on the authority of the emperor. Thus, it was easy for the dowager to forget that her son

and his regents, although more than mere puppets, were only one part of a dynastic institution whose totality transcended its individual components.

In light of her apparent affirmation of monarchical power as personalized and the submission of inferiors to superiors as absolute, it is curious that Dowager Quan does not extend this principle to herself: her husband dead and regency dissolved, a timely death as martyr may have been easier than an aimless existence as exile. Her will to survive emerges as even more baffling in light of family background. As noted in preceding chapters, the Quan clan had sired more than a single palace consort. Only a generation earlier they had also given the Southern Song court its longest reigning monarch, the controversial Lizong. Quan Jiu thereby held the distinction, rare for most harem women, of blood ties to both paternal and maternal wings of the royal family. Traditional assumptions of women placing the palace's maternal concerns before paternal interests—her own nuclear family before the extended imperial clan—scarcely applies to this woman. Moreover, childhood travels with her father exposed Quan Jiu to the male world of bureaucracy and politics. As a youth once trapped with her father at Tanzhou, where bandits had surrounded the city, she had been personal witness to the miraculous feats that loyalists of relentless resolve could accomplish.[70] Confucian ideals of "loyal commitment" (*zhong yi*) and "chaste devotion" (*jie yi*) were not, for her, empty slogans devoid of personal relevance.

Her breadth of experience with a secular world notwithstanding, the value system of Quan Jiu came increasingly in later years to be informed by Buddhist aesthetics, with its compelling denial of wealth and power and intuitive search for truth. When and how this conversion occurred is not clear, only that she eventually ended up as a nun in Beijing and her son a monk in Tibet.[71] Admittedly, monasteries had provided a safe haven for palace throwaways, especially its widowed consorts, since Tang times and earlier. Yet the religious conversions of both mother and son clearly transcend, by all indications, sheer convenience. Indeed, many an educated Song woman took to Buddhism. This grows partly out of the personal identification of women with religious icons such as Guanyin, icons that celebrate a feminized body and spirit; it grows also out of pressures from Neo-Confucian conservatives to spurn the material and the sensuous, an agenda common to the two teachings.[72]

The seriousness of purpose of Dowager Quan, in particular, is documented by visitors later in life who confirm her exceptional piety in "chanting scripture," "preaching the Law," and "sitting legs folded under

a myriad of snowflakes."[73] She seems to have converted her son to Buddhism as well. By his late teens, the former monarch comes to be characterized by acquaintances as precociously "dispassionate and detached" from the human realm.[74] He also emerges as remarkably non-material, particularly for a man born to such extraordinary privilege. He had no interest, according to contemporaries, in personally acquiring or even perusing the vast store of memorabilia and other relics retrieved from the Song palaces, materials transported to Beijing and Shangdu and readily accessible to him.[75] It was Buddhist-inspired values of this sort that seems to have saved their lives. Buddhism's affirmation of the spiritual and denial of the material, its focus on the infinite and denigration of the episodic, its stress on transformative adaptation to ever-changing conditions, and finally its propagation of a universal morality that denigrates class and gender—these all helped to neutralize the potential trauma of their tremendous loss.[76]

Another reason for Dowager Quan, in the aftermath of her dynasty's collapse, to choose life over death may relate to her responsibility as a mother of a five year old who would otherwise be orphaned. He was her only child and she emerges as understandably protective of him. Despite the numerous relocations of the next fifteen years, they would never be separated. She even accompanied him to a remote Tibet, an important center of Buddhist learning where the two, as political prisoners of a sort, could pursue spiritual interests relatively free of the usual surveillance and inhibitions. A young man of eighteen by now, he could well have gone alone.[77] Yet maternal responsibilities were probably not the overriding factor in the dowager's will to survive. Other palace women of prominence, in the absence of such commitments, still followed her example.

For women and men of the Song elite, in fact, an inverse relationship emerges between status and martyrdom—the best educated and most privileged were the least represented among loyalist ranks.[78] Grand Dowager Xie may have been childless and infirm, but there is no evidence that she even contemplated suicide, not before nor after her late summer arrival in Beijing, even though her captivity had induced one anguished nephew to take his own life.[79] The same holds for Wang Qinghui, a consort of Duzong who ended up in Manchuria as a Daoist nun. As evidenced in her widely acclaimed poetry, she identified closely with the cause of dynasty and felt profoundly despondent upon its demise. Yet even at her most vulnerable moments, while a captive heading north, Wang Qinghui's intense anger and nostalgia were tempered

by a passive resignation in this tragic turn of history.[80] Contributing substantially to her rejection of suicide may be the Daoist humanism that guided her personal life, where such acts of egotistical drama received less validation, relative to orthodox Confucianism.

Indeed, the presumption of egotistical motives behind the actions of remaining Song holdouts clearly deserves further consideration. The "monarchical mothers," as the two dowagers were sometimes dubbed endearingly, certainly concluded as much. The late spring correspondence of Xie Qiao, from her occupied capital to the Yangzhou camp of Li Tingzhi, is highly revealing in this regard. Seething with anger and indignation, the senior dowager writes:

> The aged person that I am, having met with such distressing times, recently accepted the rescript of the Emperor of the Great Yuan which permitted us to submit en masse, thereby preserving the Ancestral Altars, protecting royal clansmen, and sparing the myriad of surnames. The Great Army now occupies the capital, yet the three palaces have been spared incident, the nine temples are intact as usual, and the masses tranquil. Your independent defense of an isolated city has [heretofore] exemplified an exceptional dedication and industry. Yet the empire has already been uprooted. Of what crime are the masses guilty the extent to which you recklessly persist in a staunch defense?[81]

She obviously knew of the famine that had plagued Yangzhou since early winter, famine induced by the blockade that had cut the city off from the surrounding countryside and its supplies of food, famine that had killed off several hundred each day and reduced survivors to cannibalism.[82] But the response of Commissioner Li to local conditions seemed inexplicably cavalier. He reacted to the shortage of food by raiding private homes, carting off food for his soliders while leaving civilians to starve. He reacted to Mongol proposals for cease-fire by brutally assassinating their emissary. He hatched on his own initiative the aforementioned plot to rescue, against their will, the entourage of the deposed monarch and the junior dowager from their Mongol captors. He would also concoct, at roughly the same time, a nearly successful assassination attempt against Wen Tianxiang, a loyalist of equal dedication whom he had mistakenly identified as renegade.[83] Such reckless disregard for the lives of royalty and colleagues, not to mention the masses of innocent Yangzhou residents, genuinely baffled the Grand Dowager, much as it did the junior dowager, Quan Jiu.

The monarchy abdicated, its seals surrendered, its capital occupied,

and its regents imprisoned—by all indications, the Song imperium had expired. Admittedly, two boys of royal blood remained at large and their safe passage to Fujian circuit was common knowledge. Yet it was not until the first day of the fifth lunar month (June 14) that the eldest youth, seven year old Zhao Shi, was installed as emperor of a resuscitated Song. In the several intervening months, men like Li Tingzhi were acting on something other than the authority of the throne. Such cavalier conduct in the name of an absent authority, in any other dynasty, would most certainly be cause for apprehension—fear that unbridled ambitions might induce aspirations to the throne. But the political order of Song was organized around a wholly different set of expectations and responsibilities. The leading figures in the drama of these final years, however frustrated by regents lacking in resolve and their advisors in foresight, would never exploit conditions to their own personal advantage. The rule of Song had survived too long, its political heritage too entrenched, and subordination of the self to state too thorough to permit new apostasies of the old sort. Yet men such as Li Tingzhi could still act with the best intentions on a misguided mission where self-image weighed heavier than civic duty, his personal honor demanding a dispassionate distance from the nameless men and women in his charge. Personal vindication was particularly important for this veteran of the Xiangyang contest, who had fled the region on the heels of its collapse and under a cloud of controversy. He would brook no compromises this time around.

Among contemporaries, the inclination is to celebrate the battle-hardened Li Tingzhi as "a great man who for a decade kept the border's dust settled"; those to suffer from his caprice such as Wen Tianxiang are less generous.[84] But the two men, whatever differences in design, were cut of remarkably similar cloth. The insistence of Li Tingzhi that "instructions of surrender are beyond my ability to comprehend" could have come just as convincingly from the mouth of Wen Tianxiang.[85] Had the court not intervened, Wen Tianxiang would doubtlessly have stood firm ground at Pingjiang much as Li Tingzhi did at Yangzhou and neighboring Taizhou, and perhaps with similarly disastrous consequences. In the case of Yangzhou, a steady and agonizing decline still did not convince Commissioner Li to submit. He would ultimately be outmaneuvered by his assistant, in response to which he attempted suicide before being captured and executed.[86] Yangzhou's surrender, in August 1276, was not followed by the slaughter that many including the Grand Dowager had feared. Occupying commander Aju had insisted on re-

straint. But the city he inherited was largely depopulated all the same: the embargo and siege had claimed more lives than anyone cared to count.

ACADEME IN PARALYSIS

A rare insistence on unwavering—in fact, obsessive—political commitment also emerges in the capital at the various university campuses. The university served as more than merely a seat of militant activism. It was a leading center of Confucian fundamentalism as well, its students and faculty among the most alienated in the educated elite. Proximity to the seat of political power nurtured a particularly strong contempt for compromisers who ran the bureaucracy and monarchs who indulged them. As a consequence of university alienation from government, one would expect the fall of Linan to be received with ambivalence, if not relief. After all, students shared neither the generous salaries nor weighty responsibilities of men in office, while faculty and staff had no commission beyond keeping the campuses well ordered, academically and politically. As Mongol armies closed in on the capital and officials abandoned their posts for the safety of home, nothing prevented university students and personnel from following in their footsteps. Yet many would rally, in the end, a measure of manly courage far exceeding the bulk of bureaucrats, their ostensible leaders.[87]

That the university assumed the ethical high ground owes something to its chancellor, Yang Wenzhong. In the early weeks of 1276 when audience chambers at court stood virtually empty, this native of Sichuan was among the prominent few to persist in making the obligatory appearance.[88] He would perish a few years later in the deep south, still committed to the cause of dynasty. In audience alongside Chancellor Yang during those final days was Gao Yingsong. A former administrator at the university, he became one of the last major advisors to Dowager Xie.[89] Even in the aftermath of formal surrender, rather than return to his native Fujian, Gao Yingsong stayed on to extend final courtesies to the Grand Dowager. His last mission for the palace, whether by volition or coercion we cannot confirm, involved accompanying the imperial entourage in its journey north. Upon reaching Beijing on June 10, he began a hunger strike which soon claimed his own life.[90] That band of southern exiles, excluding the Grand Dowager who followed several months later, consisted of assorted palace celebrities from the deposed monarch to consorts and attendants, plus leading court officers—sev-

eral hundred in all. University students figured prominently among the sojourners, their ranks estimated at roughly a hundred and comparable to the number of palace women. Yet relative to others, students suffered disproportionately. Less than half of them actually reached Shangdu.[91] Many reportedly died enroute due to the neglect or abuse of their captors; a few presumably joined Gao Yingsong in committing suicide. As for the surviving minority, a handful willingly took up residence in Beijing while others eventually returned to their homes in the south.[92]

One writer suggests that students joined the sojourners not out of political principle but simple coercion. Northern occupiers, by this account, had dispatched dormitory attendants to scour halls for stray students to impress into the delegation, no doubt viewing them as just another southern commodity of potential value to the north.[93] The halls must have been largely empty in light of the small yield, which represented a tiny fraction of the several thousand students enrolled at the three metropolitan campuses. Most students had quite obviously absconded, perhaps for fear of enemy excess but also out of frustration with their own mismanaged court. The level of such absences should not be seen as simple betrayal of dynasty. Many had only recently taken leave of Linan, as with university professor Zheng Xian. He had lost his mother in the heat of enemy pursuit but persevered onward to the coastal city of Taizhou, their home to the south, to arrange suitable burial.[94] It was at her grave that he took his own life by strangulation. Martyrdom for dynasty was his declared motive, although despondency over personal losses cannot be dismissed as a contributing factor.

Also absent from the capital at the time of occupation was university student Zhong Kejun.[95] He first reacted to news of the imperial abdication by taking up arms. But scant progress had been made toward mobilizing locals for a march on Linan when time ran out—the imperial palaces had already been emptied. In a fit of frustrated anger, he drowned himself at the River of the Dragon's Gate, in the heart of his native Jiangnan West.[96] Perhaps the most moving case of student martyrdom, however, can be found in Xu Yingbiao.[97] He and his family were in residence in the capital when the occupation began. Their native Quzhou lay only several hundred kilometers to the south, but for unknown reasons they opted against a last-minute flight. Waiting until the imperial entourage had departed Linan, they instead took their own lives. The children "willingly" followed in their father's footsteps, it is said, "father and sons sitting sternly like clay statues in a temple" as fire consumed their home.[98] And when servants attempted a rescue, Xu kinsmen leapt into a well.

Members of the family had exchanged poems shortly before, in expression of shared experiences and commitment. They also offered ritual sacrifices to Yue Fei, the militant general of the preceding century, in affirmation of the political import of their deed and its place in a long historical tradition. Rallying so ritualistically around a cult hero with the impeccably martial pedigree of Yue Fei, the men seemed to be making some greater statement whose symbolism would surpass their own time and place.

More so than ordinary officials, members of the university community emerge as far more paralyzed by the fall of the dynasty: inhibited at acting in constructive ways, they turned their anger self-destructively inward. This occurred less through fault of personality and more through the crippling weight of history. Unlike other Song institutions of advanced learning, such as public colleges and private academies away from the capital, the university had a spirited tradition of going beyond mere political rhetoric and intervening aggressively in court affairs. Some of those activities, for the dynasty's last several decades, have already been noted here. But during the court's final months as the flight of bureaucrats created a dangerous vacuum, university minds could not but turn to an episode of 150 years earlier, when the naively noble aims of students culminated in deeds that brought their very loyalty into serious question. At the center of this event was Chen Dong (1085–1127), a forty-one year old student who unwittingly crossed the thin line between civil disobedience and domestic disruption.[99]

No one could miss the remarkable commonality of conditions in 1126 and 1276: alien hordes descending on the capital, contemptible bureaucrats absconding in their wake, and relocation of the royal family stirring a divisive debate. Commonality also emerges in the rhetoric of the university. In a rapid succession of memorials to the throne, Chen Dong joined by several hundred fellow students would denounce the so-called "six thugs," prominent court officials such as Cai Jing and Wang Fu and palace eunuchs like Tong Guan who promoted appeasement of the enemy: "They [Wang Fu and Tong Guan] have broken the treaties of our ancestors and have destroyed the good faith of the Middle Kingdom. They have incited border rifts and wasted our armaments. This has caused Your Majesty, newly ascended to the throne, to be suddenly saddled with the burden of turmoil along the northern border."[100] The denunciation of Tong Guan struck an especially sympathetic chord. This formidably powerful eunuch had managed to extend his influence from the palace to border commands and fiscal management to a degree un-

precedented by the conservative standards of Song. This gave Tong Guan an aggregate of power exceeding even the muddled ministers who did his bidding. He had also endorsed concessions to Jurchen invaders that only whet their appetite, in the end, for further aggression. With appeasement having failed, students demanded nothing short of the eunuch's head. Yet the compelling conviction and stirring eloquence of student rhetoric served only to intensify mass hysteria and create a tinderbox that exploded uncontrollably. Tens of thousands of ordinary Kaifeng citizens, from seemingly every class and station, soon swelled student ranks as they marched on the palace. The mob then assassinated over ten eunuchs with rare brutality, "disemboweling their bodies, severing their corpses, and grinding their bones to pulp."[101] An anxious court followed through with critical concessions, including the revival of a militant councilor favored by the university. Yet students ended up the big losers. After restoring order, the court imposed a ban on student petitions and threatened prosecution under martial law for future violators. It moved to arrest and execute several student ringleaders as well, Chen Dong among them.

The violent response of Northern Song rulers, in 1127, grew out of more than mere retaliatory impulses. They felt a greater compulsion to condemn the unorthodox tactics of the university. By accident or design, students had broken an eternal rule of political protocol under the empire: protest can be vertical but not horizontal, from individual subjects as appeals to their monarch but not from a coalition of subjects as demands. The notion of partisan alliance had never enjoyed the sanction of state or society, as the eleventh-century debate triggered by Ouyang Xiu shows.[102] The university penchant for petitioning as a group seems a prominent exception to that rule, one the court grudgingly came to accept. Yet students had gone a step further this time. Reaching beyond their campuses, they resorted to unthinkable tactics of mob pressure. A century and a half later and confronting almost identical conditions, they would not be led down the same dangerous path. Memorials to the court would continue, but students of the late Southern Song dared not take the sole step which might have spared, if only temporarily, their besieged capital—mobilizing citizens and soldiers as they had done in the past, but this time to shield rather than threaten their monarchs.

Perhaps best exemplifying the passive anger that characterized the university response to the Song demise is Zheng Sixiao (1241–1318). This native of coastal Fujian and resident of Pingjiang, an individual of ex-

ceptional literary talent, had attended the Imperial University during the dynasty's tumultuous last decade. He was also among the more vocal critics of the erratic chief councilor, Chen Yizhong.[103] When Zheng Sixiao disappeared from Linan shortly before the occupation, his mother's ill health may have provided the pretext but frustrations with an immobilized state was more likely his motive. A youthful thirty-five at the time, he would spend the next four decades eulogizing the achievements of Song and deriding its barbarian successors, his poetry and painting vociferously nationalistic. But his anger, as with so many others in that student cohort, seemed directed self-destructively inward.

Zheng Sixiao would devote his every energy to the memory of dynasty. His refusal to marry or sire a family is attributed to this obsession, as is his sale of the family estate and distribution of proceeds to friends and associates so that he might pursue a life of unfettered reclusion. In this way liberated from the mundane, he could perfect the moral impulses which now consumed him. He even insisted on an eccentric agenda of facing south whenever sleeping or sitting and covering his ears whenever northern dialects were spoken. As another expression of loyalist devotion, he changed his personal name to Sixiao, an obscure rendering for "remembering Zhao royalty." So exclusive was his use of that adopted name that his birth name remains to this day a mystery. Zheng Sixiao went so far as to fictionalize reign titles for Song and thereby avoid the Yuan standard. Yet he never overcame a profound self-hatred that grew out of acknowledged imperfections of moral courage, for he had failed on the two most critical missions of Confucian manhood. He could muster neither the measure of civic commitment to die as martyr nor familial commitment to propagate the line. In the early weeks of 1277, on the first anniversary of Linan's surrender, he writes apologetically:

> I have observed, for several generations, the dual propagation of loyalty and filial piety. My feet are planted on the earth of the Great Song while my head extends to its heaven, my body adorns the clothing of the Great Song while my mouth consumes food from its fields. . . . Yet I have an elderly mother beset with the afflictions of old age and dependent on me for the duration of her remaining years. Were I to die, then I would not succeed as a filial son; were I to live, then I would not succeed as a loyal official.[104]

Elaborating further on this point of conflicting ethical duties, "I view my body as the body of Heaven and earth, the body of my mother and father, and the body of the Middle Kingdom," he declares, "but to fully

embrace loyalty is to be inadequately filial, while being wholly filial would make me inadequately loyal."[105] Much like Wen Tianxiang, as noted in our first chapter, Zheng Sixiao found himself torn between two equally important moral imperatives; but unlike Wen Tianxiang, he could never decide which to place first. Even the death of his mother, later in 1277, did not free him to act decisively. He was an only son, after all, and propagation of the line rested solely with him. It was far easier for Wen Tianxiang, survived by younger brother and adopted son, to lay down his own life. Yet this reality seems somehow overlooked by Zheng Sixiao, who applauds his hero for a "courageous fervor that majestically radiates throughout the vast earth."[106] He saw himself in contrast as visibly inferior. If male virility is to be demonstrated either through an honorable death (*zhong*) or a profusion of heirs (*xiao*), then Zheng Sixiao was an unmitigated failure on both scores. Moreover, the expectations of his parents, with reference to civic duty, were so extraordinary as certain to frustrate as well. His father, a minor official who died when the youth was only twenty-one, refused to acknowledge any conflict between loyalty to state and family. Quite the contrary, a stern and exacting Zheng Zhen insisted that private morality cannot exist in the absence of civic commitment: filial piety is impossible without loyal devotion to state. As recollected by his son, he warned: "If you fail to serve your parents, then you are unfilial. If you fail to serve your ruler, you are also unfilial. If you fail to become accomplished, you are unfilial as well. And why? Because these bring shame to the family. If you fail to do as I say, then you are not my son."[107] And to this his mother added, "If you fail to act on your father's words, then you are better off dead." Through their civically impassioned rearing, his parents had set an almost unachievable standard of moral courage—a rigid structure with absolute commitments and little room for maneuvering. Similarly high ethical standards were set at the Imperial University, where Zheng Sixiao's education continued after the death of his father. Having failed to live up to those expectations, he never overcame his sense of inadequacy as a Confucian male. This prompted him, shortly before death, to insist that his final epitaph read "the disloyal and unfilial Zheng Sixiao."

Yet the parents of Zheng Sixiao, and indeed he himself, had embraced a standard too stringent for even the most ardently moralistic of Song thinkers. Historian Ouyang Xiu may have laid the foundation for the revolution in loyalist ethics, but his own impulses were discernibly tempered by an overarching humanism. Evidence of this can be found in his comments on the tale of Wu Zhen, a military officer with re-

spectable civilian credentials under the Later Tang. Renegades had taken captive the family of Wu Zhen and then proceeded to torture them with savage brutality. By suspending his campaign against the perpetrators, he could have saved the lives of those kinsmen, but Wu Zhen adamantly refused. For him, military duty came decidedly before personal concerns, the civic before the familial. To the extent that Wu Zhen had simultaneously presented himself as a morally circumspect Confucian, the act seemed particularly ironic and even reprehensible. Commenting in his *Historical Records of the Five Dynasties*, Ouyang Xiu writes with indignation: "Only when filial in serving one's parents can one be loyal in serving his ruler. The likes of Wu Zhen may be considered profoundly unfilial. How can he possibly be loyal?"[108] The family of Zheng Sixiao apparently viewed civic duty as a mechanism for defining the values and preserving the honor of family, as if to suggest the public precede the private. Ouyang Xiu had asserted the exact opposite: it is private values that inform public values, at times even necessitating retreat from the public realm. Civic duties can never be permitted to compromise—or as he says, "do injury to"—familial obligations. Similar equivocations can be found in the writings of Sima Guang and Zhu Xi, men who championed righteous sacrifice but warned against egotistical excess.[109] But extreme positions were not uncommon in the 1270s and beyond, when no philosophical or political authority existed to mediate normalcy in such abnormal times.

A lifelong boycott of the new regime and conformity to the customs of the old should have been adequate to satisfy the ethical expectations of family and society. Yet embedded in Zheng Sixiao's longing for martyrdom is a compulsion for ethical perfection and the inevitable frustration at being humanly imperfect. That search for perfection may relate to the fundamentalist rigor of Neo-Confucianism: prone to apply principles derived from a perfectly ordered natural world to the imperfect realm of human morality, it may have promoted ethical standards beyond the reach of most ordinary men and women. Yet a more powerful influence over Zheng Sixiao was his own unthinkably exacting and rigid family.

Interestingly, his was a family of modest means and stature. It could boast an enduring tradition of education and occasional appointment at the lowest rungs of the civil service, to be sure, but no great wealth or political power. This represents a profile typical for university students of the Song, as noted earlier, and a key factor in their idealism.[110] Zheng men had only recently migrated to the lower Yangzi from the coastal

south and, as displaced literati, probably possessed little in local re-sources.[111] Educationally accomplished but politically marginal, they had for generations criticized court leadership and the power concen-trated there in the hands of a few. These traits are unmistakably those of the outsider who aspires to be insider, men who still believe in the dy-nasty's promise of opportunity based on examination credentials, not personal contacts: precisely their strength. And despite the repeated fail-ure of the regime to live up to these expectations, Zheng men never lost faith in the dream. Their own family expectations were so closely linked to dynastic ideals, private identities so intimately intertwined with pub-lic institutions that they were utterly paralyzed by the demise of Song rule. It seemed so inexplicable to Zheng Sixiao, from his perspective as Confucian moralist, that the dynasty had exhausted its mandate—or, in the idiom of *The Changes*, the lake had drained dry. He writes in the year 1283: "My birth has proven a great misfortune, having coincided with this treacherous border conflict and the demise of empire. Since antiq-uity, when an empire expired it was invariably because its rulers had lost their virtue, causing the confidence of its people to dissipate. Yet our Great Song produced a succession of Sagely rulers who founded their empire on benevolence. How then does it end up with the disastrous invasions of Jurchen and then Mongol thugs?"[112] This retrospective on the Song may be inflated by nostalgia, but it also reflects an idealized image of the dynasty preserved in the mind of Zheng Sixiao and others of similar station, individuals who passed much of their lives in denial of the reality of dynastic change.

*Thunder repeated: the image of **arousal**.*
Thus in fear and trembling
The superior man sets his life in order
And examines himself.

The Changes, LI.

5 · Zhen:
Of Men Aroused

The virtual antithesis of a tormented and timid Zheng Sixiao was Wen Tianxiang, the impassioned statesman who emerged from the dynastic crisis as a towering hero—an outcome anything but certain based on the circumstances of his life. After all, the traits more commonly associated with heroic virtue in traditional China—austerity, sobriety, even simplicity—were scarcely inherent to him. Wen Tianxiang was, quite simply, too exquisitely endowed in riches and physical presence. As if to combine the physical stature of northern men with the elegant presence of his own south, biographers depict him as arrestingly handsome: "his physique broad and imposing, his hands delicate like jade, his eyebrows so luxurious and eyes so broad that he would glance with utter resplendence."[1] Rarely is the dynastic history for the Song, written in the 1340s under Yuan auspices, so effusive in its description of a late Song man. Wen Tianxiang possessed an imposing intellect as well, earning his doctoral credentials at a mere twenty. And his deft sense of history and politics, as revealed in earlier chapters, was complemented by a liberal flair for the literary, especially poetry in the regulated style popular in Tang times. Then, there were his material assets. Judging from the natural splendor and human enhancements of the sprawling mountain retreat that bears his name, built in 1271 and described in sumptuous detail in his collected writings, Wen Tianxiang did not want for wealth, at least not after thirty.[2] And this does not include liquid capital, much of which he would later donate to the government to defer defense expenditures. With such material bounty to complement his literary resources, he was perhaps as "bourgeois" as any Song man might be.

Through friends and associates near and far, Wen Tianxiang had more than the usual array of social diversions as well. His poetry abounds with references to abundant drink and merry feasts, leisurely solitude and extensive travel, plus the usual literati celebrations of birthdays, promotions, and partings. Carefree, extroverted, and generous—the almost universal markings of masculine nobility—he kept a high social profile in his youth, moving in circles of ever escalating exclusiveness, as permitted by his new celebrity.[3] Spouses and children had been deferred until thirty, rather late for elite men of Song times.[4] His own father's marriage at nineteen was far more typical. Once the commitment was made, however, Wen Tianxiang would focus on his new and burgeoning family with a similar totality, fathering five known children in just two years, from 1266 to 1267, several more after that. An obsessive overachiever perhaps, but nothing else seems particularly portentous about this enviably prosperous southerner, a man later to be lionized beyond all human dimensions.

He was barely forty when the Song capital fell, his eldest child just shy of ten. This was scarcely the time to confront an imminent mortality. Yet in 1279, when all hope of dynastic restoration is lost, he embraces death with an impassive resignation inexplicably anomalous for men of his youth and station. In a poem on "moral will," he writes with introspective candor on the impact of these tumultuous times on his desire to die:

Despair of a hundred years, the parameters of life are exhausted,
Distance of a myriad of miles, the journey is bitter.
Born to the wrong times, I have encountered a hundred sorrows,
To seek benevolence and obtain benevolence, what other words matter?

A single death may be as light as swansdown
Or as weighty as Mt. Tai, depending on how it is enacted.
Wives bow their heads while retaining kerchief and cap,
Men grit their teeth while swallowing sword and saw.

When life is exchanged for a cause it is not lived in vain,
For a cause that is glorious will illumine a thousand antiquities . . .
In tranquil times, who is served by the pursuit of learning?
In impending peril, what is there to fret let alone fear?[5]

Also included in this protracted poem are allusions to historical figures notoriously devoid of similar courage and conviction, causing their "crimes to reverberate to the heavens and their reputations to stink to

this very day." There is implicit here the presumption of moral discontinuity, the Confucian male's dominion over polity and society in serious jeopardy. Thus, in another poem Wen Tianxiang alludes to "stalwart men (*jian'er*) emerging victorious over a corrupt class of Confucians (*furu*)."[6] The term *ru*, in classical times and earlier, was a homonym for things "soft" or "weak."[7] When he portrays stalwart men as purging the Confucian literati of their corrupt ways, Wen Tianxiang is clearly associating this image of physical weakness with moral degeneracy—a degeneracy only to be overcome by the regeneration of a male virility uncorrupted by the effete depravities of the day. Significantly, in his view, the morally upright woman should not mimic male behavior. A virtuous man must have the courage to "swallow the sword of death," according to his poem, but a virtuous woman must preserve chaste devotion and defer to her spouse's authority by "retaining kerchief and cap." Such precepts thus serve to distinguish the sexes, while affirming the superior physical and moral vigor of males. It is, in any case, this leap from moral leadership to masculine power, from political crisis to cultural rejuvenation that is the focus of this chapter.

MATERIAL MAN OF THE SOUTH

The background and education of Wen Tianxiang shares much common ground with other prominent literati of the Southern Song. As narrated in his biographical eulogy for father Wen Yi, the family had many generations ago migrated from Chengdu to Luling county (Jizhou), from the Sichuan basin out west to the Jiangnan interior.[8] They were not displaced northerners, as was common for much of the Song elite, but displaced all the same. Sichuan was not the "south," after all, it was *Shu*—the "west."[9] Being the least "peripheral" of the various regions to the south, it was presumably the least corrupted by material excess. In celebration of those western roots, Wen Tianxiang would model much of his prison poetry on Du Fu (712–770), the Tang poet who similarly hailed from Chengdu and probably resided there simultaneously with Wen ancestors.[10] Such imitation was, for Wen Tianxiang, proud affirmation of associations beyond his adopted home to the east. A poet distinguished for literary force over frill, Du Fu personified the martial courage and political commitment commonly associated with northern culture, but given universal expression at his hand.[11] He would bear personal witness to dynastic tumult and, in consequence, knew the pain of exile and fear of cataclysmic change—expe-

riences so closely paralleling those of Wen Tianxiang that his message could easily transcend the barrier of centuries to establish common bonds of futility and dejection. But the most immediate ethical force in the early life of our Song hero was his own father, Wen Yi (1215–1256).

The senior Wen, a voracious reader and avid book collector, was a scholar of austere discipline. Entering his study at night, his son reports, he commonly emerged only after daybreak. A meticulous writer who valued brevity and precision, his composition is portrayed as "rich in maturity and substantial in constitution." Despite such rigorous training, Wen Yi seems never to have aspired to public office. "For all of his moral virtue, he was a relative unknown," according to his own son. His was a family initially marginal yet mobile, politically; prospering but not prosperous, materially; respected but not distinguished, socially. In lieu of his own aspirations to office, Wen Yi invested entirely in the next generation. He married at a youthful nineteen and devoted his remaining years to the rearing of a family of seven, a brood of four boys and three girls.[12] Instilled in them were the same values of discipline and dedication that he personally exemplified. A stern and frugal father, he was at the same time attentive and nurturing, particularly of his boys. This is reflected in his decision in 1256 to accompany, personally, his two eldest sons to a distant capital where they had both qualified to sit on the doctoral examination. The forty-one year old Wen Yi, gravely ill at the time, lay bed-ridden for most of his three months in Linan and died there only four days after the palace examination. The nineteen year old Wen Bi did not make the cut and would have to return in three years, but Tianxiang placed first on a list of 601—a distinction certain to open the highest of political doors for this family of relative unknowns.

A guilt-ridden Wen Tianxiang assumes some personal blame for his father's death in such unfamiliar surroundings. His own energies deflected by the rigors of examination, he had failed during those critical last weeks to administer medicine with the regularity required by his father's acute condition.[13] Feelings of culpability could only have been aggravated by the emotional devastation that the death initially wrought upon his mother, Zeng Deci (1214–1278), who seriously contemplated suicide when the news reached her at Luling. She chose otherwise partly due to dependent children, the youngest of whom was scarcely four years old, and an aging grandmother similarly dependent on her care. She may have been dissuaded by her own parents as well, both still alive and residing nearby. But perhaps most importantly, suicidal death seems terribly out of character for the forty-two year old Widow Zeng. As re-

vealed in a biography written by younger son Wen Bi, her commitments to family and community were far too pragmatically driven to make suicide a compelling option.[14] She apparently saw greater courage in the role of single mother rearing her own family. It is precisely this dedication that won for her the enduring respect of those children, who would later wax with unbridled ebullience on her maternal attentiveness to them and filial devotion to her own kin, her astute balancing of debt to biological kin with duties to offspring and in-laws. Widow Zeng emerges from family writings as a moral exemplar by the traditional standards of Chinese society, even by the new ethical regimen of late Song. Yet it was not Confucianism alone that informed her steady sense of moral virtue.

For the widow's father, Zeng Jue (1191–1262), there luckily exists a tomb inscription that documents a predisposition in the Zeng household for Buddhism and Daoism.[15] By curious contrast, concern for Confucian orthodoxy—so prevalent along the empire's eastern coast—was at best marginal for this particular family of the interior. The inscription also reveals that Wen Tianxiang took the unusual step of inviting Zeng Jue, his maternal grandfather, to live with him. And his grandfather stayed for several years, no doubt sometime after his father's death in 1256 and before the grandfather himself died in 1262. It is Wen Tianxiang who composes the tomb inscription and celebrates his eclectic grandfather's ruminations on Confucian rationalism in the abstract while pursuing, with still greater zest, the Daoist metaphysic of prolonging life. In character, Zeng Jue emerges as relaxed and leisured: constructing drinking games around Chinese checkers, consuming meat as frequently as fifteen times a month, and traveling extensively without the slightest social pretenses—a spontaneously unassuming man, perhaps, but also a man unapologetic about his material means. Notably lacking the scholarly discipline of Wen Tianxiang's father, he seemed more in line with the libertarian tradition of central Sichuan, the tradition of the famous Su brothers.[16] And Tianxiang emerges as equally indebted to both, his father informing his public life and his maternal grandfather inspiring the private. Of course, Confucianism has traditionally been associated with the stalwart assertiveness of the north, Daoism with the passive self-indulgence of the south—one substantially *yang* and the other fundamentally *yin*. The pacific and contemplative traits in Zeng Jue were reinforced through Buddhism, which still retained deep roots in the Jiangxi hinterland even as Confucian fundamentalism rallied elsewhere.[17] To varying degrees, all three teachings

would inform the values of Wen Tianxiang, not unlike most Song men, which might create a healthy balance in the northerner secure in his Confucian roots.[18] Yet for the geographically marginal and thus culturally defensive southerner, and especially a southerner for whom the intellectual legacies of family are so eclectic, there is the potential for overcompensation in acting on Confucian orthodoxy and its precepts of moral conservatism.

Another individual to contribute, early on, to the complexity of Wen Tianxiang's moral character is local mentor, Ouyang Shoudao (1209–1273). This native of Jizhou, the prefectural seat for Luling, emerges by the mid-thirteenth century as one of the region's premiere intellectual figures.[19] He had served the Song court in various mid-level posts, chiefly during the reign of Lizong, but his greatest commitment was to his Luling community, where many a promising young provincial knew him as teacher. This is evidenced in a stirring eulogy by Wen Tianxiang, where he refers to "the treatment of students as though they were close kin."[20] Apart from such selfless generosity, Ouyang Shoudao seemed personally to exemplify precisely the selfless charity that Confucians universally applauded in the abstract but rarely achieved in their own lives. It is this nobility that inspired Wen Tianxiang's greatest eloquence:

> The virtue of the Master lay in a beneficence akin to mother and father. He would often fret for a single person who suffered from cold or from hunger and would prefer that we not be altogether affluent nor indigent. By nature, he was calm like a shallow river and placid like ornamental jade. In bearing, he was delicate and graceful while pure in heart like a recluse. In personality, he had so perfected sincerity of heart that it could shatter mountains and conquer iron and stone.[21]

These seemingly incompatible combinations of soft yet hard, simple yet refined, spontaneous yet deliberate all suggest a character as much Daoist as Confucian. Master Ouyang also combined the *yin* qualities of mysterious refinement (placid like jade) with the *yang* qualities of strength and endurance (dense like iron and stone). He was socially aware and involved, but could be content to live as a recluse as well. Thus, converging in the single personality of Ouyang Shoudao are the divergent traits of Wen Tianxiang's father and grandfather, the impassioned Confucian and the impassive Daoist.

The same sort of selective syncretism that shaped the personal life of Ouyang Shoudao, it appears, also informed his intellectual values. His commitment to government service and research into the *Book of*

Changes places him squarely in the Confucian camp, but not necessarily the orthodoxy of the Cheng brothers and Zhu Xi, or School of the Way, with its metaphysic of moral rigor. As Wen Tianxiang would write: "The Master's learning was unadulterated like cotton or silk, legume or grain. He pursued things of benefit and utility to the age while not reverting to lofty discourse or empty talk.²² The term "lofty discourse," or abstract ideas, represents clear reference to the metaphysical speculations of the Cheng-Zhu school, which Ouyang Shoudao saw as lacking "utility." This is not to say that he similarly rejected the goals of personal and public virtue to which the new school also aspired. On the contrary, he respected many of its classical exegeses.²³ He even circulated freely among *Daoxue* proponents.²⁴ Yet he saw the school's broader vision as unacceptably skewed, too embedded in an idealized order and too removed from the human condition to offer practical solutions to pressing issues.

The School of the Way most directly influenced Wen Tianxiang and his mentor, and an array of other late Song literati, not so much in imparting definitive intellectual constructs as in informing general approaches to learning. In Tang and early Song, the large corpus of classical writing to receive recognition as cardinal texts, the so-called Five Classics, represented a highly pluralistic body of material. History found representation in the *Documents* and the *Annals*, philosophy in the *Changes*, statecraft in the *Rites*, and belles lettres in the *Odes*.²⁵ By the thirteenth century and largely through the efforts of Neo-Confucian moralists, the Five Classics had been replaced as core curriculum by the Four Books—chiefly the *Analects* of Confucius and the writings of Mencius, complemented by two shorter treatises on the "Great Learning" and "Doctrine of the Mean." Noticeably absent from this new curriculum were the early histories and poetry. According to some writers, Zhu Xi regarded these as "superficial" and "unimportant," according to others, he merely saw them as secondary to philosophical writings.²⁶ In any case, the perception of history and poetry as too tentative about moral truths and too distractive as art prompted their relegation to a second tier of classical writings. This process of narrowing the core to a few philosophically introspective works, dubbed by one scholar as "interiorization" of the classical canon, apparently has its origins in the late Tang.²⁷ Only in recent decades, however, following the 1241 sanctioning of the new metaphysic as the empire's orthodoxy for purposes of university and examination curricula, could this agenda aspire to universal propagation and acceptance.

Coincident with this reordering of the classical canon was a more sweeping refutation of other intellectual trends, most notably the production of scholarship in paralyzing profusion and the pretenses to erudition that seemed to swell with it. Zhu Xi believed intellectual breadth to have come, in recent generations, at the expense of moral focus, so he would propose the careful reading of a few good books over a cursory reading of many. "Read little but become intimately familiar with what you read," he argues, "for there are a great many books in the world, the reading of which can never be completed."[28] This seems a nostalgic reaction against the Song revolution in printing and publishing, where written materials and contending ideas proliferated to the apparent detriment of "sincere focus" (*cheng*), as espoused by Confucian moralists. Zhu Xi was hardly the first to express consternation at this dilettante approach to learning: similar sentiments had already been expressed in the eleventh and early twelfth centuries.[29] But the problem of quantity over quality seems to have worsened by his time, or so he saw it. Out of concern for restoring a moral focus to intellectual pursuits, Neo-Confucians would eventually regard history and poetry as inferior to philosophical writings—too ethically ambivalent and intellectually distractive. The Cheng-Zhu "revolution" lies precisely in its redirection of literati energies away from historical realities toward philosophical ideals, from material conditions to moral focus.[30]

Traces of this idealized vision of the human experience and the moral perfection that it advanced can readily be identified in the life and values of Wen Tianxiang. At times, he mimicks the distinctive rhetoric of *Daoxue* thinkers, extoling their introspective mission "to exhaust principle and rectify the mind," "to perfect virtue within and then extend it without."[31] He also expresses a strong personal identification with Mencius, the classical idealist whose revival in recent times had occurred largely through the efforts of Song metaphysicians. Of particular appeal was the Mencian notion of "infinite pneuma" (*haoran zhi qi*). This life force that fills both the human body and an infinite universe also makes possible moral goodness.[32] Mencius had called for the cultivation of this life force through a process more akin to self-realization than social conditioning, a notion that particularly intrigued thinkers of the Song as they struggled to enhance Confucian humanism's competitive edge against Buddhist spiritualism. The Mencian perspective had lent to Confucian thought, to wit, a metaphysical coloring heretofore missing, linking the moral conscience of man to the psychic energy of the universe. Moreover, this notion of pneuma, or *qi*, had long been associated

with martial valor and masculine courage, the same force that energizes and invigorates the human will.[33] It was this specific association of pneuma with masculine virility that inspired the title of Wen Tianxiang's "Elegy to Forthright Courage" (*Zheng qi ge*), a tribute to loyalist heroes of times past. The influence of *Daoxue* ethicists upon the political and cultural values of Wen Tianxiang is confirmation of the growing stature and appeal of the school, in late Song, to men of varied intellectual pedigree but common commitment to the rejuvenation of dynasty and regeneration of its cultural institutions.

The perception of moral virtue as modeled on a cosmic order of perfection only partially explains Wen Tianxiang's insistence on perfecting himself through the eternal sanctification of martyrdom. Such adamancy also represents an admission of nagging imperfection or inadequacy that can be redeemed or redressed only through a dramatic display of civic courage. For many a male courtier of the Southern Song, including Wen Tianxiang, defensiveness of the sort relates to dynastic roots in the southeast, a region long perceived as seriously handicapped by lifestyle and values.

In the centuries preceding the unity of Qin and Han, the "south" did not extend much beyond the domain of Chu, a region politically and culturally quite autonomous from the "central states" directly north. Having emerged along the Yangzi River, the south was a land of perilous yet pristine wilderness: a land where hunting and gathering probably surpassed agriculture; a land populated with native shamans and aboriginals, immigrant recluses and exiles; a land possessing a familiar literacy yet an unfamiliar rhetoric, similar institutions but dissimilar customs; a land endowed with an abundance of lakes and rivers but also dreaded disease and pestilence—the antithesis of everything northern.[34] It was the home of Daoism as well. This libertarian ideology, rejecting the social impositions of northern traditions like Confucianism, would advance a radical alternative agenda of individual expression and bequeath to the country, arguably, the most humane of its many philosophies. But by the time of Christ, only two centuries after the imposition of unified rule, the south generally conjures up fewer images of hostile wilderness or Daoist reclusion, northern peoples and their ways having transformed the landscape.[35] Yet from the perspective of those same northerners, the region remained irredeemably alien. Tallying the traits deemed most indecent, first-century historian Ban Gu writes: "The people live on fish and rice. Hunting, fishing, and wood-gathering are their principal activities. Because there is always enough to eat, they are

a lazy and improvident folk, laying up no stores for the future, so confident are they that the supply of food and drink will always be replenished."[36] A certain primitiveness is implicit in such comments, sedentary northerners instinctively disparaging of the hunting and gathering then common to the south. At the same time, a mild climate, sparse population, and ready supplies of water and food seemed to foster in the south radically different attitudes toward material life. Its people appear, in the mindset of northerners at least, as less industrious and frugal, more indolent and frivolous.[37] The virile discipline and self-restraint of the north—"the good heart that only labor can produce," in the words of one prominent thinker of the eleventh century—seemed altogether alien to southerners.[38] Reflecting this, their dialects tended to be soft and their food delicate. Theirs was also the land of the water buffalo, a slow and pacific animal, not the sturdy horse of the northwest nor the stubborn donkey of the northeast. Theirs was the land of sleepy junks and sedan chairs, rather passive modes of transportation.[39]

The wild and primitive traits of the south, excluding Sichuan, had virtually vanished by the fifth century. Moreover, as development of the southeast overtook the interior—as the Wu/Yue region overtook Chu as symbol of the "other"—the south emerged as a serious rival to the cultural hegemony of the north. It was the hostile sweep of north China by a succession of steppe peoples that had elevated the south initially to a place of political sanctuary, subsequently to a place of cultural conservation and rejuvenation. As a succession of northern courts were transplanted in the south, and particularly the southeast, they tended to lose their martial prowess, never fully to regain former territories. Shielded from the north by natural barriers, their armies lost the seasoned discipline that only war can instill; cut off from the gravitational energies of the north, their literati forgot the wholesome customs that only struggle can nurture. But perhaps most importantly, as possessors of a resource-rich and sparsely populated frontier, they developed a different attitude toward conflict. Traditional Chinese writers have long affirmed the region's penchant for accepting a "desperate peace" (gou'an) or "timid retrenchment" (pianan) at nearly any cost.[40] Less certain are the factors responsible for this presumed predisposition. Some modern theorists suggest that conditions of scarce resources are conducive to masculine aggression while plentitude fosters passivity and pacifism. To wit, variation in material need informs variation in the value attached to aggressive or warrior impulses, which in turn informs the validation and identity of men—the very definition of masculinity. As one writer puts it,

"when men are conditioned to fight, manhood is important; where men are conditioned to flight, the opposite is true."[41] For South China, this made compromise more reasonable than confrontation. And this penchant for compromise explains the tendency of southern courts to elevate the statesman above the warrior, artistic and literary expression above war games. A propensity for compromise may have fostered alternative notions of masculinity, where assets like wealth, pedigree, and fecundity replaced physical or aesthetic rigor as alternative symbols of male power.

Few relics of a newly emerging south so vividly exemplify its unique cultural priorities as its literary heritage. Northerners have long censured southern writers for their excessively "ornate, gaudy, and frivolous" style, one devoid of "force and vitality."[42] The southerner (*nanren*), but more specifically southeasterner, seemed too distracted by the creature comforts coincident to abundance and leisure. In a manner rare for traditional China, poetic verse could indulge ostensibly base urges toward romance and eroticism without appearing the least apologetic. The sensuality and eroticism of the *yuefu* genre as well as the romantic effusiveness of palace poetry—largely products of the southeast—would symbolize precisely this propensity for the effete,[43] inciting critics of other regions and periods. "Not suited for the gentleman," says one critic of the early Tang, outraged by the frivolity of it all.[44] Other Tang detractors, perhaps acting on self-serving and provincial interests, lampooned the sultry literature as "dissolute" and "licentious," a corrupting influence on "prevailing customs."[45] The poetry's unmanly qualities went beyond sheer adoption of an embellished idiom or admission of emotional frailty; all too frequently, southern men felt free to celebrate affections for other men, the fair countenance or delicate attire of some young boy who holds the key to an older man's heart.[46] Romantic expressions of this sort, whether heterosexually or homosexually inspired, offended Confucian moralists of the north for two reasons. On the one hand, they represented public display of sentiments which, especially for the literati class, should rightfully be kept private. Furthermore, they affirmed the emotional dependence of literati men on their social inferiors, the female suitor or male beau. This seemed an egregious infraction of the rules of social etiquette. By tradition, poetry should serve some morally edifying aim—a tradition to which sensualists of the south appeared recklessly indifferent.

The classical Chinese word for literary refinement, *wen*—the root for such key concepts as "culture" (*wenhua*) and "civilization" (*wenming*)—

conveyed a wide range of meaning, depending on proper use or improper abuse. It could imply simple literacy as well as literary embellishment, modest decoration as well as excessive adornment, candid eloquence but also cunning grandiloquence.[47] Such ambivalences of meaning and purpose notwithstanding, *wen* was considered indispensable to governance and indeed a necessary complement. As the classical philosopher Han Fei once declared:

> The myriad of objects are certain to wax or wane,
> The myriad of events are certain to relax or rigidify;
> The empire must have *wen* and *wu*,
> Just as bureaucratic order must have rewards and punishments.[48]

This injunction may have its origins in legalism, but it was echoed by contemporary Confucians as well. Lu Sheng, a third century B.C. scholar of the *Odes* who attributed the fall of earlier regimes to the excess of martial severity, would nonetheless conclude that "the mutual deployment of *wen* and *wu* represents the best approach for the long term."[49] The concept of *wen* is even elevated, in such contexts, to a craft or approach to governance. Like rewards and punishments, they seem at one level to be opposites, yet at another to be complements. Moreover, in relating *wen* to rewards and *wu* to punishments, Han Fei affirmed the maternally nurturing aspects of one and the paternally corporal aspects of the other. "The beneficent mother begets a weak child," he writes only a sentence earlier. This is an implicit critique of a Confucian order with its patriarchal facade but maternalistic core—its naive attempt to govern society through such non-coercive principles as benevolence and righteousness, reciprocity and goodness. A similar concern for instilling discipline and spurning indulgence applies to artistic and literary expression. Writing for a different time and context, a modern psychologist declares excess civility to be "inimical to the well-being of men, who need constant gratification for their aggressive drives."[50] Court historians of early China would concur. Commenting on the demise of a southern dynasty, in the fifth century, northern critics would write: "excessive reverence for literary refinement is the path to dynastic demise."[51] Such excess seemed a perennial problem for the southeast where, at least for the first millennium of imperial rule, legalist principles never developed a foothold comparable to the north. Few could convincingly embrace the austere rigor of legalism in a region where conditions, material and strategic, simply did not demand regulations of the sort.

With the rise of Song and reflecting the unique conditions attendant to that rise, a prototypically southern hostility toward the martial enterprise wins a measure of acceptance in the larger political culture that is quite unthinkable for most periods of unified rule, either before or after. Historian Ouyang Xiu, writing at the height of stability in the eleventh century, is not the least equivocal in placing *wen* before *wu*, the literary before the martial. For him, equilibrium in the *wen/wu* equation involves not balance but imbalance. In his own words:

> Martial talents (*wu*) are said to be the probe and medicine for saving a chaotic age, while literary talents (*wen*) are the fat and grain [needed to nourish recovery]. Once the chaos is settled, literary talents must be used to govern. To fail at this is tantamount to permitting a malady to do its harm before administering the probe and medicine, wherein the injury is merely compounded. Thus, the martial enables one to obtain the realm, yet employing the martial to govern the realm invariably gives rise to hegemons and brigands.[52]

The vindication of civilian prejudice against the military by associating it with criminal behavior represents more than mere rhetorical ruse. After all, no group figured more prominently in the criminal element of Song society, its soldiers often recruited among the ranks of larcenous bandits.[53] Yet the response of Ouyang Xiu and the larger civil society proved extreme. Contrary to earlier theorists, who saw *wen* and *wu* as harmonious complements, Song writers like Ouyang Xiu saw them as separate and mutually exclusive: the martial enterprise may be necessary to times of conquest, but it is ruinous to ordinary governance. Not all political leaders of the eleventh century shared his hostility toward the martial enterprise. Some like Wang Anshi and Fan Zhongyan preferred to stress a greater reciprocity or balance between the two.[54] But they all saw governance as chiefly an enterprise of the literati with the military serving a supporting role.

Efforts by Song rulers to harness military men through the deployment of civilian monitors did more than merely tarnish the self-image of those men. It also encouraged segregation of the two groups and a heightened sense of exclusiveness for each.[55] With nomination to court posts increasingly linked to examination credentials, military appointees to high civilian posts grew scarce. In the 1170s, when Emperor Xiaozong seemed modestly sympathetic and deferential toward military advisors, in some measure breaking with established tradition, Chief Councilor Shi Hao was livid in his remonstrance: "The *Way* of the Two

Emperors and the Three Kings has never been entrusted to persons with long lances and huge swords; rather, it is rightfully the domain of scholars wearing round caps and square-toed slippers."[56] Such attitudes would ultimately prompt talented individuals otherwise inclined toward military service to direct their energies elsewhere. Even at the empire's Military Academy, where advanced training was offered in martial arts and strategies, plebes commonly "abandoned their bow and arrow while practicing composition," according to the dynastic history.[57] From the mid-Southern Song, there are reports of military men, envious of the stature of their civilian counterparts, imitating their decorative apparel and lifestyle habits—all to the considerable consternation of an etiquette-conscious court.[58] At the Imperial University of late Song, student ignorance of the simplest of martial arts proved so pervasive that the government came to require basic instruction.[59]

Such celebration of the civil and denigration of the martial appears most intense in the late twelfth and early thirteenth centuries, that is, as the Southern Song entered a period of entente with the north; it was probably less pronounced in the early twelfth century, when a new string of strategic crises may have neutralized anti-military bias.[60] Nonetheless, the literati establishment's ever-tightening grip on the larger dynastic enterprise would ultimately magnify the competence gap between the civil and military bureaucracies. Relative to the other major dynasties, statesmen of Song equally accomplished in the civil and military arts—commonly dubbed "scholar-generals"—had become an endangered species. Chief councilors commonly held concurrent authority over the military bureau, particularly during the twelfth and thirteenth centuries; occasionally, they led troops into battle as well. Yet it was literary skills, not military competence, that launched them to power and informed their values. And the few councilors to make political capital of their martial interests were met with suspicion and contempt. For the thirteenth century, Han Tuozhou, Shi Songzhi, and Jia Sidao are the most visible examples of such failed cross-overs—men repeatedly assailed by cynical observers for "exploiting border conditions to advance their own careers."[61]

The civilian dominance of the military, literary eclipse of the martial, represents more than mere repudiation of an earlier age and its excesses. More importantly, it further reflects a progressive southernization of Song political culture that occurred even before the court had relocated to Linan. Perhaps the most critical first step in this process was the selection of Kaifeng as capital of the Northern Song. Located in the heart of

north China, it stood some six hundred kilometers between the old imperial capital out west at Chang'an and the Pacific coast to the east, and some seven hundred kilometers between the Great Wall to the north and the Yangzi River to the south (see Maps 1a and 1b). This placed a greater distance between the Song and its enemies along the border. But alas, it also served to separate southern troops from northern invaders, military assets from strategic threats. Moreover, the Kaifeng location brought the court closer to a commercially burgeoning southeast, linking metropolitan consumers to southern suppliers. The result was a combination of peace and prosperity, particularly for the eleventh century, that wreaked long-term havoc on the dynasty's security. Scholars have elaborated on the extraordinary material and cultural life of Kaifeng, acknowledging the assorted contributions of a resource-rich south to this metropolitan explosion.[62] Yet it was the south's cultural exports that are most often ignored, despite their critical role in shaping the aesthetic proclivities and martial disdain of the Northern Song.

A criticial institution in such cultural transfer was the prestigious Academy of Painting. Established in Kaifeng at the dynasty's outset, the Academy absorbed an initially sizable number of artists from the conquered courts of the south. Southern artists continued to flow north during the reign of Huizong (r. 1100–1126), arguably the most artistically accomplished monarch in the history of China (see Figure 3).[63] He may have been northern born and bred, but Huizong's southern sensibilities are striking. His calligraphic form is more vulnerable than vigorous, his painting style more studied than spontaneous, his political tone more ambivalent than assertive. He subsidized at utterly staggering levels the construction of metropolitan gardens resplendent with rare flowers and stones, not to mention a massive artificial mountain—the infamous Magic Marchmount.[64] Moreover, this connoisseur of rare objects and patron of the arts had acquisitive propensitites of legendary proportions. Paintings in the imperial collection, for example, swelled to over 6,000 through the forays of palace collectors.[65] Such massive building of art collections and royal gardens seemed obsessive to most observers, a sign of frivolous irresponsibility that carried ponderous political consequences.[66]

The image of effete frivolity to shadow this emperor and his age would begin with Huizong's obsession with the building of art collections and royal gardens—materialist impulses—but found confirmation in his scandalous personal behavior. He may have been serious in

his devotion to Daoism, but religious piety often seemed mere camouflage for the pursuit of lecherous fantasy.[67] For example, his favorite
Daoist priests, or "feathered guests" as these delicately-clad men were
sometimes called, were commonly afforded unrestricted access to the
palace. There, a binge of feasting and intoxication invariably followed.
Worse yet, on at least one occasion an intoxicated male guest fell asleep
with head cushioned by the emperor's lap—the two seemingly intent on
flaunting both sexual and social decorum.[68] Compared to most major
civilizations, traditional China is not known for homophobic inhibitions and taboos, particularly as in this case, where the men involved
maintain a firm footing in the heterosexual world—Huizong sired over
sixty children, after all![69] Still, indiscreet displays of the sort infuriated
court observers, experts of palace protocol quick to intuit the larger
symbolism behind the slightest imperial deed. The Huizong reign was
also tainted by a dangerous expansion in eunuch power.[70] Indeed, it was
the only time in the dynasty's long span of three centuries when such
neutered men would succeed in systematically usurping the legitimate
powers of civil servants, men to whom they should rightfully defer.
After all, proscriptions against eunuch power had been issued at the outset of the Northern Song and then reiterated at the outset of the Southern Song. The regulations were, however, to be relaxed in subsequent
reigns,[71] thus further reinforcing the image of elevated effeminacy, *yin*
in ascent over *yang*.

Taken together, trends of this sort came to symbolize everything
wrong with this once glorious age of experimentation in politics and the
arts. Reflecting retrospectively on the character of Huizong and the collapse of his government, traditional historians have often censured his
artistic style using such adjectives as "decadent" and "weak," suggesting
an effeminacy highly reminiscent of the Southern Dynasties.[72] Worse
yet, effeminacy in artistic expression seemed to carry over into literary
expression. A moralistically outraged Zhu Xi, born only a few years after
the abdication and ultimate captivity of Huizong, would link this nadir
in dynastic power to the literary trends of the day:

> At the outset of our dynasty (in the late tenth century) writing was always
> serious and mature. . . . Although at times clumsy, its expression was force-
> ful and direct. It aspired to be skillful without achieving that goal, thereby
> becoming unsophisticated and honest. . . . But by the time of Su Shi (the
> late eleventh century) writing had already begun its rush toward excessive
> cleverness and by the Zhenghe and Xuanhe eras (1111–1125), it had reached
> an extreme of gorgeous mannerism.[73]

Figure 3. "Literati Gathering." Attributed to Song Emperor Huizong (r. 1101–1126). Courtesy of National Palace Museum, Taipei, Taiwan ROC.

Zhu Xi was scarcely original in lamenting the overly sophisticated tastes of recent times and linking these to the atrophy of dynastic power: the father of Su Shi, Su Xun (1009–1066), had expressed strikingly similar concerns a century earlier.[74] Too distracted by material and aesthetic pursuits, Northern Song rulers, as both product and personification of this hybrid culture, had acquired an image of emasculated dilettantes which left their dynasty uniquely vulnerable to the assaults and insults of more vigorous nomadic predators.

Rulers of the Southern Song, for all the advantages of hindsight, proved either unwilling or unable to elude the pitfalls of predecessors in Kaifeng. Their capital at Linan, among various prospective sites in the south, was long regarded as inferior—less majestic than Jiankang, less defensible than Mingzhou, and more "peripheral" than locations out west. Worse yet, southern rulers ruthlessly perpetuated earlier policies of harnessing the military, even at the cost of a permanent fracturing of the empire. Also to augment court control, southern monarchs continued to concentrate the cream of the empire's military crop near their eastern capital. This left locations farther west perilously vulnerable—entire circuits sometimes defended by only a few thousand regulars.[75] Decision-makers at Linan, like predecessors in Kaifeng, found it cheaper and safer in the short-run to buy peace. Yet with annual subsidies to the enemy came hidden costs at home. The entire arrangement lured the Song court into a false sense of security, which in turn inhibited the needed investment in defense. It also afforded this southern empire, after a few generations, the perilous luxury of indulging its material and aesthetic impulses irrespective of political consequences.

No monarch of the Southern Song was as artistically gifted as Hui-zong, none squandered a comparable level of public funds on costly frivolities. Yet progressively over the course of the period—particularly after the transitional first and second reigns had passed—they became seduced by the bounty around them. As great consumers of bourgeois objects, foods, and festivities, they gradually assimilated into their southern environment. Following in their lead, predictably, were well-off subjects like Jia Sidao, but also men and women of far lesser station. The effects of such economic changes on the social order are documented in the writings of Yuan Cai. This twelfth-century literatus, a man of modest stature but great insight, writes with candid indigation: "Market areas, streets and alleys, tea houses and wine shops are places frequented by all kinds of inferior people. When our sort has to pass through them, we must be dignified in speech and deportment. That way we can avoid

the problem of being casually insulted by them."[76] This seems to suggest a correlation between the growth of cities and the decline of traditional distinctions between the educated elite and the illiterate masses, the empire's leaders and followers. A quiet revolution seemed underfoot in the less structured urban enclaves of the south, their material and sensual amenities eroding the barriers of class and diminishing the power of privilege.

MARKETING AN ALIEN VIRILITY

These broad changes, perceived by some as a steady deterioration in the moral fabric and political will of society, were certain to trigger a backlash. And not terribly unlike a bourgeois-capitalist West in modern times, conservative reaction in China would culminate in a retreat away from effete intellectualism and toward a rustic athleticism.[77] The setting for this reaction would be the late twelfth and early thirteenth centuries, the mid-Southern Song, and an important mirror can be found in literary expression.

Modern scholars of Southern Song literature such as Lin Shuen-fu, noting the growing popularity of a genre known as "songs on objects" (*yongwu ci*), suggest a shifting focus from the "lyrical self" to the "external object."[78] That is, the lyrical poetry of the twelfth century, with its expansive contemplation of the individual experience and its connection to the larger world and cosmos, narrows its focus in the early thirteenth century to tangible and readily defined objects. The result, so the argument goes, is the poet's retreat to a "miniature world" where the self is viewed through objects and the poetic vision progressively shrinks. This development grows substantially out of the Neo-Confucian metaphysic, with its pursuit of knowledge and moral cultivation through the "investigation of objects." It is informed as well by the increased immersion of the late Southern Song literati into an object-oriented material culture, one most visible in the prosperous coastal cities of the southeast but scarcely confined to them. Narrowing horizons also belies the heightened frustration of Song men with political action: expansion of the educated population had served to intensify competition for a finite number of civil service slots, while executives entrenched at the bureaucracy's apex obstructed the advance of others. In consequence, intellectuals shorn of greater ambitions became more reclusive in lifestyle and more insular in cognition, the poetry at once a reflection of alienation and a vehicle for subtle protest.

Critical to this theory of narrowed horizons and intellectual timidity, particularly for the early thirteenth century, is the declining visibility and influence of a literary cohort that prospered in the preceding century, a cohort fiercely nationalistic and aggressively activist. Dubbed by modern scholars as "patriotic poets," these artist-statesmen were most prominently represented by Xin Qiji (1140–1207), Lu You (1125–1210), and Yang Wanli (1127–1206), men whose poetry exhibits a venomous antipathy for the alien occupiers of north China and an indomitable will to obliterate that scourge.[79] All three men flourished in the late twelfth century and died in the first decade of the thirteenth, their vision seeming to die with them. That vision was one of dynastic restoration—revitalizing the south in order to reunify the entire empire. And consistent with longstanding tradition,[80] poetry was their chosen vehicle for articulating this agenda. Of the three, only Xin Qiji was a northern transplant, the others native to the southeast. Yet they were equally aware of the magnitude of the challenge—instilling martial aggressiveness in a traditionally pacifist region, northern dominance in a peripheral south.

With some measure of envy, southerner Lu You would revel in the vigor and virility of the north, along with the social conditions conducive to these. In the poem "Traveling the Southern Mountains," written to commemorate a trip to the border, he writes:

> This land neighboring Han and Qin, heroic in courage and customs,
> Playing swing rope and football, they divide into teams.
> Clover extending to the clouds, the hoof of horses strong.
> Willows enveloping the roads, the sound of carriages pitched.[81]

Northern virility is reflected in the popularity of athletic activities such as Chinese football and the presence of implements of war like the horse and carriage. At the same time, the three men believed it possible to cultivate similarly aggressive customs in southern men, despite a radically different context. This required, as a critical first step, raising the ethnic consciousness of Chinese men, while dehumanizing the alien enemy—playing on primitive instincts of survival and fear of the foreign. In pursuit of such racially based differentiation and exclusion, they employ in their poetry a host of derogatory adjectives in depictions of Jurchen occupiers: "insane" and "slave-like," "wild" and "rapacious," "treacherous" and "deceitful."[82] The metaphor of animal or animalistic behavior is used as well. In one highly effective use of this rhetorical skill, Lu You likens northern occupiers to fierce tigers who feed on humans.[83] The

author here is clearly exploiting the longstanding use of tiger as metaphor for rapacious bandits and tax-collectors, individuals scarcely human and only to be despised.

Further to convince southern men of their potential as men of war, historical precedent is employed. Lu You writes:

> Now, deteriorating illness confines me to bed;
> Shaking my fist, I still long to contribute to the campaign.
> Southern men, who says they know nothing of war?
> In times past, it was the three clans of Chu that annihilated Qin.[84]

In reaching back to classical times and then elevating Chu as representative of the entire south—a convention not used for many centuries—a defensive Lu You has latched onto a precedent too remote from the Song reality to be rhetorically credible.[85] He surely understood and agonized over this. Thus, his own personal example of martial commitment assumed greater symbolism as vindication of southern manhood. The virility that he exhibits—infirm and bed-ridden yet still thirsting for the enemy's blood—emerges as almost superhuman or at least super*man*ly.

Apart from setting personal examples of martial grit, these loyalist zealots acknowledged that propagating martial values in the south required a conscious suppression of indigenous impulses toward literary refinement. This stands in contradistinction to Ouyang Xiu, a century earlier, who expressly linked the redemption of the Song literatus to the rejuvenation of *civilian* virtues, literary skills representing a key component of these. The dramatic shift from a "literary culture," for the eleventh century, to an "ethical culture" for the twelfth and thirteenth has been documented by intellectual historians.[86] This reputed "counterculture" owes much to Confucian fundamentalism and its repudiation of moral and political expedience. Yet at the hands of patriotic poets, these ethical tendencies become vastly distorted and assume an anti-literary coloring. In an ironic use of the highest literary form—poetry—to attack the prevailing literary culture, Yang Wanli writes:

> Don't read books!
> Don't chant poetry
> When you read books your eye balls wither away, leaving bare sockets.
> When you chant poems your heart drains out slowly with each word.[87]

Going a step further, Lu You even attempts to distance himself from the intellectual establishment to which he belongs, having grown to detest

its pedantic proclivities. Indeed, something approaching self-hatred emerges in the following passage:

> The heartland so long lost to invaders,
> a man of spirit must drown his chest in tears.
> Don't despise me for a bookish scholar—
> a horse under me, I could strike down the foe![88]

Xin Qiji joins in the chorus as well, suggesting the irrelevence of intellectual pursuits to the enterprise of dynastic reconstruction:

> How I regret, of poetry and classics,
> Ten thousand volumes cannot help me to serve the empire
> While the land is sinking![89]

Later in the same poem, Xin Qiji enjoins young men "to renounce the aspiration to don the tassels of officialdom." It is the powerful chief councilors, after all, who have consistently impeded intervention up north. His words are echoed by Lu You, who laments the potentially "brave warriors who senselessly waste their years of youthful vigor" due to the appeasement policies of court officers.[90] This anti-elitist and almost self-abasing hostility goes well beyond the more moderate militancy of the preceding generation. The female poet Li Qingzhao (b. 1083), for example, was profoundly frustrated and angry as she wrote, in the mid-twelfth century, the following passage:

> Alive we need heroes among the living
> Who when dead will be heroes among the ghosts.
> I cannot tell how much we miss Xiang Yu
> Who preferred death to crossing East of the River.[91]

Nonetheless, in lamenting the nadir in martial courage of the mid-twelfth century, Li Qingzhao does not direct that anger against her own class. Even the militant moralist Zhu Xi, his aforementioned attacks against literati pretenses notwithstanding, emerges as far less rabidly anti-intellectual than these patriotic zealots of his own day.

These men and their poetic pyrotechnics aspired to more than mere critique of status quo policies. Permeated with themes of heroic revelry and abandon, it represents a nostalgic romanticization of primitive man and his warrior roots as rare for the preceding eleventh century as it was for the subsequent thirteenth.[92] A stirring "Song to the Stalwart Soldier," by Lu You, is highly representative of this genre:

Soldiers resent their poor and humble station, distinctions of pedigree,
Rich and powerful nowhere to be found, their hair now a resplendent
    white!
'Tis better to serve the empire by campaigning a myriad of miles away
Where the bitter cold cracks the skin and the wind kicks up sand.

Pledging to risk death to requite the Son of Heaven,
Metal helmets the color of armored shields, the color of water,
A real man falls to the ground, shooting in every direction.
How can one withdraw to a mountain retreat like recluse Yuan Qi?

The clouds of the frontier are vast, the Yellow River deep,
The new walls of Liangzhou as high as eighty feet.
The sojourner who bites the wind and sleeps with dew, so bitter a life!
This is a test of the normal heart, one hardened like iron and stone.[93]

The reader is immediately struck by the inhumanly harsh conditions of
the western frontier—a seemingly infinite expanse of desolate plains
and desert, as severe in its daytime heat as in its nighttime cold. Yet the
invincible warrior succeeds in conquering such natural obstacles and
then proceeds, with steel nerves and superior marksmanship, quite consciously to jeopardize his own life in the pursuit of maximum kill. A
dedication to honor exceeding his love of life—a primitive consciousness where reflex supplants reason, the heart supplants the mind—is
what makes this warrior "a real man," or *nan'er* in the idiom of Lu You.
He is unmistakably young as well, as evidenced by his exceptional
strength and dexterity. Peculiarly, such warriors are often cast in a phys-
iognomy distinctively alien, especially to the man of south China. In
another poem, Lu You describes his hero-warrior as sporting "a beard
like porcupine bristles and a face like angular quartz"—undeniable
markings of hardened men of the steppe.[94] It seems curious that writers
who relish in dehumanizing aliens in one passage would elsewhere celebrate, almost enviously, the most primitive of their physical traits and
survival instincts. They obviously separated, in their minds, the physical characteristics of barbarians from the people possessing them.

Related to this veneration of physical strength is a celebration of
youth rare for any dynasty, but especially the Song. Wars have long been
fought by the young, including boys in their mid-teens, but for China's
late imperial period, masculinity tended to manifest itself more through
strength of character than muscular mass. By challenging such traditions, these patriotic poets were engaged in a cultural subversion of
sorts. Their mission might even be seen as politically subversive. After

all, entrenched in the civil service establishment was a coterie of senior pacifists whose policies would scarcely be swayed by a small group of radical writers and their flights of heroic fantasy. Yet our patriotic poets, in speaking to an audience of impressionably romantic youth, had sought to inspire future generations who might subvert the timid policies of the old. And indeed, the greater frequency of court violence in the thirteenth century—particularly violence emanating from the academic circuit and directed at perceived pacifists—may well reflect the measure of their success at reaching the empire's youth and stirring them to acts of political subterfuge.

With reference to Wen Tianxiang, the influence of these militant poets is unmistakable, despite the decades separating their lives from his. It is reflected in his advocacy of an athletically disciplined and virile literati, in his denunciation of state controls on the military and popular prejudices against soldiers, in his egotistically exaggerated sense of personal duty and sacrifice. It is also reflected in his nostalgia for the militarized order of Tang when regional commanders seemed aggressive protectors of local interests, not the timid and paranoid managers of his own day. Specific terms such as "real man" or "heart of iron," while not original to our lyrical patriots, apparently came to Wen Tianxiang through them and appears repeatedly in his writings. The irony of their legacy lies in its relatively circumscribed influence in the generations more immediate to them. Save for university campuses in the capital, a broader appeal would only occur as the dynasty entered its last desperate decades. Modern literary scholars might attribute this to a shifting aesthetic focus: the prospective readers of the early thirteenth century, arguably, lacked the expansive vision and extroverted impulses of earlier generations. Yet the sad reality is that these romanticizers of dynastic virility, however dazzling their verse, were all too familiar to contemporary audiences as political time bombs, too ideologically rigid to offer an acceptable agenda of action.

The patriotic fervor of these twelfth-century poets did not exist, after all, in a political vacuum. It was informed partly by the militant sympathies of the emperor himself. When the thirty-three year old Xiaozong came to power in 1162, war had been raging for over a half year. It was a war initiated by the Jurchen, but once begun would incite expansionist elements in the south. Their emerging spokesman at court, the impassioned scholar-general Zhang Jun (1096–1164), even won the emperor's endorsement of a surprise offensive. The end result, a speedy and decisive rout, left a humiliated Song pleading for peace and Zhang Jun

demoted in disgrace.[95] Our three poets, young contemporaries of the commander, were strong supporters both during his campaign and even after its stunning failure. The political climate would later turn moderate, but never their political platform, which in subsequent decades grew glaringly anachronistic and naïve, eventually even irrelevant. Forty years later, when a new and not-so-illustrious chief of state promoted a second northern offensive, it seemed almost farcical that the two surviving poets would again lend their endorsement. The Kaixi War, of 1206, ended less than two years later in even greater disaster and its architect, Han Tuozhou, vilified by all but a minority.[96] And this new failure marks the further eclipse of militant politicians by cautious managers, an eclipse destined to last over a half century.[97] The revanchist agenda had been undone, in effect, by the blind zeal of its own advocates.

Among these rabid militants, consistently poor political judgment was compounded by a dangerously cavalier and even abusive use of official powers. Historical records allude to a number of such indiscretions, but none so dangerous as the actions of Xin Qiji. While prefect of Tanzhou in the early 1180s, for example, he set out to organize thousands of local men into "Flying Tigers" militia, a reserve unit of skilled fighters ready for emergency deployment.[98] His motives were doubtlessly noble, but he had acted without authorization from the court and despite the considerable cost of support services; and he implemented the scheme in a region far removed from the border, at a time of long-standing peace. A palace anxious about undue waste ordered an immediate halt in the project; Xin Qiji responded by concealing court orders and accelerating his program. A breach of official protocol of this magnitude could well have landed him in prison, a risk he knowingly took with rather reckless abandon. For precisely such reasons, it took some time for the misguided deeds of the well-intended to be gradually lost on the consciousness of policymakers, established and aspiring alike. But as the fortunes of dynasty waned and its martial inadequacies became magnified, the agenda of once discredited radicals acquired a newly seductive lustre.

VISUALIZING THE PRESENT THROUGH THE PAST

Generations hence it would be their "heroic vigor" (*haojie*) or "courageous temperament" (*qijie*), not any specific deed, for which these patriotic poets were most endearingly remembered.[99] To the Chinese reader, not unlike their counterparts elsewhere, these represent virtues quite

specific to men.[100] The sole woman writer in Song times described in similar fashion, Li Qingzhao, is also acknowledged as uncommonly masculine in literary style—a remarkable feat but surely an ideal to which few other women of her day aspired.[101] After all, as the male population of the late Song times struggled to reclaim the primitive virility of the past, an extra measure of diligence came to be exerted to distance themselves from potentially corrupting influences of their environment. This demanded, on the one hand, a new commitment to nurturing a martial aggressiveness and sensual temperance in men—a rigorous regimen of self-denial that borders on masochism.[102] On the other hand, the edification of the Confucian male required more socially circumspect conduct by Song women—female conformity to traditional norms being a sign of deference to male leadership. Reflected in these urges to realign gender relations are insecurities whose roots lie beyond the south and before the twelfth century.[103]

It was not only current conditions that informed the dynamic between Song men and women, but also the recent past—the Tang and Five Dynasties. Based on the revisionist histories of Ouyang Xiu, both written in the mid-eleventh century, it is abundantly clear that many men of Song saw the instability of the preceding period as a function of *yin* in ascent over *yang*, feminine over masculine forces. This is reflected in the romantic naivete of male rulers and the exploitation of such vulnerabilities by assertive eunuchs and women of the palace.

Palace women of Tang were among the most politically daring of China's entire history, triggering unthinkable acts of mutiny in the military and usurpation of the throne. This was owed partly to their own considerable resourcefulness, partly to a relationship of greater equality with husbands. But it is also due to a succession of "muddled and senile" emperors, according to historian Ouyang Xiu, men of the mid-Tang whose insatiable appetite for the sensual had permitted an illicit encroachment on the imperial sway by unworthy female favorites. Elaborating in his *New History of the Tang*, he writes:

> Alas, the calamity of women in the world is grave indeed! In the several decades from Gaozong to Zhongzong (649–709), the empire again incurred the calamity of women and the Tang imperium had, in fact, expired before being revived. Zhongzong was not spared his own life and Empress Wei subsequently saw her entire clan exterminated. Xuanzong (r. 712–756) had a personal hand in suppressing the disorder and ample opportunity to reflect on it all, yet he too fell victim to a woman.[104]

In sum, rulers of mid-Tang, not fit for governing their women, had themselves invited the political turmoil that tainted the entire era. Yet restoring balance to the political order was quite simple: it required little more than the restitution of male dominance over public affairs.

Apart from such political indecencies, palace women of preceding centuries could be scandalous in their personal indiscretions. In the late seventh century, Empress Wu Zetian (d. 705) brazenly schemed to enter the harem of two separate monarchs, father and son. Tantamount to incest, this act turned out to be mere prelude to a half century of infractions of every conceivable convention, political and social.[105] She eventually ruled as "emperor" of her own dynasty. The moral turpitude of powerful women seemingly persisted into the Five Dynasties, some three centuries later. The consort of Zhuangzong (r. 923–926), Lady Liu, won initial elevation to empress through similar acts of palace intrigue. And following her husband's death, she dared to take up with another man. Still more controversial was Lady Wang, the consort of Mingzong (r. 926–933) whose wily machinations were responsible for numerous royal deaths. She would survive the prevailing violence and even the collapse of the Later Tang house, but moving into the palaces of new dynasts seemed the ultimate infidelity in the eyes of male observers. Her wish may have been merely to retain the regal lifestyle to which she had grown accustomed, yet appearances suggested otherwise. Palace indiscretions of this sort seemed egregious even to contemporaries: it suggested a dangerous irreverence among elite women toward the political institution of monarchy, the social institution of marriage, and longstanding conventions about sexual propriety. Yet under the Song, male historians would reserve an inordinate measure of righteous fury for such women, attributing the fall of most of the Five Dynasties to the intoxication of royal men with the alluring wiles of women.

Factors other than sensual appeal were responsible, on the other hand, for the inclination of emperors of the seventh to tenth centuries to place their trust in another community of controversial insiders and symbol of *yin* power—palace castrati. For this group Ouyang Xiu reserved a special measure of rhetorical venom. Many a Tang eunuch had infiltrated the highest levels of government, especially the metropolitan armies, where they led men into battle and bartered military might for political advantage. Subversion of civil service practice aside, Ouyang Xiu took greater offense to "their emasculated spirit that lacks vigor and soft sentiments that fluctuate." This is reference to the effeminate body and mind of castrated men, physical deformities having ostensibly

induced distemper and caprice.[106] Growing out of such deformity is also the presumption of a moral bankruptcy exceeding even the most base of women. In his *Historical Records of the Five Dynasties*, Ouyang Xiu writes:

> Since antiquity, the roots of eunuch havoc on the human world lay deeper even than the ravages of women. For women, it lies merely with sensuality, but the harm done by eunuchs has no single source. Involved in matters of state, they grow close and familiar while their minds tend to be brooding and dispassionate. Through trifling good turns they can identify the wishes of others and through petty confidences they can secure the heart of others, the monarch inevitably seduced into trust and intimacy with them.[107]

Confucian literati could have more easily countenanced an emperor's exploitation of eunuchs for mere sexual sport—as commonly occurred in the West—in which case favor would focus on individual lovers and likely die with them. Yet for China, bonds between the two tended to be principally emotional. As men insulated from the outside world and naive about contacts with peers, emperors and eunuchs shared a common dysfunction as social beings. Moreover, the former were easily seduced by the nurturing qualities of the latter—men whose "sweet talk" is commonly contrasted against the "courageous candor" of the dedicated male advisor. In this competition between maternal indulgence and paternal discipline, literati discipliners rarely prevailed. The invincibility of eunuchs had also grown, historically, out of institutional supports within the palace. Thus, the deaths of neither the imperial patron nor a few favored eunuchs could dislodge them, once their tentacles were securely latched onto the reins of power. In sheer durability, eunuch power differed radically from consort power, yet the two shared a personal intimacy with the monarch, one emotional and the other sensual, in either case introducing an irrational unpredictability to palace affairs that was certain to trigger spasmic tirades within the civil service.

The Song was scarcely immune to the knavery of eunuchs and consorts, but neither faction ever accumulated the enduring clout of earlier dynasties. Wary bureaucrats proved too jealous in protecting their own powers while institutional checks proved too elaborate. Only occasionally did individual consorts and eunuchs emerge as potent powerbrokers and this inevitably triggered a viscerally intense response from an historically conscious civil service. For the thirteenth century, such palace surrogates surfaced chiefly under monarchs exceptionally alienated or ambivalent toward royal responsibilities. Alienation was cer-

tainly the case for Emperor Ningzong, a muddled man raised in a violent household and harangued by senior statesmen. Turning reclusive, he deferred to an exceedingly astute wife, Empress Yang. By mid-century, under the sensually distracted Lizong, empresses were eclipsed by eunuchs—Dong Songchen perhaps the most hated of these illicit surrogates of the emperor. With this shift, literati grew increasingly alarmed, seeing in the ascent of eunuch power a more compelling symbol of dynastic emasculation.

There is no concrete evidence of "unnatural" intimacies between Emperor Lizong and his castrated favorite, but their unusually close bonds conveyed an image of political impotence all the same. Twice in the late 1250s, Wen Tianxiang petitioned the court in remonstrance against the rise of *yin* over *yang*, feminine over masculine forces. In his daring essay for the palace examination, this young man of twenty writes: "When not focused on Heaven, it is said, we focus on man. When not focused on reason, we focus on desire. When not focused on the clarity of *yang*, we focus on the dullness of *yin*. . . . When the clarity of *yang* is inadequate to prevail over the dullness of *yin*, then a clear *yang* will contrarily be subverted by a dull *yin*."[108] In effect, Wen Tianxiang added a naturalized dimension to this perceived imbalance of politics as he castigates the rulers of Han and Tang for failing to be "pure in heart," permitting personal inadequacies compounded by their "intimacy with eunuchs and women" to obscure universal truth and reason. He similarly criticized eunuch influence under his own dynasty which, left unchecked, was certain to wreak havoc. In preceding centuries, historian Ouyang Xiu had sought to curb the illicit behavior of palace women by "strictly securing the screens and curtains." A more recent social thinker, Yuan Cai, had sought to control the wives and daughters of elite households by confining them to the "inner courtyards." In a similar vein, Wen Tianxiang proposed harnessing the influence of *yin* forces through scrupulous monitoring and timely purge.[109] Yet in the true spirit of Confucian humanism, he also aspired to a system of volitional controls acquired through social conditioning. When he declares the mission of national salvation as "not something to which a mere woman should aspire," Wen Tianxiang seeks to clarify for the feminine courtier—explicitly women but implicitly eunuchs—the limits of their legitimate involvement in political affairs.[110]

The accession of child monarchs beginning in 1274 would restore women to centerstage politics. The first dowager regency in nearly two centuries, it was certain to trigger an instinctively defensive response in

male statesmen, especially in light of recent confrontations with palace eunuchs. Even though the dowagers seemed not to covet their unexpected catapult to power, literati close to the center nonetheless expended considerable energy articulating the limits of female regents. Such concerns are highlighted in assorted public pronouncements composed by Wen Tianxiang for the Grand Dowager, Xie Qiao.[111] On the one hand, frequent reference occurs to classical models for the political woman, stressing the themes of deference to male authority and impassiveness to power. He repeatedly alludes, for example, to women in the life of King Wen, one of the founding fathers of an illustrious Zhou over two millennia ago. The king's virtuous wife, according to tradition, had given freely of her political council but invariably in the spirit of subtle deference to male authority; his proper mother had proven perennially mindful of her son and daughter-in-law.[112] Shifting to the present, Wen Tianxiang lavishes praise on the Grand Dowager herself and her embrace of a stolid solitude, a Daoist-like reclusiveness that ultimately empowers her male handlers. On the other hand, he frequently reminds her of the awesome weight of history to praise or censure depending on the degree of a regent's conformity to political traditions. He writes in one passage: "For rectifying customs and reinforcing the norms of humanity, the world will sing eternal praises to the virtue of Your Highness."[113] He is confirming, in effect, the dual responsibilities of both dowagers to a world of contemporary observers and an eternity of critical historians— men scrupulous and harsh in their moralistic judgments.

By the early thirteenth century, mere reiteration of the boundaries between outer and inner court—the legitimate realms of male and female—would seem insufficient. Wen Tianxiang thus insisted on a "dynamic regeneration" or "potent uplifting" of manly courage, his objective being to make men of his own day less vulnerable to the sweet and sensuous. Images such as "potent uplifting" (*zhuang zheng*) are markedly masculine and the message of male revelry unmistakable. Nonetheless, he did not fabricate his heroes in the manner of the patriotic poets discussed earlier. In the tradition of Confucian realism, Wen Tianxiang looked instead to the past for bona fide models. Perhaps most illustrative of this historical-mindedness is his highly celebrated "Elegy to Forthright Courage" (*Zhengqi ge*), written during his final years of captivity. Spanning more than a millennium, he provides pithy profiles for a succession of courageous men who knowingly risked their own lives for a higher political principle, generally the cause of dynasty. Many died in violent retribution, some suffered a seemingly interminable incarcera-

tion or exile, others served as lightning rods for instilling valor in others. For each reference there is an untold story, stories familiar to the Song reader and strung together with consummate coherence and eloquence:

Heaven and Earth have this Courageous Spirit
And, intermingling with them, it infuses various shapes and forms.
Below, it forms rivers and cliffs,
Above, it shapes the sun and stars,
In humans, it is known as the endless flow....
Yet only in times of despair is it made manifest
Through the vivid vignettes of one man, then another.

It emerges—
　In Qi, through the inscriptions of the grand historian [murdered for
　　his veracity],
　In Jin, through the brush of Dong Hu [ostracized for his reproof],
　In Qin, through the cudgel of Zhang Liang [killed for conspiring
　　against evil],
　In Han, through the pennant of Su Wu [jailed as emissary to the
　　enemy].

It is evidenced—
　Through the head of Commander Yan Yan [severed out of loyalty],
　Through the blood of Chamberlain Ji Shao [spilt while protecting his
　　king],
　Through the teeth of Zhang Xun of Suiyang [crushed in anger against
　　treachery],
　Through the tongue of Yan Gaoqing of Changshan [mangled for hav-
　　ing cursed rebel captors].

It may appear in the cap [of recluse Guan Ning] of Liaodong, with an
integrity pure like ice and snow.

Or in [Zhuge Liang's] Dispatch to Departing Troops,
Whose robust valor moved the Spirits to tears.

It may appear in the paddle [of Zu Ti] beaten against the water, in passage,
As he made chivalrous vows to swallow the barbarous Jie.
Or in the mace [of Duan Xiushi] used to pummel bandits
And split the skulls of accomplices to sedition.

The times of these wise men may now seem remote,
Their paradigm may lie in the past;
But as I open a book to read under shadowed eaves,
The way of the ancients is reflected on my face.[114]

Among the dozen or so individuals alluded to, explicitly or implicitly, roughly half are of military stock, the others mostly distinguished courtiers. The former perished largely in the combustive context of military confrontation, the latter more so in the dedicated execution of their political charge—yet all knew the violent cost of conviction. A balance between men of civilian and military background was quite conscious. It reflects, in part, the author's commitment to refurbishing the currently tarnished image of martial men by highlighting their historical record of chivalrous courage. It also serves to confirm, more importantly, the potential for loyalist dedication even among literarily inclined Confucians. The *Historical Records of the Five Dynasties* had initially questioned that dedication by exposing civilian officers of the tenth century as utterly devoid of loyalist impulses.[115] Author Ouyang Xiu had employed a combination of guilt and shame, in effect, to impugn the loyalist record of literati past and ultimately incite those of his own day to aspire to a higher ethical standard. Wen Tianxiang would not contest outright the historical accuracy of Ouyang Xiu's generalization about a void of civilians among tenth-century loyalists, even though the exceptions were numerous and widely known.[116] He assumed, instead, a more positive approach of indoctrination through edification. Enumerating a long list of civilian martyrs for Han, Tang, and the intervening periods of disunion, he could implicitly challenge Ouyang Xiu while retaining the deference due a thinker he otherwise respected. An ongoing dialogue with Ouyang Xiu is especially apparent in another passage, where Wen Tianxiang presents loyalists of his own day as almost exclusively civilians.[117] This is the exact opposite of Ouyang Xiu's findings for the tenth century and just as historically inaccurate. Rhetorical fervor had gotten the better of both men.

At the same time that he held up one-time civilian officers as loyalist worthies, Wen Tianxiang seemed to anticipate his own dynasty as destined to set for posterity a radically new and inspiring record of loyalist principle. It had already set other records of political and cultural attainment far exceeding most other dynasties. Even before its emperors had abdicated and nostalgia set in, Wen Tianxiang would boast of the historic triumphs of Song: the inimitable vigor and purity of its philosophical orthodoxy, the cordial and deferential reciprocity between rulers and statesmen, and the exceptional governing talents of most monarchs. In the "liberal" and "decisive" Xiaozong, for example, he saw an emperor who compared favorably with the all-time best.[118] Such enlightened and beneficent rule created unique bonds between Con-

fucian literati and the royal house, and demanded reciprocity in the form of loyalty to state.[119] In light of the Song chauvinism implicit in statements of the sort, it seems curious that his "Elegy to Forthright Courage" contains no moral exemplars of his own dynasty. It was certainly not for lack of compelling models, who win plenty of praise from Wen Tianxiang elsewhere in his writings. Rather, the omission seems quite consciously intended to illustrate the potent power of history to immortalize men so remote as otherwise to be forgotten. As he writes elsewhere:

> Since time immemorial men have died,
> Yet the loyal and righteous for long do not perish.

And again,

> The son of man was born to perform public deeds,
> The chivalrous hero dies to bequeath a noble reputation.[120]

For the public man, it is as though moral repute can replace even progeny as the vehicle for conquering death.

Another striking anomaly with reference to Wen Tianxiang's "Elegy" is the paucity of southern men among his pillars of loyalism. We have noted earlier this southern man's veritable obsession with validating himself and his region, especially as they relate to martial propensities. Yet his single-most celebrated writing is dominated by men and contexts distinctively northern: only two of his twelve heroes can be even remotely related to a southern cause.[121] This may well be a function of sheer historiography, southern men being heretofore underrepresented in historical sources. It may also reflect this southerner's need to prove himself culturally conversant with northern traditions, a century and a half of political division having shaken the confidence of Southern Song intellectuals as mediators of mainstream values. Concern with linking southern men to northern values is reflected in the very title of his elegy—the same *zhengqi* rendered earlier as "proper energy"—as if to suggest that the south's future redemption lies in mimicking northern models of ethics and manhood. Finally, in the last months of his life as he confronted an imminent death, Wen Tianxiang probably sought to stress themes both universal and eternal. His Elegy would have to transcend the parochialism of time and region, rather than be corrupted by these.

THE FUGITIVE HERO

It may seem something of a cliché to characterize the literati of imperial China, relative to the educated elsewhere, as more "historically conscious"—well versed in oral and written traditions of the past and sensitive to their own future standing within those traditions. Lacking an indigenous religion to harness the human ego and increasingly hostile to an imported Buddhism, the censure of history acquired ever greater gravity to Song intellectuals. Yet Wen Tianxiang, by no overstatement, transformed this benign consciousness into a baneful obsession. Nearly half of his extant writings, written in jail as he awaited execution, were clearly informed by this obsession with historical standing. At one point, he eulogizes a martyr of the early twelfth century and then ponders, "Today, I mourn this gentleman. In the future, who will grieve for me?"[122] It was not enough to be mourned by a surviving wife and brother, nor even by a nephew now adopted as son and the progeny he would provide. Wen Tianxiang required more importantly the recognition of peers, men of similar station who could relate personally to his own moral dilemma. This urge grows out of a perception of himself as an agent of history, which at times energized him to fight on and ultimately impelled him to die for dynasty.

In many ways, Wen Tianxiang personifies precisely the heroic dedication that Lu You and cohort had idealized through loyalist lyric a century earlier. His defiant exchange with Bayan during the February 1276 negotiations at enemy barracks, discussed in the preceding chapter, represents merely his initiation into loyalist heroics. Another dramatic milestone came only a month later, during his timely flight from enemy captors. That escape of considerable daring, near the Yangzi city of Zhenjiang, had occurred while enroute to Beijing and through the assistance of a small band of dedicated royalists.[123] He must not have been under particularly heavy guard, for the initial release was considerably less perilous than security afterwards. Northern ships commanded the Yangzi, northern troops held surrounding lands, and southern residents fretted to harbor a fugitive of such celebrity. Travel by day ran the risk of ready detection, although the nighttime alternative was scarcely safer due to strict curfews. Wen Tianxiang writes of coming perilously close to discovery by sentries on the roadways and patrols on the water. They were eluded through a combination of fortuitous circumstance and clever disguise, this journey of only a few kilometers having consumed much of a day.

"At seeing the attire of the Middle Kingdom, I felt like the prodigal son returning to the old home," the fugitive writes with exhilaration of his arrival at Zhenzhou, on the Yangzi River's northern bank. The city, still secure as loyalist stronghold, should have offered safe sanctuary. It did not. Scarcely three days after Wen Tianxiang's arrival, a conspiracy against him was exposed. Its prime mover was Li Tingzhi, a fellow loyalist ensconced at neighboring Yangzhou. Perhaps he acted out of personal frustration over the limited support extended to him by Song courtiers, consumed as they were by developments closer to Linan; or maybe he sought retribution for the unpardonable concessions of peace emissaries at Gaoting mountain, of which Wen Tianxiang was one. Motives aside, Li Tingzhi had finally met his match in Wen Tianxiang, who undaunted, not only dissuaded his would-be assassins, but then proceeded west to Yangzhou for a personal meeting with the conspirator himself. He never made it through the layers of sentries and blockades, and instead set out east for the ocean in search of new purpose.

Much of the third lunar month would be spent in hiding or in flight, his perseverance only reinforced with each ordeal. Wen Tianxiang had learned, even before his escape, of the two royal sons still unapprehended in the far south. Joining them in promoting the cause of dynastic restoration thus quickly became his singular mission. On a ship destined for the high seas, he compares his own unwavering heart to the magnetic compass, instinctively lured south (away from the earth's poles) by a force greater than man or machine. He writes:

I roam for several days the north seas, drifting with the wind,
And return to cross the mouth of the Yangzi River.
My heart is like a single mass of magnet:
If not pointing south, it cannot rest.[124]

In another poem from the same period, he ponders the well-being of his wife and family. Their separation now a year old, he admits to dreaming of them frequently.[125] Nonetheless, as befitting the stout-hearted hero in Chinese biography, a single-minded Wen Tianxiang consciously relegates such family concerns to political commitment.[126] No engagement could compete with his rendezvous with imperial exiles. After several stops enroute, that rendezvous finally occurred on July 9 at Fuzhou, where only a few weeks earlier the seven year old Zhao Shi had been enthroned as heir to a resuscitated Song. The reunion would prove poignant and painful, as revealed in another poem:

With pennant in hand, the officer of Han returns;
In hemp sandals, greeting the Son of Heaven.
Passions stirred even unto the four corners,
While the tears of stout warriors fall like rain.[127]

Simple nostalgia for the past and anxiety over the future offers only partial explanation for those tears. Wen Tianxiang was doubtlessly reacting to the new political landscape at Fuzhou as well, which did not augur well for him. Already entrenched at the reconstituted court was the triumvirate of Chen Yizhong, Lu Xiufu, and Zhang Shijie. All three men had known a history of acrimonious exchange with this effusive and opinionated hero and none would particularly welcome a power-sharing relationship with him. It surprised no one, least of all himself, that Wen Tianxiang would linger at Fuzhou for scarcely a month. Honored as nominal officer at the military bureau, he moved on to the interior where he could operate independently of the center.

To preserve his image of moral integrity and heroic idealism, it was indeed in Wen Tianxiang's best interests to be consigned to the interior. Militarily, the center was too weak to anchor itself in any secure sanctuary; politically, it proved too contentious to convince most skeptics of its own viability. Among the numerous negatives working against the regime was the ubiquitous Chen Yizhong. His untimely flight from Linan, only several months earlier as the Mongols closed in, suggested a serious deficiency in political courage. He was least qualified in consequence for instilling a broader confidence in the new order. Yet as chief councilor, that responsibility fell squarely upon his shoulders. A cloud of incredulity also hung over the monarchy itself. The child emperor Duanzong, born to a secondary consort of Duzong, was not ideally suited as heir. And his mother Yang Juliang, lacking the title of empress, made a less than ideal regent. For a court with imperial pretenses to be located at the coastal fringe of the Asian continent seemed equally unpropitious. Thus, the struggle to maintain a foothold in the interior, led principally by Wen Tianxiang, was of greater import to the legitimacy and survival of the fledgling regime than its decisionmakers would willingly admit.

For the next two and a half years, he operated chiefly within the hinterland of the coastal circuits Fujian and Guangnan East, plus a landlocked Jiangnan West. Much of this represents mountainous terrain where the movement of men and materiél would demand exceptional industry and imagination. The scarce resources attendant to such to-

pography would also impede the two most critical tasks: recruiting warriors and requisitioning provisions. A local population composed substantially of aboriginal peoples with little affinity for Chinese dignitaries
presented additional challenges unique to this region. For all of these obstacles, Wen Tianxiang's consolidation of power progressed with remarkable speed. His tenure in the Fujian hinterland at Tingzhou, for
example, lasted only a month or two. Yet he was fully prepared to intervene in the summer of 1277, over a half year after his departure, to put
down a major insurrection.[128] Led by an obscure but ambitious Huang
Guangde, "a bogus Son of Heaven" as Wen Tianxiang calls him, the
movement threatened the Song cause in more than strategic ways. Operating in the same general locality as Song royalists while assuming imperial aspirations, the pretenders presented a dangerous political threat.
Little else is known about their power base or agenda. But the suppression would span several months and involve armies up to several hundred kilometers away, clearly suggesting a dangerously expansive insur-
gency. Locals apparently led the final suppression, yet Wen Tianxiang
probably played an equally critical role in coordinating reinforcements
from outside. And the speedy success of the effort, especially in the context of scarce resources and short tempers, represents an impressive
achievement for the embattled Song regime.

Apart from his decisiveness in deploying armies, Wen Tianxiang could
mobilize men around the loyalist cause with brutal proficiency. In the
fourth month of 1277, on the eve of a new campaign and in the spirit
of martial revelry, he publicly executed two of his own commanders.[129]
These subordinates had committed some unnamed infraction of military regimen and, by responding harshly their leader clearly sought to set
an example of them. He would liken the execution's impact to "pound-
ing the drums of war," suggesting the calculated rallying of his rank-and-
file as another motive. And indeed the action did reinforce his image as
ruthlessly dedicated—a decided short-term asset, militarily, although its
long-term value politically may well be questioned.

If such extraordinary acts of martial discipline and dedication are a
manifestation of heroic virtue, still more can be found in Wen Tianxiang's unique prioritizing of civic duty before family obligations. Sometime in the year 1276, as he rallied men in southern Fujian, he arranged
for his immediate family to be relocated to the neighboring circuit of
Guangnan East. Farther removed from their imperiled home in the deep
interior and closer to the coast, the location was a scant one to two hundred kilometers from his own base of operations. Still, not until April

1277 would Wen Tianxiang rendezvous with them at Meizhou, by which time they had been separated for three long years. To be sure, he kept a hectic schedule in the years preceding their reunion and lived under conditions too harsh and dangerous for most civilian dependents. Pragmatic concerns of personal safety notwithstanding, no less critical to the family's prolonged separation were considerations of political and historical image.

Relative to most Chinese literati, after all, Wen Tianxiang seems more insistent on compartmentalizing family responsibilities. He married rather late, almost immediately took two concubines, and produced a progeny of eight or nine in the short span of a few years. From the late 1260s to early 1270s, activities centering on family and community seemingly consumed his every energy, his political career having entered a hiatus. Once opportunities for renewed activism reemerged in 1274, his focus shifted dramatically and exclusively to public service. No new births occurred, nor visits to his native Luling. This entire episode emerges as remarkably reminiscent of Yu the Great, an exemplar of the ancient Xia who "toiled with utmost dedication to the state while managing his family with utmost temperance."[130] In his stout dedication to taming torrential waters, Yu the Great had reportedly passed his own home on three separate occasions without stopping for a visit with wife and children. The three years of Wen Tianxiang's separation from family, in its close parallel to this familiar legend of several millennia earlier, is no mere coincidence. He consciously modeled his personal life, like his writings, on historic heroes like Yu the Great—precisely the sorts of men who appear in his Elegy. Through the almost superhuman totality of his devotion to public virtue, Wen Tianxiang would win liberation from the trivial distractions of family, but also and perhaps more importantly, liberation from the paralyzing burden of human sentimentality.[131] Emotional restraint and sexual abstinence—an athletic purity of sorts—emerge as critical to moral perfection no less for Wen Tianxiang than for the heterosexual heroes of other civilizations.[132] Added inspiration undoubtedly came from Buddhism, whose celibate clergy provided another model for male purity through sensual restraint and segregation from women.

Perhaps even more compelling than the image of self-denial, as a stamp of loyalist heroism, is Wen Tianxiang's identification with unjust victimization and staggering personal loss. In the words of literary scholar Kan-i Sun Chang, the magnitude of his suffering was of such

"aesthetic totality" as to acquire a rare "purity and grandeur."[133] That added image of victim was cast in September 1277 when most of his family fell into enemy hands—wife, two concubines, two daughters, and youngest son.[134] He had brought them back to the interior, their native Jiangnan West, only months earlier following a royalist rally in the circuit. This had enabled the Song to reclaim many a strategic county in the southern half of the circuit, having almost entirely retreated earlier in the year. But the new gains were never secure and it was premature for him, so soon into the rally, to relocate family members from Meizhou to Ganzhou.

Wen Tianxiang probably acted out of anxiety over his family's well-being. It was widely rumored that the enemy planned personal reprisals against him, including the unthinkable—excavation of family tombs in his native Luling, now under enemy occupation.[135] Moreover, Song control over the coastal area was scarcely more secure by now than the hinterland, while an alien dialect and unfamiliar environment made for a vulnerable conspicuousness in Guangnan East. Assuming peril to lurk in every corner, then the familiar corner is preferable to the unfamiliar. How could he have anticipated the determination of northern armies, directed in this particular theater by Li Heng, so thoroughly to obliterate all vestiges of Song power? But in his enthusiasm for advancing northward toward his native prefecture, Wen Tianxiang got lured too deeply into the circuit and, in retreat, was trapped just south of Square Rock Ridge.[136] He miraculously slipped through the enemy's net, but without wives and younger children. The two known to have joined him in flight, his mother and eldest son, would not survive the coming year.

The year 1277 proved fateful for the personal fortunes of Wen Tianxiang, but also the larger cause that energized him. It started out with the loss of Fuzhou, the emergency capital only recently evacuated by imperial occupants. Worse yet, there emerged no secure alternative to the Fuzhou site. Cities farther south along the coast had come under equally forceful attack. A variety of coastal locations offered temporary sanctuary—Huizhou, Zhangzhou, Jing'ao, and Gangzhou—none sufficiently stable however to last more than a month or two. (See map 4.) The most obvious alternative was Guangzhou (Canton), a sprawling commercial entrepôt of nearly a million souls that sits strategically at the corner of the continent. It could be easily accessed by the still sizable southern navy, but unfortunately by northern ships as well, which felled

the city twice that year. Song forces proved more adept at reclaiming Guangzhou, as they did repeatedly, than retaining it over the long haul. Something seemed terribly remiss, if not about southern strategy itself then surely the men behind it.

Wen Tianxiang blamed this interminable retreat and itinerancy on Zhang Shijie, the manager of coastal operations. This "incompetent," he charges, "knows only about managing ships, not defending territory."[137] He had leveled a similar charge against Li Tingzhi sometime earlier. "He knows only about shutting the gates and entrenching himself," Wen Tianxiang said of the staunch loyalist of Yangzhou, "not saving the empire."[138] Admittedly, he had a history of policy and personal differences with both men; he also had a penchant for arrogant condescension toward those less stellarly credentialed. Yet the criticisms of Wen Tianxiang certainly have their objective reason. While colleagues clung slavishly to the familiar strategies of reinforcing the walls of cities and then deploying masses of men to protect them, his own approach could be more flexibly imaginative. Consolidating control over surrounding subprefectures before challenging prefectural seats, he preferred to build from the bottom up. Exploiting secure bases as launching pads for neighboring lands, he advanced an aggressively expansive defense. He refused to focus obsessively on fixed positions and insisted on employing men in a manner adaptively mobile. Thus, at the same time that he criticized Li Tingzhi for positional inflexibility, he attacked Zhang Shijie for indifference to positional priorities. Wen Tianxiang demanded a dogged defense, but not to the extent of suicidal confrontation. He had vehemently opposed relocation of the former capital, for example, only to reverse himself in those final desperate days.

In 1277, beset with an unstable court on the retreat and an unrelenting enemy on the advance, Song defenders nonetheless managed to reclaim a few major cities while stalling or sabotaging northern armies at every turn. But for 1278, fewer favorable events occurred to brighten an already bleak horizon. Under additional naval pressures, the shipbound court would carry its retreat to the very edge of the Chinese realm, an island several hundred kilometers west of Guangzhou and east of Vietnam, near the Leizhou peninsula. It was on this island of Gangzhou, on May 9, that the young emperor passed away. Having nearly drowned several months earlier, he apparently died of related illnesses. Chen Yizhong had already absconded by now, ostensibly to prepare a sanctuary for Song royals in Vietnam. The court never heard from him again. In his absence, Zhang Shijie and Lu Xiufu enthroned the royal

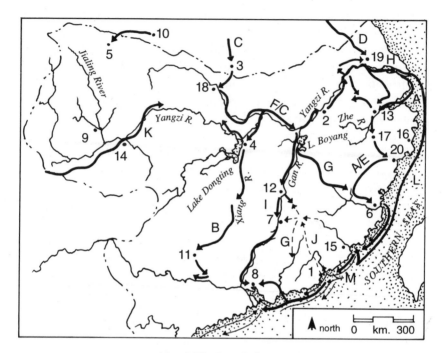

Map 4. The Song Defense

Key to City Names

1=Chaozhou
2=Chizhou
3=Dengzhou
4=Ezhou
5=Fengzhou
6=Fuzhou
7=Ganzhou
8=Guangzhou
9=Hezhou
10=Jingzhao
11=Jingjiang
12=Jizhou
13=Linan
14=Peizhou
15=Quanzhou
16=Tanzhou
17=Wuzhou
18=Xiangyang
19=Yangzhou
20=Yongjia

Key to Personal Names

A=Acihan
B=Alihaiya
C=Azhu
D=Bayan/Boluo
E=Dong Wenbing
F=Fan Wenhu
G=Li Heng
H=Li Tingzhi
I=Lü Shikui
J=Wen Tianxiang
K=Wuliang Hetai
L=Zhang Hongfan
M=Zhang Shijie

family's last surviving son, six year old Zhao Bing (Modi), his step-mother Yang installed as regent. (Historical records are mute as to the whereabouts of the child's biological mother, Consort Yu, at the time.) It was also their decision, following fresh setbacks on the Leizhou peninsula, to relocate Modi and his entourage of thousands to another island stronghold. Yaishan would be their final destination, the dynasty's last stand. Closer to Guangzhou and the loyalist resistance on the Chinese mainland, the move seemed to signal a rejection of further flight or remote exile.

Wen Tianxiang, never consulted about this succession of springtime decisions, was anxious to air his views. Repeatedly, he requested a court audience and adamantly he was refused.[139] Operating for the first half of 1278 out of Huizhou (Guangnan East), only three hundred kilometers east of Yaishan and convenient to the coast, the journey would have required relatively little time. Yet it would never be made, except many months later as a captive on enemy ships. His views had been anticipated in advance and intentionally preempted. He had become, by now, wholly excluded from the new inner circle. Sadly, political setbacks of the sort coincided with another onslaught of personal mishaps: his son died late in the summer, his mother early in the fall. Even in the face of these traumatic events, he proved inexplicably resilient. Not the previous loss of wives and children, nor the current loss of his mother would dampen his zeal for the cause of dynasty and culture. By social custom, the death of either parent demanded withdrawal from public service and three years of mourning. But the court promptly moved to waive the obligation, in line with an equally timeless convention—political expediency. In a matter of weeks, Wen Tianxiang had returned to the front at Huizhou (Guangnan East).

The region had come under increased pressure from the navies of Zhang Hongfan, forcing remnant southern troops to seek sanctuary in the nearby hills of Haifeng county. There, on 2 February 1279 a weary and ailing Wen Tianxiang was overpowered by enemy pursuers. Only a few weeks later, his fellow royalists and monarch would similarly succumb, a spectacle to which he bore personal witness from the brig of northern ships. In those initial weeks of captivity, according to personal record, he repeatedly sought to commit suicide. The opportunity never came. Unrelenting efforts to goad captors into killing him failed as well, as did a hunger strike of eight day's duration while enroute north. Instead, he would journey thousands of kilometers and wait four long years before his wishes were honored. The details of his final heroic tri-

umph, on the execution grounds of Beijing, have been elaborated earlier. But his story is not complete without one final reflection on the complex array of motives, explicit and implicit, that led him there—as a man, not a woman; a southerner, not a northerner; a litterateur, not a soldier.

Thunder over the lake:
*The image of the **Betrothed Woman**.*
Thus the superior man understands the transitory
In the light of the eternity to the end.

The Changes, LIV.

6 · Guimei:
And Their Betrothed

It was scarcely a month after his November 1279 arrival in Beijing that officers of the military bureau summoned Wen Tianxiang for interrogation. Bureau chief Boluo, having weeks earlier locked him in shackles and cangue before confining him to a dark and desolate pit, had thought his spirit broken. Boluo probably never expected to make a convert of him, but neither did he want another martyr on his hands. The audience quickly grew stormy, however, beginning with a confrontation over kowtow etiquette that evolved into a debate on the ethics of officeholding in a morally invigorated Middle Kingdom. Wen Tianxiang had exploited the occasion, predictably, to indulge personal vanity, much as he had done in the presence of Bayan three years earlier. This time around, however, his tenor seemed far more defensive as his audience shifts from present captors to an eternity of future historians. Beginning with a statement on loyalist principle, a combative, even theatrical Wen Tianxiang declares:

> In the affairs of the world, there is ascent and descent. Since antiquity, when a monarchy perished its military and civilian leaders were liquidated. In what era is it not so? In my own case, only out of continuing loyalty to the dynastic altars of Song have I come to this. And I would consider myself fortunate should you resolve the matter expeditiously. By virtue of my office as councilor of Song, the demise of empire demands my death. Moreover, the conditions of my current incarceration makes execution a legal imperative. What else matters?[1]

Boluo and cohort seemed genuinely baffled that a mind so historically conscious could be so self-delusively blind to the inevitability of dynastic change. If all political entities are doomed by the convergence of forces, human and natural, beyond any one individual's ability to change, why persist in denying the inevitable through suicidal death? This prompts Wen Tianxiang to lecture his alien captors on the implacable sense of civic duty that had inspired his actions from the outset:

> Formerly, I declined an appointment as chief councilor and accepted instead a commission as emissary to the camp of Bayan. I would soon be forceably detained while traitors handed over the empire. I should have died then [in 1276], except for my desire to rush to the aid of the two sons of Duzong, still at large in eastern Zhedong, and my aging mother in Guangnan.

A persistent Boluo, taking aim at the recent record of Song royalists in a distant south, charges them with improprieties tantamount to sedition. By abandoning the deposed Deyou Emperor and installing a lesser brother, they had intervened illicitly in the sacred matter of dynastic succession. Wen Tianxiang responds with a rather radical stand on political priorities and deft insight into the object of loyalist devotion:

> The Deyou Emperor [Gongdi] is indeed my ruler, but his tragedy was to lose the empire. At such times, the altars are important, the ruler unimportant. To install another monarch in the interests of the ancestral shrines and dynastic altars of Song is precisely what makes for the loyal official. [In the fourth century,] those who proceeded north with captive Emperors Huai and Min were not loyal, true loyalists being those to follow Yuandi. [In the eleventh century,] those who proceeded north with captive Emperors Hui and Qin were not loyal, true loyalists being those to follow Gaozong.

Herein lies the answer, precisely, to the question posed by Dowager Quan to would-be liberator Li Tingzhi, several years earlier—the monarchy abdicated, "on whose behalf do you persist in fighting?" It took enormous courage and insight for Wen Tianxiang to pronounce individual monarchs as mere symbols of authority, merely one link in a chain of royal descent. He owed his fidelity to the chain—the institution of dynasty—and placed perpetuation of the institution above all else. At the same time that monarchs are sheer symbols, their right to rule enjoys the sanctity of Heaven and cannot be capriciously manipulated by mere mortals. Thus, Wen Tianxiang proceeds to defend the legitimacy of the two boys, now dead, whose catapult to power seemed so clandestinely orchestrated. Suggesting royal sanctioning for his actions, he declares:

The Jingyan Emperor [Zhao Shi] was the eldest son of Emperor Duzong, the elder brother of the Deyou Emperor. How can this be, as you charge, "illegitimate"? His accession occurred only after Deyou had been dethroned. How can this be "usurpation"? Chief councilor Chen, in supervising the departure of the two princes from Linan, did so with the expressed consent of the Grand Dowager. How is this "unauthorized"?

This is the only source, to my knowledge, that confirms unequivocally for Dowager Xie an active role in the flight of royal sons. And her participation was critical to dispelling suspicions of self-interested opportunism on the part of concerned bureaucrats. Her support also made it easier, no doubt, for Wen Tianxiang to undertake a mission that he personally acknowledges as doomed from the outset. The certainty of defeat cannot itself justify surrender, for the loyal subject, as he states,

> . . . serves his ruler like a son serves his father. The father may be struck with an illness for which, clearly, no cure exists. Yet how can one fail to exhaust every effort in administering medicinal treatment? If he is still not saved, then Heaven has mandated so. This is the point that I have reached today, death the only option. What more can be said?

The parallel of political loyalty to filial piety, public duty to private virtue, is hardly new. It was rare, however, for a statesman of any dynasty to act out these ethical impulses on so visible a political platform, in full view of court recorders and metropolitan observers—the eyes of history. Boluo refused to "convenience" him with the execution he demanded. Returned to jail instead, Wen Tianxiang would languish there for another three years.

It is significant that this Song loyalist, like most others, would consciously cast his own will initially to survive and later to perish in purely political terms. By accepting the privileges of office under the dynasty, Wen Tianxiang presumably accepted a life-long and life-threatening responsibility for its well-being. He establishes no explicit relationship between his own death and some larger cultural mission. There is no reference here to ritualized celebration of region or gender—southern manhood—as occurs elsewhere. Nor is loyalist fervor explicitly linked to social station: the literati elite were not more obligated to the established order than those less privileged in wealth or station. Yet implicit in his comments is a hierarchy of obligations that hinges principally on political status. As nominal chief of state, the imperative of death was greater for him than brother Wen Bi, for example, who similarly held high office under a waning Song but not at the councilor level. Such

equivocation, however, was scarcely universal. "Those who live on the emoluments of Song," begins a phrase frequently reiterated in the relevant literature, "must be prepared to die in its defense." Other martyrs insist that "having lived as officials of Song, we will die as ghosts of Song." Elsewhere, "when a ruler is imperiled his officers should rally, when he is humiliated they should die."[2] The expressions may vary from text to text, verbal transmissions having preceded the written, yet they all seem to share remarkably similar content. They suggest a near contractual relationship between the government and its civil servants, one that grows out of officeholding and remuneration. Moreover, it makes no distinction between high and low, the administrative elite and their tens of thousands of subordinates. Not even students are exempt from responsibility, for they similarly drew stipends and other perquisites of ranked officiary. This still leaves the vast majority of the male population—educated as well as uneducated, rich as well as poor—ostensibly free of commitment to defense of dynasty. But curiously, the links between social station and loyalist deed, privilege and duty, were not always as expected. Those obliged did not always respond, while those to respond were often the least obligated.

THE PROFILE OF LOYALIST SUICIDES

Heretofore, my approach has been more qualitative than quantitative, more focused on specific individuals and contexts than vast clusters of nameless men and women. After all, any effort to quantify loyalist suicides for the closing years of Song will raise more problems than it answers. The task of defining suicide and then fixing motivation as civic is not as easy as it might seem. Wen Tianxiang clearly relinquished his life for political cause, for example; but having died at the hands of Yuan executioners, strictly speaking, he does not belong to the suicide category. The same can be said for many dozens, perhaps hundreds, of others. Yet to the extent that our focus is on alienation and its resolution through willful death, the inclusion of those who died under less voluntary conditions seems problematic. Apart from this rather restrictive definition of suicide, I have been forced to limit my consideration of loyalist suicides (see Appendix C) to individuals motivated preeminently by political or cultural concerns—that is, civic duty. This is certain to entail the serious underrepresentation of women, whose motivation in the traditional historiography is most often attributed to marital fidelity or re-

lated private agendas. Sections in the dynastic history devoted to so-called "loyalists" (*zhongyi zhuan*), some ten chapters long in the *History of the Song*, are reserved exclusively for men; and in its solitary chapter on "Notable Women" (*Lie nü zhuan*), only a handful of entries have even a hint of civic motivation. Historiographic bias is at the heart of other concerns, and not just selective exclusion. No less important is selective inclusion: what sorts of individuals have centuries of historians deemed worthy of mention? We see the late Song, in fact, through the filters of male historians of the Yuan, Ming, and Qing who were most likely to make heroes of men like themselves, giving rise to serious imbalances of class, gender, and regional representation. Fully aware of the historiographic biases of the sources and the methodological prejudices of my own, I have nonetheless found certain political and social trends in the data for the late Song too striking to ignore.

Perhaps the most stunning revelation of the data recovered on the loyalist suicides listed in Appendix C, and summarized on Table 1 below, is the underrepresentation of metropolitan officials. These are the men in positions of high visibility but also vulnerability as enemy targets, individuals for whom the likelihood of making it into historical sources is greatest. Yet only about 18 percent of such martyrs (20 among 110) were metropolitan officials of any rank, at the time of their deaths. Of these, the majority were indeed high-level officials, doubtlessly reflecting the disproportionate attention that status-conscious historians have afforded this political elite; but even within this group, most came from family backgrounds of notably less pedigree. Similar to Wen Tianxiang and Chen Yizhong, they were more politically accomplished than socially entrenched. The dynasty's premiere political clans are noticeably absent. The Shi of Mingzhou, for example—a political dynasty in its own right for the thirteenth century—shed little blood in defense of Song rule, as I have shown elsewhere.[3] The same apparently holds for the kinsmen of Jia Sidao. The legacy, in this regard, seems only slightly better for scions of the dynasty's cultural leaders, its great thinkers and scholars. The preeminent exception is perhaps Zhu Jun, the great grandson of Confucian luminary Zhu Xi.[4] A one-time fiscal commissioner for the lower Yangzi, he had returned to his native Fujian when northern armies swept the region, in late 1276 or soon thereafter. Refusing "humiliation at the hands of the enemy," he poisoned himself to death. But the pressures on Zhu Jun were well out of the ordinary: more than just the great grandson of the man whose values had received sanction by the

TABLE 1 The Political Status of Loyalist Suicides*

Metropolitan officials ranked 1-3	16
Metropolitan officials ranked 4-6	2
Metropolitan officials ranked 7-9	2
Regional officials ranked 1-3	13
Regional officials ranked 4-6	28
Regional officials ranked 7-9	29
Unspecified official status	12
Commoner without official rank	8

*Data missing for 5 of 110 cases

Song court as state orthodoxy, he was also husband to a princess of the Zhao royal clan. Duty to the dynasty's ethical culture had converged with duty to family in rather paralyzing ways.

The paucity of metropolitan officials and pedigreed families within our cluster of loyalist suicides relates partly to the surrender without deadly confrontation of the Song capital at Linan, but also other cultural centers in the vicinity, such as Pingjiang and Mingzhou, Shaoxing and Taizhou (Huainan East). The shift of this military contest away from the capital, in the mid-1270s, to localities of strategic but not necessarily cultural import helps to explain another phenomenon: over half of the 110 suicide cases cited above and in Appendix C involve regional officials, most of them middle-to-lower rank. Some were civilian or military administrators seeking to uphold professional honor in the face of imminent defeat; but many others, as we have seen in earlier chapters, were local literati without political office. They acted on a more convoluted set of motivations where civic concerns and private pressures converged in informing their death wish. Those most directly involved in the daily life of the localities, therefore, were apparently the ones to sacrifice the most in their defense. This does not necessarily include the highest of local administrators—military commissioners or fiscal intendants, for example—who tended to govern from the safe distance of circuit seats. The strong ties of loyalists to their communities can explain another curiosity in our data: a total of 20 cases involved either confirmed commoners or individuals of unspecified and presumably marginal literati standing—a number equivalent to metropolitan officials at the opposite end of the social spectrum. Recognizing that historical bias tends to favor those of greatest stature, we can expect a higher level of historical inclusion or overrepresentation for court officers, while com-

TABLE 2 Regional Background of Loyalist Suicides*

Chengdu circuit	6	Fujian circuit	10
Guangnan East circuit	6	Guangnan West circuit	0
Huainan East circuit	6	Huainan West circuit	7
Jiangnan East circuit	16	Jinghu North circuit	5
Jinghu South circuit	10	Jiangnan West circuit	8
Jingxi circuit	4	Kuizhou circuit	5
Lizhou circuit	3	Tongchuan circuit	4
Zhedong circuit	14	Zhexi circuit	3

*Regional background uncertain in 3 cases

moners should be seriously underrepresented, which makes their even modest visibility here all the more remarkable. This only confirms, in the end, the social diversity of late Song martyrs. There is geographic diversity as well, as exemplified in Table 2.

Loyalist suicides are documented for all sixteen circuits of the Southern Song empire, with the singular exception of a remote and sparsely populated Guangnan West. A significant cluster of cases, 30 in all, emerges in the two circuits of Jiangnan East and Zhedong, one directly to the west and the other to the east of the Song capital. These were areas in the path of advancing Yuan armies. Being close to the empire's political seat, their local literati were perhaps drawn more intensely into this drama of dynastic dissolution. This seems certainly true for the circuits with the second largest cluster of loyalist suicides—Fujian, Jinghu South, and Jiangnan West—with a total of 28 known incidents. By no coincidence, a coastal Fujian was seat to the Song government-in-exile, in late 1276; nor is it coincidental that the two remaining circuits in the interior, Jinghu South and Jiangnan West, were the homes of loyalist extraordinaires Li Fu and Wen Tianxiang. This all serves to confirm the fundamental power of politics in motivating men and women to take their own lives, however compelling their secondary agendas.

Another observation, with reference to the geographic distribution of Song loyalists, relates to data from the far west. For the four Song circuits that comprise the modern province of Sichuan—Chengdu, Kuizhou, Lizhou, and Tongchuan—I have been able to identify 18 loyalist suicides. This may seem rather unexceptional for a region containing over 18 percent of the Southern Song landmass and 23 percent of its population.[5] But late Song data for this region in the form of local gazetteers, collected writings, and memorabilia is no rival to similar sources

for the east. Sichuan's resistance to the northern campaign, on the other hand, had been epochal in dimension: it bore the brunt of successive waves of northern campaigns in the 1250s, holding its own; it again fought off Yuan armies with valor in 1277, as they pummeled celebrated hold-out cities like Chongqing and Hezhou—the former only relented in 1278, the latter in February 1279, less than a month before the fall of Yaishan.[6] A dogged devotion to dynasty and staggering loss of life is not in question. Maybe more Sichuan men died in battle than at their own hand or perhaps, being more removed from the political center to the east and less defensive about the cultural legacies of the west, they responded less deliriously to the end of dynasty. But more likely, the problem is merely one of documentation.

LOYALIST LITERATURE AS A MIRROR ON GENDER RELATIONS

The aforementioned diversity of class and region among loyalist men for the late Song is remarkable but not unthinkable, for to varying degrees most enjoyed privilege under the dynasty. This cannot be said for the one group categorically excluded from polity and society—ordinary women—a significant number of whom did die for political causes. Yet most Song men adamantly refused to acknowledge any political consciousness in women of the day. Wen Tianxiang, for example, as a captive passing through his native Jizhou, jotted down the following poem:

> The royal custodians cast aside, the poles of earth lopsided;
> Wives and concubines coveting life, make bandits of themselves.
> The man of valor dragged by the wrist, his whiskers red with anger;
> Of loyal blood, each day anticipating death at his northern terminus.[7]

Seeking to highlight the contrasting agendas of men and women—himself calmly "anticipating death" while Song women "covet life"—he seems more smug than angry. Those women of the royal family, but women of the elite generally, were never expected to exhibit his own death-defying courage.

It was a similar lack of esteem for the moral potential of women that prompted other literati men, prior to taking their own lives, to kill off their spouses and dependents. With a lifelong focus on the nuclear family, women were considered incapable of standing firm on political principle. When they commit suicide, therefore, it is almost invariably de-

picted by male historians in terms of devotion to their husbands, even when political conviction is an important contributing factor. Typical of such historical re-characterization is the story of Lady Yong, wife of Zhao Maofa, the loyalist whose death is described in Chapter 3. Reconstructed from the dynastic history and other sources is the following dialogue between husband and wife, which ostensibly occurred several days before their deaths in the second month of 1275:

> Knowing that his defense would fail, Maofa set up a banquet for friends and relatives as parting ceremony. To his wife, he then said: "The city is about to fall and, as officiating administrator, I cannot leave. But perhaps you should flee beforehand."

> Lady Yong responded: "Your Lordship was fated to be an official and I was fated to be a wife. And if Your Lordship is to be a loyal official, will you deny me the role of wife to that loyal official?"

> With a sigh, Maofa queries: "How can this be something of which a mere wife or woman is capable?"
> Her response: "Then allow me, My Lord, to precede you in death."
> Maofa simply laughed and dissuaded her.[9]

A critical reader might reasonably question whether the above passage reflects accurately the thrust of this presumably private exchange between husband and wife. Far more meaningful than textual accuracy, however, is historical intent. Regardless of her own words, her own husband but also later chroniclers felt compelled to impose political indifference on Lady Yong through the utterances of her husband. In this way, her hearty display of moral will subverts neither the family dominance of her husband nor the moral leadership of other males.

The proclivity among traditional historians to cast the motives of female martyrs in strictly personal terms is more subtly expressed in the biography of the Chaste Woman Wang, Wang Zhenfu. As narrated in the official dynastic history, *Song shi*, under "Notable Women":

> The Chaste Woman Wang was, by marriage, native to Linhai [Taizhou]. In the winter of the second year of Deyou [1276], as the forces of the Great Yuan penetrated Zhedong circuit, the Woman was taken captive along with her maternal uncle, paternal aunt, and husband. The uncle, aunt, and husband had already been killed when the chief commander, finding the Woman stunningly attractive, wished to claim her as spouse. The Woman, letting out a loud wail, wanted to commit suicide, but was compelled against acting on her wishes. That night, orders to arrest her were issued and she was randomly

incarcerated. The Woman then said to the chief commander, furtively, "Those who would take me as spouse would doubtlessly expect me to provide the master of the home a lifetime of proper service. For my uncle, aunt, and husband to die without my mourning them is not natural (*butian*). And what use could you conceivably make of someone who acts unnaturally? I seek only to complete the terms of mourning before accepting my fate. Should you fail to honor my request, then I would die in the end without ever becoming your wife." The commander, fearing she might be sincere about dying, honored her request but placed her under strict surveillance.

In spring of the next year, troops returned and she was taken away. At reaching the Qingfeng Mountains of Sheng county [a hundred kilometers north of Linhai], as they stopped to look out on a ravine, the Woman waited for the escort to lose his guard, whereupon she bit her finger to draw blood and scribbled some characters on the face of a rock. Then facing south, she wept bitterly before leaping over a cliff to her death.[10]

The motivations of Woman Wang are clearly complex, although historians here have intentionally crafted this as a simple story of marital fidelity. Still, inadvertently included in their narrative are signs of some greater social and political consciousness. Ritualistically "facing south" might suggest political inspiration, for the Song court-in-exile was operating out of Guangnan East at the time of her death, in early 1277. That the Woman Wang would wish to leave a written message reveals that she was reasonably literate and thus came from a family of some privilege, on the one hand, but also that she intuited her actions as having some historical import, on the other. In most of the extant literature for the late Song, it is the male martyr who insists on leaving behind some written message, as farewell to kinsmen or as a document for future historians. In the absence of more information about the Woman Wang's family background or even the nature of the message she left to posterity, the picture to emerge here is decidedly one-dimensional and likely a misrepresentation of her actions.

One of the rare exceptions to the rule of rigidly recasting loyalist women into the mold of devoted spouses is the Lady Lin. A native of coastal Fuzhou, she hailed from a small but politically mobile family: her father had apparently held lesser office while brother Lin Tong, with a doctoral degree, had penetrated the middle ranks of the civil service.[11] Husband Liu Quanzi was less stellarly credentialed, it seems. Yet as member of the local literati establishment, he joined Lin Tong in mobilizing nearby men and materiél behind the child-emperor of Song, ensconced at the prefectural seat. The Fuzhou resistance proved short-lived, stamped out by the Mongols in December 1276, the brother and hus-

Figure 4. Calligraphy on album of Yang Yan (1162–1232), Empress to Emperor Ningzong.
Courtesy of The Metropolitan Museum of Art, Bequest of John M. Crawford, Jr.

band of Lady Lin perishing in the process. Just prior to his death, however, a defiant Lin Tong had painted with his own blood a pledge "to die as a loyal ghost of Song." His sister would allude to that blood-stained wall when she refuted, sometime later, the charge of sedition lodged vindictively by Yuan authorities against her. Confident and proud, she declared:

> The two families of Lin and Liu, having served for generations as Song officials, had sought to repay the empire with loyal devotion. Our failure is due to Heaven. How is this "sedition"? Are you familiar with the person, only last year, who wrote a message with his own blood before dying? That person was my brother! My brother and I are of one heart in our loyal devotion. In death, I can at least seek retaliation against you in the underworld. Why should I go on living and be humiliated by you?[12]

Predictably, the young widow did not survive this strident exchange. Yet her actual death may be less noteworthy, from our perspective, than the rhetoric that preceded it. Her strong sense of personal identification with the moral traditions of both families, but especially her own blood kin, suggests an independence of her husband that women of traditional China must have found difficult to articulate, due to the conflicting sets of duties expected by biological kin and in-laws.[13] By paralleling her own loyal heart with brother Lin Tong, she is affirming political conviction, not marital fidelity, as principal motive for her death wish.

The reticence of late Song men to acknowledge the civic consciousness of women and their jealously diligent guard against female intrusion into the political domain may well relate to far broader changes in gender relations—perception that women had somehow come to threaten the hegemony of men over political, cultural, or social life. It was not necessary to look beyond the imperial palaces for evidence of women empowering themselves, and not merely as surrogates for incompetent men.

In the collection of art and artifacts by the imperial palace, for example, empresses and dowagers are known to have figured quite prominently. Based on seals and colophons affixed to extant paintings, usually a sign of ownership, art historians have identified most empresses of the Southern Song as involved in acquiring or commissioning an assortment of masterpieces for the palace.[14] Emerging as especially renowned as both collector and patron is Yang Yan. This influential wife of Ningzong, who reigned as empress for three full decades, was also an accomplished calligrapher in her own right (see Figure 4). There are traces of Empress

Figure 5. "Woman and Children Playing by the Lotus Pond," a 13th-century painting.
Courtesy, Museum of Fine Arts, Boston, Denman Waldo Ross Collection.

Xie's involvement in the arts as well, although to a lesser degree. Thus, the Song government's expanded role in collecting art presented its royal women with new opportunities for dialogue with the male world of art production and acquisition, precisely as opportunities for other sorts of dialogue beyond the walls of palaces and compounds seemed to be shrinking for most elite women.

Yet opportunities for cultural development were not confined to women of the palace. After all, the primary wives of Song literati were almost always literate, especially in religious scripture and poetic writings.[15] The most celebrated female poet of the dynasty, the early twelfth-century Li Qingzhao, was not only a remarkably articulate student of history and politics, but also an avid collector of paintings and books.[16] And not being confined by palace protocol, she could interact more freely with literati men. Other educated women became involved in religious art, particularly related to Guanyin, the matriarch behind the Song boon in painting and statuary.[17] Some women were less pious in motivation, finding conditions in crowded cities conducive to interacting with men on the most sordid of terms. As an escape from the abuse or poverty of home, they found sanctuary in the city's various taverns and teahouses, many of them establishments of prostitution.[18] Other women sought less to flee home than to flaunt social convention. One source from the twelfth century, translated by Jacques Gernet, alludes to sexual promiscuity that seems, despite its pervasiveness, to have gone without serious censure from male spouses and kin: "So many husbands prefer to shut their eyes to the behavior of their wives and comply with their having lovers, who are called 'complementary husbands.' Some ladies have as many as four or five of this kind and those who live near Buddhist monasteries sometimes have monks as lovers."[19] This is an allusion, doubtlessly exaggerated, to life in the premiere city of the south, Linan, and may well reflect a distinctly southern phenomenon. It seems to echo, in fact, reports dating back to Tang times and earlier, where southern women were similarly censured by northern men for the "indecency" of traveling and socializing with minimal restrictions from their men.[20] Worse yet, moral laxity of the sort in Song times appears at every social level, including the empire's most respected families. There was, as example, the scandal of the Woman Lin, concubine of the powerful Chief Councilor Shi Miyuan, who on the heels of his death in 1233, took up residence in one of the capital's most disreputable of precincts, permitting her thereby "to do as she pleased."[21] The incident proved painfully embarrassing for survivors of the statesman, whose only re-

Figure 6. "Eighteen Scholars": listening to music.
Courtesy of the National Palace Museum, Taipei, Taiwan ROC.

course was to entreat the Woman to return home. A broader spectrum of educated women turned to Buddhist monasteries as cover for various illicit acts, as reflected in the aforementioned quote. Suspicion of sexual misconduct on monastic grounds was clearly behind Zhu Xi's proscriptions, at coastal Zhangzhou, against the mixing of men and women on those grounds.[22] It was also behind his move to close the city's nunneries, where the congregation of sizable numbers of single women had for centuries prompted accusation and inuendo. The scope of non-conformist activity may be exaggerated by male critics, its female perpetrators may be unrepresentative of their class. Yet the picture to emerge for urban areas of the Song in general, and more acutely for southern cities like Linan, is one where women are extending the limits of social tolerance as they pursue paths that often depart from traditional models of sexual segregation and deference to gender hierarchies—subverting the power and prestige of men.

As greater numbers of elite families took up residence in urban areas with their less regulated and more populous spaces, more artificial means of insulating women seemed necessary. Zhu Xi's demand for a heightened diligence within the home to separate the sexes is but one expression of this impulse by late Song men.[23] His proposal may have been justified on the grounds of preventing illicit sex, the same justification given for parallel efforts to separate Buddhist monks from nuns, as noted earlier. But segregation based on gender would also serve, implicitly, to formalize relations within the household as a mirror of an abstract ritual and social order beyond the home, as idealized by Confucian purists. To achieve this ideal of domestic order, a radical overhaul in the physical layout of literati domiciles occurred. Beginning in Song times, fixed walls would replace the sliding panels that formerly divided rooms, according to cultural historian Robert van Gulik.[24] This created conditions more conducive to the regulation of residents in general. But with the lives of women focused narrowly on the household, any change in domestic structures was certain to have its greatest impact on them.

Another innovation in the lifestyle of Song women, and an indicator of increased circumspection, can be seen in changes of costume. For the eleventh century, the garb of elite women largely conformed to the relaxed and sensuous models of Tang, Robert van Gulik observes. Long robes were worn with wide sleeves, broad scarf loosely swagged the shoulders and extended toward the floor, and highly ornate headdress complemented a grandly inflated chignon.[25] Completing the adornment was a face generously powdered in white and highlighted with round spots

Figure 7. "Eighteen Scholars": playing chess.
Courtesy of the National Palace Museum, Taipei, Taiwan ROC.

of bright rouge on the forehead and cheeks. With the twelfth century, however, the costume is emphatically shorn of more sensuous components. Beneath outer garments with a fuller cut, women now wore short jackets with high collars, clearly intended to conceal more of their neck and breasts. Also, rouge came to be applied with greater economy, other adornments such as headdress soon to follow suit (see Figure 5).

The impulse of late Song men to impose a new moral regimen on women is also reflected in pressures against the remarriage of widows. Literature extolling the virtues of chaste widowhood may have preceded the dynasty, but the Song represents the beginning of an escalating effort at indoctrinating women in their subordination to men.[26] Then, as an added expression of male dominance, there is the practice of footbinding—perhaps the cruelest of Song China's many inventions.

Howard Levy has traced the origin of footbinding to the tenth century, the Five Dynasties-Song transition; but propagation of the practice with the conscious intent of inhibiting the movement and activity of women apparently originated with the Southern Song.[27] Only then is the custom, as it shifts from imperial palaces to the larger society, transformed from aesthetic enhancement to debilitating deformity. Robert van Gulik and Patricia Ebrey similarly associate the heightened popularity of the practice with the Southern Song.[28] This growing popularity may be more a consequence of the aesthetics of fashion than the dominance of men, but such teleological matters aside, the effects of footbinding are irrefutable: the contortions necessary to produce "golden lotuses" of three-to-four inches made movement slow and painful, while care of the bandaged foot consumed a prodigious measure of time and energy. Intentionally or not, these developments served to augment male control. An equally important consequence of footbinding was to accentuate a woman's physical frailty at a time when her male complement, introverted and urbane, had decidedly declined in physical presence relative to Tang times. The less active and more cerebral lifestyle of men demanded, in effect, commensurate changes in the physical presence of women.[29] Obviously, these assorted changes in feminine lifestyles could not occur without the willful participation of women themselves: they had to find personal value, or empowerment, in the contrivances of men. This complex dynamic lies beyond the scope of our inquiry, although I find compelling Patricia Ebrey's recent exploration of class privilege— well-to-do women seeking to distinguish their own lifestyle from that of lesser sorts—as impetus for the widespread acceptance of such socially conservative practices as footbinding.[30]

Figure 8. "Eighteen Scholars": practicing calligraphy.
Courtesy of the National Palace Museum, Taipei, Taiwan ROC.

These various lifestyle changes of the twelfth and thirteenth centuries are documented chiefly for the affluent southeast and grew out of conditions unique to that region. Yet such conservative restrictions received further sanction in the fundamentalistic brand of Confucianism then on the ascent, which lambasted the material and moral decadence of the day. The urge to impose new social controls was informed by political climate as well. The Song government, after an initial century of exceptional tolerance, grew progressively autocratic in subsequent times. Increasingly, powerless outsiders were victimized by privileged insiders—purged from office, proscribed from publishing, stripped of noble honors and material assets.[31] Those insiders, for the thirteenth century, were more often free-wheeling chief councilors than despotic emperors, but for the bureaucratic rank-and-file, the consequent sense of disempowerment was the same. In this context of political emasculation, it only stands to reason that frustrated male literati would impose similar controls on their own households, the domain of their defenseless women. Elite men of the sort may have acted on conditioned impulse or perhaps displaced aggression, but authoritarian controls on top made the heightened regulation below seem somehow more understandable, if not altogether acceptable.

For all their effort to restore a regimen of hierarchy and discipline to their domestic orders, elite men of the Southern Song could never conquer the image of inadequacy that shadowed them. Nor did they win much empathy from later historians, who could be merciless in attacking the invirility of the political structure as well as the larger culture behind it. Authors of the official history, *Song shi*, would attribute the dynasty's collapse to an excess of humanistic idealism that sapped the empire of all vitality. In the fourteenth century and under the watchful eye of Mongol patrons, these court historians write contemptuously, "The Zhao line of Song may have arisen through martial prowess, but after founding the enterprise and establishing order, it employed benevolent policies to perpetuate the line. But the malady of benevolence lies in its propensity for weakness, while the malady of literary refinement lies in its propensity for sophistry."[32] It seemed a cruel twist of irony that an empire founded on benevolence, Confucianism's most cardinal of civic virtues, would ultimately be undone by precisely this. Yet the message of Yuan historians rings clear: the southern polity in general, but its literati leadership in particular, had lost both the physical and spiritual vigor necessary to fend off stronger adversaries to the north. For Chinese intellectuals in active service to a regime bent on world domination

Figure 9. "Eighteen Scholars": painting.
Courtesy of the National Palace Museum, Taipei, Taiwan ROC.

through martial conquest, such harsh judgment of an old foe may seem somewhat self-serving. But Yuan historians were scarcely alone in their caustic critique of the Song.

With a greater measure of hindsight, seventeenth-century historian Wang Fuzhi places the perceived deficiencies of Song literati culture, especially as it pertains to masculine virtues, into a larger perspective where identities of culture and gender converge. "When the early kings molded elite men (*shi*)," he writes, "they honored them with feasts and educated them with archery, restrained them through ritual and harmonized them through music."[33] It was precisely such conditioning through the so-called "six crafts" (*liuyi*), he then argues, that augmented the "vital force" or courageous spirit of the literati male in early China. The historical decline and fall of a succession of weaker empires, by this argument, is due to the neglect or dissipation of this vital force, which for the Song was a direct consequence of state policies that ignored martial conditioning. It should be noted that the "early kings" ruled over a feudal order where the male elite, or *shi*, consisted principally of warriors who doubled as government functionaries.[34] The martial arts, figuring prominently in their early training, ostensibly infused in them a virility originating in physical strength which ultimately shaped their spiritual and moral essence. In such a context, honor and courage are highly valued, while the bonds of allegiance and fidelity seem nearly unalterable. Power being personalized, so are political loyalties. Thus, proper conditioning goes beyond the martial arts to include the communal celebration of a shared masculinity over food and drink. At the same time, as Wang Fuzhi observes, rituals are employed to "restrain" the human ego by reinforcing respect for hierarchy, while music serves to "harmonize" the human spirit by harnessing passions. In this way, when martial aggressiveness is nurtured it is also channeled in politically constructive ways. Interestingly, the "six crafts" of classical times also included writing and counting—intellectual pursuits that Wang Fuzhi consciously chose to slight. After all, like writers of *Song shi*, he had witnessed in his own life the fall of another Chinese dynasty to alien conquerors, the literarily refined Ming succumbing to a martially vigorous Qing. It all suggested a need for new priorities and mechanisms for molding an invigorated male, where corrosive intellectualism is eschewed and gallant civilism prevails.

The Song dynasty never devised a workable formula for reconciling the humanistic aspirations of Confucianism with the brutal realities of political and diplomatic life, for realizing the intellectual potential of its

male citizenry without eschewing physical vigor, for maintaining the old aura of male invincibility while shorn of the paraphenalia associated with it. If proficiency at war provides initial justification for the division of labor and male dominance over women is symbolized by the implements of war, then we would expect these symbols to figure visibly in daily life, as they do in many civilizations. Yet for centuries elite men of China, more comfortable with chessboard and zither, had been separated from the tools of violence (see Figures 6–9). Their formal attire had been shorn of the once familiar sword and spear by longstanding laws against the bearing of arms, at least in cities.[35] Moreover, beginning with the Song, even martial sport such as archery and horseback-riding came to be neglected. Relying chiefly on professional soldiers and strategists to secure its borders, there was less pressure on government or society to promote those skills more widely. Even athletic pastimes like polo, so wildly popular within the aristocratic elite of Tang times, would succumb to the same sort of professionalization over the course of Song, evolving into a spectator sport for entertainment, not exercise, according to historian James T.C. Liu. The last Song emperor known to take the sport seriously, Guangzong, died in the year 1200, precisely as the dynasty entered a new level of assimilation into its southern environment.[36] In the absence of the ancient coliseum or the modern sports arena—important institutions for cultivating martial aggressiveness and heterosexual wholesomeness in an otherwise tranquil and materially comfortable West—the literate male of late Song times seemed to suffer from an "attenuated vigor," as Wang Fuzhi puts it. The need to find alternative symbols of male power may partly explain the urge of Song men, in the dynasty's last years, to make a prominent display of masculine virtues and virility through heroic deeds like martyrdom. It reflected an interweaving of private and public agendas—a meeting of political, social, and cultural needs—the full complexity of which even they must have found difficult to fully fathom.

Appendices

List of Abbreviations Used in the Appendices

AHTZ   [*Chongxiu*] *Anhui tongzhi*, 1877, He Shaoji, Shen Baozhen
BXZ   *Baxian zhi*, 1760, Wang Erjian
CSFZ   *Changsha fuzhi*, 1741, Zhang Xiongyuan, Lü Xioagao
FJTZ   [*Chonguan*] *Fujian tongzhi*, 1871, Cheng Zuluo
GYZZ   *Gaoyou zhouzhi*, 1783, Yang Yilun
HBTZ   *Hubei tongzhi*, 1804, Wu Xiongguang
HNTZ   *Hunan tongzhi*, 1885, Li Hanzhang
HZFZ   *Hangzhou fuzhi*, 1922, Li Rong
HZFZ(2) *Huizhou fuzhi*, 1502, Peng Ze
NSS   *Nan Song shu*, N.d., Qian Shisheng
QZZ   *Qizhou zhi*, 1536, Gan Ze
RCXZ   *Rongchang xianzhi*, 1883, Shi Xuehuang
SJZYL   *Songji zhongqi lu*, N.d., Wan Sitong
SMSC   *Songmo sichuan zhanzheng shiliao xuanbian*, Hu Zhaoxi
SNXZ   *Suining xianzhi*, 1878, Sun Hai
SS   *Song shi*, Tuo Tuo
SSXB   *Songshi xinbian*, N.d., Ke Weiqi
SSY   *Songshi yi*, N.d., Lu Xinyuan
SZFZ   *Suzhou fuzhi*, 1883, Li Mingwan
SZZ   *Shouzhou zhi*, 1550, Li Yonglu
WSXSQJ *Wenshan xiansheng quanji*, N.d., Wen Tianxiang
XZZTJ   *Xu zizhi tongjian*, Bi Yuan
YS   *Yuan shi*, Song Lian
YZZ   *Yizhen zhi*, 1718, Lu Shi
ZJTZ   [*Chixiu*] *Zhejiang tongzhi*, 1736, Fu Wanglu
ZJTZ   *Zhejiang tongzhi*, Fu Wanglu, Ji Zengyun
ZSZP   *Zhaoshi zupu*, 1937, Zhao Xinian
ZZL   *Zhao zhong lu*, N.d.

Appendix A

Emperor Gongdi (Zhao Xian, 1271–1323), r. 1274–1276

Emperor Duanzong (Zhao Shi, 1268–1278), r. 1276–1278

Emperor Bing/Modi (Zhao Bing, 1272–1279), r. 1278–1279

Appendix B

1200
Death of Neo-Confucian Zhu Xi, 3rd month
Death of Empress Li, 6th month and husband Guangzong, 8th
  month

1205
Song initiates Kaixi War against the Jin empire, in the spring

1206
Mutiny of Wu Xi erupts in Sichuan, 12th month

1207
Assassination of military councilor Han Tuozhou, 10th month

1208
Peace restored to the border, in the spring
Shi Miyuan is named right-chief councilor, 10th month (tenure ends
  1233/10th)

1211
Mongols inaugurate raids on the Jin empire

1217
The Jin begins sporadic raids along the Song border, 3rd month

1224
Accession of Emperor Lizong and purge of step-brother Zhao Hong, intercalary 8th month

1225
Zhao Hong, Prince Ji, dies during rebellion, 1st month

1227
Mongols complete conquest of Xixia empire, 6th month

1230
Xie Qiao is installed as empress to Lizong, 11th month

1231
Mongols raid the northwestern border of Song, 8th month

1232
Death of Yang Yan, Empress to Ningzong, 12th month

1233
Song allies with Mongols against Jin, 10th month

1234
Jin is conquered in Song/Mongol campaign, 1st month
Song attempts to reclaim northern capitals of Kaifeng and Luoyang, triggering war with Mongols, 7th month

1239
Shi Songzhi becomes right-chief councilor, 1st month (tenure ends in 1244/9th)

1247
Death of Consort Jia, favorite of Lizong, 2nd month

1256
Wen Tianxiang passes doctoral examination, 5th month
Censor Ding Daquan replaces Dong Huai as right-chief councilor, 6th month

1258
Under direction of Möngke, the Mongols expand their campaign against Sichuan

1259

Jia Sidao is named right-chief councilor, 10th month

Mongols continue campaign against Sichuan

1260

Khubilai accedes to power in the north, 1st month

1261

Inauguration of Public Fields program by Jia Sidao

1264

Lizong dies and is succeeded by Duzong, 10th month

1267

Quan Jiu is installed as empress to Duzong, 6th month

Jia Sidao promoted to military councilor, 2nd month

Yang Juliang is installed as imperial consort to Duzong, 6th month

1270

Li Tingzhi appointed commissioner for Jinghu region

1273

Lü Wenhuan surrenders Xiangyang to the Mongols, 2nd month

1274

Mongols commit over 100,000 men to a three-pronged offensive
against the Song heartland, 2nd month

Emperor Lizong dies and is succeeded by Zhao Xian (Gongdi), Dowager Xie begins regency at court, 7th month

Landslides at Tianmu mountains kills hundreds by drowning, 8th month

Empress Xie issues *qinwang* summons, 12th month

1275

Jia Sidao is routed at Dingjiazhou, 2nd month

Dismissal of Jia Sidao as military councilor, 2nd month; he is assassinated, 9th month

Jiang Wanli perishes at Raozhou, 2nd month

Palace Guardsman Han Zhen is assassinated; Public Fields program rescinded, 3rd month

Changzhou falls to Mongols, 3rd month; again in 11th month

Chen Yizhong is named left-chief councilor, Liu Mengyan named right-chief councilor, and Wang Yue named military councilor, 6th month

Battle of Jiaoshan, 7th month

Zhang Shijie assumes general command of Song forces, 8th month

Liu Mengyan named left-chief councilor, Chen Yizhong named right-chief councilor, 10th month

1276

Li Fu perishes at Tanzhou, Chen Yizhong flees Linan, Song officially surrenders to Yuan, Wen Tianxiang named right-chief councilor, royal princes Zhao Shi and Zhao Bing depart Linan, 1st month

Zhao Shi installed as emperor at Fuzhou, Chen Yizhong named left-chief councilor, 5th month

Song court-in-exile relocates to Huizhou, 12th month

1277

Song court relocates to Zhangzhou, 1st month

Guangzhou falls to Mongols, 2nd month; falls again, 11th month

Suppression of "bogus Son of Heaven" at Tingzhou, 5th month

Song court relocates to Xiushan and Jing'ao, 11th month

Chen Yizhong abandons emperor at Jing'ao for flight to Vietnam, 12th month

1278

Zhao Shi dies at Gangzhou, to be succeeded by step-brother Zhao Bing, 4th month

Song court relocates to Yaishan, 6th month

Wen Tianxiang is captured near Haifeng, 12th month

1279

Song holdouts perish at Yaishan, 2nd month

1283

Wen Tianxiang is executed in Beijing on Jan. 9, 1283 (12th month, 1282)

Appendix C

LIST OF LOYALIST SUICIDES FOR THE LATE SONG[a]

Name	Native Place[b]	Political Status[c]	Primary Biographical/ Historical Sources[d]
Bian Juyi	JX	5	NSS 60:5 SJZYL 4:20a–21a SS 450:13250–51 XZZTJ 180:4931 YS 8:157, 127:3100–01
Cao Chi	KZ	5	BXZ 8:21b–22a NSS 59:11a–11b SJZYL 6:17a SS 451:13283, 13310
*Ms. Chen[e] Imperial Consort	ZD	–	XZZTJ 183:4985
Chen Cun	JX	1	ZJTZ 163:25b
Chen Ge (died at GE)	FJ	3	SJZYL 8:19b
Chen Jiaobo	FJ	6	FJTZ 190:4b SJZYL 8:18b–19a
Chen Jizhou (died at JN)	JW	6	NSS 61:5b SJZYL 5:22a–22b SS 454:13352
Chen Longzhi	CD	5	NSS 59:11a–11b XZZTJ 170:4635
Chen Ta	JE	2	NSS 61:9b SJZYL 5:25a–25b SS 454:13348

Name	Native Place[b]	Political Status[c]	Primary Biographical/ Historical Sources[d]
Chen Wenlong	FJ	1	FJTZ 190:36a–39a NSS 59:5a–6a SJZYL 3:30a–32b SS 451:13278–80 SSXB 175:685a–685b XZZTJ 183:4996/5001 ZZL 31a–32a
Chen Xin	JE	7	WSXSQJ 19:509
Chen Yin (died at LZ)	CD	5	NSS 60:2b SJZYL 4:9b–11a SS 447:13237–38 ZZL 1b
Chen Yisun	JN	6	CSFZ 20:39a
Chen Yuzhi	ZD	7	SJZYL 8:13b–14a SSY 31:25b ZJTZ 166:11b
Chen Zhongqiu	TC	5	RCXZ 12:1a
Cheng Zhu	JE	6	AHTZ 204:3a–3b SSY 31:20a–20b
Deng Deyu (died at GW)	CD	4	NSS 60:7a SJZYL 6:13a–13b XZZTJ 183:4997
Deng Guangjian (died at GE)	JW	1	NSS 60:7b
Er Nai	JX	5	SJZYL 4:19b
Fan Tianshun	JX	4	NSS 59:34a–3b XZZTJ 180:4915 ZZL 14a
Feng, Commander	HE	4	SJZYL 9:11b YS 9:182 YZZ 19:10a
Gao Gui (died at GE)	JE	1	SJZYL 7:20b SSXB 175:685b
Gao Yingsong (died at Beijing)	FJ	1	FJTZ 190:4b NSS 61:9b SJZYL 6:2a SS 454:13347 SSXB 175:686a XZZTJ 183:4985 ZZL 28b–29a
Ge Tiansi	ZX	3	HZFZ 130:9a–9b
Gong Ji	HE	6	GYZZ 10:50a SZFZ 71:19a
Gong Xin (died at JW)	HW	4	NSS 61:5b SJZYL 5:23a–23b

			SS 454:13353
			WSXSQJ 19:491
He Dajie	HW	5	SS 449:13245
Hu Gongzhen	FJ	6	SJZYL *bulu*:18a
			SS 47:935
			XZZTJ 182:4968
Hu Jiangui	JE	6	HZFZ (2) 9:9a
Hu Menglin	JW	5	SJZYL 9:9b
			SS 47:925
			XZZTJ 181:4938
Huang Zhen	ZD	7	*Jianming songshi,* Zhou Baozhu
Jia Chunxiao (died at GE)	TC	1	SNXZ 3:51a–51b
			SS 449:13238
Jiang Wanli	JE	1	NSS 59:1a–3a
			SJZYL 3:1a–3b
			SS 47:926, 418:12523–25
			SSXB 175:683a–683b
			XZZTJ 181:4943–44
			ZZL 15a
Jiang Youzhi	JE	6	AHTZ 204:3b
			SSY 32:12b
Li Fu	JS	4	CSFZ 20:38b–39a
			NSS 59:13a–14a
			SJZYL 6:4b–8a
			SS 47:936, 450:13253–56
			XZZTJ 181:4945, 182:4965/4972
			ZZL 23a–24b
*Lin, Lady	FJ	–	SS 452:13309, 460:13492–93
Liu Dingguo (died at GE)	JE	1	SJZYL 7:21a–21b
Liu Dingsun (died at GE)	JN	1	HBTZ 67:4b
			NSS 61:7a
			SJZYL 6:19b
			SSXB 175:685b
Liu Rongshu	JS	8	CSFZ 28:34b
Liu Rui	LZ	5	NSS 59:10b–11a
			SJZYL 4:11b–12a, 4:15b
			SS 449:13239/13242
Liu Shiyong (died at JX)	HW	4	NSS 61:11a
			SS 451:13274–75
			XZZTJ 182:4977
Liu Shizhao	JW	8	NSS 59:15b
			SS 454:13356
			SSXB 175:686a
			WSXSQJ 19:510

Name	Native Place[b]	Political Status[c]	Primary Biographical/ Historical Sources[d]
Liu Tongzi	FJ	4	NSS 66:7a SJZYL 6:4a–4b ZZL 32b–33b
Liu Xu	ZD	6	SSY 32:24b ZJTZ 165:14a
Lu Xiufu (died at GE)	HE	1	SJZYL 3:24b–30a SS 451:13275–77 SSXB 175:685a XZZTJ 184:5025–28 ZZL 34b–37a
Luo Kaili	JW	6	SSY 32:19b
Ma Fa	GE	5	SJZYL 7:19b–20a
Mao Xiang (died at GE)	FJ	1	SJZYL 7:21a
Miao Chaozong (died at JW)	HE	5	SJZYL bulu: 5a SS 418:12538 WSXSQJ 19:506
Niu Fu (died at JX)	HW	5	NSS 60:5b SJZYL 4:19b–20a SZZ 7:40b–41a XZZTJ 180:4915 ZZL 13b
Pan Fang	ZD	6	SJZYL 6:3a SS 454:13344
Pang Yanhai	KZ	4	XZZTJ 178:4867
Qi Xinglong	north	7	SJZYL 7:4b
Ruan Yingde	ZX	6	SJZYL 9:9b SS 47:927 XZZTJ 181:4948
Shao Yuan	ZD	6	ZJTZ 165:2b
Shen Zhong	JS	6	CSFZ 20:39a NSS 59:13b SJZYL 6:7b XZZTJ 182:4972–73 ZZL 23b–24a
Sima Mengqiu	JN	6	HBTZ 62:14b–15a NSS 60:6a SJZYL 6:16b–17a SS 47:927, 452:13309
Song Yinglong	HE	7	NSS 59:4a SJZYL 5:8a–8b SS 421:12602–03, 454:13349 SSXB 175:683a XZZTJ 183:4992

Sun Huchen	HE	5	SJZYL *bulu*:17a
			XZZTJ 182:4964
			YZZ 19:9a–9b
Tang Taiyu	JE	7	AHTZ 206:2b
Wang Fu	JE	5	SJZYL 4:20a
(died at JX)			SZZ 7:41a
			XZZTJ 180:4915
Wang Guixing	CD	6	SJZYL 7:11b
(died at JE)			SSY 32:6a–6b
Wang Jue	HW	5	ZJTZ 165:2b
Wang Lixin	HW	5	CSFZ 20:38a
(died at JS)			NSS 59:7a–9a
			SZZ 7:38a–38b
			XZZTJ 180:4927–28,
			181:4946–47
			ZZL 15b–16a
Wang Shichang	TC	4	SJZYL 8:24b, 9:8a
			SS 451:13283
			XZZTJ 183:5010
Wang Weichong	JE	1	AHTZ 204:4a
			HZFZ (2) 9:9b–10a
Wang Xian	KZ	5	NSS 60:3b
			SJZYL 4:14b–15a
			SS 452:13310
Wang Yanming	HW	8	QZZ *di*:6a
Wang Yu	CD	6	NSS 59:11b
			SJZYL 4:14b–15a
			SS 449:13242
			ZZL 5a–6a
Wei Hengzhong	ZD	8	ZJTZ 166:3b
Xia Yi	JE	5	AHTZ 241:3b
(died at HW)			SJZYL 7:3b–4a
			SS 47:925
			SSY 32:14b
			XZZTJ 181:4939
Xian Long	KZ	4	SS 451:13283
Xie Xu	ZX	7	HZFZ 130:8b–9a
			NSS 59:2a–2b
			ZJTZ 163:6b
Xiong Fei	GE	7	SJZYL *bulu*:20b
			SS 47:941
			XZZTJ 183:4994–95
Xu Biaosun	CD	6	NSS 59:11a–11b
(died at TC)			SS 449:13240
			ZZL 11a–11b

Name	Native Place[b]	Political Status[c]	Primary Biographical/ Historical Sources[d]
Xu Daolong (died at ZX)	ZD	5	SJZYL 5:15b–16a SS 451:13267 ZJTZ 165:13b–14a ZZL 27b–28b
Xu Yingbiao	ZD	7	NSS 61:9a–9b SJZYL 6:1a–1b SS 451:13277 SSXB 14:55b, 175:686a XZZTJ 182:4981 YS 9:180 ZZL 33b
Xu Zongren (died at GE)	?	1	SS 425:12680–81 SSXB 14:57a, 175:685b
Yan Yingyan	JS	6	CSFZ 20:39a, 28:33b–34a
*Yang Juliang Imperial Consort (died at GE)	ZD	–	SS 243:8662 XZZTJ 184:5027 ZSZP 1:70a
Yang Mengdou (died at HE)	FJ	7	FJTZ 190:4a SSY 31:21a
Yang Shu	ZD	6	ZJTZ 164:12a
Yang Ting	JS	6	CSFZ 28:35a–35b SS 450:13258–59
Yang Zhen	JS	4	NSS 59:13b–14b SJZYL 6:9b–10b SS 47:936, 450:13256 SSXB 175:682b XZZTJ 182:4972–74
Yin Gu	JS	5	NSS 59:13b–14a SJZYL 6:8a–9b SS 47:936, 450:13256–57 SSXB 175:682b XZZTZ 182:4972–73 ZZL 24b
Yin Yuexiu	JS	7	ZZL 24b
*Yong, Lady	JN	–	NSS 59:9a SS 450:13259
Yuan Tianyu	JS	8	SSXB 175:684b
Yuan Yong	ZD	8	SJZYL 8:9a–9b SSY 32:2b–4a ZJTZ 164:2b
Zeng Fenglong (died at GE)	JW	5	SJZYL 7:18a–18b
Zeng Ruji	JS	5	HNTZ 96:12a SJZYL 7:7b–8a

Zhang Jue (died at TC)	LZ	4	NSS 60:3a–3b SJZYL 8:21b–25b SMSC 494–497 SS 451:13280–83 XZZTJ 183:5009–10, 185:5041 YS 9:188 ZZL 29a–29b
Zhang Zhensun	GE	5	XZZTJ 183:5010
Zhang Zi	TC	5	SJZYL 9:9a SS 47:922
Zhao Li	KZ	5	BXZ 9:17a–17b NSS 60:3b SJZYL 6:17a SS 451:13283–84
Zhao Liangchun (died at ZX)	JE	5	NSS 40:13b–14a SJZYL 5:14a–15b SS 47:937, 451:13265–66 ZZL 27b–28b
Zhao Maofa (died at JE)	JN	5	HZFZ 130:8a–8b SJYZL 5:8b–10a SS 47:925, 450:13259 SSXB 175:682b XZZTJ 181:4941 YS 8:161, 127:3104 ZZL 14a–14b
Zhao Qian	JE	8	NSS 59:5a
Zhao Qiao	GE	1	SJZYL 7:20b SSXB 175:685b
Zhao Shijian	JE	6	AHTZ 209:3b SJZYL 7:2a SSY 32:8b
Zhao Shikua	GE	6	SJZYL 7:6b
Zhao Xiji	GE	4	SJZYL 5:18a–18b
Zhao Youtai (died at KC)	?	5	SS 451:13283
Zhao Zaisun (died at ZX)	JE	8	ZZL 28b
Zheng Bingsun	LZ	6	SJZYL 9:5b
Zheng Xian	ZD	2	SJZYL 8:6a
Zhong Kejun	JW	7	SJZYL 7:5a
*Zhu, Imperial Consort (died at Beijing)	ZD	–	XZZTJ 183:4985
Zhu Jun	FJ	1	FJTZ 190:13a–13b SJZYL 8:16b SSY 31:15a ZZL 32b

Name	Native Place[b]	Political Status[c]	Primary Biographical/ Historical Sources[d]
Zou Feng (died at GE)	JW	1	SJZYL 5:19b–20a SS 418:12538 SSXB 175:684a WSXSQJ 19:505 XZZTJ 184:5021

Notes: [a]This category includes men and women who died at their own hands or committed suicide through the assistance of family and friends. Thus, Wen Tianxiang has been excluded, in that he died at the hands of Yuan executioners. Also excluded are men such as Xie Fangde (1226–1289), individuals who purportedly committed suidice out of loyalist devotion to Song but waited many years to do so, which raises issues beyond the scope of this book.

[b]CD = Chengdu circuit   FJ = Fujian circuit
GE = Guangnan East circuit   GW = Guangnan West circuit
HE = Huainan East circuit   HW = Huainan West circuit
JE = Jiangnan East circuit   JN = Jinghu North circuit
JS = Jinghu South circuit   JW = Jiangnan West circuit
JX = Jingxi circuit   KZ = Kuizhou circuit
LZ = Lizhou circuit   TC = Tongchuan circuit
ZD = Zhedong circuit   ZX = Zhexi circuit

An additional note will stipulate those occasions when a martyr has died outside of his or her native circuit, these being exceptional cases.

[c]1 = high-level court officer (rank 1–3)
2 = mid-level court officer (rank 4–6)
3 = low-level court officer (rank 7–9)
4 = high-level regional officer (rank 1–3)
5 = mid-level regional officer (rank 4–6)
6 = low-level regional officer (rank 7–9)
7 = unspecified official status
8 = commoner without official standing

[d]This is a select bibliography. My preference here is for sources most immediate in time to the Song; Ming and Qing references are included only in the absence of earlier documentation or when they add valuable information not found elsewhere. For additional secondary sources, the reader should consult the relevant footnotes accompanying the text.

[e]Asterisk (*) indicates female martyr.

Notes
List of Works Cited
Glossary
Index

Notes

CHAPTER 1: *SHI*

1. This and subsequent headings for each chapter are quoted, with slight modification, from Richard Wilhelm and Cary F. Baynes, trans., *The I Ching, or Book of Changes* (Princeton: Princeton University Press, 1969), pp. 33, 76, 171, 182, 198, and 209, respectively.

2. On the location of Yaishan, see Jian Youwen, *Songmo erdi nanqian nianlu kao* (Hong Kong: Mengjin shuwu congshu, 1957), pp. 90–92; Li Tianming, *Song Yuan zhanshi* (Taipei: Shihuo chubanshe, 1988), vol. 2, p. 1439; Luo Xianglin, "Song wangtai yu songji zhi haishang xingchao," in *Songshi yanjiu ji* (Taipei: Zhonghua congshu, 1977), vol. 9, pp. 99–146 (esp. 109–111); Tan Qixiang, ed., *Zhongguo lishi ditu ji* (Shanghai: Ditu chubanshe, 1982), vol. 6, pp. 65–66. Some scholars suggest a location slightly farther west, but still in modern Guangdong province. On the debate, see Jennifer W. Jay, *A Change in Dynasties: Loyalism in Thirteenth-Century China* (Bellingham: Western Washington University, Center for East Asian Studies, 1991), p. 85; Jian Youwen, *Song huangtai jinian ji* (Hong Kong: Rongfeng, 1960), pp. 175–206.

   More precisely, Yaishan in Song times was merely a mountain range on the southern end of an island off the coast of Xinhui county, which in turn was subordinate to Guangzhou prefecture, Guangnan East circuit. But historians often refer to the entire island by the name of the southern region where Song armies were concentrated and the confrontation with Yuan forces occurred.

3. On the Yaishan debaucle, see *Songji sanchao zhengyao* (Congshu jicheng edition), juan 6, pp. 70–71; Jian, *Songmo erdi nanqian*, p. 90; Zhao Xinian, *Zhaoshi zupu* (Hong Kong, 1937), juan 1, pp. 74b–75a, juan 1, p. 80b; Qian Shisheng, *Nansong Shu* (n.d.), juan 6, p. 15b; Xu Qianxue, *Zizhi tongjian houbian* (Siku quanshu edition), juan 152, pp. 10b–11a; Bi Yuan, *Xu zizhi tongjian* (Beijing: Guji chubanshe, 1957), juan 184, p. 5015; Otto Franke, *Geschichte des Chinesischen Reiches: Eine Darstellung seiner Entstehung, seines Wesens und seiner Entwicklung bis zur Neuesten Zeit* (Berlin: Verlag von Walter de Gruyter and Co., 1948), vol. 4, pp. 348–349; Horst Wolfram Huber, "Between Land and Sea: The End of the Southern Sung," *Analecta Husserliana*, vol. 19 (1985), pp. 101–128.

4. Tuo Tuo [Toghto], et al., *Song Shi* (Beijing: Zhonghua shuju, 1977), juan 243, p. 8662; Zhao, *Zhaoshi zupu*, juan 1, p. 70a.

5. For biographical information on Lu Xiufu and Zhang Shijie, see Tuo Tuo, *Song Shi*, juan 451, pp. 13275–13277; Wan Sitong, *Songji zhongyi lu* (Siming congshu edition), juan 3, pp. 21a–24b, juan 3, pp. 24b–30a; Jiang Yixue, *Lu Xiufu nianpu* (Shanghai: Shangwu yinshukuan, 1936).

6. Song Lian, et al., *Yuan Shi* (Beijing: Zhonghua shuju, 1976), juan 129, pp. 3155–3159, juan 156, pp. 3679–3684.

7. On this decisive battle, see Jiang, *Lu Xiufu nianpu*, pp. 23–27; Chen Bangzhan, Feng Qi, *Songshi jishi benmo* (Beijing: Zhonghua shuju, 1977), juan 108, pp. 1180–1182; Huang Jin, *Huang wenxiangong ji* (Congshu jicheng edition), juan 3, pp. 111–113; Li, *Song Yuan zhanshi*, vol. 3, pp. 1477–1482; Luo, "Song wangtai," pp. 103–104; Bi, *Xu tongjian*, juan 184, pp. 5024–5028; Umehara Kaoru, *Ben Tenshō* (Tokyo: Jimbutsu yukikisha, 1969), pp. 247–252.

8. A prominent secondary source, authored by Liu Boji and based upon a variety of primary materials, suggests 700 ships on the Yuan side. My lower estimate of 300–400 is based on the eyewitness account of Wen Tianxiang, formerly chief councilor and military commander of the Song. At the time of the Yuan assault on Yaishan, he was prisoner on a nearby enemy ship and reports of over 1,000 ships on the Song side, "a very great many of them large." Yuan assets, however, he reports at only 500 ships of all sizes, the bulk presumably small, of which 200 had already been lost at sea and unavailable for deployment. See Liu Boji, *Songdai zhengjiao shi* (Taipei: Taiwan zhonghua shuju, 1971), vol. 1, p. 520; Wen Tianxiang, *Wenshan xiansheng quanji* (Shanghai: Shijie shuju, 1936), juan 16, p. 405.

9. Li, *Song Yuan zhanshi*, vol. 3, p. 1479.

10. Edward H. Schafer, *The Vermilion Bird: T'ang Images of the South* (Berkeley: University of California Press, 1967), p. 105.

11. Wen, *Wenshan quanji*, juan 15, p. 384.

12. Wen, *Wenshan quanji*, juan 14, p. 350. My translation but also interpretation of this poem differs rather dramatically from another proposed by literary scholars; see Yoshikawa Kojiro, *Five Hundred Years of Chinese Poetry, 1150–1650*, translated by John T. Wixted (Princeton: Princeton University Press, 1989), p. 51.

13. Li E, *Songshi jishi* (Taipei: Dingwen shuju, 1971), juan 81, p. 33a.

14. Tuo Tuo, *Song Shi*, juan 47, p. 945; Song Lian, *Yuan Shi*, juan 129, p. 3158; Chen, *Songshi jishi benmo*, juan 108, p. 1182; Li, *Song Yuan zhanshi*, vol. 3, p. 1481.

    This figure is very likely exaggerated. The first-hand account by Wen Tianxiang refers to "tens of thousands having died by drowning," as evidenced by their floating bodies. Yet he seems to be conflating the numbers for those killed *before* entering the water (genuine suicide cases) with those to die *afterwards* (war casualties), for the bodies of actual drowning victims would have taken a minimum of several days to surface. Nonetheless, the implication here is that *total deaths* did not exceed thirty to forty thousand, one-third the official number. A similar casualty count is confirmed by Huang Jin, a contemporary of Wen Tianxiang who based upon first-hand sources depicts deaths, on the Song side, as numbering in the "tens of thousands." See Wen, *Wenshan quanji*, juan 16, p. 404; Huang, *Huang wenxiangong ji*, juan 3, p. 113.

15. Tuo Tuo, *Song Shi*, juan 449, p. 13238; Sun Hai, et al., *Suining xianzhi* (1878 edition) juan 3, pp. 51a–51b.

16. See biography of Lu Xiufu in *Zhao zhong lu* (Baibu congshu jicheng edition), p. 36a.

17. Tuo Tuo, *Song Shi*, juan 243, p. 8662, juan 451, p. 13274; Bi, *Xu tongjian*, juan 184, p. 5027.

18. Most sources portray the drowning of Zhang Shijie as accidental, but one source insists that he drank himself to death out of depression over recent setbacks. See Wan, *Songji zhongyi lu*, juan 3, p. 24b.

19. Cheng Minzheng, *Song yimin lu* (Baibu congshu jicheng edition) juan 10, pp. 8b–14a.

20. For biographical information, see Wan, *Songji zhongyi lu*, juan 11, pp. 30a–32a; Jay, *Change of Dynasties*, pp. 157–167.
21. This translation is based on the poem as it appears in Yuan Youzong, *Aiguo shici xuan* (Taipei: Taiwan shangwu yinshuguan, 1982), pp. 414–415. The text varies slightly in other editions of Fang Feng's collected works; see *Cunyatang yigao* (Siku quanshu edition), juan 1, p. 6b.
22. Wen, *Wenshan quanji*, juan 14, p. 350. See alternative translation in Yoshikawa, *Five Hundred Years of Chinese Poetry*, p. 51.
23. Our idiom derives not from Wen Tianxiang, but Alfred Lord Tennyson ("Tiresias").
24. Wen, *Wenshan quanji*, juan 17, p. 460, juan 19, p. 494; William Andreas Brown, *Wen T'ien-hsiang, A Biographical Study of a Sung Patriot* (San Francisco: Chinese Materials Center Publications, 1986), pp. 151, 158–59, 216, 218.
25. Wen, *Wenshan quanji*, juan 17, pp. 461–462; Brown, *Wen T'ien-hsiang*, pp. 160–162, 219–221.
26. Wen, *Wenshan quanji*, juan 15, p. 384.
27. Wen, *Wenshan quanji*, juan 15, p. 385.
28. Wen, *Wenshan quanji*, juan 15, p. 387. The use of literary works, in Song times, to foster virtues of civic duty is evidenced in the novel *Master Tung's Western Chamber Romance: A Chinese Chantefable*, by Tung Chieh-yuan (New York: Columbia University Press, 1994).
29. Wen, *Wenshan quanji*, juan 15, p. 385.
30. Tuo Tuo, *Song Shi*, juan 419, p. 12540; Brown, *Wen T'ien-hsiang*, p. 168.
31. Jay, *Change of Dynasties*, p. 126.
32. Brown, *Wen T'ien-hsiang*, pp. 142–143, 213; Wen, *Wenshan quanji*, juan 16, p. 433, juan 17, p. 457, juan 19, p. 491; Bi, *Xu tongjian*, juan 183, p. 5005; Li An, *Song Wen chengxiang tianxiang nianpu* (Taipei: Taiwan shangwu yinshuguan, 1980), pp. 72–73; Wan Shengnan, *Wen Tianxiang zhuan* (Henan: Henan renmin chubanshe, 1985), pp. 166–168.
33. Wen, *Wenshan quanji*, juan 16, p. 431, juan 17, p. 457; Brown, *Wen T'ien-hsiang*, p. 143n284.
34. Brown, *Wen T'ien-hsiang*, p. 215; Li, *Song Wen chengxiang*, p. 74.
35. Wen, *Wenshan quanji*, juan 16, pp. 432–433; Wan, *Wen Tianxiang zhuan*, p. 260; Wu Pei-yi, *The Confucian's Progress: Autobiographical Writings in Traditional China* (Princeton: Princeton University Press, 1990), p. 38.
36. Wan, *Wen Tianxiang zhuan*, pp. 220–221; Brown, *Wen T'ien-hsiang*, pp. 46, 224.
37. Most traditional writings suggest that Wen Tianxiang and his younger brother passed the same doctoral examination, in 1256, but a recent study has argued convincingly to the contrary. See Brown, *Wen T'ien-hsiang*, p. 97n8.
38. For an informative funeral inscription, see Liu Yueshen, *Shenzhai liu xiansheng wenji* (Zhibuzu zhai edition), juan 10, pp. 1a–4a; Li, *Song Wen chengxiang*, p. 82; Wan, *Wen Tianxiang zhuan*, pp. 250–251. One writer suggests, in the case of Wen Bi, a more "reluctant" defection to the Mongols; see Jay, *Change in Dynasties*, p. 135.
39. Zheng Sixiao, *Tie'han xinshi* (Sibu kanyao edition) (rpt. Taipei: Shijie shuju, 1970), juan 2, p. 12a.
40. Wen, *Wenshan quanji*, juan 15, p. 393. Cf. translations in Brown, *Wen T'ien-hsiang*, pp. 162–164n375; Jay, *Change in Dynasties*, p. 112.
41. Wan, *Wen Tianxiang zhuan*, pp. 235–236; Wu, *The Confucian's Progress*, pp. 34–35.
42. Wen, *Wenshan quanji*, juan 16, p. 431.
43. Li, *Songshi jishi*, juan 67, p. 7b.
44. Wen, *Wenshan quanji*, juan 16, p. 433, juan 16, p. 432, respectively; Wu, *The Confucian's Progress*, p. 38.
45. Wen, *Wenshan quanji*, juan 16, p. 432, juan 16, p. 434.

46. Wen, *Wenshan quanji*, juan 15, p. 386, juan 15, p. 385, respectively.
47. Liu, *Shenzhai wenji*, juan 10, p. 1a, juan 10, p. 4a. Italics added.
48. D. C. Lau, translator, *Mencius* (New York: Penguin, 1970), p. 125 [IV/A/19].
49. Confucius, *Analects*, p. 121 [XIII/18].
50. Cf. translation by D. C. Lau, in Confucius, *Analects*, p. 59 [I/2].
51. *Xiao jing* (Sibu congkan edition) juan 1, p. 3b.
52. Based on translation by James Legge, with modifications; see *Li Chi: Book of Rites: An Encyclopedia of Ancient Ceremonial Usages, Religious Creeds, and Social Institutions*, edited by Ch'u Chai and Winberg Chai (New Hyde Park, N.Y.: University Books, 1967), vol. 2, pp. 236–237 [XXII/2]; *Liji* (Sibu congkan edition) juan 14, pp. 15b–16a.
    Only when I differ substantively with a translator over meaning or presentation, will the Chinese original be cited alongside the English translation.
53. Ouyang Xiu, *Wudai shiji* [*Xin wudai shi*] (Beijing: Zhonghua shuju, 1974), juan 15, p. 162. Italics added.
54. Wan, *Songji zhongyi lu*, juan 7, pp. 5b–6b; Wen, *Wenshan quanji*, juan 19, p. 510.
55. Wan, *Songji zhongyi lu*, juan 8, pp. 13b–14a; Lu Xinyuan, *Song Shi yi*, 1906 edition (rpt. Taipei: Dingwen shuju, 1978), juan 31, p. 25b; Fu Wanglu, et al., [*Chixiu*] *Zhejiang tongzhi* (1735 edition), juan 116, p. 11b.
56. Lu, *Song Shi yi*, juan 32, p. 12b; He Shaoji, et al., [*Chongxiu*] *Anhui tongzhi* (1877 edition) juan 204, p. 3b.
57. Lu, *Song Shi yi*, juan 32, pp. 2b–4a; Wan, *Songji zhongyi lu*, juan 8, pp. 9a–9b; Fu, *Zhejiang tongzhi*, juan 164, p. 2b.
58. On the collapse of Ningbo, known in Song times as Mingzhou, see Dai Mei, et al., [*Xinxiu*] *Yinxian zhi* (1887 edition), juan 14, p. 40b, juan 15, p. 1a.
59. Andrew C.K. Hsieh and Jonathan D. Spence, "Suicide and the Family in Pre-modern Chinese Society," in Arthur Kleinman and Tsung-yi Lin, eds., *Normal and Abnormal Behavior in Chinese Culture* (Dordrecht, Holland: D. Reidel Publishing Co., 1981), pp. 29–47 (esp. 31).
60. Wei Shou, *Wei Shu* (Beijing: Zhonghua shuju, 1974), juan 87, p. 1889.
61. For one such example of a marginal loyalist, see biography of Liu Dunru, in Liu Xu, et al., *Jiu Tang shu* (Beijing: Zhonghua shuju, 1975), juan 187b, pp. 4910–4911.
62. Ouyang Xiu, et al., *Xin Tang shu* (Beijing: Zhonghua shuju, 1975), juan 191–193.
63. I will offer no more elaborate a definition of "loyalism" (*zhongyi*) than this. A recent author, while similarly avoiding a fixed definition, nonetheless seeks to characterize their behavior by dividing loyalists into three categories: 1) martyrs who died, willfully or not, for the Song cause; 2) survivors who out of devotion to the old order boycotted the new (the permanently disenfranchised); 3) survivors who identified with the old order but eventually entered the service of the new (the marginally disenfranchised). See Jay, *Change of Dynasties*, pp. 10–11. Characterizations of this sort appear consistent with scholarship for other periods; see Lynn A. Struve, "Ambivalence and Action: Some Frustrated Scholars of the K'ang-hsi Period," in Jonathan D. Spence and John E. Wills, Jr., eds., *From Ming to Ch'ing: Conquest, Region, and Continuity in Seventeenth-Century China* (New Haven: Yale University, 1979), pp. 323–365 (esp. 326–327); Tom Fisher, "Loyalist Alternatives in the Early Ch'ing," *Harvard Journal of Asiatic Studies*, vol. 44, no. 1 (June, 1984), pp. 83–122 (esp. 83–84).
64. Tuo Tuo, *Song Shi*, juan 446, p. 13149. On Fan Zhi and Wang Pu, see biographies by Jack L. Dull in Herbert Franke, et al., *Sung Biographies* (Wiesbaden: Franz Steiner Verlag GMBH, 1976), pp. 310–321, 1131–1137. As for Han Tong and Wei Yong, see Tuo Tuo, *Song Shi*, juan 484, pp. 13968–13970, juan 482, pp. 13941–13942; and Wang Gungwu biography of the former in Franke, *Sung Biographies*, pp. 384–387.
65. For an overview of these changes and modern assessments of their significance, see

James T.C. Liu and Peter J. Golas, *Change in Sung China: Innovation or Renovation?* (Boston: D.C. Heath & Co., 1969).

66, James T.C. Liu, "Sung Roots of Chinese Political Conservatism: The Administrative Problems," *Journal of Asian Studies*, vol. 26, no. 3 (May, 1967), pp. 457–463.

67. Tuo Tuo, *Song Shi*, juan 47, p. 935; Song, *Yuan Shi*, juan 127, pp. 3100–3101, juan 127, p. 3107, juan 128, p. 3127; Bi, *Xu tongjian*, juan 170, p. 4635, juan 180, pp. 4930–4931, juan 183, p. 4968, juan 182, pp. 4980–4981, juan 183, p. 5007, juan 183, p. 5011; Hu Zhaoxi, Tang Weimu, *Songmo sichuan zhanzheng shiliao xuanbian* (Chengdu: Sichuan renmin chubanshe, 1984), p. 441; Li Zhen, et al., *Zhongguo lidai zhanzheng shi* (Taipei: Sanjun lianhe canmou daxue, 1968), Section 6, vol. 11, p. 427.

68. Song, *Yuan Shi*, juan 8, pp. 155–156; also see Chapter 4, below.

69. Tuo Tuo, et al., *Jin Shi* (Beijing: Zhonghua shuju, 1976), juan 123, p. 2688.

70. This conclusion is based on a survey of the "loyalist" chapters in the dynastic history. There are a few notable exceptions. A commoner of Chinese ethnicity, Guo Xiama, with high standing in the Jin military establishment, reportedly orchestrated mass death for himself, his family, and fellow defenders when the dynasty fell in 1234. A reported 500 military men, most apparently of Jurchen ethnicity, are claimed to have committed suicide with the last emperor of Jin, as well. See Tuo Tuo, *Jin Shi*, juan 121–124, esp. juan 124, pp. 2708–2711; Bi, *Xu tongjian*, juan 167, pp. 4555–4556.

71. Ouyang Xiu, *Wudai shiji*, juan 54, p. 611.

72. Hoyt Cleveland Tillman, "Proto-Nationalism in Twelfth-Century China? The Case of Ch'en Liang" *Harvard Journal of Asiatic Studies*, vol. 39, no. 2 (Dec. 1979), pp. 403–428 (esp. 417–419).

73. Chen Liang, *Chen Liang ji* (Sibu kanyao edition), juan 1, p. 3. The presumption of geomantic inferiority does not necessarily lead to fatalism for Chen Liang, a man native to the southeast. "Although a peripheral land," he writes, "never has the [pent-up] energy of peripheral lands gone five to six hundred years without releasing itself." (Ibid., juan 1, p. 8) The southeast having failed for centuries to act on an agenda of dynastic aggression has now, in effect, the reserve power to succeed.

74. For further elaboration on their views on the "peripheralness" of the southeast vs. southwest, see Winston Wan Lo, *The Life and Thought of Yeh Shih* (Gainesville: University Presses of Florida, 1974), pp. 58–59; Wang Fuzhi, *Song Lun* (Sibu kanyao edition), juan 14, pp. 253–255.

75. Information below on Linan and its material amenities are based upon Patricia Buckley Ebrey, ed., *Chinese Civilization and Society: A Sourcebook* (New York: The Free Press, 1981), pp. 100–106; Gernet, *Daily Life*, pp. 22–58.

76. Chen, *Chen Liang ji*, juan 1, p. 7.

77. In his Historical Records of the Five Dynasties, for example, Ouyang Xiu affirms the consumption and debauchery of the Wu region as the most pronounced of the entire south. See *Wudai Shiji*, juan 61, p. 747, juan 67, p. 843.

78. Lo, *Life and Thought of Yeh Shih*, p. 49; Wang Jianqiu, *Songdai taixue yu taixuesheng* (Taipei: Taiwan shangwu yinshuguan, 1965), pp. 232–238.

79. Wen, *Wenshan quanji*, juan 15, p. 388; also see, juan 10, p. 249.

80. Wm. Theodore de Bary, "Chu Hsi's Aims as an Educator," in Wm. Theodore de Bary and John W. Chaffee, ed., *Neo-Confucian Education: The Formative Stage* (Berkeley: University of California Press, 1989), pp. 186–218 (esp. 202).

81. For a useful critique of the relevant literature, see Arthur Brittan, *Masculinity and Power* (Oxford: Basil Blackwell, 1989), pp. 1–18, 77–107.

82. Empress Renxiao [née Xu], *Nei xun* (Congshu jicheng edition), p. 476b. Although written in 1406, the *Nei xun* represents codification of earlier precepts on female behavior. Also see R.H. van Gulik, *Sexual Life in Ancient China* (Leiden: E.J. Brill, 1974), p. 99.

83. For a fascinating perspective on the links between material abundance and reactionary

militancy, see Jeffrey Herf, *Reactionary Modernism: Technology, Culture, and Politics in Weimar and the Third Reich* (Cambridge: Cambridge University Press, 1984) p. 24.

84. On the "moral rigorism" of Southern Song Confucianism and its spreading appeal, see Wm. Theodore de Bary, *Neo-Confucian Orthodoxy and the Learning of the Mind-and-Heart* (New York: Columbia University Press, 1981), pp. 98–131.

85. Ouyang Xiu, *Wudai shiji*, juan 54, p. 612.

86. Wang Gung-wu, "Feng Tao: An Essay on Confucian Loyalty," in Arthur F. Wright and Denis Twitchett, ed., *Confucian Personalities* (Stanford: Stanford University Press, 1962), pp. 123–145.

87. Ouyang Xiu, *Wudai shiji*, juan 54, p. 614.

88. For a useful critique of the historian's approach to gender, see Michael Roper and John Tosh, eds., *Manful Assertions: Masculinities in Britain since 1800* (London: Routledge, 1991), Introduction, pp. 1–16.

89. Song, *Yuan Shi*, juan 127, p. 3108.

CHAPTER 2: *GU*

1. Bi, *Xu tongjian*, juan 180, p. 4928.

2. On the population of Linan, see Jacques Gernet, *Daily Life in China on the Eve of the Mongol Invasion, 1250–1276* (Stanford: Stanford University Press, 1962), pp. 29–30. Gernet's estimate of a million or so residents for the "whole area" of Linan is quite conservative. A good many scholars in Asia estimate a considerably larger population. On the controversy, see Yoshinobu Shiba, "Urbanization and the Development of Markets in the Lower Yangtze Valley," in John Winthrop Haeger, ed., *Crisis and Prosperity in Sung China* (Tucson: University of Arizona Press, 1975), pp. 22–23; Lin Zhengqiu, *Nansong ducheng linan* (Hangzhou: Xiling yinshe, 1986), pp. 174–185.

3. Even within the 1271 gazetteer for Linan, there exists considerable discrepancy about the height and area of Tianmu Shan. On these, see Qian Yueyou, [*Xianchun*] *Linan zhi* (Songyuan difangzhi congshu edition) juan 25, p. 1, juan 26, pp. 1a–1b.

4. Watson, Burton, *The Columbia Book of Chinese Poetry: From Early Times to the Thirteenth Century* (New York: Columbia University Press, 1984), p. 217.

5. Li You, *Guhang zaji* (Congshu jicheng edition), p. 1.

6. Qian, *Linan zhi*, juan 25, p. 1a. For a valuable discussion of monarchical interest in and subsidy of local gods, see Valerie Hansen, *Changing Gods in Medieval China, 1127–1276* (Princeton: Princeton University Press, 1990).

7. Li, *Guhang zaji*, p. 1.

8. Drawing upon earlier chronicles, Qing historian Bi Yuan characterizes Zhao Qi in the following manner: "his words were always consistent with proper measure" (*yan bi he du*). This was apparently the inspiration for his rather unusual posthumous name. See Bi, *Xu tongjian*, juan 178, p. 4853.

9. Ding Chuanjing, *Songren yishi huibian* (reprint Taipei: Taiwan shangwu yinshuguan, 1982), juan 3, p. 102, juan 18, pp. 1013–1014; Ebrey, *Inner Quarters*, p. 181.

10. On these criticisms, see Tuo Tuo, *Song Shi*, juan 46; Bi, *Xu tongjian*, juan 179, p. 4893, juan 180, p. 4927; Huang Zhen, *Huangshi richao gujin jiyao yibian* (Congshu jicheng edition), pp. 11–14; Ding, *Songren yishi huibian*, juan 3, p. 103. See also my detailed narrative for the Duzong reign, forthcoming in *The Cambridge History of China*, vol. 5.

11. Song, *Yuan Shi*, juan 8, pp. 155–156. On Khubilai's role in the 1259 campaign of Möngke and negotiations with the Song, see Morris Rossabi, *Khubilai Khan, His Life and Times* (Berkeley: University of California Press, 1988), pp. 48–50, 81.

12. Tuo Tuo, *Song Shi*, juan 46, pp. 918–919.

13. For 25 of its 166 years, the Northern Song had female regencies—most of them fairly stable. No repetition occurred in Southern Song times, prior to 1274, chiefly for two

reasons: incapacitated emperors tended to abdicate (as with Gaozong, Xiaozong, and Guangzong), while heirless rulers tended to adopt more mature heirs (Gaozong, Ningzong, and Lizong). See Priscilla Ching Chung, *Palace Women in the Northern Sung, 960–1126* (Leiden: E.J. Brill, 1981), p. 6; Zhang Bangwei, *Songdai huangqin yu zhengzhi* (Chengdu: Sichuan renmin chubanshe, 1993), pp. 143–146.

14. The personal name and dates for Empress Xie vary slightly from source to source. Information within the dynastic history is not altogether consistent and these inconsistencies are reflected in secondary works. See Tuo Tuo, *Song Shi*, juan 243, pp. 8658–8660; Zhao, *Zhaoshi zupu*, juan 1, p. 69a; Zheng, *Tie'han xinshi*, juan 2, p. 33b; Franke, *Sung Biographies*, biography by Priscilla Ching Chung and H. Chiba, vol. 1, pp. 410–412; Deng Guangming, *Zhongguo lishi da cidian: Song Shi* (Shanghai: Shanghai cishu chubanshe, 1984), p. 477.

15. Tuo Tuo, *Song Shi*, juan 394, pp. 12038–12041, esp. juan 394, p. 12038.

16. For biographical information on Empress Yang, see Richard L. Davis, *Court and Family in Sung China, 960–1279* (Durham: Duke University Press, 1986), pp. 84–105; Franke, *Sung Biographies*, biography by Priscilla Ching Chung and H. Chiba, pp. 1222–1226; Tuo Tuo, *Song Shi*, juan 243, pp. 8656–8658; Zhao, *Zhaoshi zupu*, juan 1, p. 67a.

17. I have dealt rather extensively with Empress Li, wife of Guangzong (r. 1189–1194), and her violent outbursts of jealousy in my political narrative for *The Cambridge History of China*, vol. 5 (forthcoming). Also see Bi, *Xu tongjian*, juan 152, p. 4079; Tuo Tuo, *Song Shi*, juan 36, p. 701.

18. Tuo Tuo, *Song Shi*, juan 243, p. 8659. Some might interpret as possibly vindictive the decision by Dowager Xie, in 1275, to confiscate the lands attached to monasteries where two consorts of her former husband once lived. In light of the court's economic desperation at that time, however, this impresses me as chiefly an economic decision. See Tuo Tuo, *Song Shi*, juan 47, p. 933.

19. Tuo Tuo, *Song Shi*, juan 469, p. 13675.

20. Tuo Tuo, *Song Shi*, juan 243, p. 8659; Bi, *Xu tongjian*, juan 175, p. 4789.

21. Chung, *Palace Women*, pp. 73 ff.

22. On the Zhao Hong affair, see Davis, *Court and Family*, pp. 95–105. At least two prominent officials are recorded as having memorialized the throne, in 1275, to address the posthumous status of the dead prince; see Bi, *Xu tongjian*, juan 181, p. 4954, juan 182, p. 4969; Tuo Tuo, *Song Shi*, juan 47, p. 934, juan 421, p. 12597.

23. For biographical information, see Tuo Tuo, *Song Shi*, juan 41, p. 783, juan 243, pp. 8660–8661; Zhao, *Zhaoshi zupu*, juan 1, p. 68a, juan 1, pp. 69b–70a.

24. Chung, *Palace Women*, pp. 24–29.

25. Ding, *Songren yishi huibian*, juan 3, p. 104.

26. The full exchange is quoted in Tuo Tuo, *Song Shi*, juan 243, p. 8661. An abbreviated and slightly modified rendering of that meeting can be found elsewhere (juan 45, pp. 878–879) in the same source.

27. The two standard translations differ rather significantly; see Lau, *Analects* [I/3], p. 59; Legge, *Analects*, p. 139.

28. For biographical information, see Tuo Tuo, *Song Shi*, juan 243, p. 8662; Zhao, *Zhaoshi zupu*, juan 1, p. 70a.

29. A number of sources, including the memorabilia of the Song anecdotist Zhou Mi, have made this claim. This is a consequence, no doubt, of two men sharing the same rather familiar name, Yang Zhen, and being related to palace consorts of the mid-thirteenth century. But a careful examination of the dates for the various persons and their ostensibly convoluted relationship to one another seems to discredit this theory, as does the low status of Consort Yang when she entered the harem of Duzong. See Ding, *Songren*

yishi huibian, juan 18, p. 1027; Tuo Tuo, *Song Shi*, juan 248, pp. 6789–6790; Zhao, *Zhaoshi zupu*, juan 1, p. 70a; Jian, *Songmo erdi*, p. 6.

30. Jay, *Change of Dynasties*, pp. 201–202.
31. Bi, *Xu tongjian*, juan 183, p. 5007.
32. Zhao, *Zhaoshi zupu*, juan 1, p. 70a.
33. Lien-sheng Yang, "Female Rulers in Imperial China," in John L. Bishop, ed., *Studies of Governmental Institutions in Chinese History* (Cambridge: Harvard University Press, 1968), pp. 155–169 (esp. 55–56); Chung, *Palace Women*, pp. 71–72; Franke, *Sung Biographies*, vol. 1, pp. 494–498; Tuo Tuo, *Song Shi*, juan 242, pp. 8612–8616.
34. Chung, *Palace Women*, pp. 72–74; Yang, "Female Rulers," pp. 55–56; Tuo Tuo, *Song Shi*, juan 242, pp. 8625–8627.
35. Davis, *Court and Family*, pp. 84–104; Tuo Tuo, *Song Shi*, juan 243, pp. 8656–8658.
36. Tuo Tuo, *Song Shi*, juan 243, p. 8658, juan 248, pp. 8789–8790, juan 474, pp. 13779–13780; Bi, *Xu tongjian*, juan 165, p. 4494; Franke, *Sung Biographies*, p. 203.
37. Ding, *Songren yishi huibian*, juan 18, p. 1008.
38. Assorted anecdotes on the social and material life of Jia Sidao, and the principal source for the following paragraph, have been conveniently assembled by Ding Chuanjing; see *Songren yishi huibian*, juan 18, pp. 1006–1025. For a partial translation of this source, including some material on Jia Sidao's material lifestyle, see Ting Ch'uan-ching, *A Compilation of Anecdotes of Sung Personalities*, trans. by Chu Djang and Jane C. Djang (Collegeville, Mn.: St. John's University Press, 1989), pp. 720–730. Also see Zhou Mi, *Qidong yeyu* (Baibu congshu jicheng edition) juan 19, pp. 12a–13b; Li, *Songshi jishi*, juan 96, pp. 34b–38a.
39. Ding, *Songren yishi huibian*, juan 18, p. 1018.
40. Davis, *Court and Family*, pp. 70–71, 111–112, 137–138.
41. On these pronouncements, see Patricia Buckley Ebrey, *The Inner Quarters: Marriage and the Lives of Chinese Women in the Sung Period* (Berkeley: University of California Press, 1993), pp. 101–103; Chu Hsi, *Chu Hsi's Family Rituals: A Twelfth-Century Chinese Manual for the Performance of Cappings, Weddings, Funerals, and Ancestral Rites*, trans. by Patricia Buckley Ebrey (Princeton: Princeton University Press, 1991), pp. 55–56.
42. Chu, *Family Rituals*, p. 56. Interestingly, a parallel association of masculine ornateness to femininity appears in Western writings. In his *Social Contract*, for example, Jean-Jacques Rousseau, claims that military virtue among the Romans died out when "they became connoisseurs of paintings, engravings, jeweled vessels and began to cultivate the fine arts." Thus, he admonishes, "let all kinds of womanish adornment be held in contempt. And if you cannot bring women themselves to renounce it, let them at least be taught to disapprove of it, and view it with disdain in men." Jean Bethke Elshtain, *Women and War* (New York: Basic Books, 1987), p. 61.
43. Chu Hsi and Lü Tsu-ch'ien, *Reflections on Things at Hand: The Neo-Confucian Anthology compiled by Chu Hsi and Lü Tsu-ch'ien*, trans. by Wing-tsit Chan (New York: Columbia University Press, 1967), pp. 135, 137–138.
44. Liu Zijian, "Luelun songdai wuguanchun zai tongzhi jieji zhong di diwei," in *Aoyama hakushi koki kinen: Sōdaishi ronsō* (Tokyo: Seishin shobo, 1974), p. 481.
45. de Bary, *Neo-Confucian Orthodoxy*, p. 128.
46. de Bary, *Neo-Confucian Orthodoxy*, pp. 109–110; Zhen Dexiu, *Xishan wenji* (Siku quanshu edition), juan 29, p. 26a.
47. Franke, *Sung Biographies*, vol. 1, p. 412.
48. Liu, "Luelun songdai wuguanchun," pp. 477–487 (esp. 479).
49. Another prominent exception to this rule of exclusion, a half-century earlier, is Han Tuozhou—and he was similarly ostracized by the degree-holding establishment. See Davis, *Court and Family*, pp. 84–92.

50. On the Public Fields program, see Herbert Franke, "Chia Ssu-tao (1213–1275): A 'Bad Last Minister'?" in Arthur F. Wright and Denis Twitchett, ed., *Confucian Personalities* (Stanford: Stanford University Press, 1962), pp. 217–234 (esp. 229–231); Jay, *Change of Dynasties*, pp. 20–21; Tuo Tuo, *Song Shi*, juan 173, pp. 4194–4195; Bi, *Xu tongjian*, juan 177, p. 4837 *passim*; Zhang Yinlin, "Nansong wangguo shi bu," *Songshi yanjiu ji*, vol. 2 (Taipei: Zhonghua congshu, 1964), pp. 105–122 (esp. 117–122); Chen Dengyuan, *Zhongguo tudi zhidu* (Shanghai: Shangwu yinshuguan, 1935), pp. 195–200. I have also dealt rather extensively with Jia Sidao's tenure as chief councilor and this controversial reform in my survey of the Lizong and Duzong reigns for *The Cambridge History of China*, vol. 5 (forthcoming).

51. In addressing the problem of land accumulation, early Southern Song rulers would go no further than to order land surveys and monitor tax payments; see *Cambridge History of China*, vol. 5 (forthcoming), chapters by Ching-shen Tao and Richard L. Davis. On the broader conservatism of the late Song government, in reaction to the tumultuous reforms of the late eleventh and early twelfth centuries, see James T.C. Liu, "Sung Roots of Chinese Political Conservatism: The Administrative Problems," *Journal of Asian Studies*, vol. 26, no. 3 (May 1967), pp. 457–463.

52. Mark Elvin, *The Pattern of the Chinese Past* (Stanford: Stanford University Press, 1973), pp. 164–178.

53. Quan Hansheng, "Songmo di tonghuo pengzhang ji qi duiyu wujia di yingxiang," *Songshi yanjiu ji*, vol. 2 (Taipei: Zhonghua congshu, 1964), pp. 263–325 (esp. 286–287); Tuo Tuo, *Song Shi*, juan 423, pp. 12634–12636.

54. Robert M. Hartwell, "The Imperial Treasuries: Finance and Power in Song China," *The Bulletin of Sung Yuan Studies*, no. 20 (1988), pp. 16–89 (esp. 72–78).

55. In his collected writings, Wen Tianxiang alludes to this special fund established by Emperor Lizong and reserved for emergency military expenses. See *Wenshan quanji*, juan 3, p. 48.

56. Jian, *Songmo erdi nanqian*, p. 90; Bi, *Xu tongjian*, juan 184, p. 5015; Zhao, *Zhaoshi zupu*, juan 1, p. 74b.

57. Estimates of some 93,000 households—400,000 to 500,000 individuals—for the prefectural population of Xiangyang is based on Aoyama Sadao, "Zui Tō Sō sandai ni okeru kosu no chiiki teki kōsatsu, *Rekishigaku kenkyū*, vol. 6 (1936), no. 4, pp. 411–446, no. 5, pp. 529–554 (esp. p. 539). Yet only 50–60% of that total population probably lived within the walls of the city.

For a useful chart on the area and walled defenses of Southern Song cities, the source of this estimate on the area of Xiangyang, see Huang Kuanchong, "Songdai chengguo di fangyu sheshi ji cailiao," in *Nansong junzheng yu wenxian tansuo* (Taipei: Xin wenfeng chuban gongsi, 1990), pp. 183–224 (esp. 213). Also see Herbert Franke, "Siege and Defense of Towns in Medieval China," in Frank A. Kierman, Jr., ed., *Chinese Ways and Warfare* (Cambridge: Harvard University, East Asian Research Center, 1974), pp. 151–194 (esp. 181).

58. On the battle at Xiangyang, see Morris Rossabi, *Khubilai Khan: His Life and Times* (Berkeley: University of California, 1988), pp. 82–88; Zhou Mi, *Guixin zazhi* (Baibu congshu jicheng edition), bieji (B), pp. 34a–43b; Bi, *Xu tongjian*, juan 178, pp. 4875–4876, juan 178, p. 4481, juan 179, p. 4883, juan 179, p. 4886, juan 179, p. 4888, juan 179, p. 4890, juan 179, pp. 4898–4909, juan 180, pp. 4911–4917; Chen, *Songshi jishi benmo*, juan 106, pp. 1131–1157; Hu Zhaoxi, Zou Chonghua, *Song/Meng (Yuan) guanxi shi* (Chengdu: Sichuan daxue chubanshe, 1992), pp. 317–330; Huang Kuanchong, *Nansong shi yanjiu ji* (Taipei: Xin wenfeng chuban gongsi, 1985), pp. 1–18; Li, *Yuanshi xinjiang*, vol. 2, pp. 274–285; Liu Boji, *Songdai zhengjiao shi* (Taipei: Taiwan zhonghua shuju, 1971), vol. 1, pp. 494–505.

59. Li, *Yuanshi xinjiang*, vol. 2, p. 279; Li, *Song Yuan zhanshi*, vol. 2, p. 1008.

60. These additional appropriations are recorded throughout juan 46 of the dynastic history; see Tuo Tuo, *Song Shi*.

61. Song, *Yuan Shi*, juan 161, p. 3788; Chen, *Songshi jishi benmo*, juan 106, p. 1137.

62. Li, *Song Yuan zhanshi*, vol. 2, p. 1031. I assume this technology to be relatively new due to the novelty implicit in contemporary depictions.

63. Ibid., vol. 2, pp. 1028, 1031; Bi, *Xu tongjian*, juan 179, p. 4908.

64. One prominent and fairly recent example of such hereditary power in the Southern Song military establishment can be found in the Wu clan of modern Sichuan, which flourished in the late twelfth and early thirteenth centuries. I have discussed them at length in my narrative for the *Cambridge History of China*, vol. 5, Guangzong/Ningzong chapter (forthcoming). Also see Liu, "Luelun songdai wuguanchun," pp. 482–483.

65. By "special military councilor," I refer specifically to *pingzhang junguo zhongshi*, an ad hoc post which is in many ways superior to the chief councilorship (*tong zhongshu menxia pingzhang shi*). I find terribly awkward the standard translation offered by Charles Hucker, "manager of important national security matters," and have thus chosen a simplified version. On the evolution and significance of this office in Song times, see Charles O. Hucker, *A Dictionary of Office Titles in Imperial China* (Stanford: Stanford University Press, 1985), p. 386; Lin Tianwei, "Songdai quanxiang xingcheng zhi fenxi," in *Songshi yanjiu ji*, vol. 8 (Taipei: Zhonghua congshu, 1976), pp. 141–170 (esp. 154–159).

66. On Lü Wende's background and associations, see Fang Zhenhua, "Wansong bianfang yanjiu," M.A. Thesis, National Taiwan Normal University, 1992, pp. 127–132; Huang, *Nansong shi yanjiu ji*, pp. 7–14; Ke Weiqi, *Songshi xinbian* (rpt. Taipei: Xin wenfeng, 1974), juan 189, pp. 739a–739b; Ke Shaomin, *Xin Yuan Shi* (bonaben edition), juan 177, p. 17a; Li, *Song Yuan zhanshi*, vol. 2, pp. 970–971, 986–987, 1065; Tu Ji, *Mengwu'er shiji*, 1934 edition (Taipei: Dingwen shuju, 1976), juan 7, p. 22b, juan 111, pp. 3a–4b.

67. Tu, *Mengwu'er shiji*, juan 111, p. 3b.

68. On the political and military autonomy of Sichuan, see Paul J. Smith, *Taxing Heaven's Storehouse: Horses, Bureaucrats, and the Destruction of the Sichuan Tea Industry, 1074–1224* (Cambridge: Council on East Asian Studies, Harvard University, 1991), chap. 3; and my own narrative for the Guangzong/Ningzong era, *Cambridge History of China*, vol. 5 (forthcoming).

69. Tuo Tuo, *Song Shi*, juan 421, pp. 12599–12603; Wan, *Songji zhongyi lu*, juan 3, pp. 16a–21a; Li Qingya, "Shu Li Tingzhi," *Wenshi zazhi* (Hong Kong), vol. 1, no. 11 (May 16, 1941), pp. 61–68.

70. Zhou, *Guixin zazhi*, Bieji (B), p. 36a.

71. Bi, *Xu tongjian*, juan 176, p. 4812; Liu, "Luelun songdai wuguanchun," p. 483.

72. Tuo Tuo, *Song Shi*, juan 421, p. 12601; Tu, *Mengwu'er shiji*, juan 112, pp. 1a–3b.

73. Scrupulous avoidance of the enemy is characteristic of Fan Wenhu's behavior for most of his three-year term in the region, but admittedly for the first year, 1271, his contribution to Xiangyang's defense was more substantial. See Tu, *Mengwu'er shiji*, juan 7, pp. 22a–22b.

74. Tu, *Mengwu'er shiji*, juan 111, p. 4a; Ke, *Songshi xinbian*, juan 189, p. 739a.

75. Huang, *Nansong shi yanjiu ji*, p. 14; Li, *Song Yuan zhanshi*, vol. 2, pp. 1037–1039; Tu, *Mengwu'er shiji*, juan 111, p. 7b.

76. Rossabi, *Khubilai Khan*, p. 88.

77. Zhou, *Guixin zazhi*, Bieji (B), p. 41b.

78. Tu, *Mengwu'er shiji*, juan 111, p. 4a.

79. For biographical information, see Zhou, *Qidong yeyu*, juan 18, pp. 17b–19b; idem, *Guixin zazhi*, Bieji (B), pp. 34b–43b; Li, *Song Yuan zhanshi*, vol. 2, pp. 1027–1034; Bi, *Xu tongjian*, juan 179, pp. 4908–4909, juan 180, pp. 4911–4912; Tuo Tuo, *Song Shi*, juan 450, pp. 13248–13249.

Certain modern sources, including Bi Yuan's *Xu tongjian* and Li Tianming's *Song Yuan zhanshi*, have erroneously suggested that our two Zhang heroes were natives of the Shanxi region, what would either be northwest China or one of two Shanxi mountain ranges in South China but far removed from the Jinghu region. This represents, however, a misreading of the original citation in Zhou Mi's *Guixin zazhi*, a late thirteenth-century text, where the two men are acknowledged as native to *xishan* (a generic designation for western mountains), not Shanxi (the proper name for a province). Further confirmation that the Zhang men were locals can be found in *Songshi jishi benmo* (juan 106, p. 1135). This late-sixteenth century text, compiled by Chen Bangzhan and Feng Qi, associates Zhang Shun and Zhang Gui with the western mountain ranges between Xiangyang and nearby Yingzhou. Unfortunately, the punctuators of Bi Yuan's famous *Xu tongjian* interpreted *shanxi* as a proper name and their error gets duplicated elsewhere.

80. Tu, *Mengwu'er shiji*, juan 112, pp. 1a–1b; Li, *Song Yuan zhanshi*, vol. 2, p. 1033.

81. *Zhao zhong lu*, p. 13b; Qian Shisheng, *Nansong Shu* (n.d.), juan 60, p. 5b; Li, *Song Yuan zhanshi*, vol. 2, pp. 1058–1059; Bi, *Xu tongjian*, juan 180, p. 4915; Tuo Tuo, *Song Shi*, juan 450, p. 13250; Wan, *Songji zhongyi lu*, juan 4, pp. 19b–20a.

82. *Zhao zhong lu*, p. 14a; Qian, *Nansong Shu*, vol. 59, pp. 3a–3b, vol. 60, p. 5b; Bi, *Xu tongjian*, vol. 180, p. 4915; Tuo Tuo, *Song Shi*, vol. 450, pp. 13249–13250. Based upon Bi Yuan's authoritative *Xu tongjian*, I have concluded that Fan Tianshun died in the first lunar month at Fancheng, but another body of literature suggests that he died a month later at Xiangyang. For a useful presentation of such discrepancies and their duplication in an array of primary and secondary sources, see Li, *Song Yuan zhanshi*, vol. 2, p. 1074n3.

83. With some 3,000 soldiers remaining in Fancheng, the total population of residuals, military and civilian, very likely stood well in excess of 10,000. See Li, *Song Yuan zhanshi*, vol. 2, pp. 1059–1061.

84. An historian of the Yuan, noting the one and a half months separating the fall of Fancheng and then Xiangyang, suggests that the surrender of the latter was chiefly due to additional military pressure, in particular the Mongol display of devastatingly powerful missiles. He makes no mention of the massacre at Fancheng and its strategic consequences. Yet Xiangyang's delay in capitulating could also be explained, as noted earlier, by the negotiations which Lü Wenhuan conducted with his opponents, negotiations clearly of some duration and most likely begun soon after the fall of Fancheng. See Rossabi, *Khubilai Khan*, p. 86.

85. Tuo Tuo, *Song Shi*, juan 451, p. 13278.

86. Translation based on Tuo Tuo, *Song Shi*, juan 418, p. 12534. Also see Wen, *Wenshan quanji*, juan 17, p. 448.

CHAPTER 3: *GOU*

1. The term *qin wang* has its origins in the *Chun qiu* [Spring and Autumn Annals], *Zuozhuan* [Narrative of Zuo]. The standard translation by James Legge, "to show an earnest interest in the king's behalf," is both awkward and misleading. The reader, therefore, may need to consult the original. See James Legge, *The Chinese Classics*, vol. 5, "The Ch'un Ts'ew with The Tso Chuen," (rpt. Hong Kong: Hong Kong University Press, 1960), pp. 194–195; Yang Bojun, ed., *Chunqiu zuozhuan zhu* (Beijing: Zhonghua shuju, 1981), vol. 1, p. 431 [Xigong 25].

2. The edict has been preserved in the collected writings of Wen Tianxiang; see *Wenshan quanji*, juan 17, pp. 448–449. The date he ascribes to promulgation of the edict is the eleventh lunar month of 1274. The twelfth month, given here, is based upon the Song dynastic history and most other authoritative sources; see Tuo Tuo, *Song Shi*, vol. 47, p.

924. I should also note that to my own rendering of this passage differs significantly from the partial translation of Jay; see *Change of Dynasties*, pp. 29–30.

3. Tuo Tuo, *Song Shi*, juan 418, p. 12534.

4. For the text of the 1125 edict by Emperor Qinzong, see Li Tao, *Xu zizhi tongjian changbian* (rpt. Taipei: Shijie shuju, 1974), juan 51, pp. 1a–2b; Tuo Tuo, *Song Shi*, juan 22, p. 417.

5. On the precise dating for important Song events, see James M. Hargett, "A Chronology of the Reigns and Reign–Periods of the Song Dynasty (960–1279), *Bulletin of Sung–Yuan Studies*, no. 19 (1987), pp. 26–34.

6. Jay, *Change of Dynasties*, pp. 30–31.

7. Tuo Tuo, *Song Shi*, juan 418, p. 12534.

8. For biographical information, see Jay, *Change of Dynasties*, pp. 41–60; Yin Dexin, et al., *Lidai jiaoyu biji ziliao*, vol. 2 (Beijing: Zhongguo laodong chubanshe, 1991), pp. 22–25; Tuo Tuo, *Song Shi*, juan 418, pp. 12529–12532; Bi, *Xu tongjian*, juan 175, p. 4764. On the political import of the university and the social composition of its students, see Thomas H.C. Lee, *Government Education and Examinations in Sung China* (Hong Kong: The Chinese University Press, 1985), pp. 55–103.

9. Zhou, *Qidong yeyu*, juan 19, p. 2a.

10. On this incident, see Tuo Tuo, *Song Shi*, juan 44, p. 857, juan 405, p. 12242, juan 414, p. 12432, juan 418, p. 12529, juan 474, p. 13778–13779; Bi, *Xu tongjian*, juan 174, pp. 4761–4762, juan 175, p. 4764; Wang, *Songdai taixue*, pp. 309–310. I have also dealt with this particular incident, as well political activism at the university in general, in my narrative for the Lizong reign in the *Cambridge History of China*, vol. 5 (forthcoming).

11. Tuo Tuo, *Song Shi*, juan 418, p. 12529.

12. The background and policies of these men have been discussed in my narrative of the Duzong reign in *The Cambridge History of China*, vol. 5 (forthcoming).

13. The authority of Jia Sidao, as special military councilor, to "instruct" his two chief councilors was clearly acknowledged by the court; see Tuo Tuo, *Song Shi*, juan 47, p. 923. There is also evidence of court documents being regularly reviewed in his private residence, the extent to which formal audiences were less necessary; see Liu, *Songdai zhengjiao shi*, vol. 1, p. 495.

14. Tillman, *Utilitarian Confucianism*, p. 176; also see McKnight, "Chu Hsi and His World," pp. 422–425.

15. Lo, *Life and Thought of Yeh Shih*, pp. 57–74; Tillman, *Utilitarian Confucianism*, pp. 169–180.

16. Tuo Tuo, *Song Shi*, juan 425, pp. 12680–12681, juan 474, p. 13779; Bi, *Xu tongjian*, juan 175, p. 4776.

17. Much of the university memorial indicting Shi Songzhi has been translated by me in *Court and Family*, pp. 149–155.

18. Julia Ching, "Chu Hsi on Personal Cultivation," in *Chu Hsi and Neo-Confucianism*, pp. 273–291; Brian McKnight, "Chu Hsi and His World," pp. 408–436.

19. Tuo Tuo, *Song Shi*, juan 450, pp. 13375–13378; Wang, *Songdai taixue*, p. 305.

20. Wang, *Songdai taixue*, p. 354; Davis, *Court and Family*, pp. 84–92.

21. On the affair and events leading up to it, see Li, *Song Yuan zhanshi*, vol. 2, pp. 1182–1185; Bi, *Xu tongjian*, juan 181, pp. 4944–4947; Tuo Tuo, *Song Shi*, juan 47, pp. 925–926, juan 418, p. 12530, juan 474, p. 13786; Wang, *Songdai taixue*, pp. 318–319.

22. Bi, *Xu tongjian*, juan 181, p. 4944. Although we lack exact figures on the size of the Imperial Clan Academy at the dynasty's close, an estimate of at least several hundred seems quite reasonable. In the early thirteenth century, only 100 slots were allocated for the institution, but this is also a century of massive expansion in the size of educational institutions in Linan, the academy scarcely exempt from this expansion. Still, this leaves

the Imperial Clan Academy only a fraction of the size of the Imperial University. See Song Xi, "Songdai di zongxue," in *Songshi yanjiu luncong* (Taipei: Zhongguo wenhua yanjiusuo, 1980), pp. 13–40.

23. This exchange is quoted with slight discrepancies in the dynastic history; see Tuo Tuo, *Song Shi*, juan 243, p. 8659, juan 474, p. 13786.

24. Chen Yizhong would later arrest and then murder the assassin of Jia Sidao at Fuzhou, which may not be sufficient proof of implication in the original conspiracy against Jia, but involvement in the second assassination raises suspicion of a cover-up attempt and some measure of guilt behind it. For a convenient summary of the relevant literature, see Hu, *Song/Meng guanxi shi*, pp. 399–401.

25. The Han Zhen affair is richly detailed by anecdotist Zhou, *Guixin zazhi* (Qianji), pp. 34a–34b, 47a–48b. Also see Li, *Song Yuan zhanshi*, vol. 2, p. 1189; Bi, *Xu tongjian*, juan 181, p. 4947.

26. Zhou Mi, *Guixin zazhi* (Qianji), pp. 34a–34b, 48a.

27. Tuo Tuo, *Song Shi*, juan 243, p. 8659.

28. Tuo Tuo, *Song Shi*, juan 418, pp. 12528–12529.

29. Bi, *Xu tongjian*, juan 181, p. 4948; Tuo Tuo, *Song Shi*, juan 47, p. 930.

30. Bi, *Xu tongjian*, juan 181, p. 4950.

31. Tuo Tuo, *Song Shi*, juan 47, pp. 930, 932.

32. Brian E. McKnight, *Law and Order in Sung China* (Cambridge: Cambridge University Press, 1992), p. 322.

33. Bi, *Xu tongjian*, juan 180, pp. 4927–4928.

34. Li, *Song Yuan zhanshi*, vol. 2, pp. 1178–1180.

35. On Zhao Maofa and the demise of Chizhou, see Song, *Yuan Shi*, juan 8, p. 161, juan 127, p. 3104; Tuo Tuo, *Song Shi*, juan 47, p. 925, juan 450, pp. 13259–13260; *Zhao zhong lu*, pp. 14a–14b; Li, *Song Yuan zhanshi*, vol. 2, pp. 1182–1183; Bi, *Xu tongjian*, juan 181, p. 4941.

36. *Zhao zhong lu*, p. 14b; Li, *Song Yuan zhanshi*, vol. 2, p. 1183.

37. It should be noted that the location of Anqing in Song times differs from the modern city after which it is named: the Song city was nestled some sixty kilometers in the interior and accessible to the Yangzi by a tributary; the modern city is farther south and sits along the Yangzi River in the heart of Anhui province. For maps, see Tan, *Zhongguo lishi ditu ji*, vol. 6, pp. 59–60.

38. On Xia Yi, see Tuo Tuo, *Song Shi*, juan 47, p. 925; Lu, *Song shi yi*, juan 32, p. 14b; Bi, *Xu tongjian*, juan 181, p. 4939; Wan, *Songji zhongyi lu*, juan 7, p. 3b–4a.

39. He, *Anhui tongzhi*, juan 141, p. 3b.

40. On the death of Jiang Wanli at Raozhou, see Tuo Tuo, *Song Shi*, juan 47, p. 926, juan 418, pp. 12523–12525, juan 450, pp. 13260–13261; Wan, *Songji zhongyi lu*, juan 3, pp. 1a–3b; Bi, *Xu tongjian*, juan 181, pp. 4943–4944; Li, *Song Yuan zhanshi*, vol. 2, pp. 1191–1192.

41. Tuo Tuo, *Song Shi*, juan 418, p. 12525.

42. Song, *Yuan Shi*, juan 8, pp. 166–167; Li, *Song Yuan zhanshi*, vol. 2, p. 1216.

43. Tuo Tuo, *Song Shi*, juan 47, p. 928.

44. Li, *Song Yuan zhanshi*, vol. 2, pp. 1193, 1222–1223.

45. Bi, *Xu tongjian*, juan 182, p. 4969.

46. Tuo Tuo, *Song Shi*, juan 451, p. 13272.

47. Tuo Tuo, *Song Shi*, juan 421, p. 1201, juan 451, pp. 13272–13273; Li, *Song Yuan zhanshi*, vol. 2, pp. 1222–1228.

48. On the battle at Jiaoshan, see Bi, *Xu tongjian*, juan 181, p. 4958; Song, *Yuan Shi*, juan 156, p. 3671, juan 156, p. 3681; Tuo Tuo, *Song Shi*, juan 451, pp. 13272–13273; Hu, *Song/Meng guanxi shi*, pp. 402–403; Li, *Song Yuan zhanshi*, vol. 2, pp. 1225–1227, vol. 4, maps 156, 157; Liu, *Songdai zhengjiao shi*, vol. 1, p. 510.

The name Aju [Azhu] is synonomous with Ashu, an alternative transliteration common in earlier Chinese sources.

49. Tuo Tuo, *Song Shi*, juan 418, p. 12531.
50. Wen, *Wenshan quanji*, juan 16, p. 401. "Carnivores" is a reference to the Mongol military leaders at Jiaoshan, men whose combined stipends represented taxes from several hundreds of thousands of households.
51. Elvin, *Chinese Past*, pp. 84–90; Joseph Needham, *Science in Traditional China; a Comparative Perspective* (Cambridge: Harvard University Press, 1981), pp. 27–56.
52. Elvin, *Chinese Past*, pp. 88–89.
53. On the "erudite litterateur" examination (or "polymaths and resonant prose" to employ the literal translation of *boxue hongci* proposed by one scholar), see Bradford C. Langley, "Wang Yinglin (1223–1296): A Study in the Political and Intellectual History of the Demise of Song," Ph.d. diss., Indiana University, 1980, pp. xxiv-xxv, 150–179, 549–558. For further information on the life and career of Wang Yinglin, see Franke, *Sung Biographies*, biography by Bradford C. Langley, vol. 2, pp. 1167–1176; Tuo Tuo, *Song Shi*, juan 438, pp. 12987–12991; Huang Zongxi, *Song Yuan xue'an* (Taipei: Shijie shuju, 1973), juan 85, pp. 1614–1622; Song Xi, "Nansong zhedong di shixue," in *Songshi yanjiu ji* (Taipei: Zhonghua congshu, 1983), vol. 14, pp. 9–52 (esp. 34–36).
54. Chen Liang, *Chen Liang ji*, juan 4, pp. 40–48; Song Dingzong, *Chunqiu Songxue fawei*, revised edition (Taipei: Wenshizhe, 1986), pp. 112–114; Tillman, "Proto-Nationalism in Twelfth-Century China?" pp. 410–411.
55. A number of his writings have been summarized in English; see Yves Hervouet, *A Sung Bibliography (Bibliographie des Sung)* (Hong Kong: The Chinese University of Hong Kong, 1978), pp. 27, 64, 71, 176, 189, 231, 261, 329; Langley, "Wang Yinglin," pp. 476–489.
56. de Bary, *Neo-Confucian Orthodoxy*, pp. 1–66.
57. On the increased overlap, in the thirteenth century, between erudites such as Wang Yinglin and Neo-Confucian metaphysicists, see Hoyt C. Tillman, "Encyclopedias, Polymaths, and Tao-hsueh Confucians: Preliminary reflections with special reference to Chao Ju-yü," in *Journal of Sung-Yuan Studies*, no. 22 (1990–1992), pp. 89–108 (esp. 104–108). Another pivotal figure in the merging of *Daoxue* and *Xinxue* values, during the post-Zhu Xi era, is Zhen Dexiu; see de Bary, *Neo-Confucian Orthodoxy*, pp. 67–131.
58. Wang Yinglin's interest in historical astronomy is confirmed in his miscellaneous writings; see *Kunxue jiwen (jizheng)* (rpt. Taipei: Taiwan shudian, 1960), juan 9; *Liujing tianwen bian* (Congshu jicheng edition), juan 1 and 2; Hervouet, *Sung Bibliography*, pp. 231, 261.
59. The decline in Song times of speculative theories on interactive resonance is perhaps best demonstrated in historical writings; see John B. Henderson, *The Development and Decline of Chinese Cosmology* (New York: Columbia University Press, 1984), pp. 89–136; Bol, *"This Culture of Ours,"* pp. 191–201; Richard L. Davis, "Sung Historiography: Empirical Ideals and Didactic Realities," *Chinese Culture* (Taipei), vol. 29, no. 4 (Dec. 1988), pp. 67–80; Zheng Han, "Ouyang Xiu tianrenguan shitan," in *Songshi lunji* (Henan: Zhongzhou shuhuashe, 1983), pp. 363–377. Recent scholarship suggests, for North China under Jurchen rule, something of a revival of interest in speculative theories; see Hok-lam Chan, *Legitimation in Imperial China: Discussions under the Jurchen-Chin Dynasty (1115–1234)* (Seattle: University of Washington Press, 1984), pp. 51–81.
60. Tuo Tuo, *Song Shi*, juan 47, p. 934; Bi, *Xu tongjian*, juan 182, p. 4969.
61. I have dealt with the 1224 succession and its implications for the imperial clan in my narratives for the Ningzong, Lizong, and Duzong reigns; see *Cambridge History of China*, vol. 5 (forthcoming).
62. Tuo Tuo, *Song Shi*, juan 418, pp. 12528–12529; Bi, *Xu tongjian*, juan 181, p. 4948.

63, Franke, *Sung Biographies*, vol. 2, p. 1174; Langley, "Wang Yinglin," pp. 403–408; Tuo Tuo, *Song Shi*, juan 438, p. 12991; Bi, *Xu tongjian*, juan 182, p. 4969.

64. On the activities of Wang Yinglin, after leaving the court, see Jay, *Change in Dynasties*, pp. 173–178; Langley, "Wang Yinglin," pp. 457–473.

65. Tuo Tuo, *Song Shi*, juan 418, pp. 12525–12528; Huang, *Song Yuan xue'an*, juan 80, p. 1520.

66. Bi, *Xu tongjian*, juan 181, pp. 4949, 4957.

67. Bi, *Xu tongjian*, juan 181, p. 4949.

68. According to one writer, Chen Yizhong did reside briefly in the capital during the eighth lunar month, but this seems poorly documented. See Li, *Song Yuan zhanshi*, vol. 2, p. 1237.

69. Tuo Tuo, *Song Shi*, juan 425, p. 12687.

70. Tuo Tuo, *Song Shi*, juan 418, p. 12531; Bi, *Xu tongjian*, juan 181, pp. 4960–4961.

71. Tuo Tuo, *Song Shi*, juan 418, p. 12528.

72. Some technical aspects of this story are clearly in error, although the story itself seems credible. See Tuo Tuo, *Song Shi*, juan 418, p. 12531; Bi, *Xu tongjian*, juan 182, p. 4965.

73. Bi, *Xu tongjian*, juan 182, p. 4964.

74. Tuo Tuo, *Song Shi*, juan 418, p.12535.

75. Wen, *Wenshan quanji*, juan 3, pp. 53–62. Military governorships akin to Tang models were briefly established for the border region in the 1130s, but subsequently abolished. In the early thirteenth-century, similarly drawing inspiration from the Tang, the eminent utilitarian thinker Ye Shi made a new call for relaxation of central controls on the military and more regional autonomy; see Lo, *Life and Thought of Yeh Shih*, pp. 57–90, 111–135; Tao Ching-shen, *Cambridge History of China*, vol. 5 (forthcoming), narrative for Gaozong. One finds a similar assault on the excessive centralization of military power in the writings of Southern Song philosopher Chen Liang (1143–1193); see *Chen Liang ji*, juan 1, p. 5.

76. Bol, *"This Culture of Ours,"* pp. 48–58, 148–155; McKnight, *Law and Order in Sung China*, pp. 191–198; Edmund H. Worthy, "The Founding of Sung China, 950–1000: Integrative Changes in Military and Political Institutions," Ph.D. diss., Princeton University, 1976; Chen, *Songshi jishi benmo*, juan 2, p. 7–12.

77. Wen, *Wenshan quanji*, juan 19, p. 496; Wan, *Wen Tianxiang zhuan*, p. 79.

CHAPTER 4: *KUN*

1. Song, *Yuan Shi*, juan 158, pp. 3715–3716.

2. Li, *Yuanshi xinjiang*, vol. 2, p. 309.

3. Franke, *Sung Biographies*, biography by Y. Shiba, vol. 2, pp. 1060–1062; Chen, *Songshi jishi benmo*, juan 6, pp. 29–36 (esp. juan 6, p. 32); Tuo Tuo, *Song Shi*, juan 258, pp. 8977–8983 (esp. juan 258, p. 8979); Ding, *Songren yishi huibian*, juan 4, pp. 128–129.

4. For one lively example of such hagiographic embellishment, see Rossabi, *Khubilai Khan*, pp. 25–26.

5. On the Changzhou conflict, see *Zhao zhong lu*, 22b–23a; Liu Minzhong, *Ping Song lu* (Baibu congshu jicheng edition) juan 2, pp. 31–3b; Song, *Yuan Shi*, juan 127, p. 3107; Tuo Tuo, *Song Shi*, juan 450, pp. 13251–13253, juan 451, pp. 13274–13275; Chen, *Songshi jishi benmo*, juan 106, pp. 1156–1157; Langley, "Wang Yinglin," pp. 399–401; Hu, *Song/Meng guanxi shi*, p. 404; Li, *Song Yuan zhanshi*, vol. 2, pp. 1238–1244; Li, *Yuanshi xinjiang*, vol. 2, p. 321; Bi, *Xu tongjian*, juan 182, p. 4966.

6. Li, *Song Yuan zhanshi*, vol. 2, pp. 1239–1240, 1243.

7. Zhao, *Zhongyi ji*, juan 4, p. 8a.

8. Liu, *Ping Song lu*, juan 2, p. 3b.

9. Tu, *Mengwu'er shiji*, juan 90, pp. 21b–22a; Li, *Song Yuan zhanshi*, vol. 2, pp. 1244–1245.

10. Yin Tinggao, *Yujing qiaochang* (Siku quanshu edition) juan 1, p.15a; Li, *Song Yuan zhanshi*, vol. 2, p. 1244.

11. Shi Nengzhi, *Xianchun Piling zhi*, 1268, (Song Yuan difangzhi congshu edition), (Taipei: Zhongguo dizhi yanjiuhui, 1978), juan 16, p. 1a.

12. On the educational attainments of this region in late Southern Song, see Davis, *Court and Family*, pp. 190–193; idem, "Custodians of Education and Endowment at the State Schools of Southern Sung," *Journal of Sung-Yuan Studies*, no. 25 (1995), pp. 95–119.

13. On the surrender of Pingjiang, see Liu, *Ping Song lu*, juan 2, p. 4a; Tuo Tuo, *Song Shi*, juan 418, p. 12535; Wen, *Wenshan quanji*, juan 17, pp. 449, 452; juan 19, pp. 488, 496–497; Li, *Song Yuan zhanshi*, vol. 2, pp. 1245–1247, 1250; Yang De'en, *Wen Tianxiang nianpu* (Shanghai: Shangwu yinshuguan, 1947), pp. 187–188.

The aforementioned sources serve to document a sizable force which accompanied Wen Tianxiang from Pingjiang to Linan. Yet he personally admits to taking only 2,000 men to Linan. The smaller number may reflect mere textual error or it may represent the number of regulars, as opposed to informal militia, in his entourage. See Wen, *Wenshan quanji*, juan 13, p. 311.

14. Tao Zongyi, *Nancun Zhuogeng lu* (Beijing: Zhonghua shuju, 1959), juan 1, p. 15; Tuo Tuo, *Song Shi*, juan 47, p. 938.

15. Lin Yutang, *The Gay Genius: The Life and Times of Su Tungpo* (New York: The John Day Company, 1957), pp. 305–306.

16. Chen, *Songshi jishi benmo*, juan 56, p. 593.

17. The early conflict between Song and Yuan has been discussed at length in my narrative for the Lizong reign in *The Cambridge History of China*, vol. 5.

18. On these early conflicts, see Charles A. Peterson, "Old Illusions and New Realities: Sung Foreign Policy, 1217–1234," in Morris Rossabi, ed., *China Among Equals: The Middle Kingdom and its Neighbors, 10th–14th Centuries* (Berkeley: University of California Press, 1983), pp. 204–239.

19. Rossabi, *Khubilai Khan*, p. 56; Song, *Yuan Shi*, juan 157, pp. 3708–3709.

20. Rossabi, *Khubilai Khan*, p. 81; Bi, *Xu tongjian*, juan 169, p. 4611, juan 176, p. 4802.

21. On these views, see Tuo Tuo, *Song Shi*, juan 405, p. 12237, juan 406, p. 12263, juan 412, p. 12374; Bi, *Xu tongjian*, juan 169, p. 4611.

22. Franke, "Chia Ssu-tao," pp. 226–229; Rossabi, *Khubilai Khan*, p. 56.

23. Song, *Yuan Shi*, juan 127, p. 3104; Tuo Tuo, *Song Shi*, juan 474, p. 13785; Bi, *Xu tongjian*, juan 181, p. 4940.

24. Liu, *Ping Song lu*, juan 1, pp. 9b–10b; Chen, *Songshi jishi benmo*, juan 106, pp. 1152–1153; Bi, *Xu tongjian*, juan 181, pp. 4953–4954.

25. Li, *Yuanshi xinjiang*, vol. 2, p. 322; Bi, *Xu tongjian*, juan 182, pp. 4970–4971.

26. Tuo Tuo, *Song Shi*, juan 243, p. 8660; Bi, *Xu tongjian*, juan 182, p. 4975.

27. Bi, *Xu tongjian*, juan 182, p. 4970.

28. Bi, *Xu tongjian*, juan 182, p. 4969. One highly credible sources makes the incredulous claim of nearly 200,000 troops in the Song capital at the time of its fall. Yet even assuming a last-minute induction into military service of massive numbers of commoners, so large a force remains inconceivable for a city whose residents had been fleeing for months. See *Zhao zhong lu*, p. 28b.

29. Tuo Tuo, *Song Shi*, juan 47, pp. 935–937; Ke, *Songshi xinbian*, juan 175, p. 685b; Li, *Song Yuan zhanshi*, vol. 2, p. 1255.

30. Li, *Song Yuan zhanshi*, vol. 2, pp. 1250, 1256–1257; Bi, *Xu tongjian*, juan 182, p. 4976.

31. Tuo Tuo, *Song Shi*, juan 451, p. 13273; Wen, *Wenshan quanji*, juan 13, p. 311.

32. Tuo Tuo, *Song Shi*, juan 47, p. 937; Hu, *Song/Meng guanxi shi*, pp. 410–411; Li, *Song Yuan zhanshi*, vol. 2, p. 1256–1257.

33. Song, *Yuan Shi*, juan 9, pp. 176–177. The rescript also appears, but in abbreviated form, in the Song dynastic history; see Tuo Tuo, *Song Shi*, juan 47, pp. 937–938.

34. Ke, *Songshi xinbian*, juan 189, p. 739b.

35. The population of Tanzhou, under the Northern Song was roughly one and a half million, but this grew substantially under the Southern Song. On the eve of the Mongol conquest, commander Arigh Khaya refers to "several million" as populating the city. See Song, *Yuan Shi*, juan 128, p. 3127; Wang Cun, et al., *Yuanfeng jiuyu zhi* (Guoxue jiben congshu edition), juan 6, pp. 287–288.

36. Tuo Tuo, *Song Shi*, juan 450, p. 13254.

37. On Li Fu (Fei) and the collapse of Tanzhou, see *Zhao zhong lu*, pp. 23a–24b; *Songji sanchao zhengyao*, juan 5, p. 63; Tuo Tuo, *Song Shi*, juan 47, p. 936, juan 450, pp. 13253–13256; Song, *Yuan Shi*, juan 9, p. 175, juan 128, pp. 3126–3127; Zhang Xiongyuan and Lü Xiaogao, *Changsha fuzhi* (1747 edition), juan 20, pp. 38b–39a; Qian, *Nansong Shu*, juan 59, pp. 13a–13b; Li, *Song Yuan zhanshi*, vol. 2, pp. 1279–1286; Bi, *Xu tongjian*, juan 181, p. 4945, juan 182, p. 4965, juan 182, pp. 4972–4973; Wan, *Songji zhongyi lu*, juan 6, pp. 4b–8a.

38. Zeng Guoquan, et al., *Hunan tongzhi*, 1885 edition, juan 87, pp. 8b–19a.

39. Zheng, *Tie'han xinshi*, juan 1, p. 23b.

40. Tuo Tuo, *Song Shi*, juan 450, pp. 13256–13259; Qian, *Nansong Shu*, juan 59, pp. 13b, 14a–14b; Bi, *Xu tongjian*, juan 182, pp. 4972–4974; Wan, *Songji zhongyi lu*, juan 6, pp. 9b–10b.

41. *Zhao zhong lu*, p. 24b; Tuo Tuo, *Song Shi*, juan 47, p. 936, juan 450, pp. 13256–13257; Qian, *Nansong Shu*, juan 59, pp. 13b–14a; Ke, *Songshi xinbian*, juan 175, p. 682b; Bi, *Xu tongjian*, juan 182, pp. 4972–4973; Wan, *Songji zhongyi lu*, juan 6, pp. 8a–9b.

42. Tuo Tuo, *Song Shi*, juan 450, p. 13256.

43. Zhou Nanrui, *Tianxia tongwenji* (Siku quanshu edition), juan 13, p. 2a.

44. Chen Yan, *Yuanshi jishi* (Shanghai: Guji chubanshe, 1987), juan 4, p. 37.

45. Zhou, *Tianxia tongwenji*, juan 13, p. 2b; Li, *Song Yuan zhanshi*, vol. 2, p. 1284–1285.

46. Song, *Yuan Shi*, juan 128, pp. 3126–3127.

47. In the official historiography, Chen Yizhong and Zhang Shijie are portrayed not as cooperating, during their last days in Linan, but parting in anger and hostility. This does not adequately consider, however, Chen Yizhong's sudden reversal on the relocation issue, resulting in the eleventh-hour release of the imperial sons which Zhang Shijie had requested. A recent author, Jennifer Jay, has independently confirmed the probability of the two men cooperating on this scheme. See Jay, *Change of Dynasties*, p. 47; Bi, *Xu tongjian*, juan 182, p. 4976.

48. Wen Tianxiang has narrated, in rare detail, his role in the negotiations; see *Wenshan quanji*, juan 13, pp. 311–319, juan 17, pp. 449–450; Li, *Song Yuan zhanshi*, vol. 2, pp. 1257–1259; Horst Huber, "Wen T'ien-hsiang (1236–1283): Vorstufen zum Verständnis seines Lebens," Ph.d. Diss., Universität zu München, 1983, pp. 179–180.

49. Wen, *Wenshan quanji*, juan 13, p. 315.

50. Wen, *Wenshan quanji*, juan 13, p. 315. Emphasis added.

51. Jay, *Change of Dynasties*, p. 36.

52. Wen Tianxiang's anxiety over southern manhood is similarly suggested by Umehara Kaoru; see *Ben Tenshō*, pp. 270–277.

53. On the occupation of Linan, see Liu, *Ping Song lu*, juan 2, pp. 6b–9b; Song, *Yuan Shi*, juan 9, p. 177, juan 127, p. 3109; Tuo Tuo, *Song Shi*, juan 47, p. 938; Bi, *Xu tongjian*, juan 182, pp. 4977–4981; Zhou Baozhu, et al., *Jianming songshi* (Beijing: Renmin chubanshe, 1985), pp. 440–443.

54. Yoshikawa Kojiro, *An Introduction to Sung Poetry*, Translated by Burton Watson (Cambridge: Harvard-Yenching Institute, 1967), p. v; Wang Yuanliang, *Shuiyun ji*, Wulin

wangzhe yizhu edition, (Taipei: Yiwen yinshuguan, 1971), juan 1, p. 1a. The Watson translation substantially modified.

55. Song, *Yuan Shi*, juan 127, p. 3109.

56. Bi, *Xu tongjian*, juan 97, p. 2566.

57. Robert A. Rorex and Wen Fong, *Eighteen Songs of a Nomad Flute: The Story of Lady Wen-chi* (New York: The Metropolitan Museum of Art, 1974), Introduction; Ebrey, *Inner Quarters*, pp. 21–23.

58. Qian, *Nansong Shu*, juan 7, p. 6b; Ke, *Songshi xinbian*, juan 14, p. 55b; Bi, *Xu tongjian*, juan 182, p. 4981; Ding, *Songren yishi huibian*, juan 3, pp. 104–105.

59. One of the women to make the journey north and survive, Zheng Huizheng, would years later write a poem where she alludes specifically to Cai Yan and the contemporary parallels. See Wang Yuanliang, *Song jiugongren shici* (Congshu jicheng edition), p. 2.

60. Bi, *Xu tongjian*, juan 183, p. 4985.

61. Wang, *Shuiyun ji*, pp. 19a–19b; and addendum (*fulu*), pp. 1a–1b.

62. Wing-tsit Chan, *Chu Hsi: New Studies* (Honolulu: University of Hawaii Press, 1989), p. 540. For further elaboration on this issue, see Bettine Birge, "Chu Hsi and Women's Education," in Wm. Theodore de Bary & John W. Chaffee, ed., *Neo-Confucian Education: The Formative Stage* (Berkeley: University of California, 1989), pp. 325–367 (esp. 338–341); Ebrey, *Inner Quarters*, pp. 188–203.

63. Ding, *Songren yishi huibian*, juan 3, p. 105.

64. A Chinese woman's perception of obligation to follow her husband in death, according to recent secondary scholarship, seems to relate directly to the degree of moral propriety in her spouse; see Hsieh and Spence, "Suicide and the Family," p. 31.

65. Li, *Songshi jishi*, juan 90, p. 31b.

66. Ouyang, *Wudai shiji*, juan 13, pp. 127–132, juan 14, p. 141–147, juan 15, pp. 157–161, juan 16, p. 171, juan 17, pp. 175–181, juan 18, pp. 191–192, juan 19, pp. 197–199.

67. Chan, *Chu Hsi: New Studies*, p. 540.

68. On the incident, see Tuo Tuo, *Song Shi*, juan 421, pp. 12601–12602, juan 451, p. 13268; Qian, *Nansong Shu*, juan 59, p. 3b; Li, *Song Yuan zhanshi*, vol. 2, pp. 1264–1265, 1299–1300; Bi, *Xu tongjian*, juan 182, p. 4982.

69. Tuo Tuo, *Song Shi*, juan 421, p. 12602.

70. Tuo Tuo, *Song Shi*, juan 243, pp. 8660–8661.

71. On the lives of Dowager Quan and her son, after the abdication, see Liu, *Ping Song lu*, juan 2, pp. 10b–11a; Tuo Tuo, *Song Shi*, juan 418, p. 12539; Zhao, *Zhaoshi zupu*, juan 1, pp. 69b–70a, juan 1, p. 71b; Jay, *Change of Dynasties*, pp. 89, 145; Ke, *Songshi xinbian*, juan 14, p. 55b; Bi, *Xu tongjian*, juan 186, pp. 5072–5074, juan 186, p. 5086, juan 188, p. 5144; Ding, *Songren yishi huibian*, juan 3, pp. 105–107.

72. Barbara E. Reed, "The Gender Symbolism of Kuan-yin Bodhisattva," in José I. Cabezón, ed., *Buddhism, Sexuality, and Gender* (Albany: State University of New York, 1992), pp. 159–180 (esp. 162); Birge, "Chu Hsi and Women's Education," pp. 357–359.

73. Wang Yuanliang, *Hushan leigao* (Siku quanshu edition) juan 3, pp. 9a–9b.

74. Ding, *Songren yishi huibian*, juan 3, p. 107.

75. Wang, *Shuiyun ji*, addendum (*fulu*), juan 2, p. 3a.

76. Reed, "The Gender Symbolism of Kuan-yin Bodhisattva," pp. 159–180.

77. Contemporary Wang Yuanliang confirms that Dowager Quan departed for Tibet in 1288, but she probably returned to Beijing shortly thereafter. See Wang, *Hushan leigao*, juan 3, p. 9b. On the subsequent whereabouts of Gongdi and the legends to grow up around him, see Jennifer W. Jay, "Memoirs and Official Accounts: The Historiography of the Song Loyalists," *Harvard Journal of Asiatic Studies*, vol. 50, no. 2 (Dec. 1990), pp. 589–612 (esp. 610–611).

78. See Chapter 6, below.

79. Qian, *Nansong Shu*, juan 59, pp. 21–2b; Ding, *Songren yishi huibian*, juan 3, p. 101.

80. Yoshikawa, *Five Hundred Years of Chinese Poetry*, pp. 58–59; Yuan, *Aiguo shici xuan*, pp. 376–377. On her increased resignation in later years toward the plight of captivity, see Li, *Songshi jishi*, juan 84, pp. 5b–6a; Wang, *Song jiugongren shici*, pp. 1, 3.

81. Liu, *Ping Song lu*, juan 3, p. 1a.

82. Tuo Tuo, *Song Shi*, juan 421, p. 12602.

83. Tuo Tuo, *Song Shi*, juan 418, p. 12536. According to one contemporary writer, whose argument I do not find particularly convincing, the assassination attempt against Wen Tianxiang is the mere fiction of dynastic historians, writing under Mongol rule, who sought to denigrate the loyalist record of Li Tingzhi. See Li Qingya, "Shu Li Tingzhi," pp. 65–66.

84. Li, *Songshi jishi*, juan 81, p. 32b; Wen, *Wenshan quanji*, juan 13, p. 328.

85. Tuo Tuo, *Song Shi*, juan 421, p. 12602.

86. Song, *Yuan Shi*, juan 128, p. 3123; Tuo Tuo, *Song Shi*, juan 421, pp. 12602–12603; Li, *Song Yuan zhanshi*, vol. 2, pp. 1204–1205; Bi, *Xu tongjian*, juan 183, pp. 4991–4992.

87. Terada Gō, *Sōdai kyōikushi gaisetsu* (Tokyo: Hakubunsha, 1965), pp. 319–323.

88. Tuo Tuo, *Song Shi*, juan 425, p. 12687.

89. *Zhao zhong lu*, pp. 28b–29a; Tuo Tuo, *Song Shi*, juan 454, p. 13347; Jay, *Change of Dynasties*, p. 39.

90. One source suggests that Gao Yingsong died not in Beijing but Shangdu, which seems in error. See Bi, *Xu tongjian*, juan 183, p. 4985.

91. Anon., *Sanchao yeshi* (Congshu jicheng edition), pp. 9a–9b; Song, *Yuan Shi*, juan 9, p. 182; Jay, *Change of Dynasties*, p. 40; Wang, *Songdai taixue*, pp. 340–341.

92. Bi, *Xu tongjian*, juan 183, p. 4993.

93. *Sanchao yeshi*, pp. 9a–9b.

94. Wan, *Songji zhongyi lu*, juan 8, p. 6a.

95. Wan, *Songji zhongyi lu*, juan 7, p. 5a.

96. The aforementioned source gives Longtou (Dragon's Head) as the name of the river where Zhong Kejun died, but this seems a textual corruption of Longmen (Dragon's Gate), the only such river in the region. See Tan, *Zhongguo lishi ditu ji*, vol. 6, p. 61.

97. *Zhao zhong lu*, p. 33b; Song, *Yuan Shi*, juan 9, p. 180; Tuo Tuo, *Song Shi*, juan 451, p. 13277; Jay, *Change of Dynasties*, p. 40; Ke, *Songshi xinbian*, juan 175, p. 686a; Bi, *Xu tongjian*, juan 182, p. 4981; Wan, *Songji zhongyi lu*, juan 6, pp. 1a–1b; Wang, *Songdai taixue*, pp. 360–361.

98. Reference to "sitting sternly like clay statues in a temple" seems more Buddhist in inspiration than Confucian and indeed, for the pre-Song period, scholars have shown that Buddhism's proclivity for trivializing human life may have encouraged suicide as well. See Jacques Gernet, "Les Suicides par le feu chez les Bouddhistes Chinois du ve au xe siècle," *Melanges publies par L'institut des Hautes Etudes Chinoises*, vol. 2 (Paris: Presses Universitaires de France, 1960), pp. 527–558.

99. On the student movement of 1126, see Chen Dong, *Shaoyang ji* (Siku quanshu edition) juan 6, pp. 4b–12b; Tuo Tuo, *Song Shi*, juan 455, pp. 13359–13362; Yin, *Lidai jiaoyu biji ziliao*, vol. 2, p. 25; Franke, *Sung Biographies*, narratives by Edward H. Kaplan and Brian E. McKnight, pp. 124–132, 1090–1097; Huang Xianfan, *Songdai taixuesheng jiuguo yundong* (Shanghai: Shangwu yinshuguan, 1936), pp. 12–20; Lee, *Government Education and Examinations*, pp. 190–192; Wang, *Songdai taixue*, pp. 270–282.

100. Chen, *Shaoyang ji*, juan 1, p. 6b. The entire memorial has been translated by a former student of mine, Ari Levine, as an Appendix to his B.A. thesis, "Kneeling at the Gates: Chen Dong (1085–1127) and the Loyalist Student Movement of the Northern Song in Context" (Brown University, 1994).

101. Wang, *Songdai taixue*, p. 277.

102. For the radical argument of Ouyang Xiu, which defended certain factional activity as politically constructive, see Wm. Theodore de Bary, ed., *Sources of Chinese Tradition* (New York: Columbia University Press, 1960), vol. 1, pp. 391–393; James T.C. Liu, *Ou-yang Hsiu: An Eleventh-Century Neo-Confucianist* (Stanford: Stanford University Press, 1967), pp. 52–64.

103. On this celebrated figure, see Zheng Sixiao, *Zheng suonan xiansheng wenji* (Congshu jicheng edition), pp. 40–41 ff.; Cheng, *Song yimin lu*, juan 13, pp. 1a–9a; Ke, *Xin Yuan Shi*, juan 241, pp. 2b–3a; Li, *Songshi jishi*, juan 80, pp. 1a–6a; Lu, *Song shi yi*, juan 34, pp. 17a–18a; Huber, "Wen T'ien-hsiang," pp. 62–81; Jay, *Change of Dynasties*, pp. 186–189; Frederick W. Mote, "Confucian Eremitism in the Yuan Period," in Arthur F. Wright, ed., *The Confucian Persuasion* (Stanford: Stanford University Press, 1960), pp. 202–240 (esp. 234–235); Su Wending, *Songdai yimin wenxue yanjiu* (Taipei: Xuesheng shuju, 1979), pp. 121–148.

104. Zheng, *Tie'han xinshi*, juan 1, p. 25b. This passage is partly translated in Mote, "Confucian Eremitism," p. 235.

105. Zheng, *Tie'han xinshi*, juan 1, p. 72a.

106. Zheng, *Tie'han xinshi*, juan 1, p. 41a. For other commentary on Wen Tianxiang, see Ibid., juan 2, pp. 7a–15b, 42b–43b; Horst Wolfram Huber, "The Hero as the Spiritual Legacy of his Culture: Wen T'ien-hsiang and his Admirers," *Analecta Husserliana*, vol. 21 (1986), pp. 309–336 (esp. 325–331).

107. Zheng, *Tie'han xinshi*, juan 1, p. 79b.

108. Ouyang, *Wudai shiji*, juan 26, pp. 279–280.

109. Schneider, *Madman of Ch'u*, pp. 77–79.

110. For this insight, I am indebted to Thomas H.C. Lee's paper on "The Fulfillments of Education—Social Alienation and Intellectual Dissent in Paradox," presented at a conference on Confucian Intellectuals: Ideals and Actions (With Emphasis on the Sung), The Chinese University of Hong Kong, July 1990.

111. For biographical information on the Zheng family, see Zheng, *Zheng suonan wenji*, pp. 37–39.

112. Zheng, *Tie'han xinshi*, juan 2, p. 44a.

CHAPTER 5: *ZHEN*

1. Tuo Tuo, *Song Shi*, juan 418, p. 12533. The translation offered by William A. Brown has been largely overhauled; see *Wen T'ien-hsiang*, p. 96.

2. On the mountain retreat, dubbed Wenshan, see Wen, *Wenshan quanji*, juan 9, pp. 212–213; Umehara, *Bun Tenshō*, pp. 81–86. One biographer in the People's Republic, clearly seeking to downplay the bourgeois lifestyle of this cultural hero, insists on more humble beginnings (Wan, *Wen Tianxiang zhuan*, pp. 20–21). His documentation is rather weak and the argument not fully convincing. To accumulate, in only a decade or so, the levels of wealth documented for the early 1270s would require involvement in some extraordinarily lucrative activities—either commercial endeavors or political corruption—neither of which fit the profile of this particular man.

3. Writing on the Balkans, anthropologist David D. Gilmore reports that "the category of 'real men' is clearly defined. A real man is one who drinks heavily, spends money freely, fights bravely, and raises a large family"—personifying an "'indominitable virility' that distinguishes him from effeminate counterfeits"; see *Manhood in the Making: Cultural Concepts of Masculinity* (New Haven: Yale University Press, 1992), pp. 16, 220–231.

4. On the marriage age of Song men, see Ebrey, *Inner Quarters*, p. 75.

5. Wen, *Wenshan quanji*, juan 14, p. 350.

6. Wen, *Wenshan quanji*, juan 16, p. 439.

7. The locus classicus is apparently the *Shuowen jieci*, an etymological dictionary written

in the first century A.D. See Zhang Qiyun, *Zhongwen da cidian*, rev. edition (Taipei: Huagang chuban youxian gongsi, 1976), vol. 1, p. 1238.

8. Wen, *Wenshan quanji*, juan 11, pp. 266–269. For further information on Wen Yi, see Liu, *Shenzhai wenji*, juan 10, pp. 1a–4a; Li, *Song Wen chengxiang nianpu*, pp. 2–15.

9. Exactly when *nanren*, southerner, acquired the specific meaning of southeasterner is not altogether clear. Plenty of documentation exists for such usage in Mongol times, although the practice is much older. See Ch'en Yuan, *Western and Central Asians in China under the Mongols*, trans. by Ch'ien Hsing-hai and L. Carrington Goodrich (Los Angeles: Monumenta Serica at the University of California, 1966), p. 2.

10. In prison when he wrote this large collection of poetry, he clearly had no access to his personal library and apparently composed largely from memory, that massive corpus of Du Fu poetry committed to memory in his youth. See Wen, *Wenshan quanji*, juan 16, pp. 397–441; Wu, *The Confucian's Progress*, p. 37.

11. David R. McCraw, *Du Fu's Laments from the South* (Honolulu: University of Hawaii Press, 1992), pp. 149–165.

12. Wen Tianxiang personally speaks of only three sons in the family, but brother Wen Bi confirms a fourth son who died before maturity. See Wen, *Wenshan quanji*, juan 11, p. 269, juan 18, p. 470.

13. Wen, *Wenshan quanji*, juan 11, p. 266.

14. Wen, *Wenshan quanji*, juan 18, pp. 469–471.

15. Wen, *Wenshan quanji*, juan 11, pp. 272–273.

16. Hoyt Cleveland Tillman, *Utilitarian Confucianism: Ch'en Liang's Challenge to Chu Hsi* (Cambridge: Council on East Asian Studies, Harvard University, 1982), pp. 45–46; Bol, *"This Culture of Ours,"* pp. 254–299.

17. Tillman, *Utilitarian Confucianism*, p. 58.

18. In her synthetic and comprehensive treatment of Daoism under the empire and its relationship with Confucian and Buddhism, Anna Seidel points to the highly syncretic interweaving of the three teachings into the lives of Song emperors, courtiers, and even Confucian conservatives like Zhu Xi. Yet the highest level of religious tolerance and syncretic borrowing, I would note, occurred during the Northern Song. By contrast, Southern Song rulers and thinkers alike tended to be more cautiously selective, in terms of public displays of religious piety, while intensifying their public rhetoric against Buddhism and Daoism. See Anna Seidel, "Chronicle of Taoist Studies in the West, 1950–1990," *Cahiers d'Extreme-Asie (Revue bilingue de l'Ecole Française d'Extreme-Orient)*, vol. 5 (1989–90), pp. 223–347.

19. Huang, *Song Yuan xue'an*, juan 88, pp. 1664–1666; Tuo Tuo, *Song Shi*, juan 411, pp. 12364–12366.

20. Wen, *Wenshan quanji*, juan 11, pp. 282–283.

21. Wen, *Wenshan quanji*, juan 11, p. 282.

22. Wen, *Wenshan quanji*, juan 11, p. 282.

23. Ouyang Shoudao, *Xunzhai wenji* (Siku quanshu edition), juan 12, pp. 1a–5a, juan 21, pp. 4b–5b.

24. Huber, "The Hero as Spiritual Legacy," p. 313.

25. Hsiao Kung-chuan, *A History of Chinese Political Thought*, trans. by F. W. Mote (Princeton: Princeton University Press, 1979), vol. 1, p. 509; David McMullen, *State and Scholars in T'ang China* (Cambridge: Cambridge University Press, 1988), pp. 72–79 ff.

26. For the former view, see Chu Hsi, *Learning to be a Sage: Selections from the Conversations of Master Chu, Arranged Topically*, trans. by Daniel K. Gardner (Berkeley: University of California Press, 1990), pp. 152–153. For the latter more favorable view, see de Bary, "Chu Hsi's Aims as an Educator," pp. 207–208; Conrad Schirokauer, "Chu Hsi's Sense of History," in Hymes, *Ordering the World*, pp. 193–220.

27. McMullen, *State and Scholars*, p. 70.

28. Chu Hsi, *Learning to be a Sage*, p. 131. Translation modified.
29. Susan Cherniack, "Book Culture and Textual Transmission in Sung China," *Harvard Journal of Asiatic Studies*, vol. 54, no. 1 (June, 1994), pp. 5–121.
30. My own views, in this regard, have recently echoed elsewhere; see Hymes and Schirokauer, *Ordering the World*, p. 12.
31. Wen, *Wenshan quanji*, juan 10, p. 255.
32. Wen, *Wenshan quanji*, juan 9, pp. 216–217. On this concept of *haoran zhi qi*—variously translated as "passion nature," "blood-and-*qi*," or "psychophysical energy/substance"—see Lau, *Mencius*, pp. 24–26, 77 [II/A/2]; Ann-ping Chin and Mansfield Freeman, translators, *Tai Chen on Mencius: Explorations in Words and Meanings* (New Haven: Yale University Press, 1990), pp. 33–35, 41–44, 114–136.
33. Benjamin I. Schwartz, *The World of Thought in Ancient China* (Cambridge: Harvard University Press, 1985), pp. 269–278.
34. Qu Yuan, *The Songs of the South: An Ancient Chinese Anthology of Poems by Qu Yuan and Other Poets*, trans. by David Hawkes (New York: Penguin Books, 1985), pp. 14–28; Schneider, *Madman of Ch'u*, pp. 13–14, 68–69. For other regions of the remote southeast, similar characterizations emerge in the literature of the early empire; see Schafer, *Vermillion Bird*, pp. 18–78, 130–134. Interestingly, these crude and unspoiled qualities continue to be identified with the Chu region, as literary convention, long after real conditions had radically changed. For such depictions of the south in Tang times, see McCraw, *Du Fu's Laments from the South*, pp. 61–80, 166–179.
35. It would take many more centuries, of course, before such civilizing effects would be felt upon the remote south, the Guangdong region; see Schafer, *Vermillion Bird*, pp. 87–90.
36. Hawkes, *Songs of the South*, p. 18. I must admit to attempting to locate this quote in the Chinese original (Ban Gu, *Han shu*), but without success.
37. Schafer, *Vermillion Bird*, p. 35 ff; Chen, *Chen Liang ji*, juan 1, pp. 4–7.
38. George Hatch, "Su Hsun's Pragmatic Statecraft," in Hymes and Schirokauer, *Ordering the World*, pp. 59–75 (esp. 71).
39. The Neo-Confucian moralist Zhu Xi, in personally refusing to use the sedan chair, suggested a negative connotation although there is some ambiguity about his motives. See Chan, *Chu Hsi: New Studies*, p. 54.
40. For a typical example of secondary scholarship that presumes a predisposition toward pacifism in the southeast, see Zhang Junrong, *Nansong Gaozong pianan jiangzuo yuanyin zhi tantao* (Taipei: Wenshizhe chubanshe, 1986).
41. Gilmore, *Manhood in the Making*, p. 221.
42. Xiao Tong, *Wen xuan, or Selections of Refined Literature*, trans. by David R. Knechtges (Princeton: Princeton University Press, 1982), vol. 1, pp. 11–21. For further assistance in clarifying ambiguous notions such as "decadence" in the traditional literature, I should acknowledge the contribution of a graduate student in Comparative Literature at Brown University, Wu Fusheng, who quite recently made available to me several chapters of his 1994 Ph.d. dissertation on "Decadence as Theme in Chinese Poetry of the Six Dynasties and Tang Period."
43. Xiao, *Wen xuan*, p. 41; Kang-i Sun Chang, *Six Dynasties Poetry* (Princeton: Princeton University Press, 1986), pp. 146–157; John Marney, *Liang Chien-wen Ti* (Boston: Twayne Publishers, 1976), pp. 98–117.
44. Anne Birrell, *New Songs from a Jade Terrace: An Anthology of Early Chinese Love Poetry* (New York: Penguin Books, 1986), p. 26.
45. Marney, *Liang Chien-wen Ti*, pp. 115–116.
46. For examples of such homoerotic poetry, see Birrell, *New Songs*, pp. 165, 200–201, 213, 285, 292. Also see Bret Hinsch, *Passions of the Cut Sleeve: The Male Homosexual Tradition in China* (Berkeley: University of California Press, 1990), pp. 55–76.
47. In the words of Su Shi, one of the great literary craftsman of the eleventh century, *wen*

can be "harmonious yet strong, ornate yet normative, as brilliant as a design of the five colors, as variegated as a symphony of the eight tones." See Peter K. Bol, *"This Culture of Ours,"* p. 298.

48. Han Fei, *Han Fei Zi* (Sibu congkan edition), juan 6, p. 9a.
49. Sima Qian, *Shi Ji* (Beijing: Zhonghua shuju, 1959), juan 97, p. 2699.
50. Brittan, *Masculinity and Power*, p. 83.
51. Shen Yue, *Song Shu* (Beijing: Zhonghua shuju, 1974), juan 9, p. 190.
52. Ouyang, *Xin Tang Shu*, juan 198, p. 5637.
53. McKnight, *Law and Order in Sung China*, pp. 69–73, 197.
54. Liu Zijian, "Luelun songdai wuguanchun," pp. 480.
55. Fang, "Wan Song bianfang yanjiu," pp. 109–120; Huang Kuanchong, "Zhongguo lishi shang wuren diwei di zhuanbian: yi songdai wei li," in *Nansong junzheng yu wenxian tansuo* (Taipei: Xin wenfeng chuban gongsi, 1990), pp. 387–399.
56. Davis, *Court and Family*, p. 69.
57. Tuo Tuo, *Song Shi*, juan 157, p. 3686.
58. Liu Zijian, "Luelun songdai wuguanchun," p. 481.
59. Yin, *Lidai jiaoyu biji ziliao*, vol. 2, pp. 17–18.
60. On "scholar-generals" during their heyday, in the early Southern Song, see Yang Dequan and James T.C. Liu, "The Image of Scholar-Generals and a Case in the Southern Sung," *Saeculum*, vol. 37 (1986), pp. 182–191.
61. I have dealt extensively with each in my narrative for *The Cambridge History of China*, vol. 5 (forthcoming); also see Davis, *Court and Family*, pp. 84–92, 142–157.
62. Ihara Hiroshi, *Chūgoku kaihō no seikatsu to saiji: egakareta Sōdai no toshi seikatsu* (Tokyo: Yamakawa shuppansha, 1991); Zheng Shoupeng, *Songdai kaifengfu yanjiu* (Taipei: Zhonghua congshu, 1980); K. C. Chang, *Food in Chinese Culture: Anthropological and Historical Perspectives* (New Haven: Yale University Press, 1977), chapter on Song by Michael Freeman, pp. 143–176; Michael H. Finegan, "Urbanism in Sung China," Ph.D. dissertaion, University of Chicago, 1976; E. A. Kracke, Jr., "Sung K'ai-feng: Pragmatic Metropolis and Formalistic Capital," in John Winthrop Haeger, ed., *Crisis and Prosperity in Sung China* (Tucson: University of Arizona Press, 1975), pp. 49–77.
63. The William Rockhill Nelson Gallery of Art and Mary Atkins Museum of Fine Arts, Kansas City, *Eight Dynasties of Chinese Painting* (Bloomington: Indiana University Press, 1980), essay by Wai-kam Ho, pp. xxv–xxx.
64. Hargett, James M., "Huizong's Magic Marchmount: The Genyue Pleasure Park of Kaifeng," *Monumenta Serica*, vol. 38 (1988–1989), pp. 1–48.
65. Ibid., p. xxviii; Ting, *Compilation of Anecdotes*, pp. 60–70.
66. For the late Ming, one witnesses a parallel case where aesthetic indulgence is associated with a disintegrating social order; see Joanna F. Handlin Smith, "Gardens in Ch'i Piaochia's Social World: Wealth and Values in Late-Ming Kiangnan," *The Journal of Asian Studies*, vol. 51, no. 1 (Feb. 1992), pp. 55–81.
67. On the unusual devotion of Emperor Huizong to religious Daoism, see Patricia B. Ebrey and Peter N. Gregory, *Religion and Society in T'ang and Sung China* (Honolulu: University of Hawaii Press, 1993), pp. 1–44.
68. Ting, *Compilation of Anecdotes*, p. 64.
69. With 19 consorts, 31 sons, and 33 daughters (Priscilla Chung reports 29 sons and 34 daughters)—the largest progeny for any Song emperor—there is no question about Huizong's fundamentally heterosexual character. See Priscilla Chung, "Palace Women," pp. 10, 22; Zhao, *Zhaoshi zupu* juan 1, pp. 58a–58b.
70. On eunuch power under Huizong, see biographies of Chen Dong and Tong Guan, in Franke, *Sung Biographies*, narratives by Edward H. Kaplan and Brian E. McKnight, pp. 124–132, 1090–1097. On the influence of eunuchs over the fiscal machinery of the

Northern Song, see Hartwell, "Imperial Treasuries," pp. 16–89. For a broader survey of eunuch power under the Song, see Zhang, *Songdai huangqin,* pp. 263–303.

71. Twitchett, *The Cambridge History of China,* vol. 5 (forthcoming), narrative for the Gao-zong reign by Tao Ching-shen; Chung, "Palace Women," p. 3.

72. Franke, *Sung Biographies,* narrative by T. Yoshida, pp. 461–464.

73. Richard John Lynn, "Chu Hsi as Literary Theorist and Critic," in *Chu Hsi and Neo-Confucianism,* pp. 337–354 (esp. 342–343).

74. Hatch, "Su Hsun's Pragmatic Statecraft," pp. 68–72.

75. McKnight, *Law and Order in Sung China,* p. 248.

76. Ebrey, *Family and Property,* p. 258.

77. Segal, *Slow Motion,* chap. 5 (esp. pp. 106–107).

78. Shuen-fu Lin, *The Transformation of the Chinese Lyrical Tradition: Chiang K'uei and Southern Sung Tz'u Poetry* (Princeton: Princeton University Press, 1978), pp. 3–61 (esp. 11).

79. For a useful English-language narrative on these men, replete with bibliography, see Michael S. Duke, *Lu You* (Boston: Twayne Publishers, 1977); Irving Yucheng Lo, *Hsin Ch'i-chi* (New York: Twayne Publishers, 1971); J. D. Schmidt, *Yang Wan-li* (Boston: Twayne Publishers, 1976); Franke, *Sung Biographies,* narratives by D. R. Jonker, pp. 691–704, 1238–1245. For additional poems by these and other so-called "patriotic poets," see Xu Yuan Zhong, trans., *Songs of the Immortals: An Anthology of Classical Chinese Poetry* (New York: Penguin, 1994).

80. Schneider, *Madman of Ch'u,* pp. 44–45.

81. Lu You, *Lu fangweng quanji: Jiannan shigao* (Beijing: Zhongguo shudian, 1986), juan 3, p. 43. My translation differs radically from Michael Duke; see *Lu You,* p. 22.

82. Huang Wenji, *Song nandu ciren* (Taipei: Xuesheng shuju, 1985), pp. 63–64.

83. Duke, *Lu You,* p. 26.

84. Lu, *Jiannan shigao,* juan 14, p. 234. For alternative translation, see Duke, *Lu You,* p. 26.

85. By pre-Song literary convention, the term "south" was often a synonym for Chu, al-though beginning with the Southern Song, the practice grew less common. See McCraw, *Du Fu's Laments from the South,* pp. 61–80.

86. Bol, *"This Culture of Ours,"* p. 338.

87. Yang Wan-li, *Heaven My Blanket, Earth My Pillow,* trans. by Jonathan Chaves (New York: Weatherhill, 1975), p. 70.

88. Burton Watson, *The Columbia Book of Chinese Poetry: From Early Times to the Thirteenth Century* (New York: Columbia University Press, 1984), p. 316.

89. Lo, *Hsin Ch'i-chi,* p. 63.

90. Duke, *Lu You,* p. 69.

91. Rexroth, *Li Ch'ing-chao,* p. 65.

92. On the "knight-errant" tradition and its limited appeal beyond this small coterie of men, see James J.Y. Liu, *The Chinese Knight-Errant* (Chicago: University of Chicago Press, 1967), pp. 68–71. It is fascinating that in Japan, at roughly the same time, a similar den-igration of "effete aristocrats" and celebration of "manly warriors" was well underway, but the movement would win a much wider degree of acceptance over the long haul. See William W. Farris, *Heavenly Warriors: The Evolution of Japan's Military, 500–1300* (Cambridge: Council on East Asian Studies, Harvard University, 1992), pp. 311 ff.

It is important to remember that the anti-intellectualism and martial revelry, so unique to this coterie of Song poets, is not altogether new to Chinese history. In the pre-ceding Tang dynasty, for example, in the aftermath of the An Lushan rebellion, poet Li Shangyin conveys a similar message. Written as a "Poem for My Little Boy," he writes:

"Your father once was fond of reading books;
sweating, slaving, he wrote some of his own;
going on forty now, worn and tired,

no meat for his meals, cringing from fleas and lice—
Take care, my son—do not copy your father,
studying, hoping for first or second on the exam!
Rangju's *Rules of the Marshal,*
Zhang Liang's *Yellow Stone Strategy,*
these will make you a teacher of kings;
waste no time on trash and trifles!
See Watson, *Chinese Poetry,* pp. 288–290.

93. Yuan, *Aiguo shici xuan,* p. 339. Italics added.
94. Duke, *Lu You,* p. 73.
95. Davis, *Court and Family,* pp. 62–67.
96. The exceptional opponent to Han Tuozhou was Yang Wanli. The Kaixi War of 1206 has been discussed in my narrative for the Ningzong reign in *The Cambridge History of China,* vol. 5 (forthcoming); also see Duke, *Lu You,* pp. 22–23; Franke, *Sung Biographies,* pp. 699, 1242; Lo, *Hsin Ch'i-chi,* p. 36; Schmidt, *Yang Wan-li,* p. 35.
97. Some might view the abortive Song attempt, in 1234, to regain the northern capitals of Kaifeng and Luoyang as representing a brief revelry for revanchist politics. Yet inspiring Chief minister Zheng Qingzhi was not so much revanchist idealism with its sweeping agenda of dynastic restoration, but rather political opportunism. These issues have been addressed in my narrative for the Lizong reign in *The Cambridge History of China,* vol. 5 (forthcoming).
98. Lo, *Hsin Ch'i-chi,* pp. 29–30.
99. Lo, *Hsin Ch'i-chi,* pp. 58–65.
100. On the links between moral courage and masculine virility, as established in classical times in the West, see Jean Bethke Elshtain, *Women and War* (New York: Basic Books, 1987), pp. 49–56.
101. Zhang Jingqiu, "Titang you zhangfu qi," in *Li Qingzhao yanjiu lunwen ji,* pp. 245–252.
102. de Bary, "Chu Hsi's Aims as an Educator," p. 192.
103. Similar heroics as an expression of gender insecurity has been observed in other cultures; see Gilmore, *Manhood in the Making,* pp. 9–29.
104. Ouyang, *Xin Tang Shu,* juan 5, p. 154.
105. On these women and their critics, see Denis Twitchett, ed., *The Cambridge History of China,* vol. 3, Part I (Cambridge: Cambridge University Press, 1979), pp. 242–273, 290–321; Ouyang, *Wudai shiji,* juan 14, pp. 143–147, juan 15, pp. 158–160.
106. Ouyang, *Xin Tang Shu,* juan 207, p. 5856.
107. Ouyang, *Wudai shiji,* juan 38, p. 406.
108. Wen, *Wenshan quanji,* juan 3, p. 46.
109. On these several views, see Ouyang, *Xin Tang Shu,* juan 76, p. 3468; Wen, *Wenshan quanji,* juan 3, pp. 63–65; Ebrey, *Family and Property,* p. 286.
110. Wen, *Wenshan quanji,* juan 10, p. 249.
111. On these communications, see Wen, *Wenshan quanji,* juan 4, pp. 70–91.
112. On these women, see Legge, *The She King,* pp. 438, 436 [III/A/3.2, III/A/6.1].
113. Wen, *Wenshan quanji,* juan 4, p. 76.
114. Wen, *Wenshan quanji,* juan 14, pp. 375–376. For a well annotated version, see Yuan, *Aiguo shici xuan,* pp. 380–386. A full translation, with modest annotation, can be found in Yoshikawa, *Five Hundred Years of Chinese Poetry,* pp. 53–55.
115. Ouyang, *Wudai shiji,* juan 33, p. 355.
116. It was in response to Ouyang Xiu's glaring misrepresentation of loyalism during the Five Dynasties that writers of the Song dynastic history sought to correct that oversight by including, quite inappropriately at the very end of their work, several Later Zhou loyal-

ists whose biographies are extraneous to the history of the Song but had heretofore been ignored. See Tuo Tuo, *Song Shi*, juan 484, pp. 13967–13979.

117. Wen, *Wenshan quanji*, juan 16, p. 407.

118. On these views, see Wen, *Wenshan quanji*, juan 3, p. 63, juan 9, p. 222, juan 10, p. 255.

119. Wen, *Wenshan quanji*, juan 3, p. 54.

120. Wen, *Wenshan quanji*, juan 14, p. 362, juan 1, p. 12, respectively.

121. Yuan, *Aiguo shici xuan*, pp. 383n14, 384n17; Yoshikawa, *Five Hundred Years of Chinese Poetry*, p. 54.

122. Wen, *Wenshan quanji*, juan 14, p. 368.

123. On the escape, see Wen, *Wenshan quanji*, juan 13, pp. 319, 323–332; Yang, *Wen Tianxiang nianpu*, pp. 201–216.

124. Wen, *Wenshan quanji*, juan 13, p. 343.

125. Wen, *Wenshan quanji*, juan 13, p. 339.

126. Wu, *The Confucian's Progress*, pp. 12, 38.

127. Wen, *Wenshan quanji*, juan 16, p. 412.

128. On Wen Tianxiang's role in the suppression, see Huber, "Wen T'ien-hsiang," pp. 192–194; Li, *Song Wen chengxiang nianpu*, pp. 72–73; Wen, *Wenshan quanji*, juan 17, pp. 456–457; Yang, *Wen Tianxiang nianpu*, pp. 243–250. In the collected writings of Wen Tianxiang, the rebel is referred to as Huang Cong, but Huang Guangde is given in another highly credible source, which I have chosen to follow; see Li, *Song Yuan zhanshi*, vol. 2, pp. 1416, 1428n26.

129. Wen, *Wenshan quanji*, juan 17, p. 456; Yang, *Wen Tianxiang nianpu*, pp. 246–247.

130. Legge, *The Shoo King*, p. 60 [II/B/2.14].

131. For a discussion of changing Chinese attitudes toward sentimentality and the cult of hero, see Kang-i Sun Chang, *The Late-Ming Poet Ch'en Tzu-lung: Crises of Love and Loyalism* (New Haven: Yale University Press, 1991), pp. 9–37.

132. Michel Foucault, *The History of Sexuality*, vol. 2, "The Use of Pleasure," translated by Robert Hurley (New York: Vintage, 1990), pp. 20, 78–93.

133. Chang, *The Late-Ming Poet Ch'en Tzu-lung*, pp. 106, 116–117.

134. Wen, *Wenshan quanji*, juan 17, pp. 456–457; Li, *Song Yuan zhanshi*, vol. 2, pp. 1423–1424; Yang, *Wen Tianxiang nianpu*, pp. 251–252.

135. Li, *Song Yuan zhanshi*, vol. 2, p. 1422.

136. Li, *Song Yuan zhanshi*, vol. 2, pp. 1415–1416, 1422–1423.

137. Wen, *Wenshan quanji*, juan 16, p. 403.

138. Wen, *Wenshan quanji*, juan 16, p. 402.

139. Wen, *Wenshan quanji*, juan 19, p. 500; Li, *Song Yuan zhanshi*, vol. 2, p. 1440.

CHAPTER 6: *GUIMEI*

1. Wen, *Wenshan quanji*, juan 17, pp. 461–462. The entire exchange has been translated into German by Horst Huber; see, "Wen T'ien-hsiang," pp. 214–218.

2. For a varied sampling of such phrases, see Tuo Tuo, *Song Shi*, juan 446, p. 13164, juan 450, p. 13250, juan 452, p. 13300, juan 454, p. 13345; Wan, *Songji zhongyi lu*, juan 4, p. 24b, juan 7, p. 21b.

3. Davis, *Court and Family*, pp. 163–168.

4. Cheng Zuluo, [*Chongzuan*] *Fujian tongzhi*, 1871 edition, juan 190, pp. 13a–13b; Lu, *Song shi yi*, juan 31, p. 15a; *Zhao zhong lu*, p. 32.

5. Liang Fangzhong, *Zhongguo lidai hukou, tiandi, tianfu tongji*, (Shanghai: Renmin chubanshe, 1980) p. 164.

6. Hu, *Song/Meng guanxi shi*, pp. 433–437; Hu, *Songmo sichuan*, pp. 472–506; Li, *Song*

Yuan zhanshi, vol. 3, pp. 1449–1460; also see my narrative for the Duzong reign in *The Cambridge History of China*, vol. 5 (forthcoming).

7. Wen, *Wenshan quanji*, juan 14, p. 353.
8. Wen, *Wenshan quanji*, juan 17, p. 457.
9. Tuo Tuo, *Song Shi*, juan 450, p. 13259; Qian, *Nansong Shu*, juan 59, p. 9a.
10. Tuo Tuo, *Song Shi*, juan 460, pp. 13489–13490.
11. This account is based on the Song dynastic history, but two separate sections which are not in total agreement. (See Tuo Tuo, *Song Shi*, juan 452, p. 13309, juan 460, pp. 13492–13493) I have followed here the lead of modern scholars, who conclude that the dynastic history is wrong is assuming Lin Tong to be the father, not the brother, of Lady Lin. See Chang Bide, et al., *Songren zhuanji ziliao suoyin* (Taipei: Dingwen shuju, 1976), vol. 2, p. 1337.
12. Tuo Tuo, *Song Shi*, juan 460, p. 13493.
13. Hsieh and Spence, "Suicide and the Family," p. 31.
14. William Rockhill Nelson Gallery of Art, *Eight Dynasties of Chinese Painting*, pp. 51, 72–76.
15. Birge, "Chu Hsi and Women's Education," pp. 352–359; Pei-yi Wu, "Education of Children in the Sung," in Wm. Theodore de Bary and John W. Chaffee, eds., *Neo-Confucian Education: The Formative Stage* (Berkeley: University of California, 1989), pp. 307–324 (esp. 318–319).
16. Ebrey, *Inner Quarters*, pp. 122–123, 158–160; Li Ch'ing-chao, *Li Ching-chao, Complete Poems*, trans. by Kenneth Rexroth and Ling Chung (New York: New Directions Books, 1979), p. 89; Hu Ping-ch'ing, *Li Ching-chao* (New York: Twayne Publishers, 1966), pp. 28–40. For a useful collection of essays and a valuable Chinese bibliography on this prominent poet, see Jinan shi shehui kexue yanjiusuo, *Li Qingzhao yanjiu lunwen ji* (Beijing: Zhonghua shuju, 1984).
17. Reed, "The Gender Symbolism of Kuan-yin Bodhisattva," p. 162.
18. Gernet, *Daily Life*, pp. 96–99.
19. Gernet, *Daily Life*, p. 164.
20. van Gulik, *Sexual Life in Ancient China*, pp. 103–104; Schafer, *Vermillion Bird*, pp. 79–86.
21. Davis, *Court and Family*, p. 285n28.
22. Birge, "Chu Hsi and Women's Education," p. 359; Chan, *Chu Hsi: New Studies*, pp. 543–544.
23. Chu Hsi, *Family Rituals*, p. 29; Ebrey, *Inner Quarters*, pp. 23–29.
24. van Gulik, *Sexual Life in Ancient China*, p. 235.
25. van Gulik, *Sexual Life in Ancient China*, pp. 236–238.
26. Ebrey, *Inner Quarters*, pp. 204–216.
27. Howard S. Levy, *Chinese Footbinding: The History of a Curious Erotic Custom* (New York: W. Rawls, 1966), pp. 40–46.
28. van Gulik, *Sexual Life in Ancient China*, pp. 212–222; Ebrey, *Inner Quarters*, pp. 37–44.
29. A recent publication has independently confirmed my own views in this regard, see Ebrey, *Inner Quarters*, pp. 41–42.
30. Ebrey, *Inner Quarters*, pp. 1–20, 261–271.
31. F. W. Mote, "The Growth of Chinese Despotism: A Critique of Wittfogel's Theory of Oriental Despotism as Applied to China," *Oriens Extremus*, vol. 8, no. 1 (1961), pp. 1–41.
32. Tuo Tuo, *Song Shi*, juan 47, p. 938.
33. Wang, *Song Lun*, juan 14, p. 252.
34. Schwartz, *The World of Thought in Ancient China*, pp. 57–59.
35. McKnight, *Law and Order in Sung China*, p. 291.

36. James T.C. Liu, "Polo and Cultural Change: From T'ang to Sung China," *Harvard Journal of Asiatic Studies*, vol. 45, no. 1 (June 1985), pp. 203–224. Interestingly, Jurchen rulers and aristocrats in the north were fully conscious of the links between athletic sport and military prowess. In the words of Shizong (r. 1161–89), as recorded in the Jin dynastic history: "Our ancestors conquered the country by military might—should we neglect it in time of peace? About twenty years ago, under the previous [reign], a ban was placed on polo and similar games. People at the time criticized the ban as a mistake. We thought so ourselves. This is why we use the game [today] to impress upon the country the significance of martial arts." (Liu, "Polo and Cultural Change," p. 214).

List of Works Cited

Allsen, Thomas T. *Mongol Imperialism: The Policies of the Grand Qan Möngke in China, Russia and the Islamic Lands, 1251–1259.* Berkeley: University of California Press, 1987.

Aoyama Sadao 青山定雄. "Zui Tō Sō sandai ni okeru kosū no chiiki teki kōsatsu" 隋唐宋三代における戸数の地域的考察 (Regional study of populations for the three dynasties of Sui, Tang, and Song) *Rekishigaku kenkyū* 歴史學研究, vol. 6, no. 4, pp. 411–446; vol. 6, no. 5, pp. 529–554 (1936).

Baibu congshu jicheng 百部叢書集成. Taipei: Yiwen yinshuguan, 1965.

de Bary, Wm. Theodore. "Chu Hsi's Aims as an Educator," in Wm. Theodore de Bary and John W. Chaffee, eds., *Neo-Confucian Education: The Formative Stage.* Berkeley: University of California Press, 1989.

——. *Neo-Confucian Orthodoxy and the Learning of the Mind-and-Heart.* New York: Columbia University Press, 1981.

——, ed. *Sources of Chinese Tradition.* 2 vols. New York: Columbia University Press, 1960.

Bi Yuan 畢沅. *Xu zizhi tongjian* 續資治通鑑 (Sequel to *The Comprehensive Mirror for Aid in Governance*). Beijing: Guji chubanshe, 1957.

Birge, Bettine. "Chu Hsi and Women's Education," in de Bary and Chaffee, eds., *Neo-Confucian Education* (q.v.).

Birrell, Anne. *New Songs from a Jade Terrace: An Anthology of Early Chinese Love Poetry.* New York: Penguin Books, 1986.

Bol, Peter K. "Government, Society, and State: On the Political Visions of Ssu-ma Kuang and Wang An-shih," in Hymes and Schirokauer, eds., *Ordering the World* (q.v.).

——. *"This Culture of Ours": Intellectual Transitions in T'ang and Sung China.* Stanford: Stanford University Press, 1992.

Bona ben 百衲本. Shanghai: Shangwu yinshuguan, 1937.

Brittan, Arthur. *Masculinity and Power.* Oxford: Basil Blackwell, 1989.

Brown, William Andreas. *Wen T'ien-hsiang: A Biographical Study of a Sung Patriot.* San Francisco: Chinese Materials Center Publications, 1986.

Chan, Hok-lam. *Legitimation in Imperial China: Discussions under the Jurchen-Chin Dynasty (1115–1234)*. Seattle: University of Washington Press, 1984.

Chan, Wing-tsit. *Chu Hsi: New Studies*. Honolulu: University of Hawaii Press, 1989.

Chang Bide 昌彼得, Wang Deyi 王德毅, et al. *Songren zhuanji ziliao suoyin* 宋人傳記資料索引 (Index to biographical materials for Song personages). Taipei: Dingwen shuju, 1976.

Chang, K. C., ed. *Food in Chinese Culture: Anthropological and Historical Perspectives*. New Haven: Yale University Press, 1977.

Chang, Kang-i Sun. *The Late-Ming Poet Ch'en Tzu-lung: Crises of Love and Loyalism*. New Haven: Yale University Press, 1991.

——. *Six Dynasties Poetry*. Princeton: Princeton University Press, 1986.

Chen Bangzhan 陳邦瞻 and Feng Qi 馮琦. *Songshi jishi benmo* 宋史紀事本末 (A topical summary of events from the Song History). Beijing: Zhonghua shuju, 1977.

Chen Dengyuan 陳登原. *Zhongguo tudi zhidu* 中國土地制度 (The system of land tenure in China). Shanghai: Shangwu yinshuguan, 1935.

Chen Liang 陳亮. *Chen Liang ji* 陳亮集 (The writings of Chen Liang), Sibu kanyao edition.

Chen Shisong 陳世松, et al. *Song Yuan zhanzheng shi* 宋元戰爭史 (A history of wars for the Song-Yuan epoch). Chengdu: Sichuansheng shehuikexue yuan chubanshe, 1988.

Chen Yan 陳衍. *Yuanshi jishi* 元詩紀事 (Historical events as recorded in Yuan poetry). Shanghai: Guji chubanshe, 1987.

Ch'en, Yuan. *Western and Central Asians in China under the Mongols*. Ch'ien Hsing-hai and L. Carrington Goodrich, trs. Los Angeles: Monumenta Serica at the University of California, 1966.

Cheng Minzheng 程敏政. *Song yimin lu* 宋遺民錄 (Record of loyal survivors of Song). Baibu congshu jicheng edition.

Cheng Zuluo 程祖洛, et al. *Fujian tongzhi* 福建通志 (Comprehensive gazetteer for Fujian), 1871 edition.

Cherniack, Susan. "Book Culture and Textual Transmission in Sung China." *Harvard Journal of Asiatic Studies,* vol. 54, no. 1, pp. 5–121 (1994).

Chin, Ann-ping and Mansfield Freeman, eds. and trs. *Tai Chen on Mencius: Explorations in Words and Meanings*. New Haven: Yale University Press, 1990.

Ching, Julia. "Chu Hsi on Personal Cultivation," in Wing-tsit Chan, ed., *Chu Hsi and Neo-Confucianism*. Honolulu: University of Hawaii Press, 1986.

Cholakian, Patricia Francis. "Rewriting History: Madame de Villedieu and the Wars of Religion," in Helen M. Cooper, et al., eds, *Arms and the Woman: War, Gender, and Literary Representation*. Chapel Hill: University of North Carolina Press, 1989.

Chu, Hsi. *Learning to Be a Sage: Selections from the* Conversations of Master Chu, Arranged Topically. Daniel K. Gardner, tr. Berkeley: University of California Press, 1990.

——. *Chu Hsi's* Family Rituals: *A Twelfth-Century Chinese Manual for the Performance of Cappings, Weddings, Funerals, and Ancestral Rites*. Patricia Buckley Ebrey, tr. Princeton: Princeton University Press, 1991.

—— and Lü Tsu-ch'ien, comps. *Reflections on Things at Hand: The Neo-Confucian Anthology Compiled by Chu Hsi and Lü Tsu-ch'ien*. Translated with notes by Wing-tsit Chan. New York: Columbia University Press, 1967.

Chung, Priscilla Ching. *Palace Women in the Northern Sung, 960–1126*. Leiden: E. J. Brill, 1981.

Confucius. *The Analects*. D. C. Lau, tr. New York: Penguin, 1979.

Congshu jicheng xinbian 叢書集成新編. Taipei: Xin wen feng chuban gongsi, 1985.

Dai Mei 戴枚, et al. [*Xinxiu*] *Yinxian zhi* 新修鄞縣志 (Gazetteer of Yin county, newly revised), 1887.

Davis, Richard L. *Court and Family in Sung China, 960–1279: Bureaucratic Success and Kinship Fortunes for the Shih of Ming-chou*. Durham: Duke University Press, 1986.

——. "Custodians of Education and Endowment at the State Schools of Southern Sung." *Journal of Sung-Yuan Studies*, vol. 25, pp. 95–119 (1995).

——. "The Eclipse of Imperial Leadership: Kuang-tsung and Ning-tsung (1189–1224)," "Ventures Foiled and Opportunities Missed: The Times of Li-tsung (1224–1264)," "Dynasty Besieged: Tu-tsung and Successors (1264–1279)," in Denis C. Twitchett, ed. *The Cambridge History of China*, vol. 5. Cambridge: Cambridge University Press, forthcoming.

——. "Sung Historiography: Empirical Ideals and Didactic Realities." *Chinese Culture* (Taipei), vol. 29, no. 4, pp. 67–80 (Dec. 1988).

Deng, Guangming. "Cultural Splendor and Cultural Policies of the Song Dynasty." *Social Sciences in China*, vol. 12, no. 1, pp. 169–174 (Jan. 1992).

—— 鄧廣銘. *Zhongguo lishi da zidian: Song Shi* 中國歷史大辭典：宋史 (An historical dictionary for China: Song history). Shanghai: Shanghai cishu chubanshe, 1984.

Ding Chuanjing, 丁傳靖, comp. *A Compilation of Anecdotes of Sung Personalities* (*Sung jen i shih hui pien*), Chu Djang and Jane C. Cjang, trs. Collegeville, Mn.: St. John's University Press, 1989.

——. *Songren yishi huibian* 宋人軼事彙編 (A collection of anecdotes for person-alities of Song). Taipei: Taiwan shangwu yinshuguan, 1982.

Duke, Michael S. *Lu You*. Boston: Twayne Publishers, 1977.

Ebrey, Patricia Buckley, ed. *Chinese Civilization and Society: A Sourcebook*. New York: The Free Press, 1981.

——, tr. *Family and Property in Sung China: Yuan Ts'ai's Precepts for Social Life*. Princeton: Princeton University Press, 1984.

——. *The Inner Quarters: Marriage and the Lives of Chinese Women in the Sung Period*. Berkeley: University of California Press, 1993.

—— and Peter N. Gregory, eds. *Religion and Society in T'ang and Sung China*. Honolulu: University of Hawaii Press, 1993.

Eight Dynasties of Chinese Painting: The Collections of the Nelson Gallery-Atkins Museum, Kansas City, and the Cleveland Museum of Art, with essays by Wai-kam Ho, et al. William Rockhill Nelson Gallery of Art and Mary Atkins Museum of Fine Arts. Bloomington: Indiana University Press, 1980.

Elshtain, Jean Bethke. *Women and War.* New York: Basic Books, 1987.

Elvin, Mark. *The Pattern of the Chinese Past.* Stanford: Stanford University Press, 1973.

Fang Feng 方鳳. *Cunyatang yigao* 存雅堂遺稿 (Extant documents from the Cunya Pavilion). Siku quanshu edition.

Fang Zhenhua 方震華. "Wansong bianfang yanjiu (A.D. 1234–1275)" 晚宋邊防 研究 (Study of border defense during the late Song). M.A. thesis, National Taiwan Normal University, 1992.

Finegan, Michael H. "Urbanism in Sung China." Ph.D. diss., University of Chicago, 1976.

Fisher, Tom. "Loyalist Alternatives in the Early Ch'ing." *Harvard Journal of Asiatic Studies,* vol. 44, no. 1, pp. 83–122 (1984).

Foucault, Michel. *The History of Sexuality,* vol. 1: *An Introduction,* Robert Hurley, tr. New York: Vintage Books, 1980.

———. *The History of Sexuality,* vol. 2: *The Use of Pleasure,* Robert Hurley, tr. New York: Vintage Books, 1990.

Franke, Herbert. "Chia Ssu-tao (1213–1275): A 'Bad Last Minister'?" in Arthur F. Wright and Denis Twitchett, eds., *Confucian Personalities.* Stanford: Stanford University Press, 1962.

———. "Siege and Defense of Towns in Medieval China," in Frank A. Kierman, Jr., and John K. Fairbank, eds., *Chinese Ways and Warfare.* Cambridge: Harvard University Press, 1974.

———, ed. *Sung Biographies.* 4 vols. Wiesbaden: Franz Steiner Verlag Wiesbaden GmbH, 1976.

Franke, Otto. *Geschichte des Chinesischen reiches: eine darstellung seiner entstehung, seines wesens und seiner entwicklung bis zur neuesten zeit.* Volume 4. Berlin: Verlag von Walter de Gruyter and Co., 1948.

Fu Wanglu 傅王露 and Ji Zengyun 稽曾筠, et al [*Chixiu*] *Zhejiang tongzhi* 敕修 浙江通志 (Comprehensive gazetteer for Zhejiang, further revised), 1735.

Gan Ze 甘澤, et al. *Qizhou zhi* 蘄州志 (Gazetteer for Qizhou), 1536, Academia Sinica rare edition.

Gernet, Jacques. *Daily Life in China on the Eve of the Mongol Invasion, 1250– 1276,* H. M. Wright, tr. Stanford: Stanford University Press, 1962.

———. "Les Suicides par le Feu chez les Bouddhistes Chinois du ve au xe siècle." In *Mélanges publiés par L'institut des Hautes Études Chinoises.* Vol. 2. Paris: Presses Universitaires de France, 1960.

Gilmore, David D. *Manhood in the Making: Cultural Concepts of Masculinity.* New Haven: Yale University Press, 1990.

Gulik, R. H. van. *Sexual Life in Ancient China: A Preliminary Survey of Chinese Sex and Society from ca. 1500 B.C. till 1644 A.D.* Leiden: E. J. Brill, 1974.

Guoxue jiben congshu 國學基本叢書. Taipei: Shangwu yinshuguan, 1956.

Han Fei 韓非. *Han fei zi* 韓非子 (Master Han Fei). Sibu congkan edition.

Handlin Smith, Joanna F. "Gardens in Ch'i Piao-chia's Social World: Wealth and Values in Late-Ming Kiangnan," *The Journal of Asian Studies,* vol. 51, no. 1, pp. 55–81 (Feb. 1992).

Hansen, Valerie. *Changing Gods in Medieval China, 1127–1276.* Princeton: Princeton University Press, 1990.

Hargett, James M. "A Chronology of the Reigns and Reign-Periods of the Song Dynasty (960–1279)," *Bulletin of Sung-Yuan Studies,* Vol. 19, pp. 26–34 (1987).

——. "Huizong's Magic Marchmount: The Genyue Pleasure Park of Kaifeng," *Monumenta Serica,* vol. 38, pp. 1–48 (1988–1989).

Hartwell, Robert M. "The Imperial Treasuries: Finance and Power in Song China," *Bulletin of Sung-Yuan Studies,* vol. 20, pp. 16–89 (1988).

Hatch, George. "Su Hsun's Pragmatic Statecraft," in Hymes and Schirokauer, eds., *Ordering the World.*

He Shaoji 何紹基 and Shen Baozhen 沈葆禎, et al. [*Chongxiu*] *Anhui tongzhi* 重修安徽通志 (Comprehensive gazetteer for Anhui, further revised), 1877.

Henderson, John B. *The Development and Decline of Chinese Cosmology.* New York: Columbia University Press, 1984.

Herf, Jeffrey. *Reactionary Modernism: Technology, Culture, and Politics in Weimar and the Third Reich.* Cambridge: Cambridge University Press, 1984.

Hervouet, Yves. *A Sung Bibliography (Bibliographie des Sung).* Hong Kong: The Chinese University of Hong Kong, 1978.

Hinsch, Bret. *Passions of the Cut Sleeve: The Male Homosexual Tradition in China.* Berkeley: University of California Press, 1990.

Hong Zaixin 洪再新. "Songdai fengsu hua" 宋代風俗畫 (Lifestyle Paintings for the Song Dynasty). *Xin meishu* 新美術, No. 21, pp. 60–67 (1985).

Hsiao, Kung-chuan. *A History of Chinese Political Thought.* F. W. Mote, tr. Princeton: Princeton University Press, 1979.

Hsieh, Andrew C. K., and Jonathan D. Spence. "Suicide and the Family in Pre-Modern Chinese Society," in Arthur Kleinman and Tsung-yi Lin, eds., *Normal and Abnormal Behavior in Chinese Culture.* Dordrecht, Holland: D. Reidel Publishing Company, 1981.

Hu, Ping-ch'ing. *Li Ch'ing-chao.* New York: Twayne Publishers, 1966.

Hu Zhaoxi 胡昭曦, Zou Chonghua 鄒重華. *Song/Meng (Yuan) guanxi shi* 宋蒙 (元)關系史 (History of relations between the Song and Yuan). Chengdu: Sichuan daxue chubanshe, 1992.

—— and Tang Weimu 唐唯目, eds. *Songmo sichuan zhanzheng shiliao xuanbian* 宋末四川戰爭史料選編 (Selection of source materials on wars in Sichuan at the end of Song). Chengdu: Sichuan renmin chubanshe, 1984.

Huang Jin 黃溍. *Huang wenxiangong ji* 黃文獻公集 (Collected writings for Mr. Huang), Congshu jicheng edition.

Huang Kuanchong 黃寬重. *Nansong junzheng yu wenxian tansuo* 南宋軍政與文獻探索 (A study of Southern Song military affairs and the relevant literature). Taipei: Xin wenfeng chuban gongsi, 1990.

——. *Nansong shi yanjiu ji* 南宋史研究集 (Collected essays on Southern Song history). Taipei: Xin wenfeng chuban gongsi, 1985.

Huang Wenji 黃文吉. *Song nandu ciren* 宋南渡詞人 (Song lyricists after the dynasty's relocation south). Taipei: Xuesheng shuju, 1985.

Huang Xianfan 黃現璠. *Songdai taixuesheng jiuguo yundong* 宋代太學生救國運動 (The patriotic activism of students at the Imperial University of Song times). Shanghai: Shangwu yinshuguan, 1936.

Huang Zhen 黃震. *Huang shi richao gujin jiyao yibian* 黃氏日抄古今紀要逸編 (The diary of Mr. Huang: An extant collection of basic materials for the past and present), Congshu jicheng edition.

Huang Zongxi 黃宗羲. *Song Yuan xue'an* 宋元學案 (Intellectual biographies for the Song and Yuan). Taipei: Shijie shuju, 1973.

Huber, Horst Wolfram. "Between Land and Sea: The End of the Southern Sung," *Analecta Husserliana,* vol. 19, pp. 101–128 (1985).

——. "The Hero as the Spiritual Legacy of his Culture: Wen T'ien-hsiang and his Admirers," *Analecta Husserliana,* vol. 21, pp. 309–336 (1986).

——. "Wen T'ien-hsiang (1236–1283): Vorstufen zum Verständnis seines Lebens." Ph.D. diss., Universität zu München, 1983.

Hucker, Charles O. *A Dictionary of Office Titles in Imperial China.* Stanford: Stanford University Press, 1985.

Hymes, Robert P., and Conrad Schirokauer, eds. *Ordering the World: Approaches to State and Society in Sung Dynasty China.* Berkeley: University of California Press, 1993.

The I Ching, or Book of Changes. German translation by Richard Wilhelm rendered into English by Cary F. Baynes. 3rd edition. Princeton: Princeton University Press, 1967.

Ihara Hiroshi 伊原弘. *Chūgoku kaihō no seikatsu to saiji: egakareta sōdai no toshi seikatsu* 中國開封の生活と歲時：描かれた宋代の都市生活 (Life and Seasons in the Chinese city of Kaifeng: A depiction of metropolitan life under Song rule). Tokyo: Yamakawa shuppansha, 1991.

Jay, Jennifer W. *A Change in Dynasties: Loyalism in Thirteenth-Century China.* Bellingham: Western Washington University, Center for East Asian Studies, 1991.

——. "Memoirs and Official Accounts: The Historiography of the Song Loyalists," *Harvard Journal of Asiatic Studies,* vol. 50, no. 2, pp. 589–612 (1990).

Jian Youwen [Ren Youwen] 簡又文. *Songmo erdi nanqian nianlu kao* 宋末二帝南遷輦路考 (Study of the passage south of the last two emperors of Song). Hong Kong: Mengjin shuwu congshu, 1957.

——. *Song huangtai jinian ji* 宋皇台紀念集 (A commemorative for the Song royal esplanade). Hong Kong: Rongfeng hang, 1960.

Jiang Yixue 蔣逸雪. *Lu Xiufu nianpu* 陸秀夫年譜 (Chronology for Lu Xiufu). Shanghai: Shangwu yinshuguan, 1936.

Jinan shi shehuikexue yanjiusuo 濟南市社會科學研究所, *Li Qingzhao yanjiu lunwen ji* 李清照研究論文集 (Collection of essays on Li Qingzhao). Beijing: Zhonghua shuju, 1984.

Ke Shaomin 柯劭忞, et al. *Xin Yuan Shi* 新元史 (A new history of the Yuan), Bonaben edition.

Ke Weiqi 柯維騏. *Songshi xinbian* 宋史新編 (A new history of the Song). Taipei: Xin wenfeng chuban gongsi, 1974.

Kracke, E. A., Jr. "Sung K'ai-feng: Pragmatic Metropolis and Formalistic Capital." In John Winthrop Haeger, ed., *Crisis and Prosperity in Sung China.* Tucson: University of Arizona Press, 1975.

Kuhn, Annette, and Ann Marie Wolpe, eds. *Feminism and Materialism: Women and Modes of Production.* London: Routledge and Kegan Paul, 1978.

Langley, Bradford C. "Wang Yinglin (1223–1296): A Study in the Political and Intellectual History of the Demise of Song." Ph.D. diss., Indiana University, 1980.

Lee, Thomas H. C. *Government Education and Examinations in Sung China*. Hong Kong: The Chinese University Press, 1985.

——. "The Fulfillments of Education—Social Alienation and Intellectual Dissent in Paradox." Paper presented at the Conference on Confucian Intellectuals: Ideals and Actions (With Emphasis on the Sung), The Chinese University of Hong Kong, July 1990.

Legge, James. *The Chinese Classics*. 2d rev. ed. 7 vols. Hong Kong: Hong Kong University Press, 1960.

——, tr. *Li chi: Book of Rites: An Encyclopedia of Ancient Ceremonial Usages, Religious Creeds, and Social Institutions*. Ch'u Chai and Winberg Chai, eds. Hyde Park, N.Y.: University Books, 1967.

Levy, Howard S. *Chinese Footbinding: The History of a Curious Erotic Custom*. New York: W. Rawls, 1966.

Lewis, Mark Edward. *Sanctioned Violence in Early China*. Albany: State University of New York Press, 1990.

Li An 李安. *Song Wen chengxiang tianxiang nianpu* 宋文丞相天祥年譜 (A chronology for Wen Tianxiang, chief minister of Song). Taipei: Taiwan shangwu yinshuguan, 1980.

Li, Ch'ing-chao. *Li Ch'ing-chao, Complete Poems*. Kenneth Rexroth and Ling Chung, trs. New York: New Directions Books, 1979.

Li E 厲鶚. *Songshi jishi* 宋詩紀事 (Historical events as recorded in Song poetry). Taipei: Dingwen shuju, 1971.

Li Hanzhang 李瀚章, et al. *Hunan tongzhi* 湖南通志 (Comprehensive gazetteer for Hunan), 1885 edition.

Li Ji 禮記 (Book of Rites), Sibu congkan edition.

Li Mingwan 李銘皖, et al. *Suzhou fuzhi* 蘇州府志 (Prefectural gazetteer for Suzhou [Soochow]), 1883 edition.

Li Qingya 李青厓. "Shu Li Tingzhi" 述李庭芝 (A narrative on Li Tingzhi). *Wenshi zazhi* 文史雜誌, vol. 1, no. 11, pp. 61–68 (May 16, 1941).

Li Rong 李榕, et al. *Hangzhou fuzhi* 杭州府志 (Prefectural gazetteer for Hangzhou), 1922 edition.

Li Tao 李燾. *Xu zizhi tongjian changbian* 續資治通鑑長編 (A detailed sequel to *The Comprehensive Mirror for Aid in Governance*). Taipei: Shijie shuju, 1974.

Li Tianming 李天鳴. *Song Yuan zhanshi* 宋元戰史 (A history of wars between Song and Yuan). 4 vols. Taipei: Shihuo chubanshe, 1988.

Li Yonglu 栗永祿. *Shouzhou zhi* 壽州志 (Gazetteer for Shouzhou), 1550, Academia Sinica rare edition.

Li You 李有. *Guhang zaji* 古杭雜記 (Miscellaneous notes for ancient Hangzhou), Congshu jicheng edition.

Li Zefen 李則芬. *Yuanshi xinjiang* 元史新講 (A new interpretation of Yuan history). 4 vols. Taipei: Zhonghua shuju, 1978.

Li Zhen 李震, et al. *Zhongguo lidai zhanzheng shi* 中國歷代戰爭史 (A history of Chinese wars through the Ages). Taipei: Sanjun lianhe canmou daxue, 1968.

Liang Fangzhong 梁方仲. *Zhongguo lidai hukou, tiandi, tianfu tongji* 中國歷代戶口、田地、田賦統計 (Statistical overview of population, land area, and taxes for Chinese history). Shanghai: Renmin chubanshe, 1980.

Lin, Shuen-fu. *The Transformation of the Chinese Lyrical Tradition: Chang K'uei and Southern Sung Tz'u Poetry.* Princeton: Princeton University Press, 1978.

Lin Tianwei 林天蔚. "Songdai quanxiang xingcheng zhi fenxi" 宋代權相形成之分析 (Analysis of the emergence of powerful ministers in Song times). In *Songshi yanjiu ji* 宋史研究集, vol. 8, pp. 141–170. Taipei: Zhonghua congshu, 1976.

Lin, Yutang. *The Gay Genius: The Life and Times of Su Tungpo.* New York: The John Day Company, 1947.

Lin Zhengqiu 林正秋. *Nansong ducheng linan* 南宋都城臨安 (A Southern Song capital: Linan). Hangzhou: Xiling yinshe, 1986.

Liu Boji 劉伯驥. *Songdai zhengjiao shi* 宋代政教史. (A history of politics and culture for the Song). Taipei: Taiwan zhonghua shuju, 1971.

Liu, James J. Y. *The Chinese Knight-Errant.* Chicago: The University of Chicago Press, 1967.

Liu, James T. C. "Luelun songdai wuguanchun zai tongzhi jieji zhong di diwei" 略論宋代武官群在統治階級中的地位 (Discussion on the status of military officials within the ruling class of the Song Dynasty). In *Aoyama hakushi koki kinen: Sōdaishi ronsō* 青山博士古稀紀念：宋代史論叢. Tokyo: Seishin shobo, 1974.

——. *Ou-yang Hsiu: An Eleventh-Century Neo-Confucianist.* Stanford: Stanford University Press, 1967.

——. "Polo and Cultural Change from T'ang to Sung China," *Harvard Journal of Asiatic Studies,* vol. 45, pp. 203–224 (1985).

——. "Sung Roots of Chinese Political Conservatism: The Administrative Problems," *Journal of Asian Studies,* vol. 26, no. 3, pp. 457–463 (May 1967).

——. "Yueh Fei (1103–41) and China's Heritage of Loyalty," *Journal of Asian Studies,* vol. 31, no. 2, pp. 291–297 (Feb. 1972).

—— and Peter J. Golas, eds. *Change in Sung China: Innovation or Renovation?* Lexington, Mass.: D. C. Heath and Company, 1969.

Liu Minzhong 劉敏中. *Ping Song lu* 平宋錄 (Record of the pacification of Song), Baibu congshu jicheng edition.

Liu Xu 劉昫, et al. *Jiu Tang Shu* 舊唐書 (Old history of the Tang). Beijing: Zhonghua shuju, 1975.

Liu Yueshen 劉岳申. *Shenzhai liu xiansheng wenji* 申齋劉先生文集 (Collected writings of Master Liu Shenzhai), Zhibuzu zhai edition, 1812.

Liu Zijian 劉子健: *See* James T. C. Liu.

Lo, Irving Yucheng. *Hsin Ch'i-chi.* New York: Twayne Publishers, 1971.

Lo, Winston Wan. *The Life and Thought of Yeh Shih.* Gainesville: The University Presses of Florida, 1974.

Lu, Sheldon Hsiao-peng. *From Historicity to Fictionality: The Chinese Poetics of Narrative.* Stanford: Stanford University Press, 1994.

Lu Shi 陸師. *Yizhen zhi* 儀真志 (Gazetteer for the Yizhen region), 1718 edition.

Lu Xinyuan 陸心源. *Song Shi yi* 宋史翼 (Supplement to the Song dynastic history), 1906. Taipei: Dingwen shuju, 1978.

Lu You 陸游. *Lu fangweng quanji: Jiannan shigao* 陸放翁全集：劍南詩藁

(Complete writings of Lu Fangweng: the Jiannan poetry). Beijing: Zhongguo shudian, 1986.

Luo Xianglin 羅香林. "Song wangtai yu songji zhi haishang xingchao" 宋王台與宋季之海上行朝 (The Royal Esplanade and the water-bound court of Song times), in *Songshi yanjiuji*, vol. 9, pp. 99–146. Taipei: Zhonghua congshu, 1977.

Lynn, Richard John. "Chu Hsi as Literary Theorist and Critic," in Wing-tsit Chan, ed., *Chu Hsi and Neo-Confucianism*. Honolulu: University of Hawaii Press, 1986.

Marney, John. *Liang Chien-wen Ti*. Boston: Twayne Publishers, 1976.

McCraw, David R. *Du Fu's Laments from the South*. Honolulu: University of Hawaii Press, 1992.

McKnight, Brian. "Chu Hsi and His World," in *Chu Hsi and Neo-Confucianism* (q.v.)

——. *Law and Order in Sung China*. Cambridge: Cambridge University Press, 1992.

McMullen, David. *State and Scholars in T'ang China*. Cambridge: Cambridge University Press, 1988.

Mencius. *Mencius*. D. C. Lau, tr. New York: Penguin, 1970.

Morgan, David. *The Mongols*. Oxford: Basil Blackwell, 1986.

Mote, Frederick W. "Confucian Eremitism in the Yuan Period," in Arthur F. Wright, ed., *The Confucian Persuasion*. Stanford: Stanford University Press, 1960.

——. "The Growth of Chinese Despotism: A Critique of Wittfogel's Theory of Oriental Despotism as Applied to China," *Oriens Extremus*, vol. 8, no. 1, pp. 1–41 (1961).

Needham, Joseph. *Science in Traditional China: A Comparative Perspective*. Cambridge: Harvard University Press, 1981.

—— and Wang Ling. *Science and Civilisation in China*, vol. 2: *History of Scientific Thought*. Cambridge: Cambridge University Press, 1956.

Ouyang Shoudao 歐陽守道. *Xunzhai wenji* 巽齋文集 (Collected writings of Mr. Xunzhai), Siku quanshu edition.

Ouyang Xiu 歐陽修, et al. *Xin Tang shu* 新唐書 (New History of the Tang). Beijing: Zhonghua shuju, 1975.

——. *Wudai shiji* 五代史記, or *Xin wudai shi* 新五代史 (Historical records [or New history] of the Five Dynasties). Beijing: Zhonghua shuju, 1974.

Pang Dexin 龐德新. *Songdai liangjing shimin shenghuo* 宋代兩京市民生活 (Daily life in the two capitals of Song). Hong Kong: Longmen shudian, 1974.

Peng Ze 彭澤, et al. *Huizhou fuzhi* 徽州府志 (Prefectural gazetteer for Huizhou), 1502 edition.

Peterson, Charles A. "Old Illusions and New Realities: Sung Foreign Policy, 1217–1234," in Morris Rossabi, ed., *China among Equals: The Middle Kingdom and its Neighbors, 10th–14th Centuries*. Berkeley: University of California Press, 1983.

Qian Shisheng 錢士升. *Nansong shu* 南宋書 (History of the Southern Song). N.d.

Qian Yueyou 潛說友, et al. [*Xianchun*] *Linan zhi* 咸淳臨安志 (Gazetteer for

Linan [ca. 1264–1274]). Song Yuan difangzhi congshu edition. Taipei: Zhongguo dizhi yanjiu hui, 1978.

Qu, Yuan. [*Chu tzu*] *The Songs of the South: An Ancient Chinese Anthology of Poems by Qu Yuan and Other Poets.* Translated and annotated by David Hawkes. New York: Penguin Books, 1985.

Quan Hansheng 全漢昇. "Songmo di tonghuo pengzhang ji qi duiyu wujia di yingxiang" 宋末的通貨膨脹及其對於物價的影響 (Inflation during the late Song and its impact on prices), in *Songshi yanjiu ji*, vol. 2, pp. 283–325. Taipei: Zhonghua congshu, 1964.

Reed, Barbara E. "The Gender Symbolism of Kuan-yin Bodhisattva," in José Ignacio Cabezón, ed., *Buddhism, Sexuality, and Gender.* Albany: State University of New York Press, 1992.

Renxiao, Empress 仁孝皇后 [née Xu 徐氏]. *Nei xun* 內訓 (Instructions for the Inner Quarters), Congshu jicheng edition.

Roper, Michael, and John Tosh, eds. *Manful Assertions: Masculinities in Britain since 1800.* London: Routledge, 1991.

Rorex, Robert A., and Wen Fong. *Eighteen Songs of a Nomad Flute: The Story of Lady Wen-chi, Fourteenth-century Handscroll in the Metropolitan Museum of Art.* New York: The Metropolitan Museum of Art, 1974.

Rossabi, Morris. *Khubilai Khan: His Life and Times.* Berkeley: University of California Press, 1988.

Sanchao yeshi 三朝野史 (Spurious history for three reigns), Congshu jicheng edition.

Schafer, Edward H. *The Vermilion Bird: T'ang Images of the South.* Berkeley: University of California Press, 1967.

Schirokauer, Conrad. "Chu Hsi's Sense of History," in Hymes and Schirokauer, eds., *Ordering the World* (q.v.).

Schmidt, J. D. *Yang Wan-li.* Boston: Twayne Publishers, 1976.

Schneider, Laurence A. *A Madman of Ch'u: The Chinese Myth of Loyalty and Dissent.* Berkeley: University of California Press, 1980.

Schwartz, Benjamin I. *The World of Thought in Ancient China.* Cambridge: Harvard University Press, 1985.

Segal, Lynne. *Slow Motion: Changing Masculinities, Changing Men.* New Brunswick, N.J.: Rutgers University Press, 1990.

Seidel, Anna. "Chronicle of Taoist Studies in the West, 1950–1990." *Cahiers d'Extreme-Asie (Revue bilingue de l'Ecole Française d'Extreme-Orient),* vol. 5, pp. 223–347 (1989–1990).

Shen Yue 沈約, et al. *Song Shu* 宋書 (History of the [Liu] Song). Beijing: Zhonghua shuju, 1974.

Shi Nengzhi 史能之, et al. [*Xianchun*] *Piling zhi* 咸淳毘陵志 (Gazetteer for Piling [1265–1274 epoch], 1268. Song Yuan difangzhi congshu edition.

Shi Xuehuang 施學煌, et al. *Rongchang xianzhi* 榮昌縣志 (Gazetteer for Rongchang county), 1883 edition.

Sibu congkan chubian 四部叢刊初編. Shanghai: Shangwu yinshuguan, 1929–1934.

Sibu kanyao 四部刊要, Yang Jialuo 楊家駱, comp. Taipei: Shijie shuju, 1959.

Siku quanshu 四庫全書, Wenyuange 文淵閣 edition, reprint Taipei: Shangwu yinshuguan, 1967.

Sima Qian 司馬遷. *Shi Ji* 史記 (Records of the Grand Historian). Beijing: Zhonghua shuju, 1959.

Siming congshu 四明叢書, Zhang Shouyong 張壽鏞, comp., 1932.

Shiba, Yoshinobu. "Urbanization and the Development of Markets in the Lower Yangtze Valley," in Haeger, ed., *Crisis and Prosperity in Sung China* (q.v.).

Smith, Paul J. *Taxing Heaven's Storehouse: Horses, Bureaucrats, and the Destruction of the Sichuan Tea Industry, 1074–1224.* Cambridge: Council on East Asian Studies, Harvard University, 1991.

Song Dingzong 宋鼎宗. *Chunqiu Songxue fawei* 春秋宋學發微 (Exploration of Song scholarship on the Spring and Autumn Annals). Rev. ed. Taipei: Wenshizhe chubanshe, 1986.

Songji sanchao zhengyao 宋季三朝政要 (A narrative summary for three reigns of the Song period), Congshu jicheng edition.

Song Lian 宋濂, et al. *Yuan Shi* 元史 (History of the Yuan). Beijing: Zhonghua shuju, 1976.

Song Xi 宋晞. "Nansong zhedong di shixue" 南宋浙東的史學 (Historical scholarship in Zhedong region during the Southern Song), in *Songshi yanjiu ji,* vol. 14, pp. 9–52. Taipei: Zhonghua congshu, 1983.

——. *Songshi yanjiu luncong* 宋史研究論叢 (Collected essays on Song history). Taipei: Zhongguo wenhua yanjiusuo, 1980.

Struve, Lynn A. "Ambivalence and Action: Some Frustrated Scholars of the K'ang-hsi Period," in Jonathan D. Spence and John E. Wills, Jr., eds., *From Ming to Ch'ing: Conquest, Region, and Continuity in Seventeenth-Century China.* New Haven: Yale University Press, 1979.

——, tr. *Voices from the Ming-Qing Cataclysm: China in Tigers' Jaws.* New Haven: Yale University Press, 1993.

Su Wenting 蘇文婷. *Songdai yimin wenxue yanjiu* 宋代遺民文學研究 (A literary study of loyalist survivors of Song). Taipei: Xuesheng shuju, 1979.

Sun Hai 孫海, et al. *Suining xianzhi* 遂寧縣志 (Gazetteer for Suining county), 1878 edition.

Sung Yuan difangzhi congshu 宋元地方志叢書. Taipei: Sung Yuan fangzhi weiyuan hui, 1978.

Tan, Qixiang 譚其驤. "The First and Last Years of Dynastic Reigns." *Social Sciences in China,* vol. 13, no. 4, pp. 92–99 (Dec. 1992).

——, ed. *Zhongguo lishi ditu ji* 中國歷史地圖集 (Historical atlas for China). Shanghai: Ditu chubanshe, 1982.

Tao, Ching-shen. "The Establishment of the Southern Sung: The Reign of Emperor Kao-tsung (1127–1162)," in Denis C. Twitchett, ed., *The Cambridge History of China,* vol. 5 (q. v.).

Tao Zongyi 陶宗儀. *Nancun Zhuogeng lu* 南村輟耕錄 (Jottings between tillings for Mr. Nancun). Beijing: Zhonghua shuju, 1959.

Terada Gō 寺田剛. *Sōdai kyōikushi gaisetsu* 宋代教育史 (An educational history for the Song dynasty). Tokyo: Hakubunsha, 1965.

——. *Sōdai no giki* 宋代の義氣 (The righteous spirit of the Song dynasty). Tokyo: Bunka shobō, 1972.

Tillman, Hoyt C. "Encyclopedias, Polymaths, and Tao-hsueh Confucians: Preliminary Reflections with special reference to Chao Ju-yü," *Journal of Sung-Yuan Studies,* vol. 22, pp. 89–108 (1990–1992).

———. "Proto-Nationalism in Twelfth-Century China? The Case of Ch'en Liang," *Harvard Journal of Asiatic Studies,* vol. 39, no. 2, pp. 403–428 (Dec. 1979).

———. *Utilitarian Confucianism: Ch'en Liang's Challenge to Chu Hsi.* Cambridge: Council on East Asian Studies, Harvard University, 1982.

Ting, Ch'uan-ching. *See* Ding Chuanjing.

Tu Ji 屠寄. *Mengwu'er shiji* 蒙兀兒史記 (Historical Records for the Mongols). 1934. Taipei: Dingwen shuju, 1977.

Tung, Chieh-yuan. *Master Tung's Western Chamber Romance: A Chinese Chantefable,* Li-li Ch'en, tr. New York: Columbia University Press, 1994.

Tuo Tuo 脫脫 [Toghto], et al. *Jin shi* 金史 (History of Jin). Beijing: Zhonghua shuju, 1976.

———, et al. *Song shi* 宋史 (History of Song). Beijing: Zhonghua shuju, 1977.

Twitchett, Denis, ed. *The Cambridge History of China.* Vol. 3: *Sui and T'ang China, 589–906, Part 1.* Cambridge: Cambridge University Press, 1979.

Umehara Kaoru 梅原郁. *Bun Tenshō* 文天祥 (Wen Tianxiang). Tokyo: Jimbutsu yukikisha, 1969.

Wan Shengnan 萬繩楠. *Wen Tianxiang zhuan* 文天祥傳 (Biography of Wen Tianxiang). Henan: Henan renmin chubanshe, 1985.

Wan Sitong 萬斯同. *Songji zhongyi lu* 宋季忠義錄 (Record of loyalists for the Song period), Siming congshu 四明叢書 edition. Taipei: 1964.

Wang Cun 王存, et al. *Yuanfeng jiuyu zhi* 元豐九域志 (Gazetteer for the empire's nine regions [1078–1085 epoch]), Guoxue jiben congshu edition.

Wang Erjian, comp. 王爾鑑. *Baxian zhi* 巴縣志 (Gazetteer for Ba county), 1760 edition.

Wang Fuzhi 王夫之. *Song lun* 宋論 (Discourse on the Song), Sibu kanyao edition. Taipei: 1984.

Wang, Gung-wu. "Feng Tao: An Essay on Confucian Loyalty," in Arthur F. Wright and Denis Twitchett, eds., *Confucian Personalities.* Stanford: Stanford University Press, 1962.

Wang Jianqiu 王建秋. *Songdai taixue yu taixuesheng* 宋代太學與太學生 (The Imperial University and its students during the Song dynasty). Taipei: Taiwan shangwu yinshuguan, 1965.

Wang Yinglin 王應麟. *Kunxue jiwen (jizheng)* 困學紀聞集証 (Reflections after arduous study), annotated by Weng Yuanqi, 1807. Taipei: Taiwan shudian, 1960.

———. *Liujing tianwen bian* 六經天文編 (Texts on Astronomy in the Six Classics), Congshu jicheng edition.

Wang Yuanliang 汪元量. *Hushan leigao* 湖山類稿 (Assorted drafts for Mr. Hushan), Siku quanshu edition.

———. *Shuiyun ji* 水雲集 (Collected writings for Mr. Shuiyun), Wulin wangzhe yizhu edition. Taipei: Yiwen yinshuguan, 1971.

———. *Song jiugongren shici* 宋舊宮人詩詞 (Poetry for former palace women of the Song), Congshu jicheng edition.

Watson, Burton, tr. and ed. *The Columbia Book of Chinese Poetry: From Early Times to the Thirteenth Century.* New York: Columbia University Press, 1984.

Wei Shou 魏收. *Wei shu* 魏書 (History of Wei). Beijing: Zhonghua shuju, 1974.

Wen Tianxiang 文天祥. *Wenshan xiansheng quanji* 文山先生全集 (Complete writings of Master Wenshan). Shanghai: Shijie shuju, 1936.

Wollstonecraft, Mary. *A Vindication of the Rights of Woman: An Authoritative Text, Backgrounds, Criticism.* Carol H. Poston, ed. New York: Norton and Company, 1975.

Worthy, Edmund H. "The Founding of Sung China, 950–1000: Integrative Changes in Military and Political Institutions." Ph.D. diss., Princeton University, 1976.

Wu, Pei-yi. *The Confucian's Progress: Autobiographical Writings in Traditional China.* Princeton: Princeton University Press, 1990.

——. "Education of Children in the Sung," in de Bary and Chaffee, eds., *Neo-Confucian Education* (q.v.).

Wu Xiongguang 吳熊光, et al. *Hubei tongzhi* 湖北通志 (Comprehensive gazetteer for Hubei), 1804 edition.

Wulin Wangzhe yizhu 武林往哲遺著. Ding Bing 丁丙, comp., Jiahuitang edition, late 19th century.

Xiao, Tong. *Wen xuan, or Selections of Refined Literature.* David R. Knechtges, tr. 2 vols. Princeton: Princeton University Press, 1982.

Xiao jing 孝經 (Classic of Filial Piety), Sibu congkan edition.

Xu Yuan Zhong, tr. *Songs of the Immortals: Anthology of Classical Chinese Poetry.* London: Penguin, 1994.

Xu Qianxue 徐乾學. *Zizhi tongjian houbian* 資治通鑑後編 (Addendum to the *Comprehensive Mirror for Aid in Governance*), Siku quanshu edition.

Yang Bojun 楊伯峻, ed. *Chunqiu zuozhuan zhu* 春秋左傳注 (Annotated edition of the *Spring and Autumn Annals* with *Narrative of Tso*). Beijing: Zhonghua shuju, 1981.

Yang De'en 楊德恩. *Wen Tianxiang nianpu* 文天祥年譜 (Chronology for Wen Tianxiang). Shanghai: Shangwu yinshuguan, 1947.

Yang, Dequan, and James T. C. Liu. "The Image of Scholar-Generals and a Case in the Southern Sung," *Saeculum*, vol. 37, pp. 182–191 (1986).

Yang, Lien-sheng. "Female Rulers in Imperial China," in John L. Bishop, ed., *Studies of Governmental Institutions in Chinese History.* Cambridge: Harvard University Press, 1968.

Yang, Wan-li. *Heaven My Blanket, Earth My Pillow.* Jonathan Chaves, tr. New York: Weatherhill, 1975.

Yang Yilun 楊宜崙, et al. *Gaoyou zhouzhi* 高郵州志 (Prefectural gazetteer for Gaoyou), 1783 edition.

Yin Dexin 尹德新, et al., comp. *Lidai jiaoyu biji ziliao* 歷代教育筆記資料 (Memorabilia sources on educational history). Beijing: Zhongguo laodong chubanshe, 1991.

Yin Tinggao 尹廷高. *Yujing qiaochang* 玉井樵唱 (Woodcutter's songs from the jade well), Siku quanshu edition.

Yoshikawa, Kōjirō. *An Introduction to Sung Poetry.* Burton Watson, tr. Cambridge: Harvard-Yenching Institute, 1967.

——. *Five Hundred Years of Chinese Poetry, 1150–1650: The Chin, Yuan, and Ming Dynasties.* Princeton: Princeton University Press, 1989.

Yuan Youzong 袁宙宗. *Aiguo shici xuan* 愛國詩詞選 (A selection of patriotic poetry). Taipei: Taiwan shangwu yinshuguan, 1982.

Zhang Bangwei 張邦煒. *Songdai huangqin yu zhengzhi* 宋代皇親與政治 (Imperial relatives and politics in Song times). Chengdu: Sichuan renmin chubanshe, 1993.

Zhang Jingqiu 張勁秋. "Titang you zhangfu qi: tan Li Qingzhao ci di yige yishu tedian" 倜儻有丈夫氣：談李清照詞的一個藝術特點 (Free-spirited in the manner of men: Discussion of a special artistic trait of Li Qingzhao's lyric verse), in Jinan shi shehui kexue yanjiusuo, comp., *Li Qingzhao yanjiu lunwen* (q.v.).

Zhang Junrong 張峻榮. *Nansong Gaozong pian'an jiangzuo yuanyin zhi tantao* 南宋高宗偏安江左原因之探討 (Inquiry into the causes for retrenchment in the eastern Yangzi under Southern Song Emperor Gaozong). Taipei: Wenshizhe chubanshe, 1986.

Zhang Qiyun 張其昀, et al. *Zhongwen da cidian* 中文大辭典 (An encyclopedic dictionary of the Chinese language). Rev. ed. Taipei: Huagang chuban youxian gongsi, 1976.

Zhang Xiongyuan 張雄圓, Lü Xiaogao 呂蕭高, et al. *Changsha fuzhi* 長沙府志 (Prefectural gazetteer for Changsha), 1747.

Zhang Yinlin 張蔭麟. "Nansong wangguo shibu" 南宋亡國史補 (Historical supplement to the fall of the Southern Song empire), in *Songshi yanjiu ji*, vol. 2, pp. 105–122. Taipei: Zhonghua congshu, 1964.

Zhao Xinian 趙錫年. *Zhaoshi zupu* 趙氏族譜 (Genealogy for the Zhao clan). Hong Kong: n.p., 1937.

Zhao zhong lu 昭忠錄 (A record of loyalism made manifest), Baibu congshu jicheng edition.

Zhen Dexiu 真德秀. *Xishan wenji* 西山文集 (Collected writings of Zhen Dexiu), Siku quanshu edition.

Zheng Han 鄭涵. "Ouyang Xiu tianrenguan shitan" 歐陽修天人觀試探 (Exploration into Ouyang Xiu's views on Heaven and Humanity), in *Songshi lunji* 宋史論集, pp. 363–377. Henan: Zhongzhou shuhuashe, 1983.

Zheng Shoupeng 鄭壽彭. *Songdai Kaifengfu yanjiu* 宋代開封府研究 (Study of Kaifeng during the Song dynasty). Taipei: Zhonghua congshu, 1980.

Zheng Sixiao 鄭思肖. *Tie'han xinshi* 鐵函心史 (History of the heart, as preserved in a metal box), Sibu kanyao edition. Taipei: Shijie shuju, 1970.

———. *Zheng suonan xiansheng wenji* 鄭所南先生文集 (Collected writings of Master Zheng Sixiao), Congshu jicheng edition.

Zhibuzu zhai congshu 知不足齋叢書. 1812. Reprint, Shanghai: Kushu liutung-chu, 1921.

Zhou Baozhu 周寶珠. *Jianming Songshi* 簡明宋史 (A simplified history of the Song). Beijing: Renmin chubanshe, 1985.

Zhou Mi 周密. *Guixin zazhi* 癸辛雜識 (Miscellaneous notes from Guixin Street), Baibu congshu jicheng edition.

———. *Qidong yeyu* 齊東野語 (Specious sayings from eastern Qi), Baibu congshu jicheng edition.

Zhou Nanrui 周南瑞. *Tianxia tong wenji* 天下同文集 (Common writings for the universe), Siku quanshu edition.

Glossary

Anqing, Huainan West 安慶
Azhu (Aju) 阿珠、阿朮

Baoyou reign 寶祐
Ban Gu 班固
Bayan 伯顏
Beijing 北京
beng 崩
Bian Juyi 邊居誼
Boluo 博羅
Boyang Lake 鄱陽湖
boxue hongci 博學宏詞
butian 不天

Cai Jing 蔡京
Cai Yan 蔡琰
Cao Bin 曹彬
Cao Qi 曹琦
Changjiang 長江
Changzhou, Zhexi 常州
Chaoyang 潮陽
Chaozhou, Guangnan 潮州
Chen, Consort 陳氏
Chen Bangzhan 陳邦瞻
Chen Cun 陳存
Chen Dong 陳東
Chen Jiaobo 陳覺伯
Chen Jizhou 陳繼周
Chen Ge 陳格
Chen Liang 陳亮
Chen Longzhi 陳隆之

Chen Shao 陳炤
Chen Ta 陳牽
Chen Wenlong 陳文龍
Chen Xin 陳莘
Chen Yin 陳寅
Chen Yisun 陳億孫
Chen Yizhong 陳宜中
Chen Yuzhi 陳虞之
Chen Zhongqiu 陳仲逷
cheng 誠
Cheng Zhu 程洙
Cheng-Zhu 程朱
Chengdu circuit 成都路
Chizhou, Jiangnan East 池州
Chu 楚
Chongqing 重慶
Cixian, Lady 慈憲

Daoxue 道學
Deng Deyu 鄧得遇
Deng Quangjian 鄧光薦
Deyou reign 德祐
Ding Daquan 丁大全
Dingjiazhou 丁家洲
Dong Hu 董狐
Dong Huai 董槐
Dong Songchen 董宋臣
Dong Wenbing 董文炳
Dongting Lake 洞庭湖
Du Fu 杜甫
Duan Xiushi 段秀實

Duanzong, Emperor 端宗
Duzong, Emperor 度宗

Er Nai 爾乃
Ezhou, Jinghu North 鄂州

Fan Tianshun 范天順
Fan Wenhu 范文虎
Fan Zhi 范質
Fan Zhongyan 范仲淹
Fancheng, Jingxi 樊城
Fang Feng 方鳳
Fangshiling, Jiangnan West 方石嶺
Feng, Commander 馮都統
Feng Dao 馮道
fu 復
Fujian circuit 福建路
furu 腐儒
Fuzhou, Fujian 福州

Gangzhou, Guangnan East 碙洲
Ganzhou, Jiangnan West 贛州
Gao, Empress of Yingzong 高皇后
Gao Gui 高桂
Gao Yingsong 高應松
Gaoting Mountain 皋 (高) 亭山
Gaozong, Emperor 高宗
Ge Tiansi 葛天思
gengyue 艮嶽
Gongdi, Emperor 恭帝
Gong Ji 龔澱
gongtian fa 公田法
Gong Xin 鞏信
Gou 姤
gou'an 苟安
gu 蠱
guai 夬
Guan Ning 管寧
Guangnan circuit 廣南路
Guangzhou, Guangnan 廣州
Guangzong, Emperor 光宗
Guifei 貴妃
guimei 歸妹
Guo, Empress of Xiaozong 郭皇后
Guo Pu 郭璞
Guo Xiama 郭蝦蟆

Haifeng, Guangnan 海豐

Han, Empress of Ningzong 韓皇后
Han Fei 韓非
Han peoples 漢人
Han River 漢水
Han Tong 韓通
Han Tuozhou 韓侂冑
Han Zhen 韓震
Hanyang, Jinghu North 漢陽
Hanzhou, Sichuan 漢州
Hao Jing 郝經
haojie 豪傑
haoran zhi qi 浩然之氣
He Dajie 何大節
Hezhou 合州
Hu Gongzhen 胡拱辰
Hu Jiangui 胡建桂
Hu Menglin 胡夢麟
Hua Yue 華岳
Huang Zhen 黃震
Huashigang 花石綱
Huai River 淮河
Huai'an, Huainan East 淮安
Huainan circuit 淮南路
Huang Guangde (Cong) 黃光德
 (黃從)
Huangzhou, Huainan West 黃州
Hubei province 湖北省
Huizhou, Jiangnan East 徽州
Huizhou, Guangnan East 惠州
Huizong, Emperor 徽宗

Ji Shao 嵇紹
Jia Chunxiao 賈純孝
Jia, Precious Consort 賈貴妃
Jia Sidao 賈似道
jian'er 健兒
Jiang Wanli 江萬里
Jiang Youzhi 江友直
Jiangnan circuit 江南路
Jiangxi province 江西省
Jiangzhou, Jiangnan West 江州
Jiankang (Nanking), Jiangnan East
 建康
Jiaoshan, Huainan East 焦山
jie yi 節義
Jing'ao, Guangnan East 井澳
Jinghu circuit 荊湖路
Jingjiang, Guangnan West 靜江

Jingxi circuit 京西路
Jingyan reign 景炎
Jizhou, Jiangnan West 吉州
Junzhou, Jingxi 均州

Kaifeng 開封
Kaixi reign 開禧
Kuizhou circuit 夔州路
kun 困

Leizhou 雷州
li 里
Li Congjing 李從璟
Li, Empress 李皇后
Li Fu 李芾
Li Heng 李恒
Li Qingzhao 李清照
Li Tingzhi 李庭芝
Li, the Woman 李氏
Li Xinchuan 李心傳
Li Zifa 李梓發
Lie nü 列女
Lin, the Lady 林夫人
Lin'an 臨安
Linhai 臨海
Lin Tong 林同
Lin, Woman 林氏
Liu Dingguo 劉定國
Liu Dingsun 劉鼎孫
Liu Dunru 劉敦儒
Liu, Empress of Zhenzong 劉皇后
Liu Jiugao 劉九皋
Liu Mengyan 留夢炎
Liu Rongshu 劉榮叔
Liu Rui 劉銳
Liu Shiyong 劉師勇
Liu Shizhao 劉士昭
Liu Tongzi 劉仝子
Liu Xu 柳敘
liuyi 六藝
Liu Yueshen 劉岳申
Lixue 理學
Lizhou circuit 利州路
Lizong, Emperor 理宗
Longmen 龍門
Longtou 龍頭
Lu Sheng 陸生
Lu Xiufu 陸秀夫

Lu You 陸游
Luling county, Jiangnan West 廬陵
Luo Kaili 羅開禮
Luoyang 洛陽
Lü Shikui 呂師夔
Lü Wende 呂文德
Lü Wenhuan 呂文煥

Ma Fa 馬發
Mao Xiang 茅湘
Meizhou, Guangnan East 梅州
Miao (Miu) Chaozong 繆朝宗
Min 閩
Mingzhou, Zhedong 明州
Modi, Emperor 末帝
mou 畝

Nan'an, Jiangnan West 南安
Nanjing (Nanking) 南京
nan'er 男兒
nanren 南人
nanzi 男子
Nie Bichuang 聶碧窗
Ningbo 寧波
Ningzong, Emperor 寧宗
Niu Fu 牛富

Ouyang, Lady 歐陽夫人
Ouyang Shoudao 歐陽守道
Ouyang Xiu 歐陽修

Pan Fang 潘方
Pang Yanhai 龐彥海
pianan 偏安
pianqi 偏氣
Pingjiang, Zhexi 平江
pingzhang junguo zhongshi 平章軍國
  重事

Qi Xinglong 齊興隆
qijie 氣節
Qiantang River 錢塘江
qin wang 勤王
Qingfeng Mountains 清風嶺
qingming 清明
Qingyuan 慶元
Qinzong, Emperor 欽宗
Quan Jiu 全玖

Quan Zhaosun 全昭孫
Quzhou, Zhedong 衢州

Raozhou, Jiangnan East 饒州
Renzong, Emperor 仁宗
Ruan Yingde 阮應得

sanren 三仁
shanxi 山西
Shangdu 上都
Shanghai 上海
Shao Yuan 邵困
Shaoxing, Zhedong 紹興
Shen Zhong 沈忠
Sheng county 嵊縣
shenling 甚令
Shi 士
Shi Hao 史浩
Shi Miyuan 史彌遠
Shi Songzhi 史嵩之
Shizong, Jurchen Emperor 世宗
Shufei 淑妃
Sichuan 四川
Sima Guang 司馬光
Sima Mengqiu 司馬夢求
Song Jing 宋京
Song Yinglong 宋應龍
Songshi 宋史
Su Shi 蘇軾
Su Wu 蘇武
Su Xun 蘇洵
Suizhou, Jingxi 隨州
Sun Huchen 孫虎臣
Suzhou (Soochow) 蘇州

Tai, Mount 泰山
Taixue 太學
Taizhou, Huainan East 泰州
Taizhou, Zhedong 台州
Taizu, Emperor 太祖
Tang Taiyu 唐泰嶽
Tang Zhen 唐震
Tanzhou, Jinghu South 潭州
Tianmu Shan, Zhexi 天目山
Tingzhou, Fujian 汀州
Tongchuan circuit 潼川路
Tong Guan 童貫
tong zhongshu menxia pingzhang shi
　同中書門下平章事

Wang, the Chaste Woman 王貞婦
Wang Anjie 王安節
Wang Anshi 王安石
Wang Fu 王福
Wang Fuzhi 王夫之
Wang Guixing 王貴行
Wang Jue 王玨
Wang Liangchen 王良臣
Wang Lixin 汪立信
Wang Ning 王凝
Wang Pu 王溥
Wang Qinghui 王清惠
Wang Shichang 王世昌
Wang Weichong 汪維崇
Wang Xian 王仙
Wang Yanming 王彥明
Wang Yinglin 王應麟
Wang Yu 王翊
Wang Yuanliang 汪元量
Wang Yue 王爚
Wei Hengzhong 魏亨中
Wei Shou 魏收
Wei Yong 衛融
wen 文
wenhua 文化
wenming 文明
Wen, King of Zhou 文王
Wen Bi 文璧
Wen Daosheng 文道生
Wen Fengniang 文奉娘
Wen Jianniang 文監娘
Wen Sheng 文陞
Wen Tianxiang 文天祥
Wen Yi 文儀
Wenzhou, Zhedong 溫州
wu 武
Wu, Empress of Gaozong 吳皇后
Wu-Yue 吳越
Wu Zhen 烏震
Wuhu, Jiangnan East 蕪湖
Wu Xi 吳曦
Wuxue 武學
Wuzhou, Zhedong 婺州

Xia, Empress of Xiaozong 夏皇后
Xia Yi 夏椅
Xian Long 鮮龍
Xianzong, Yuan Emperor 憲宗
Xiang Yu 項羽

Xiangyang, Jingxi 襄陽
xiao 孝
Xiaozong, Emperor 孝宗
Xie, Empress of Xiaozong 謝皇后
Xie Fangde 謝枋得
Xie Qiao 謝喬 (Daoqing 道清)
Xie Shenfu 謝深甫
Xie Xu 謝緒
Xin Qiji 辛棄疾
Xing, Empress of Gaozong 邢皇后
Xinghua, Fujian 興化
Xiong Fei 熊飛
xishan 西山
xiurong 修容
Xiushan, Guangnan East 秀山
Xixia 西夏
Xu Biaosun 許彪孫
Xu Daolong 徐道隆
Xu Yingbiao 徐應鑣
Xu Zongren 徐宗仁
Xuanhe reign 宣和

Yaishan, Guangnan East 厓(崖)山
Yan 燕
yan bi he du 言必合度
Yan Gaoqing 顏杲卿
Yan Yan 嚴顏
Yan Yingyan 顏應焱
yang 陽
Yang Juliang 楊巨良
Yang Mengdou 楊夢斗
Yang Shu 楊恕
Yang Ting 楊霆
Yang Wanli 楊萬里
Yang Wenzhong 楊文仲
Yang Yan 楊儼
Yang Zan 楊瓚
Yang Zhen 楊震
Yang Zhen 楊鎮
Yangzhou, Huainan East 揚州
Yangzi 揚子江
Yao Shu 姚樞
Yao Yin 姚訔
Ye Shi 葉適
yi 義
yili 義理
yin 陰
Yin Gu 尹穀
Yin Tinggao 尹廷高

Yin Yuexiu 尹岳秀
Yingzhou, Jingxi 郢州
Yingzong, Emperor 英宗
Yong, the Woman 雍氏
Yongjia, Zhedong 永嘉
yongwu ci 詠物詞
Yu, Consort 俞修容
Yu the Great 大禹
Yuan Cai 袁采
Yuan Jue 袁桷
Yuan Tianyu 袁天與
Yuan Yong 袁鏞
yuefu 樂府

Zeng Deci 曾德慈
Zeng Fenglong 曾逢龍
Zeng Jue 曾珏
Zeng Ruyi 曾如驥
zha 柵
zhang 丈
Zhang Gui 張貴
Zhang Hongfan 張弘範
Zhang Jian 章鑑
Zhang Jue 張玨
Zhang Jun 張浚
Zhang Liang 張良
Zhang Shijie 張世傑
Zhang Shun 張順
Zhang Xun 張巡
Zhang Zhensun 張鎮孫
Zhang Zi 張資
zhangfu 丈夫
Zhangzhou, Fujian 漳州
Zhao Bing 趙昺
Zhao Dun 趙惇
Zhao Gou 趙構
Zhao Hong 趙竑
Zhao Kuangyin 趙匡胤
Zhao Kuo 趙擴
Zhao Li 趙立
Zhao Liangchun 趙良淳
Zhao Maofa 趙卯發
Zhao Qi 趙禥
Zhao Qian 趙潛
Zhao Qiao 趙樵
Zhao Shen 趙慎
Zhao Shi 趙昰
Zhao Shijian 趙時踐
Zhao Shikua 趙時侉

Zhao Xian 趙㬎
Zhao Xiji 趙希泪
Zhao Youtai 趙酉泰
Zhao Yun 趙昀
Zhao Zaisun 趙載孫
Zhedong circuit 浙東路
zhen 震
Zhen Dexiu 真德秀
Zhenchao, Huainan West 鎮巢
Zhenjiang, Zhexi 鎮江
zhennan 真男
Zhenzhou, Huainan East 真州
Zheng Bingsun 鄭炳孫
Zheng Huizhen 鄭惠真
Zheng Qingzhi 鄭清之
Zheng Sixiao 鄭思肖
Zheng Xian 鄭憲
Zheng Zhen 鄭震

Zhenghe reign 政和
Zhengqi ge 正氣歌
Zhexi circuit 浙西路
Zhezong, Emperor 哲宗
zhong 忠
Zhong Kejun 鍾克俊
zhong yi zhuan 忠義傳
Zhou and Han, Princess of 周漢國
　公主
Zhou Mi 周密
Zhu, Consort 朱氏
Zhu Jun 朱浚
Zhu Xi 朱熹
Zhuge Liang 諸葛亮
zhuang zheng 壯正
Zou Feng 鄒灃
Zu Ti 祖逖

Index